D1395589

Editorial Manager	Judith Maxwell
Senior Editor	Lynne Williams
Editors	Brenda Clarke Bridget Daly
Series Designers	QED (Alastair Campbell and Edward Kinsey)
Series Consultant	Keith Lye
Production	John Moulder
Picture Research	Jenny De Gex

© Macdonald Educational Ltd. 1980
First published 1980
Macdonald Educational Ltd.
Holywell House,
Worship Street,
London EC2A 2EN

2081/3200
ISBN 0 356 07007 7

Designed and created in
Great Britain

Printed and bound by
New Interlitho, Italy

The Evolution of Life

David John

Richard Moody

Macdonald

Contents

The Evolution of Plants and Animals

The Prehistoric World

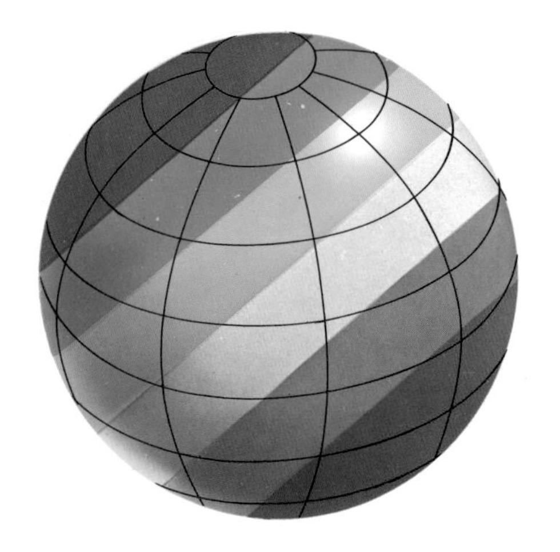

World of Knowledge

This book breaks new ground in the method it uses to present information to the reader. The unique page design combines narrative with an alphabetical reference section and it uses colourful photographs, diagrams and illustrations to provide an instant and detailed understanding of the book's theme. The main body of information is presented in a series of chapters that cover, in depth, the subject of this book. At the bottom of each page is a reference section which gives, in alphabetical order, concise articles which define, or enlarge on, the topics discussed in the chapter. Throughout the book, the use of SMALL CAPITALS in the text directs the reader to further information that is printed in the reference section. The same method is used to cross-reference entries within each reference section. Finally, there is a comprehensive index at the end of the book that will help the reader find information in the text, illustrations and reference sections. The quality of the text, and the originality of its presentation, ensure that this book can be read both for enjoyment and for the most up-to-date information on the subject.

The Evolution of Plants and Animals

Introduction

Every living thing on the Earth today has a history stretching back over millions of years, and the changes which have taken place within that time are described in **The Evolution of Plants and Animals.** Although the mystery of life's origins on Earth has not yet been solved, scientists are discovering more and more about the early Earth from its rocks and from the fossils they contain. These reveal an overwhelming diversity of life forms in our world — from simple, single cells to huge trees and enormous dinosaurs. Some of these forms are remarkably similar to plants and animals alive today. Others have died out, leaving only their remains behind. **The Evolution of Plants and Animals** also traces the course of life among individuals, explaining how one generation passes its hereditary characteristics to its offspring, and how plants and animals adapt successfully, by 'selection', to the surroundings in which they live.

Our knowledge of the chemistry of life, and the discovery of fossils in some of the world's oldest rocks, help us to understand how life may first have appeared and spread on the primeval Earth.

The Origins of Life

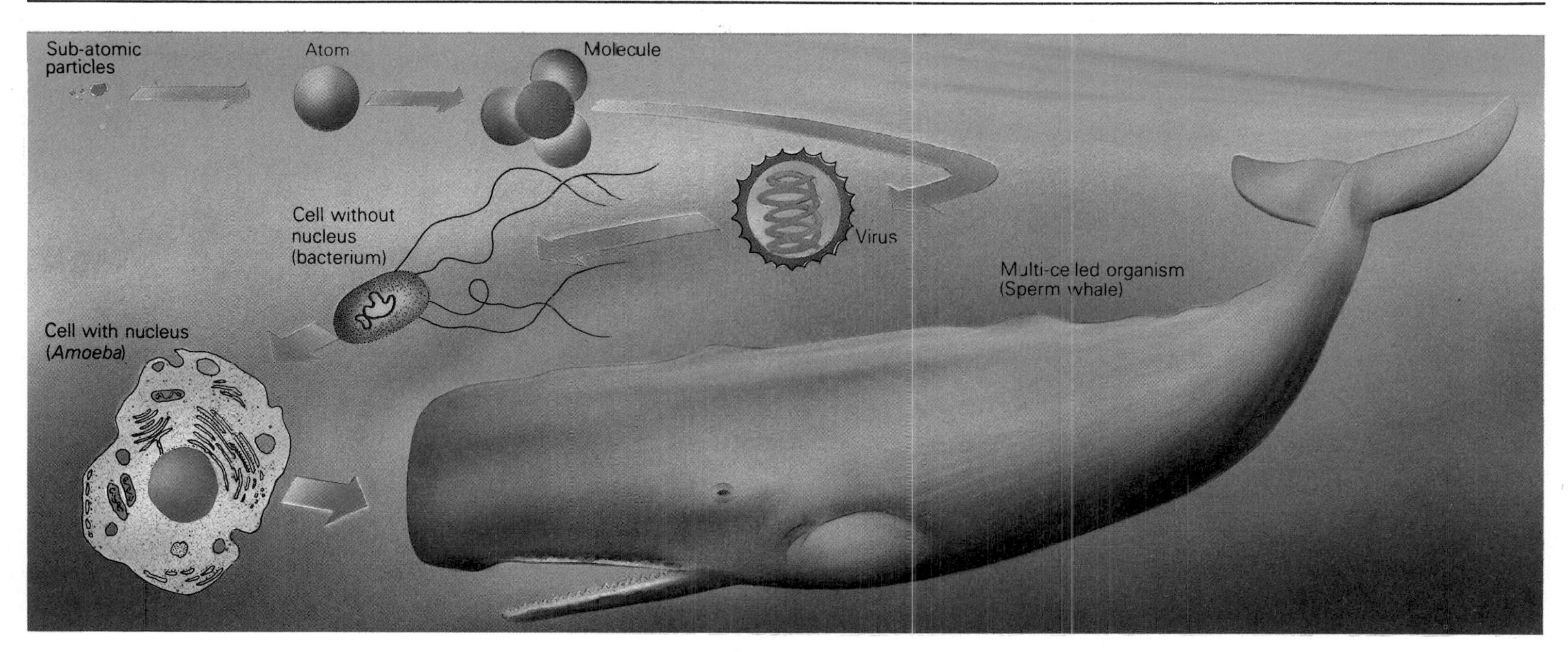

Above: Many scientists believe that matter differs simply in its degree of organization, and that 'life' results when a particular level of organization is reached. So it is possible to progress from sub-atomic particles to increasingly more complex arrangements of matter — from the atom, molecule, virus, single-celled organisms without a nucleus, single-celled organisms with a nucleus, to multi-celled organisms like the mighty whale.

Because there are obvious differences between an animal or plant and, say, a rock, many people assume that the difference between life and non-life is as easy to describe. In fact the ancient Greek philosopher Aristotle (384–322 BC) was nearer to the truth when he noted that on a scale from the smallest ATOMS to complex organisms it is hard to answer the question: what is life? Growth, reproduction and respiration (*see page 6*) could be listed as some of its properties, yet these are also known in the non-living state. On the other hand, VIRUSES, which are on the threshold of life, may show none of the three properties mentioned. It is perhaps more sensible, then, to see life as a property of matter when it reaches a particular stage of complexity.

Life on Earth

Life comprises the most plentiful elements in the universe — hydrogen, carbon, nitrogen and oxygen. However, there has been disagreement over how these first combined into living beings. The ancient Greeks believed in spontaneous generation, thinking, for example, that frogs came into being from damp earth. This view was finally shown to be wrong in the 1800s by Louis PASTEUR, who demonstrated that living organisms, including BACTERIA, were created only as offspring of parent organisms. With Charles DARWIN'S ideas on evolution, his work led to the theory, now widely accepted, that life started on the primeval Earth in a warm 'soup' of ORGANIC MOLECULES. On the other hand, a very different idea was advanced by Svante ARRHENIUS. It stated that the Earth was seeded by life from other planets and that life itself is eternal. His 'PANSPERMIA' concept does not fit the observed facts, but some astronomers have recently presented a new case for the theory that life began beyond the Earth. Finally, there remains the explanation that life was created by a supernatural force, as in the story of Genesis.

Reference

A

Aerobic means with oxygen. Nearly all EUKARYOTES need oxygen to combine with the carbon in their food and so produce energy. Carbon dioxide and water are formed as waste products.

Amber is the fossilized resin of coniferous trees and is comparatively rare. As it oozed from trees the resin often trapped insects, and a large variety of these is known from amber of the Oligocene age. The insects' outer parts are perfectly preserved, but the soft internal tissues are missing.

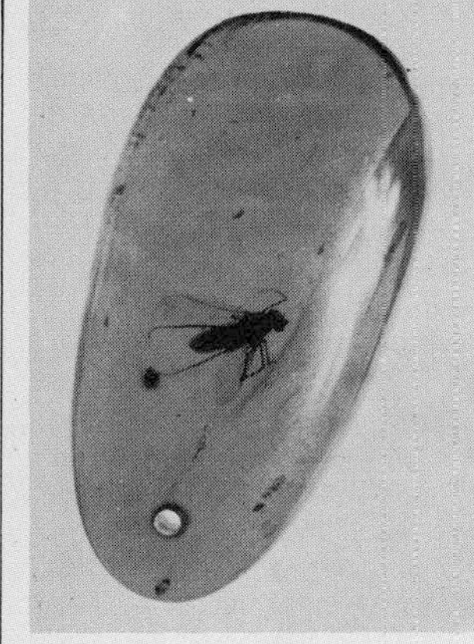

Fly fossilized in amber

Anaerobic means without oxygen. Some BACTERIA cannot reproduce or grow in the presence of oxygen — these are called obligate anaerobes. Facultative anaerobes can tolerate oxygen, but also live without it. Instead of combining the carbon in their food with oxygen, obligate anaerobes gain energy by breaking down carbon-rich substances such as glucose into simpler components. Energy is released in the process.

Aragonite is one kind of crystalline calcium carbonate (the other is calcite). Aragonite is more unstable than calcite if exposed to air or fresh water. But both kinds are often destroyed by the action of water, especially in sandy rocks. The calcium carbonate parts of organisms are therefore often only preserved as CASTS, or are replaced by another mineral such as pyrites.

Arrhenius, Svante (1859–1927) was a Swedish chemist who first set out the theory of PANSPERMIA in a number of popular books and scientific papers. According to this idea, organisms could have journeyed across space from another solar system, aided by the pressure of radiation — a sort of solar wind. In recent years variants of this theory have been put forward by several scientists.

Atoms are extremely small particles. They make up elements, the simplest components into which substances can be sub-divided. The atoms in any one element are identical, but those of different elements have

Above: This scene represents the Earth as it may have looked early in its history. Volcanic gases are generally believed to have created the Earth's atmosphere and oceans. Electrical discharges in this primitive atmosphere may have formed organic molecules which dissolved in the oceans. Such molecules are thought to have provided the raw materials from which life developed.

The first living organisms

The Earth is about 4,600 million years old, while the earliest known organisms are from rocks roughly 3,300 million years old. Assuming that life began on Earth, it must have started some time in the first 1,300 million years after the planet was formed. During this time the Earth's atmosphere and oceans were also created by huge outpourings of gases from its volcanoes. Judging from the gases emitted in volcanic eruptions today, the early atmosphere contained lots of hydrogen, ammonia and methane, and smaller amounts of carbon dioxide and nitrogen. The oxygen-nitrogen mixture we breathe today came much later, after plants evolved that were capable of PHOTOSYNTHESIS — a process in which oxygen is formed as a by-product. Without oxygen there would have been no OZONE layer in the upper atmosphere, as there is now, to filter out ULTRAVIOLET LIGHT from the Sun's rays. Therefore ultraviolet light, which is harmful to all living things, must have reached the Earth's surface. It was in this seemingly hostile setting that life is supposed to have started. The sequence of events may have been as follows.

Creation of life

Lightning flashes and ultraviolet light supplied enough energy for the relatively simple ingredients in the atmosphere to combine into more complex organic molecules. Some of these molecules are seen as the building blocks, or PRE-BIOTIC substances, from which life later developed. A similar effect has taken place in the laboratory by sending high-voltage sparks through mixtures of gases believed to resemble the Earth's primitive atmosphere. Several molecules produced in these experiments could be described as pre-biotic, since they are found in both PROTEIN and NUCLEIC ACIDS, the two essential components in every living organism. After pre-biotic substances formed in the atmosphere on the primeval Earth, they dissolved in the oceans, turning them into a thin soup.

---

different properties. Combinations of atoms are known as molecules. Oxygen and hydrogen are elements, while water is a molecule which is made up of 2 hydrogen atoms and 1 oxygen atom.

Autotrophs are organisms which can nourish themselves. They make their own food from simple non-living substances acquired from their surroundings. Green plants are the autotrophs most familiar to us. All animal life and fungi depend ultimately on autotrophs for their existence.

B

Bacteria are the simplest living organisms, and consist of a single cell. They are minute — in fact it has been worked out that one thousand billion individuals (1,000,000,000,000) of a certain bacteria could be packed into one cubic centimetre. There is another group of single-celled organisms called Protista, which includes *Amoeba,* but they have a much more complex structure. Bacteria belong to the PROKARYOTES, whereas members of the protists are EUKARYOTES.

Blue-green algae closely resemble BACTERIA (despite their name) and are otherwise known as cyanobacteria. They are made up from single cells or from cells joined end to end to form filaments. They may also be formed from colonies of individual cells or filaments held together in a jelly-like mass.

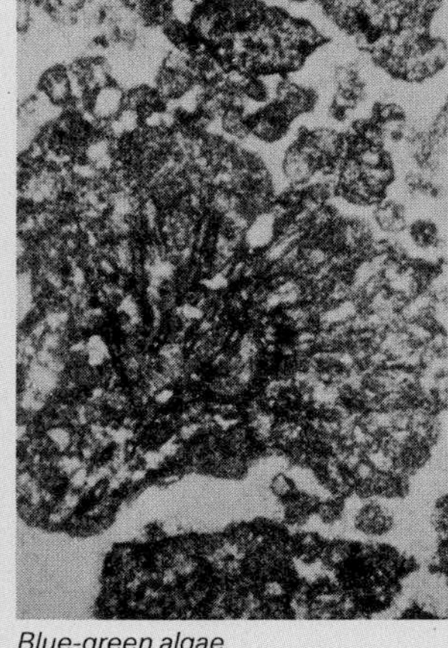

Blue-green algae

C

Cainozoic is the name of the ERA which began at the end of Cretaceous times, about 65 million years ago. It comprises the Tertiary and Quaternary PERIODS. The Tertiary includes the Palaeocene, Eocene, Oligocene, Miocene and Pliocene EPOCHS. The Quaternary is made up of the Pleistocene and Holocene (or Recent) epochs. The Holocene opened around 10,000 years ago and is the epoch in which we live.

Calcite, see ARAGONITE.

Cast, or mould, is the impression left in a rock by the inner or outer surface of a fossil. If the cast is of an outer part, a replica of the original organism can be made by pouring into it a rubber solution or plaster of Paris. Sometimes the organ-

The next stages in the sequence are only guessed at. First the pre-biotic material became more concentrated and then it was assembled into protein and nucleic acids. We know that in solutions containing water and the substances we think were present in the Earth's early oceans, droplets will form. These are rich in some of the dissolved substances, and also have an enveloping surface membrane. Such droplets, or COACERVATES, grow as they absorb more of the dissolved substances from the surrounding solution, and may then divide into smaller droplets. Perhaps something of this kind eventually evolved into the earliest cell. In any event, the concentration most likely took place beneath the surface of the oceans, for although ultraviolet light can help simple organic molecules to form, it tends to break down more complex types.

The basic organic molecules are helped to assemble in living organisms by substances called ENZYMES, which form only in the presence of nucleic acids. So in trying to explain how the first nucleic acids developed we seem to be faced with a chicken and egg cycle: enzymes cannot be formed without nucleic acids, and vice-versa. It is possible that metals such as copper, iron or vanadium may have acted instead of enzymes in the chemical reactions that led to the earliest organisms.

These ideas remain only suggestions, and we are still a long way from being able to create life in a test-tube. As we have already seen, even the idea of life evolving spontaneously in a soup of organic molecules is not universally accepted. It has been criticized on several counts, including the lack of direct proof that a soup ever existed. There is, too, the view that the origin of life was extra-terrestrial. In recent years significant amounts of organic molecules have been detected in the space between the stars and in METEORITES. From these and other observations, people have claimed that the first organisms actually developed within COMETS, which 'showered' the Earth with life. If this is true, life-bearing comets could also have seeded other planets, and life might be scattered throughout the universe.

Pre-Cambrian life

It was not until the 1950s that fossil life was confirmed in rocks older than those of the Cambrian geological period, which began about

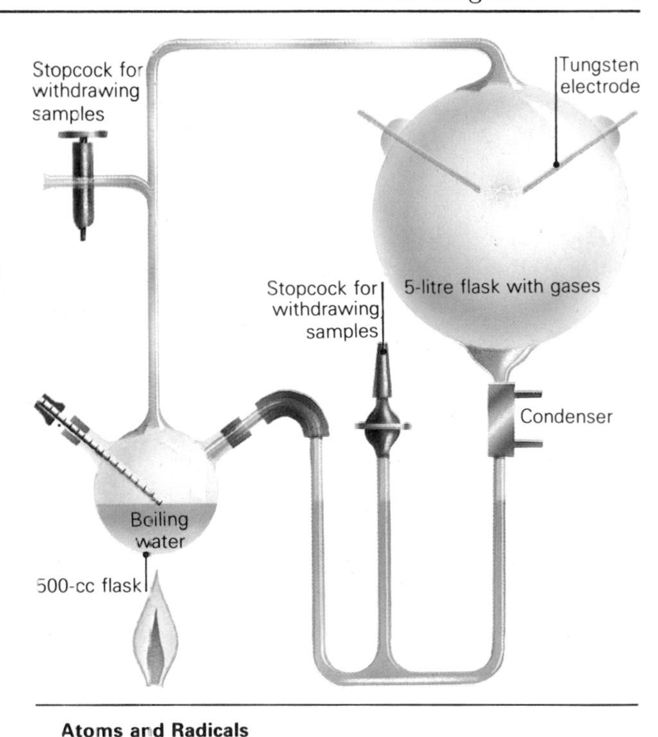

Right: Stanley L. Miller and Harold C. Urey used this equipment at the University of Chicago to simulate electrical discharges in the atmosphere of the primitive Earth. A mixture of gases thought to have been present in the atmosphere at that time were subjected to a spark discharge. The compounds that were then formed were collected in the water at the bottom of the apparatus. Water is boiled and steam is led through the system in order to circulate the gases. The heated gases in the flask are condensed and are then drawn off at intervals in order to be analysed. Electrodes inserted into the flask cause an electric current to be passed through it. The resulting spark provides energy, enabling the gases to react.

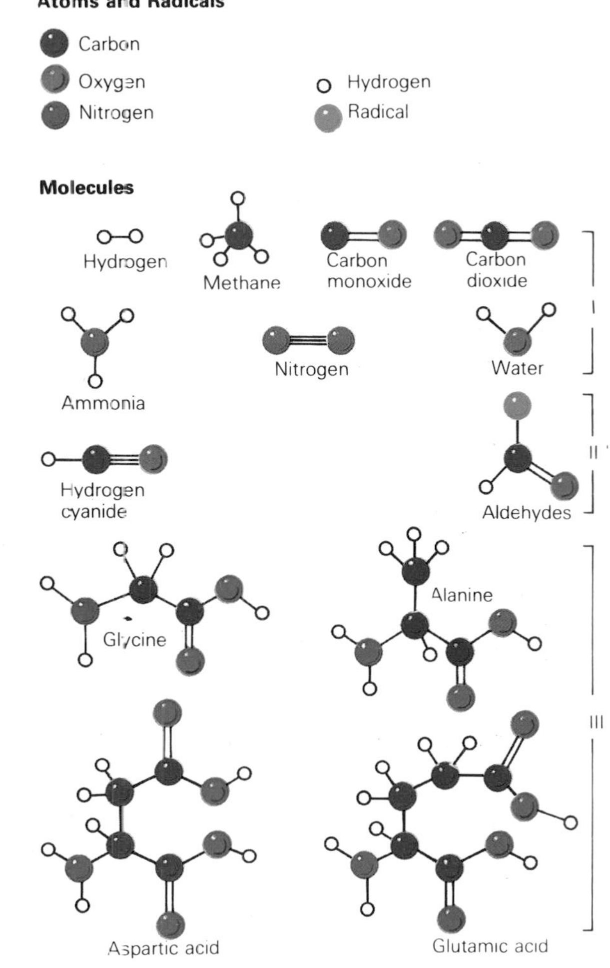

Right: Miller and Urey's spark discharge experiments started with simple products that were assumed to have been plentiful in the Earth's early atmosphere. Hydrogen cyanide and aldehydes were given off after a period of spark discharge. Continued sparking produced more complex molecules, including 4 amino acids that are commonly present in proteins — glycine, alanine, aspartic acid and glutamic acid.

ism's remains may have been filled with sediment before they were destroyed and this provides an internal mould. Casts of shells are very common, since the calcium carbonate from which they are made is easily dissolved away from porous rock which allows water to pass through.

Coacervates are small, round particles of organic material (see ORGANIC MOLECULES) dispersed in water. But they are not actually dissolved as in true solutions. Soap and detergents, for example, disperse in water the same way. It is known that many living substances can dissolve in coacervates or become attached to their surfaces. They could thus have provided important gathering sites for PRE-BIOTIC substances in the earliest oceans.

Comets travel round the Sun, but unlike the planets their orbits are elliptical. They come from a 'cloud' of cometary bodies surrounding the solar system and from time to time individual bodies plunge into it. They are made up of gas, dust and ice, and as they pass the Sun, its heat causes material to spray out and form a tail which can be seen in the night sky.

D **Darwin,** Charles (1809–82) was a British biologist. Following a voyage to South America and Australasia in HMS *Beagle* in 1831, he developed a theory of evolution (*see page 12*) based on natural selection and survival of the fittest. Only those organisms best fitted to survive, he reasoned, would reproduce and so pass on their characteristics to the next generation. The balance of characteristics in the descendants might then differ greatly from that in the original. Therefore the organisms would change, or evolve, with the passage of time.

Charles Darwin

E **Element,** see ATOM.

Enzymes are special kinds of PROTEIN which act as catalysts for chemical reactions inside cells. That is, they speed up the reactions without being changed themselves. Each enzyme performs a specific task in the cell. The fact that the same enzyme may carry out the same task in a wide

570 million years ago. Today we have ample evidence that the varied and complex creatures living in the Cambrian world were preceded by much more primitive ancestors. Their remains show that these were mostly microscopic and single-celled.

The earliest micro-fossils found are simple round cells of the PROKARYOTE type. They are apparently 3,200 million years old and occur in rocks in South Africa. Fossil colonies of prokaryote cells, called STROMATOLITES, also come from slightly younger rocks in Zimbabwe, and are relatively frequent in rocks laid down about 2,300 million years ago. The first traces of more advanced EUKARYOTE cells appear in rocks under 1,500 million years old. Macroscopic remains of multi-celled organisms enter the fossil record only in the last 100 million years of Pre-Cambrian time. These are of worms, jellyfish and possibly sponges.

Above: Living stromatolite colonies in the Bahamas.

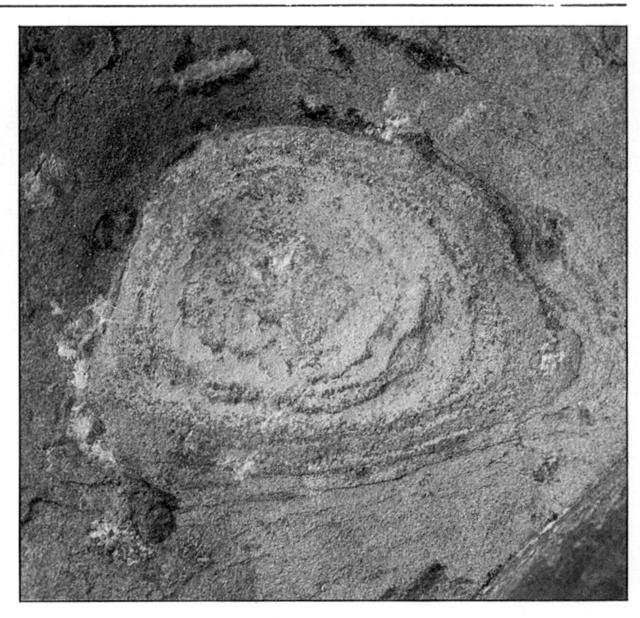

Right: This fossil stromatolite from the Lower Palaeozoic of Europe shows the structure of the algal colony.

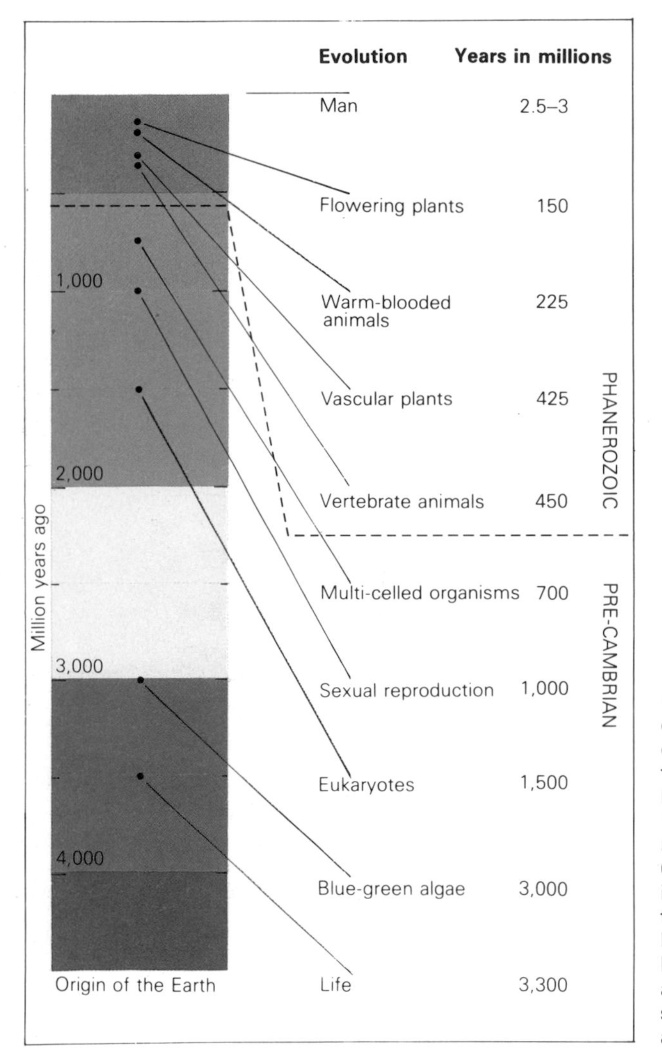

Left: Ten major events in the course of biological evolution are shown, related to the time-scale of the Earth's history. The Phanerozoic, or era of manifest life, began nearly 600 million years ago, for it is in rocks of this age that fossils of organisms with hard parts first appear. The Pre-Cambrian is referred to as the era of hidden life, since the fossil organisms are generally microscopic.

Prokaryote cells are those of the bacteria and BLUE-GREEN ALGAE; all other forms of life have eukaryote cells. The early micro-fossils seem to have been free-floating blue-green algae or their predecessors, while stromatolites were constructed by shallow-water communities of blue-green algae and bacteria. These ancient blue-green algae changed the Earth's atmosphere and in so doing affected the later course of evolution. To understand how this happened, we must first examine the way prokaryotes live.

Food and energy

Blue-green algae make their own foods and so are called AUTOTROPHS. They use sunlight to combine carbon and hydrogen into carbohydrates and release oxygen as waste. Oxygen is then employed to break down the carbohydrates in order to free energy for the organisms. The first process is called photosynthesis; the second respiration. Since both processes occur in the presence of oxygen, they are said to be AEROBIC. Some bacteria are also autotrophs, but they have different pigments for trapping sunlight and the processes are ANAEROBIC, that is, they take place without oxygen. Most bacteria, however, do not make their own food and so are called HETEROTROPHS. They gain their energy by breaking down substances already available. Again this is usually done anaerobically. As well as energy,

range of organisms suggests an evolutionary link between them.
Epochs are sub-divisions of the Tertiary and Quaternary PERIODS and are separated on the basis of fossil types.
Eras are the largest sub-divisions of recorded time. The PALAEOZOIC and MESOZOIC eras opened with the appearance of major new groups of organisms, and both closed with the mass extinctions of many descendants of these new groups. The start of the present CAINOZOIC era also coincided with sudden advances in the evolution of birds and mammals.
Eukaryotes are organisms that have cells with a NUCLEUS (see page 15). In each cell this is surrounded by CYTOPLASM (see page 13) which is relatively large and complex, with several distinct sub-divisions. All green plants, animals and fungi are eukaryotes.

F **Fossilization** is the process by which remains of organisms, or some trace of their activities, are preserved in rocks and thus form fossils.

G **Green algae** are EUKARYOTES which have CHLOROPLASTS (see page 17). They range from microscopic single-celled types to large branched seaweeds.

H **Heterocysts** are thick-walled cells found in BLUE-GREEN ALGAE. They protect nitrogen-fixing ENZYMES from coming into contact with oxygen which would slow them down or stop them altogether.
Heterotrophs are organisms which cannot make the food substances they need from simple non-living materials. Instead they depend directly or indirectly on AUTOTROPHS, mainly plants. Heterotrophs gain their energy by breaking down large, complex molecules such as starch and glucose (see ATOM) derived from autotrophs.

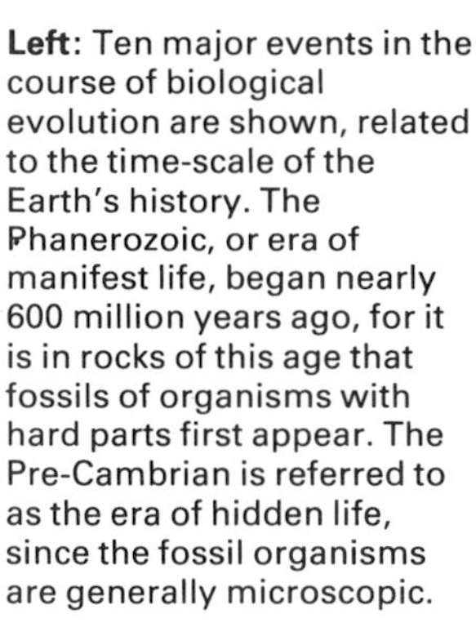

Sea-thong, green algae

I **Isotopes** of the same element have the same number of protons (positively charged particles), but a different number of neutrons (particles neither positively nor negatively charged) in their ATOMS. For instance, there are 3

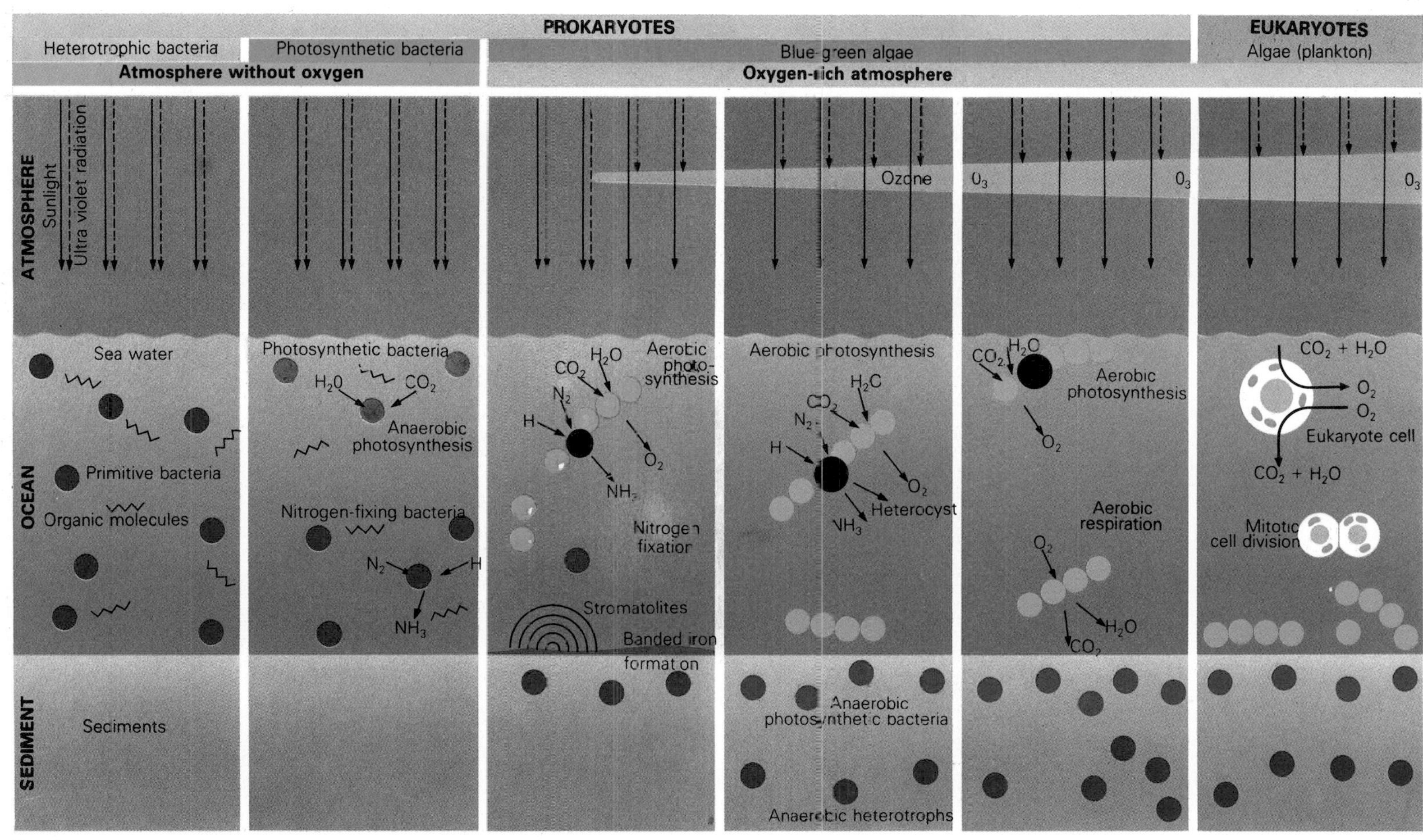

From 'Evolution of the Earliest Cells', J. W. Schopf. Copyright © 1978 by Scientific American Inc. All rights reserved.

organisms need nitrogen, to build protein. Only certain prokaryotes can 'fix' nitrogen into a form which can be used by living matter. The enzymes which bring about this fixation will not function if exposed to oxygen, so many nitrogen-fixing bacteria are adapted to oxygen-free environments. Similarly, among the blue-green algae, the enzymes in question are encased in special cells named HETEROCYSTS, to prevent contact with oxygen.

How life developed

These facts and the new fossil evidence available make it possible to reconstruct the likely development of life and of the Earth's atmosphere during the Pre-Cambrian era. The oldest organisms were almost certainly heterotrophic bacteria. These would have 'fed' on the organic molecules which had dissolved in the primeval oceans after being produced in the atmosphere with the aid of ultraviolet light. Bacteria capable of anaerobic photosynthesis and 'fixing' nitrogen probably evolved next, and it seems that from these the blue-green algae arose, perhaps as far back as 3,000 million years ago. Because stromatolite colonies of these organisms occur so often in rocks laid down around 2,300 million years ago, we can infer that oxygen in the Earth's atmosphere also reached significant proportions about then. This in turn must have led to the ozone layer emerging in the upper atmosphere (which now shields us from harmful ultraviolet rays). As the oxygen increased, the anaerobic bacteria would have retreated to the sediments on the sea-floor where there was little oxygen.

There are other indicators that oxygen was abundant roughly 2,000 million years ago. Compounds of iron and oxygen were widely deposited on the ocean floors at this time, which implies large oxygen reserves. And recently reported are perhaps the oldest fossil heterocyst cells, about 2,200 million years old.

Above: The chart illustrates the evolution of the earliest cells and the influence of an oxygen-rich atmosphere on later evolution. The first primitive bacteria probably lived by fermenting organic molecules in the Earth's early oceans. Later, bacteria capable of photosynthesis and 'fixing' nitrogen appeared. About 2 billion years ago, oxygen-producing photosynthesis began in ancestors of the blue-green algae. This added oxygen to the Earth's atmosphere, while those bacteria unable to live in oxygen retreated to the sediments of the sea-floor. When the oldest eukaryotes evolved the atmosphere was undoubtedly oxygen-rich and the protective ozone layer in the upper atmosphere was already established.

isotopes of oxygen: $^{16}_{8}O$ has 8 protons and 8 neutrons; $^{17}_{8}O$ has 8 protons and 9 neutrons; $^{18}_{8}O$ has 8 protons and 10 neutrons. O is the symbol for oxygen; the bottom number given before the symbol states the number of protons, and the top number — the atomic number — gives the sum of protons and neutrons.

K

Kelvin, William Thomson, Baron (1824–1907) was a British physicist who claimed in 1883 that the surface of the Earth had solidified as recently as 20 to 40 million years ago. This idea was strongly resisted at the time. Scientists believed it was impossible to fit into such a short time span the historical record of rocks and the evolutionary story of life they contained. Though they could not fault Kelvin's calculations, we now realize that these had been based on incomplete information.

William Thomson Kelvin, Baron

L

Lyell, Sir Charles (1797–1875) was one of the fathers of modern geology (the study of the Earth and its rocks). His book *The Principles of Geology* championed the views of James Hutton (1726–97) who developed the theory of uniformitarianism. This states that the processes which took place in rocks during the past were of the same kind as those which operate today. Although this view was highly controversial at first, the uniformitarian approach is central to much research today.

M

Mesozoic is the name given to an ERA of recorded time. It has 3 PERIODS — the Triassic, Jurassic and Cretaceous. The Mesozoic extended from 225 to 65 million years ago and is often called the 'Age of Reptiles'. But Mesozoic actually means 'middle life', for it comes between the PALAEOZOIC and the CAINOZOIC eras. All 3 coincide with that part of Earth history which is known as the Phanerozoic. This is the time of manifest life, coming after the Pre-Cambrian which until recently was regarded as the time of hidden life.

Meteorites are solid bodies which enter the Earth's atmosphere from space, and may be related to COMETS.

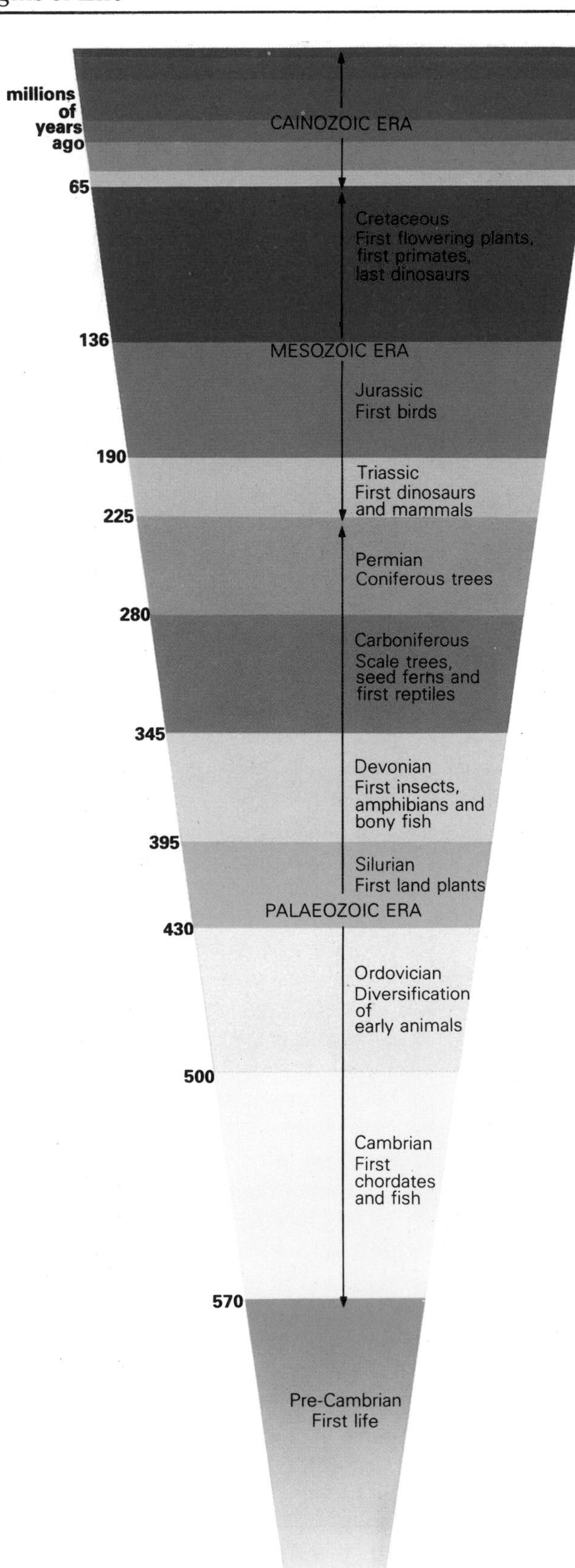

Recent or Holocene
Quaternary Pleistocene 1.6
Pliocene 7
Miocene
Tertiary 26
Oligocene 37.5
Eocene
53
Palaeocene 65

Left: Geological time is divided into eras, which are in turn divided into periods. The Tertiary and Quaternary periods are further sub-divided into epochs. The various divisions coincide with the appearance and disappearance of different groups of fossil organisms.

Everything points to the atmosphere having been oxygen-rich when the first eukaryote cells appeared, less than 1,500 million years ago. They resembled GREEN ALGAE and probably respired aerobically, as did all later eukaryotes.

The Earth's history

Rocks and fossil remains of plants or animals preserved in them provide a record of the Earth's history. They show that life has grown more varied and complex, and that great changes in climate have taken place, as has the distribution of land and sea. Where STRATA (or layers of rock) rest upon each other, the highest will be the youngest, provided the strata have not been overturned by earth movements. Therefore a study moving upwards through the strata and the fossils they contain will reveal successively younger stages of the Earth's history. Studies of this kind have led to a way of classifying rocks according to their relative — rather than their actual — ages.

The time which has elapsed since the Pre-Cambrian ERA is divided into three more eras: the PALAEOZOIC, the MESOZOIC and the CAINOZOIC. The rocks of each of these three eras are further divided into SYSTEMS which correspond to the different PERIODS of geological time. The two Cainozoic periods — the Tertiary and the Quaternary — are broken down again into EPOCHS. There are just two in the Quaternary: the Pleistocene and the Holocene. The Holocene is the epoch in which we live.

Dating of rocks

Before the relatively recent arrival of accurate geological dating, various early estimates were made of the actual ages of the Earth and its rocks. Charles LYELL worked from supposed rates of change in the fossil populations of one group of animals — the molluscs. From this he obtained

They are made up of iron or stone, or a mixture of both. Most meteorites are stony, and one group (the so-called carbonaceous chondrites) contains ORGANIC MOLECULES.

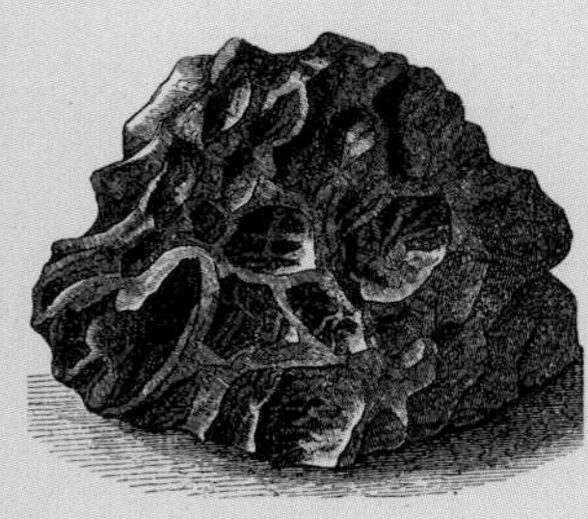

Piece of a meteorite

Mid-oceanic ridges are long narrow mountain chains which rise from the sea-floor. They mark the meeting point of the great rigid slabs which support the continents and oceans. Molten rock from the Earth's centre wells up at the ridges and, when cooled, adds new crust to the edges of the rigid plates, as they constantly spread apart from each other.

Molecules, see ATOM.

N

Nucleic acids are made up from a ribose sugar, a phosphate group and a few relatively simple nitrogen substances called bases.

O

Organic molecules contain ATOMS of carbon and hydrogen. The organic molecules essential to life also contain atoms from one or more other elements, especially nitrogen, oxygen, phosphorus and sulphur.

Ozone is a gas in which each molecule comprises 3 atoms of oxygen (hence its chemical formula O_3). Ozone is concentrated into a layer in the upper atmosphere. Unlike other components in the atmosphere it absorbs ULTRAVIOLET LIGHT, so that only small amounts manage to penetrate as far as the Earth's surface.

P

Palaeomagnetism refers to the fossil magnetization of rocks. As rocks containing iron minerals are laid down, or as molten rocks cool, they take on a weak magnetization which runs parallel to the Earth's magnetic field. The pattern of the field resembles that which a giant bar magnet would produce if placed parallel to the Earth's axis.

Palaeozoic means 'ancient life' and is the name given to an ERA of recorded time which lasted from 570 to 225 million years ago. The Palaeozoic spans 6 PERIODS – the Cambrian, Ordovician, Silurian, Devonian, Carboniferous and Permian.

Panspermia was a theory developed by ARRHENIUS. It stated that life arrived on Earth in the form of a bacterial spore which had escaped from a distant planet. In its original form the theory has been rejected, since in space the spore would have been subjected

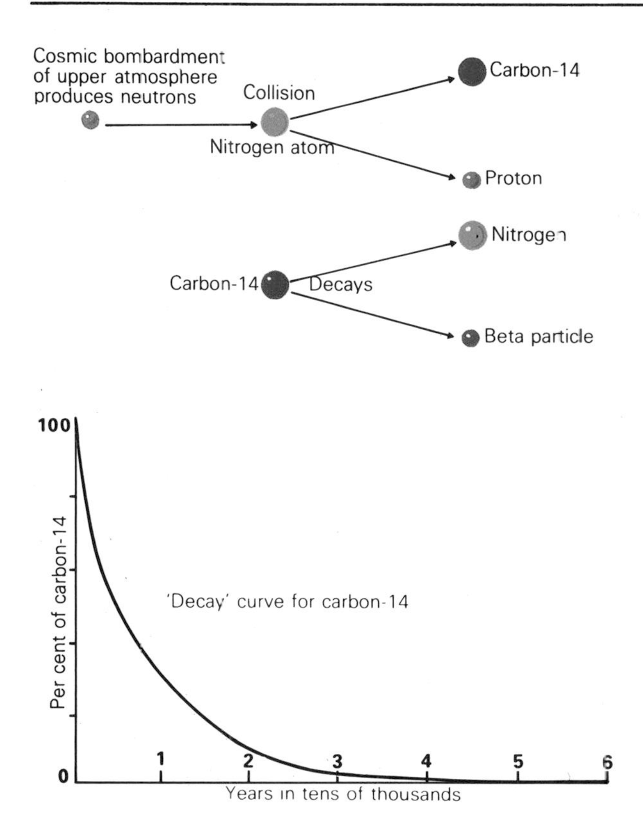

Left: This diagram shows the development of carbon-14 in the upper atmosphere. Carbon-14 can be used to date once-living materials. Cosmic bombardment of the upper atmosphere produces neutrons. These collide with atoms of nitrogen to produce carbon-14 and protons. Carbon-14 is taken up by living organisms, but after their death it decays at a constant rate into nitrogen and beta particles. The amount of carbon-14 in their remains is halved every 5,570 years. After about 55,000 years there is very little left, and so the carbon-14 dating method cannot be used for remains older than this.

which are considered to be the same age as the Earth, and of 3,400 million years for the oldest known Earth rocks. Rocks as young as 30,000 years old can also be dated by the potassium-argon method. But dates as far back as 50,000 years are gained from measuring amounts of a radioactive isotope of carbon found in the remains of organisms. The relative amounts of the isotope and of stable carbon present in the organisms while they were alive can be judged fairly accurately. So the quantity of the isotope in their remains gives a measure of their age. Practically all of the isotope decays into nitrogen in 55,000 years, which explains the limited range of carbon dating.

Radioactive dating has been applied to the studies of PALAEOMAGNETISM and SEA-FLOOR SPREADING. Alternate periods of normal and reversed magnetism in the Earth's magnetic field are recorded in cores of sediments from the sea bed. They are also recorded as parallel strips in the lavas which cover the floor of the oceans either side of the MID-OCEANIC RIDGES. These strips formed from lavas that welled up and cooled at the ridges, and were then carried away

ages of 80 million years for the start of the Tertiary period, and 240 million years for the start of the Cambrian. Another early calculation was based on the rates at which it was thought certain kinds of rocks were laid down. This put the opening of the Cambrian at about 600 million years ago. We now know that the first and the third of these estimates were surprisingly good. Yet later, in 1883, William KELVIN worked out that the Earth was no more than 40 million years old, assuming that it had cooled from an original molten state. He was mistaken partly because he did not know that the Earth contains unstable radioactive elements (see RADIOACTIVITY). As these decay they release heat and so slow down the rate at which the Earth cools.

Measurement of radioactive elements and their decay products is today the standard way to date rocks. The most useful measurement is that of an ISOTOPE of potassium as it decays into an isotope of argon. As we know the rate at which this change takes place, we can measure how much of each isotope exists in a rock and work out its age. Potassium-argon dates of 4,600 million years have been obtained for meteorites,

Right: A study of the ocean floor has revealed that on either side of the mid-oceanic ridges, iron minerals in its rocks are lined up with the Earth's magnetic field. Strips of reversed and normal magnetization form the same pattern on either side of the ridges (*top*), as the Earth's magnetic field has alternated between normal and reversed. Matching alternations are also recorded in sediments which have accumulated on the ocean floor (*below*). The epochs of normal and reversed magnetization, and the shorter reversals or events within them, have been dated by the potassium-argon method. Measuring the magnetic polarity of sea-floor sediments therefore provides a ready magnetic chronology or timescale.

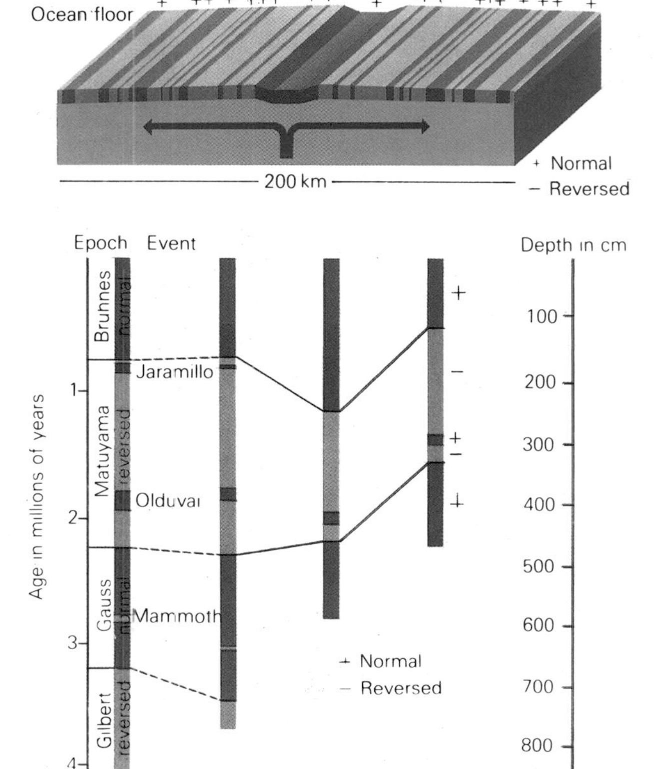

to amounts of radiation several times above that needed to kill any Earth-living spore. That a spore or cell arrived on Earth in a meteorite, however, is not so readily disproved.

Pasteur, Louis (1822–95) was a French scientist who, among other great achievements, designed experiments which finally proved wrong the theory of spontaneous generation *(see page 3).* He established that certain organic substances (*see* ORGANIC MOLECULES) are broken down by micro-organisms in the atmosphere, and that this decomposition cannot happen in their absence.

Periods are sub-divisions of ERAS and each is identified with specific fossil plants and animals.

Permafrost is the permanently frozen ground of arctic and antarctic regions, such as the tundra beyond the northern coniferous forests. During the glacial stages of the Pleistocene, permafrost was extensive in the mid-northern hemisphere. The soils in these regions often display features of former permafrost.

Permafrost in Siberia

Photosynthesis is a process by which living organisms make sugar out of water and carbon dioxide. The energy for this synthesis is provided by sunlight, which is captured by a green pigment known as chlorophyll. ENZYMES convert some of the sugar into starch for storage, and the rest is broken down to free energy during respiration *(see page 6).* In EUKARYOTES chlorophyll is concentrated in structures called chloroplasts, and some people have suggested that these are the descendants of former free-living microscopic organisms.

Pre-biotic means 'before life'. The term is often used of chemical substances which we assume formed in the atmosphere and oceans of the early Earth and from which the first living organisms are believed to have developed. Some scientists have pointed out, however, that there is no direct evidence for these pre-biotic substances being manufactured on Earth, although they do appear to be plentiful in inter-stellar space. These scientists therefore

sideways as the ocean floors expanded. As they cooled, the lavas were imprinted by the Earth's magnetic field. Potassium-argon dates for the normal and reversed periods show that the ocean floors have spread from the ridges at between 10–100 millimetres each year.

How a fossil is formed

In order for organisms or traces of their activities to appear in the fossil record they must be preserved. Many organisms are eaten by predators. The dead remains of those left will normally decompose or be destroyed by scavengers, winds, waves and currents. Even after FOSSILIZATION, the remains of an organism may still be destroyed by chemical action. In other words, fossils are rarely a representative sample of former plant and animal communities.

More distortion is introduced because usually only the hard parts of an organism, such as teeth, bones and shells, are preserved. The fossil may be of the hard part itself, or perhaps a CAST of its inside or outside. Soft parts and entirely soft-bodied organisms are known mostly from impressions left in the sediments which buried them. Very rarely indeed, such impressions may also indicate what colour the organism was. It is clear that when a group of organisms evolved hard parts their chances of being fossilized must have greatly increased. Perhaps this explains why so many new forms of life appear abruptly in the fossil record at the beginning of the Cambrian period.

Preservation is most likely where the dead organism is saved from destruction. On land this happens only in special situations. For example, insects may be entombed in tree resin which later fossilizes into AMBER. Much more common is the preservation in peat bogs of plant materials, bones and, occasionally, soft parts. But most spectacular of all are the frozen mammoths in the PERMAFROST of Siberia.

Marine fossils

Marine environments are much more favourable than the land for fossilization, as large parts of the sea-floor are continuously buried by sediment from rivers. But the remains of marine organisms are often chemically rearranged or altered during the process of fossilization. For example, some modern shells are made from one form of calcium

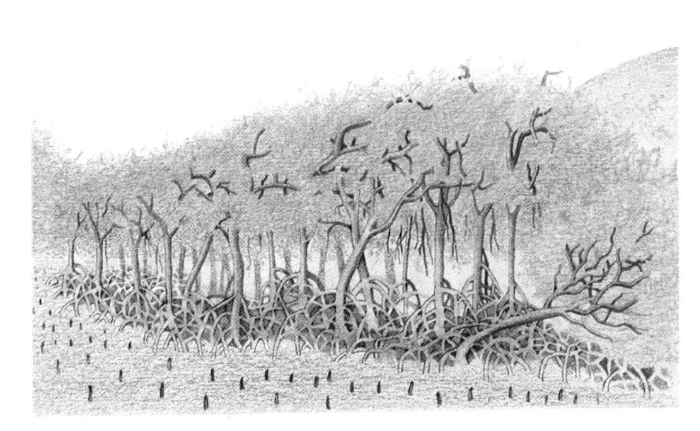

Right: The process of fossilization takes place in various ways. In the scenes shown here, for example, a mangrove swamp is gradually submerged by water, and, as sea level rises, the remains of its vegetation are eventually buried beneath marine sediments. Animals with shells, particularly gastropods, flourish in the shallow coastal waters. In turn, their remains are covered by sediments carried down by rivers. A further rise in sea level produces a deeper-water environment, in which fish are the dominant types of animal. Their skeletons accumulate in the muds of the sea floor. In time, sea level falls dramatically, and the sea floor becomes land once more. Beneath the new land surface are successive layers of rock which contain fossils of fish, the gastropods, and the trunks of trees which once grew in the mangrove swamp.

favour the idea of an extra-terrestrial origin for life.
Prokaryotes include BLUE-GREEN ALGAE, BACTERIA and a group of mould-like organisms called actinomycetes. Their cells lack a well-defined centre or nucleus. Prokaryotes multiply by ASEXUAL REPRODUCTION *(see page 12)* in a process called binary fission. EUKARYOTES reproduce by more complex processes.
Protein is the structural matter of life, and is found in all cells. Much of our vegetable and meat diet is protein. It is made up from AMINO ACIDS *(see page 12)* of which, although many are known, just 20 provide the building blocks for all proteins. In other words, the thousands of proteins found in living organisms differ only in the arrangement of these 20 amino acids.

Radioactivity is the process in which unstable ATOMS decay, either through losing particles or through discharging radiation. The rate of decay is expressed as the half-life (being the time taken for half of the atoms to break down into other substances). Because of such decay, the environment is mainly made up of stable ISOTOPES. Rates of decay vary from one isotope to another, but they are always constant in each.

Sea-floor spreading is the widening of the ocean floors either side of the MID-OCEANIC RIDGES, where new material is added to the Earth's crust by the upwelling of molten rock or magma. Sea-floor spreading has produced the oceans as we know them today.
Silica is a mineral made up

Rock strata, Lulworth Cove, England

Left: A fossil ammonite, *Anahoplites,* from the Gault Clay of south-east England. The outer form of the shell has been preserved in iron pyrites, which tends to disintegrate when exposed to air.

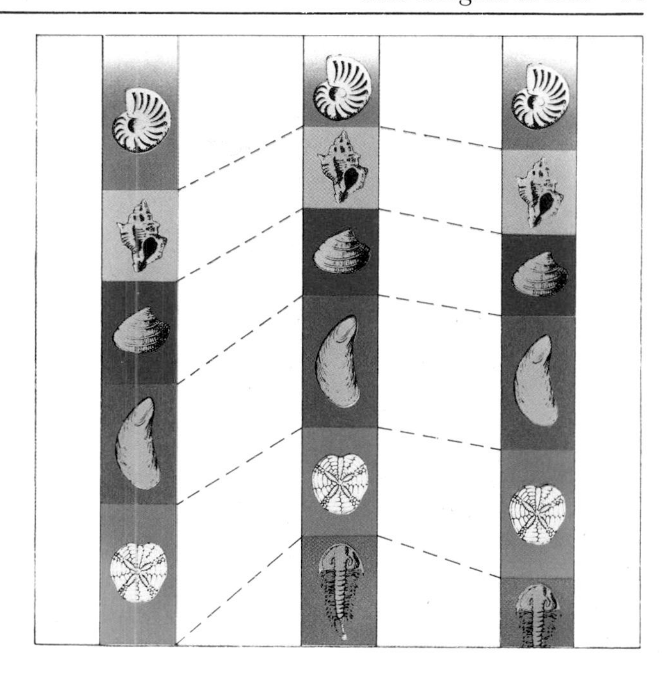

Above: Fossils are used in the relative dating of rocks. The presence of a specific type of ammonite, for example, will often allow the palaeontologist to relate the rock in which it is found to a particular zone or stage of a geological system. Fossils also help to relate strata over considerable distances (as in the matching coloured blocks in the diagram which represent successive strata), even if they look different.

carbonate known as ARAGONITE, which through time often changes into a more stable form called calcite. So although aragonite shells are common in Cainozoic rocks, and to a lesser extent in Mesozoic ones, they are hardly known in older rocks. In other cases, the hard parts are impregnated or replaced by calcite, SILICA or iron compounds from water surrounding the remains. However, the outside form of the fossil is not changed, and in those made of iron pyrites the details are often very sharp. The last kind of change is that where the soft parts lose their more volatile substances and leave a carbon-rich residue, which may trace the outline of the organism.

What fossils tell

Fossils are used to date rocks and reconstruct past environments. For example, there may be two layers of rock, one of which yields a large variety of fossils. The other may contain a much smaller variety, but of organisms known to have lived within a short geological time span. In practice, both layers could be related not only to their geological periods or epochs, but probably also to their respective STAGES and maybe to their ZONES as well. This is one of the ways in which geologists recognize different rock units and follow them across country when making geological maps. Exactly the same principle is used to identify rock layers reached in bore holes.

Below: A petrified tree trunk, in which the original wood has been replaced by silica. This specimen is from Arizona, USA.

of ATOMS of silicon and oxygen. A common form is quartz — a hard, glassy substance. The majority of sand grains on most beaches are composed of quartz.

Stages are sub-divisions of SYSTEMS, and are recognized by their particular groups of fossils. Usually a stage is a succession of ZONES.

Strata is the collective name for layers of rock, an individual layer being a stratum. Strata may vary considerably in both thickness and width.

Stromatolites are reef-like communities of ELUE-GREEN ALGAE and BACTERIA. Living examples have only recently been recognized, as sea creatures feed on them, so preventing their development into significant structures. However, such creatures had not evolved in the Pre-Cambrian era, and large stromatolite colonies were therefore quite common then.

Systems are the sequences of rocks which correspond to individual PERIODS.

U

Ultraviolet light has a shorter wavelength than that of visible light.

V

Viruses are generally much smaller than the smallest BACTERIA. They have no NUCLEUS or CYTOPLASM (*see pages 15, 13*), and consist almost entirely of DNA (*see page 13*) or RNA (*see page 15*), usually with a PROTEIN covering. All viruses live as parasites on higher organisms and cannot reproduce without the aid of the ENZYMES of their host. Since they depend on other organisms for their continued survival, some scientists believe that viruses must have evolved after cellular forms of life such as bacteria. On the other hand, their very primitive characteristics have been said to indicate an origin earlier than cells. But, because they are unable to reproduce independently, it has also been argued that they should not be seen as living organisms at all. Certainly they seem to occupy a twilight zone between life and non-life.

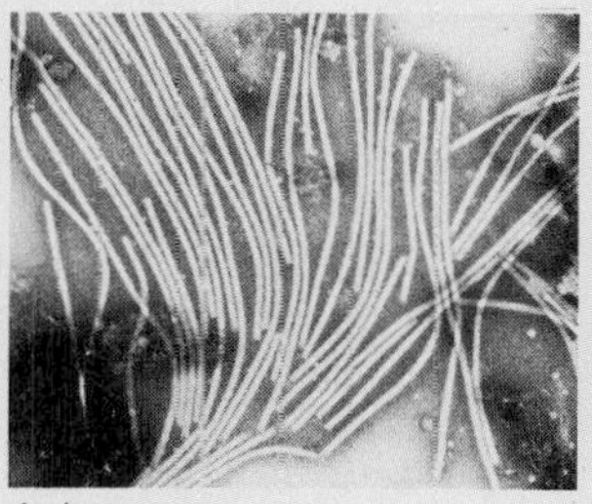

A virus

Z

Zone refers to the rock stratum or STRATA laid down in a specific interval of time and which can be identified by particular kinds of fossil organisms. Although 2 sets of strata may be very different in composition and thickness, if they have the same zonal fossils they belong to the same zone. The zones take their names from the zonal fossils.

The millions of plants and animals which live on the Earth today have evolved to their present forms throughout the history of our planet. This process involves environmental selection and biological inheritance.

Theories of Evolution

Organisms change with time and such change is called evolution. It was once widely believed that all plants and animals had been specially created in their present form. The first serious challenge to this view was made by Jean LAMARCK in the early 1800s. He thought that organisms had started by spontaneous generation (*see page 3*), but that over time each had become better adapted to its environment through inheriting acquired characteristics from its parents. According to this idea giraffe necks became longer from repeatedly stretching for tree leaves, and the added length achieved in one generation was inherited by the next.

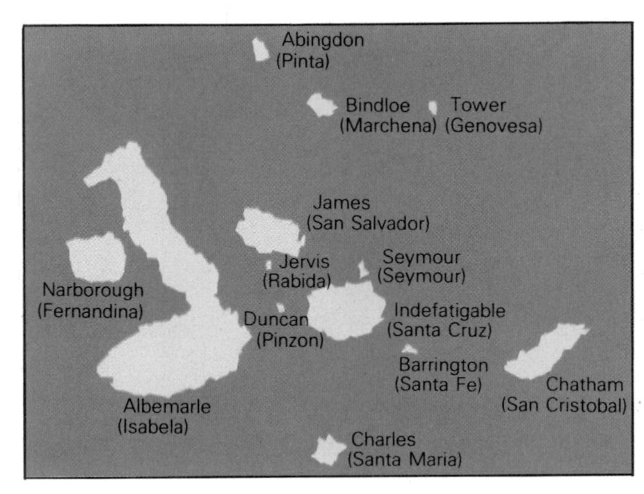

Above: Each island in the Galapagos archipelago has its own type of tortoise (*right*). The 2 longer-necked species shown live in dry places and feed on tree cacti, whereas the short-necked species lives in moist regions and feeds off more luxuriant, low-growing vegetation.

Left: Lamarck believed that giraffe necks had become longer from repeatedly stretching for tree leaves (*top*) and that the long necks achieved in one generation had been inherited by the next. According to Darwin's views, however, selection would favour individuals with the longest necks (*below*). Over the generations the length of the neck would progressively increase, but there would still be room for variations.

In 1844 DARWIN (*see page 5*) presented a different view of ADAPTIVE EVOLUTION. Put simply, all individuals in a plant or animal SPECIES vary in some way, and together they produce more offspring than can survive. The environment in which they live will determine which individuals are best fitted to survive, and only those so 'selected' will therefore reproduce. In the case of the giraffe, selection favoured individuals with the longest necks, so that over the generations the length of the neck progressively increased. Where a population of one species is broken up, say by a rise in sea-level, then the changes resulting from selection in each of the now separate groups could well differ. They might even diverge to the point where individuals from one group could no longer interbreed with those of another. This reasoning

Reference

A **Adaptive evolution** results in organisms becoming better fitted to the environments in which they live. The fit is so close that for a long time organisms were thought to have been created in their present form by a supernatural force. However, becoming adapted to an environment is the end product of a series of changes in organisms over time — changes which favoured their chances of survival through natural selection (*see page 12*). Because there was so much variation between individuals in populations which were the ancestors of living organisms, some were better equipped than others to survive. Only the survivors reproduced, so that it was their characteristics which were passed on to the next generation. The process was repeated over and over again and in this way many organisms have come to differ greatly from their predecessors. For example, speed was essential for the zebra's forebears to survive, and so down the ages their legs became progressively longer and their toes were reduced to one.

Amino acids are the chemical building blocks of PROTEIN (*see page 10*). Their general formula is R CH (NH_2) COOH, where R is a side group of any atoms, usually carbon and hydrogen. When amino acids are linked into chains to form protein, a molecule of water (H_2O) is removed at each linkage point. Twenty different amino acids are found in protein, and their number and combination control specific types of protein. Since amino acids can combine in so many different ways, it is not surprising that thousands of proteins are known.

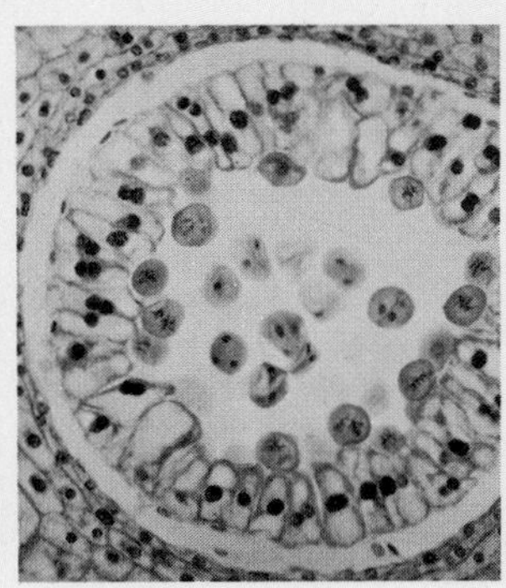

Chromosomes in a cell

Asexual reproduction occurs when one or more offspring develop from a parent organism without the aid of GAMETES, or sex cells.

C **Chromosomes** are usually included in the cell NUCLEUS. Each is made up of a central strand of one very long DNA molecule, which in turn comprises hundreds of GENES. Around the DNA molecule there are proteins called histones. Genes which are covered by

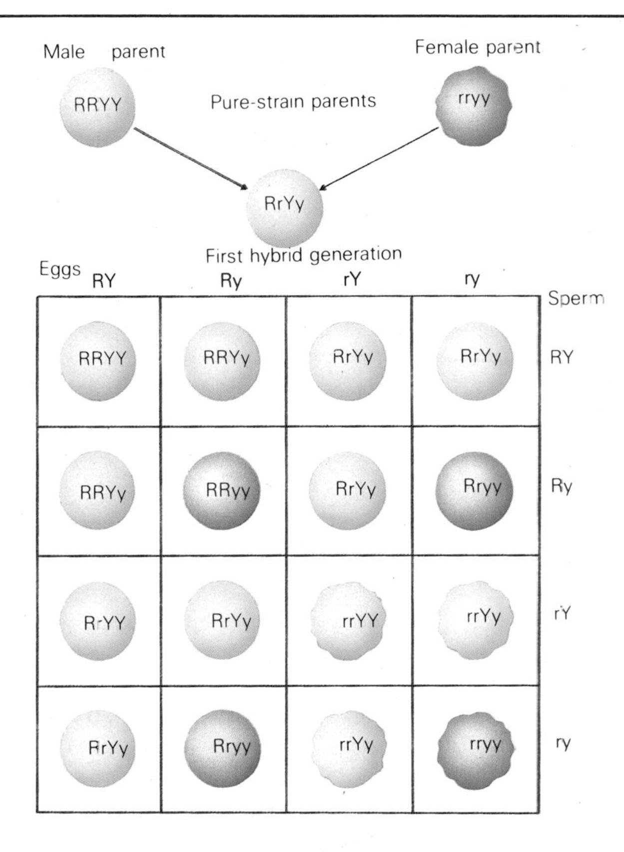

Left: If a male pea plant with only dominant genes for round, yellow (RRYY) peas is crossed with a female pea plant with only recessive genes for wrinkled, green (rryy) peas, the offspring have mixed genes, though they will only produce peas with the dominant round, yellow traits. When the first generation plants are crossed, however, the wrinkled and green traits reappear in a constant ratio to the yellow and round ones. There are always 3 times as many yellow ones and 3 times as many round ones.

was used by Darwin to explain the different but closely related species of tortoises and birds on each island in the Galapagos.

How heredity works

However, Darwin could not explain what caused the variation between individuals on which selection depends. This was made clear by Gregor MENDEL in his experiments with peas. He found that the characteristics passed on to each generation are controlled by inherited units, which we now call GENES. He cross-bred pure strains of round, yellow peas with wrinkled, green ones and found that the first generation of offspring were all round and yellow. When these in turn were crossed, four kinds of peas resulted. In every 16, 9 were round and yellow, 3 round and green, 3 wrinkled and yellow and 1 was wrinkled and green. From this he worked out that each of the original peas had two equivalent genes for colour and two equivalent genes for shape. The genes for yellow colour and round shape he described as DOMINANT; those for green colour and wrinkled shape as RECESSIVE. In the first generation of peas only the dominant genes were expressed, making all the offspring round and yellow. In the second generation the recessive green and wrinkled ones were 're-vealed', but only where they were responsible for colour or shape.

Genes make up strands called CHROMOSOMES, which in all EUKARYOTES (*see page 6*) are in the cell NUCLEUS. Just as there are pairs of equivalent genes, so in most cells there are matching sets (2N) of the basic number of chromosomes (N). In ASEXUAL reproduction the number of chromosomes doubles (to 4N) before the parent cell divides. Each daughter cell then has the correct amount (2N) of chromosomes. This process is known as MITOSIS. In SEXUAL reproduction the cell division is called MEIOSIS. Here the same chromosome doubling (to 4N) takes place, but the chromosomes segregate in a different way prior to cell division. The new cells therefore have the same number of chromosomes (2N) as the parent cell, but in different combinations. A second division then follows to produce sex cells, or GAMETES, which have 50 per cent (N) of the normal number of chromosomes (2N). When two gametes (usually a male and female) unite they

Below: Meiosis (the process of cell division in sexual reproduction) taking place in an organism with matching sets (2N) of the basic number of chromosomes (N). The result is a set of cells which has only 50% of the chromosomes of the parent cell. The parent cell may initially divide in 1 of 2 ways, so far as the combination of chromosomes is concerned. In practice, therefore, 2 different sets of sex cells, or gametes, are possible. As the cell divides, portions of matching chromosomes often stick together and genetic material is exchanged between the chromosomes. This 'crossing-over' is a further source of genetic variation.

2N = 4
4N
Either
Or
Nuclear division
First meiotic division
2N
2N
Second meiotic division
2N
2N
N N N N N N N N

histones cannot control the making of protein and vice versa. Chromosomes occur in pairs in most cells. Both members of a pair are identical in appearance and are called homologous chromosomes. The number of paired chromosomes in a cell varies from SPECIES to species. Man, for example, has 23 pairs.

Codons are non-overlapping triplets of NUCLEOTIDE bases. Each codon corresponds to an AMINO ACID. The 4 different nucleotide bases can combine into 64 possible triplets. But the 64 triplet sequences correspond to only 20 amino acids and such instructions as 'start' and 'stop'. It is therefore clear that some amino acids are dictated by more than one codon.

Cytoplasm is the material found inside the cell membrane or cell wall. It also occurs outside the NUCLEUS or (if the cell has no nucleus) the loop of DNA.

D

DNA is short for deoxyribonucleic acid. DNA occurs as giant molecules and in most organisms is the store of genetic information

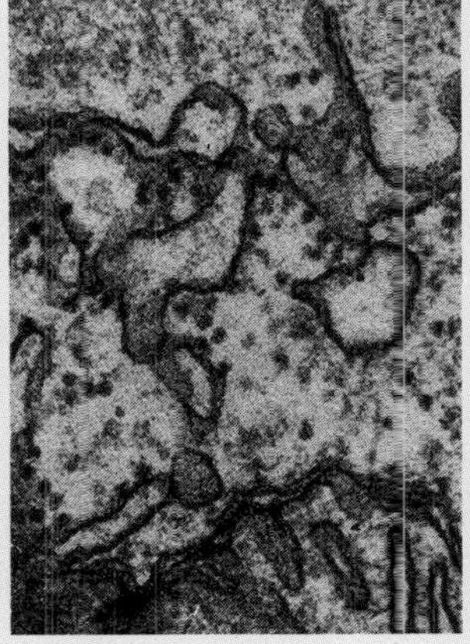

Cytoplasm

(*see* GENE) which is duplicated and passed on to the NUCLEUS of daughter cells. DNA molecules are made up of 4 different types of NUCLEOTIDES.

Dominant characteristics are those which tend to prevail in each new generation of organisms. In humans, one pair of CHROMOSOMES carries GENES for eye colour. If one parent has eye colour genes which are both brown and the other's genes are both for blue, they will always have brown-eyed children. So in this case the gene for brown eye colour is dominant over that for blue eyes.

G

Gametes are reproductive, or sex, cells. During sexual reproduction 2 gametes unite to form a ZYGOTE.

Genes are chemical codes which control the making of proteins — the structural matter of life. Each gene carries the information needed to produce one protein. A gene has more than one state, and so in practice gives rise to slightly different proteins. These different states cause variations in the same SPECIES.

form a ZYGOTE with the normal number (2N) of chromosomes, and the zygote then develops into a new organism. Sexual re-shuffling of the genes into new combinations through meiosis produced the contrasts that Mendel observed in his peas.

The genetic code

The gene strands, or chromosomes, are actually very long DNA molecules. Each molecule is shaped rather like a spiral staircase. The 'sides' are made up of two identical chains of alternate sugar and phosphate molecules. The 'steps' joining these chains each have a pair of substances called bases, of which there are four: adenine, thymine, guanine and cytosine — A, T, G and C for short. A always joins with T to form a step, and G with C. The staircase is built up first of all from units called NUCLEOTIDES. Every nucleotide has a sugar molecule and a phosphate molecule — in effect a section of one staircase side—to which one of the four bases is attached. The way in which nucleotides are arranged into DNA is therefore decided by the way in which the bases are paired. And the possible combinations of paired bases are endless. When a chromosome doubles, the DNA molecule 'unzips' itself. Unpaired bases then link up with nucleotides in the cell nucleus to form two new molecules of DNA. In this way genetic information in the chromosome is passed on, by the gametes, down through the generations.

Mendel's hereditary units correspond to segments of the DNA molecule which are identified as triplets of bases, for example: AGT, TCA, GCA or CGT. A triplet is a sort of 'code word' for making one of the AMINO ACIDS which are the sole ingredients of protein. A specific sequence of triplets is therefore a code for a certain kind of protein. Such a sequence makes one hereditary unit (or one gene). Although a multitude of proteins exists in living organisms, they are all assembled from just 20 common amino acids.

How proteins form

Protein is formed in the CYTOPLASM surrounding the cell nucleus, by a substance called RNA, a near-relative of DNA. Spirally-coiled nucleotide chains in the DNA molecule separate slightly to form a PUFF, which then travels along the molecule. While the chains are apart, nucleotides

Below: The gene strands, or chromosomes, contain all the genetic information carried in the body's cells. Every chromosome is made up of 2 chromatids, each of which is an immensely long, coiled molecule of DNA. The DNA molecule itself is rather like a spiral staircase, with sides made up of sugar and phosphate molecules. Joining these are cross-pieces, or 'steps', each of which has a pair of 4 bases—adenine, guanine, thymine and cytosine. These bases, or chemical units, can appear in an infinitely variable order, and the order of the paired links makes up the coded instructions which can be used elsewhere in the cell. When the cell is ready to divide, the DNA must be replicated exactly, so that each new cell will have the same type of DNA. This happens when the DNA splits. The chemical units which form the cross-links snap on to the ends of the split cross-links, forming 2 identical new strands of DNA.

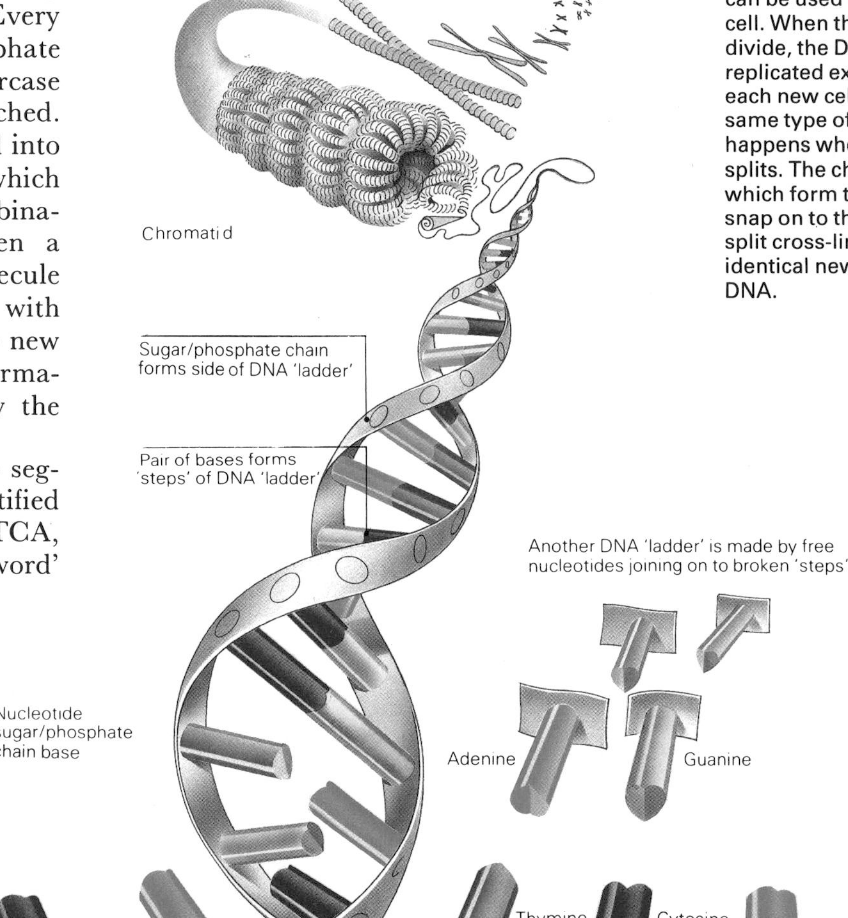

Lamarck, Jean-Baptiste (1744–1829), was a French biologist whose theory of evolution rightly recognized that organisms had become better adapted to their environments over time, and that the diversity of life was due to adaptation. But his theory was faulty as it assumed that characteristics acquired during an organism's lifetime are passed on to its offspring. Although the inheriting of acquired characteristics has not been completely disproved, it is obvious that many (such as the loss of a limb in an accident, for example) are not inherited by the next generation.

Jean-Baptiste Lamarck

Meiosis is the process of cell division which takes place at some stage in the life of all organisms with SEXUAL REPRODUCTION. It results in 4 daughter cells with nuclei containing half the number of CHROMOSOMES of the parental NUCLEUS.

Mendel, Gregor (1822–84), was an Austrian monk who founded the scientific study of heredity or genetics. From experiments in which he crossed different kinds of pea plants, he established that heredity characteristics are passed on by units which we now call GENES.

Gregor Mendel

Mitosis is the process of cell division which produces new cells or individuals with CHROMOSOMES identical to those of the parent.

Mutations are errors in duplicating DNA which may lead to the production of different proteins. Mutations may be restricted to GENES or may affect larger parts of the CHROMOSOME. If mutations occur in an organism's sex cells they can be passed on to the next generation.

line up against one of them, in a sequence decided by the positions of the bases, to form RNA. (The bases in RNA are the same as in DNA, except that thymine is replaced by the closely related uracil, or U.) As the chains connect once more, RNA is released as a strand of nucleotides with unpaired bases. It enters the cytoplasm where it acts as template, or copy, for the making of protein.

This 'messenger' RNA attaches itself to a RIBOSOME, which moves along the nucleotide strand 'reading' the coded message. At the same time molecules of another kind of RNA, transfer RNA, carry to the ribosome the amino acids that match their triplets of bases. The ribosome then assembles the amino acids into a protein chain, according to the instructions coded on the messenger RNA.

All organisms have the same set of RNA CODONS. Since there are four bases which can combine into different groups of three, there are altogether 64 triplet codons. Not only do they inform the ribosome of the order in which to assemble the amino acids, they also instruct it where to start and stop. Thus AUG serves as a 'start' signal, whereas UAA, UAG and UGA signify 'stop'. As three triplets can specify 'stop', it appears that the genetic code involves some redundancy. For instance, out of the 20 acids specified by the 64 codons, eight are each specified by four or more different triplets.

First RNA nucleotide base	Second RNA nucleotide base				Third RNA nucleotide base
	U	C	A	G	
Uracil (U)	Phenylaniline	Serine	Tyrosine	Cysteine	U
	Phenylaniline	Serine	Tyrosine	Cysteine	C
	Leucine	Serine	STOP	STOP	A
	Leucine	Serine	STOP	Tryptophan	G
Cytosine (C)	Leucine	Proline	Histidine	Arginine	U
	Leucine	Proline	Histidine	Arginine	C
	Leucine	Proline	Glutamine	Arginine	A
	Leucine	Proline	Glutamine	Arginine	G
Adenine (A)	Isoleucine	Threonine	Asparagine	Serine	U
	Isoleucine	Threonine	Asparagine	Serine	C
	Isoleucine	Threonine	Lysine	Arginine	A
	START/Methionine	Threonine	Lysine	Arginine	G
Guanine (G)	Valine	Alanine	Aspartic acid	Glycine	U
	Valine	Alanine	Aspartic acid	Glycine	C
	Valine	Alanine	Glutamic acid	Glycine	A
	Valine	Alanine	Glutamic acid	Glycine	G

Neutral · Aromatic · Basic · Acidic · Sulphur containing

From The Mechanisms of Evolution F. J. Ayala. Copyright © 1978 by Scientific American, Inc. All rights reserved.

Above: Triplets of nucleotide bases act as signals for the manufacture of 20 amino acids. They also specify 'start' and 'stop', to signal the beginning and end of the assembly of amino acids that correspond to a specific protein. For example, Uracil (first base) with Adenine (A — second base) plus Adenine (A — third base) equal 'stop'. Since only 20 amino acids are specified by 64 signals, the genetic code is highly redundant (e.g. UAA, UAG and UGA all specify 'stop').

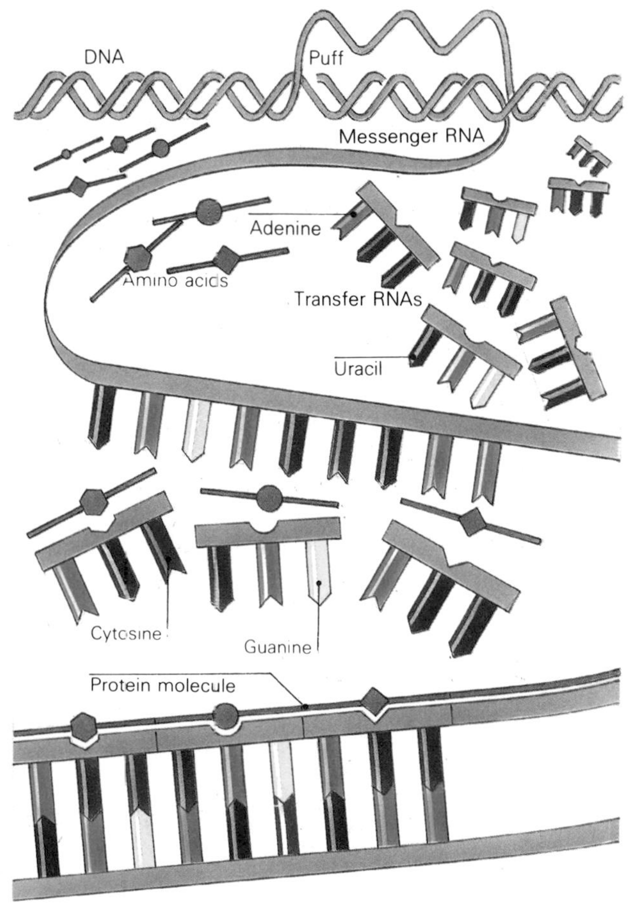

Left: How the information in the DNA molecule is used to make protein. Messenger RNA copies the genetic code from DNA when the DNA coils separate to form a puff. It then carries its copy of the code to the ribosome. As the ribosome moves along the RNA strand 'reading' the coded message, transfer RNAs convey to the ribosome the amino acids that match their triplets of bases. Here they are assembled into protein in a sequence dictated by the messenger RNA.

Mistakes in the code

Any error in producing a replica of the DNA molecule during meiosis could affect protein assembly in the developing offspring. Such errors produce MUTATIONS. In point mutations one pair of nucleotide bases replaces another. Because of the redundancy in the genetic code this need have no practical effect. But it could lead to one amino acid being substituted for another, or even to the triplet of bases being altered so as to specify the 'stop' signal. Larger mutations arise when a nucleotide is put in or taken out. Small mutations are the basic source of most variety in a population, as they spread in ever-different combinations by sexual reproduction. Natural selection eventually decides if a small mutation is of advantage to organisms. Large mutations tend not to be so.

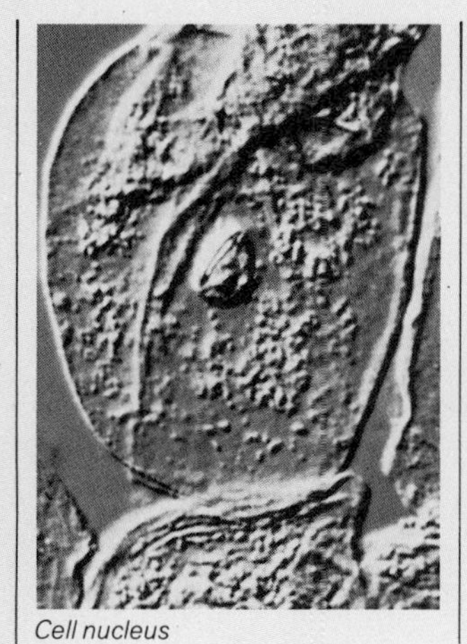

Cell nucleus

N **Nucleotides** are combinations of phosphate, sugar and 1 of 4 bases — adenine, thymine, guanine and cytosine.

Nucleus is the membrane-bound body which contains the CHROMOSOMES in a EUKARYOTE (*see page 6*) cell.

P **Puff** is that part of the DNA molecule which uncoils slightly to allow access to the information recorded in the GENE sequence of a single DNA strand. This sequence is used as a pattern to be copied for making messenger RNA.

R **Recessive** characteristics are those which are least likely to prevail in each new generation. A recessive character appears only when both GENES for that characteristic are recessive. Where a DOMINANT and a recessive gene for a characteristic occur in the same organism, it is always the dominant gene which is expressed, or revealed.

Ribosomes are the sites at which protein synthesis takes place in a cell.

RNA stands for ribonucleic acid. Messenger RNA copies the genetic code from DNA and carries it to the RIBOSOME, where it dictates the sequence in which AMINO ACIDS are assembled into proteins. Transfer RNA carries the amino acids to the ribosome.

S **Sexual reproduction** involves the fusion of male and female sex cells or GAMETES.

Species are groups of organisms which are distinct from other groups by their GENES. Members of one species can breed with each other, but not with members of other species.

Z **Zygote** is a cell formed by the union of 2 GAMETES.

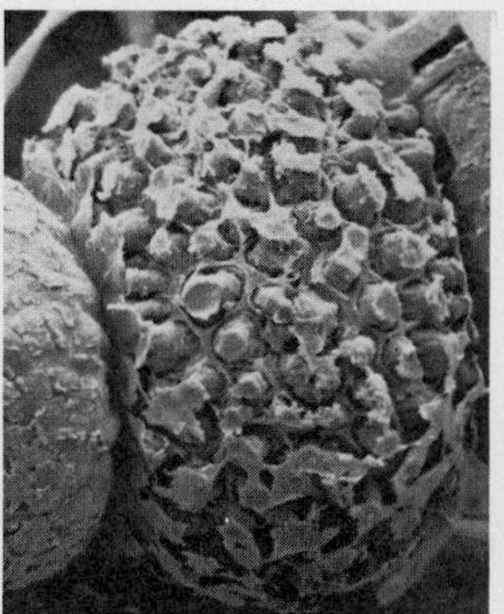

A formed zygote

From their primitive beginnings in water, plants have adapted to a way of life away from it, in all the diverse habitats of land.

Evolution of Plants

From 'Evolution of Multicellular Plants and Animals', J. W. Valentine. Copyright © 1978 by Scientific American, Inc. All rights reserved.

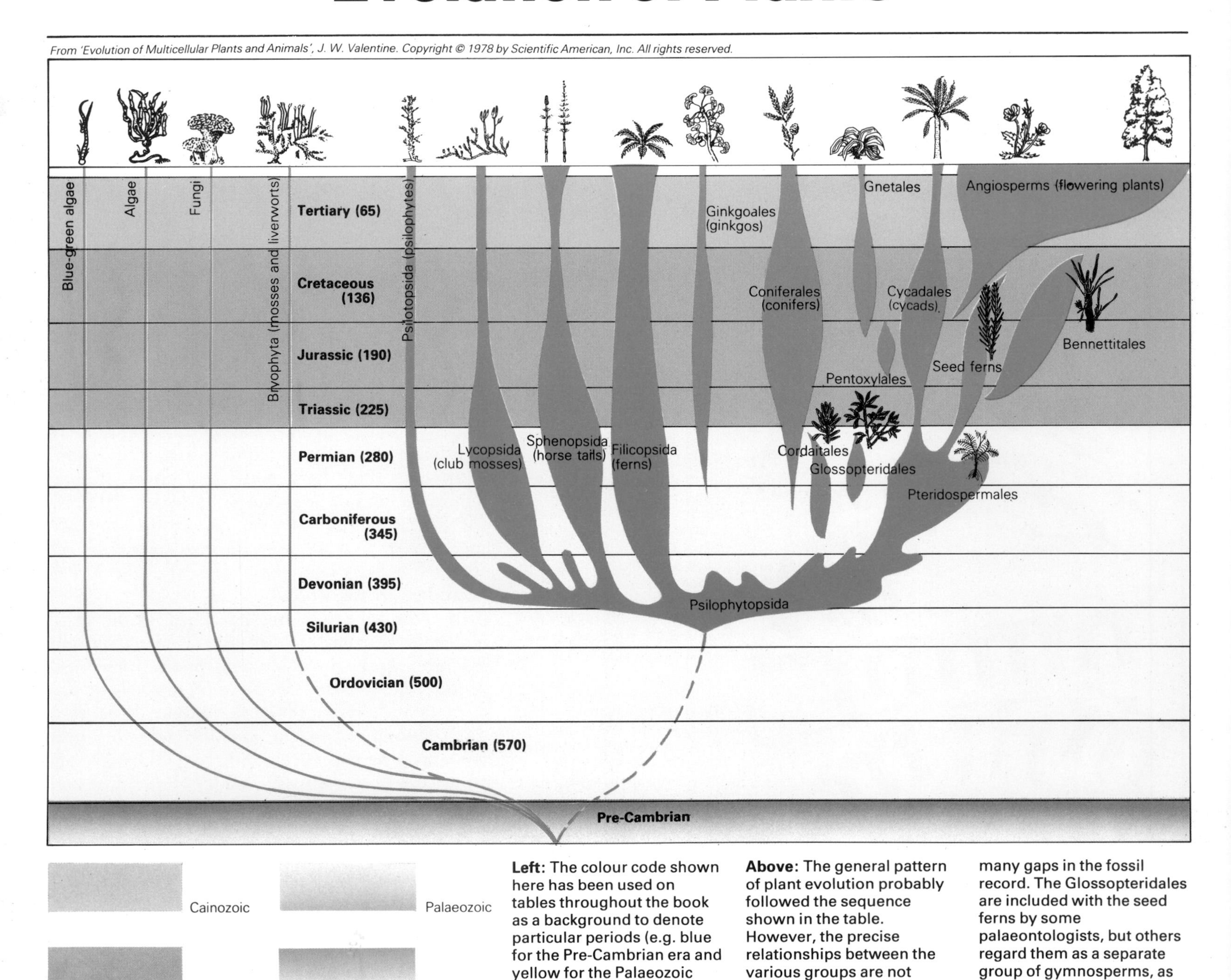

Left: The colour code shown here has been used on tables throughout the book as a background to denote particular periods (e.g. blue for the Pre-Cambrian era and yellow for the Palaeozoic era).

Above: The general pattern of plant evolution probably followed the sequence shown in the table. However, the precise relationships between the various groups are not always clear, as there are many gaps in the fossil record. The Glossopteridales are included with the seed ferns by some palaeontologists, but others regard them as a separate group of gymnosperms, as shown here.

Reference

A

Angiospermae are a sub-division of the seed plants, or SPERMATOPHYTA. The angiosperms are the highest form of seed plants. They are also known as the flowering plants, and their seeds are always enclosed in fruits.

Annularia are leaf fossils of CALAMITES in which the leaves are arranged in whorls. Unlike those in ASTEROPHYLLITES, however, the leaves tend to stand out at right angles from the stem and are shaped like elongated ovals.

Asterophyllites are leaf fossils of CALAMITES in which the leaves are arranged in whorls. Each whorl has needle-like leaves, which tend to be cupped upwards.

B

Bennettitales are an extinct order of the GYMNOSPERMAE. They were palm-like plants with reproductive organs that strongly resembled the flower of ANGIOSPERMAE. They lived from the Triassic up until Cretaceous times.

Bryophyta are a division of the plant kingdom which includes the mosses and liverworts. They lack VASCULAR TISSUES but possess anchoring RHIZOIDS. These plants have 2 alternate generations — GAMETOPHYTE and SPOROPHYTE. Unlike PTERIDOPHYTA, in bryophytes the gametophyte generation is the adult plant. It is necessary for this to live in moist places since the male sex cells it produces need to make use of a film of water in order to swim to the female sex organs, which are on the same adult plant.

C

Calamites are fossil CASTS *(see page 4)* of the inner stems of plants belonging to the SPHENOPSIDA. They thrived in the Carboniferous and many looked like a giant version of EQUISETUM.

Calamites

Carpels are the female structures found in the centre of most flowers. A single carpel consists of an OVARY which contains one or more OVULES which in turn contain the sex cells. The top of the ovary is drawn up into

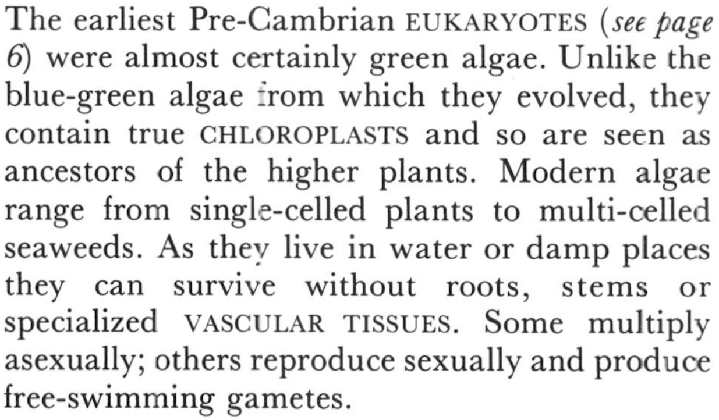

Left: Internal mould of a *Calamites* stem, from the Carboniferous coal swamps. This specimen was found at Snowden Colliery in Kent, south-east England.

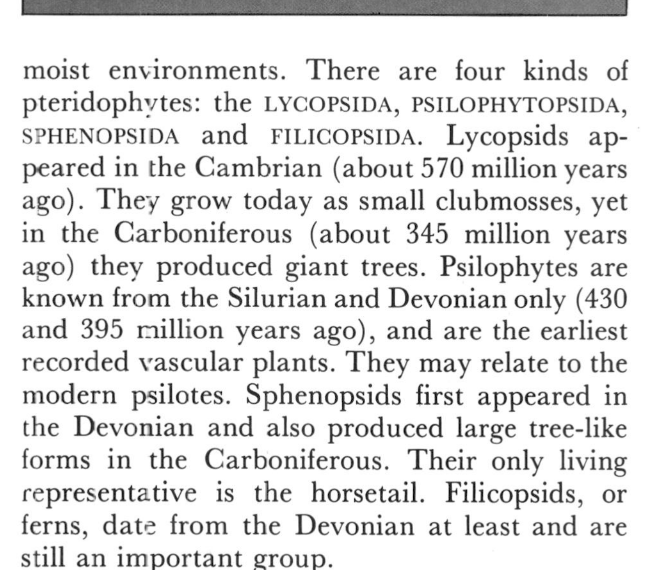

Right: *Stigmaria ficoides*, a fossil root of the giant tree *Lepidodendron*, showing the points where rootlets were attached.

The earliest Pre-Cambrian EUKARYOTES (*see page 6*) were almost certainly green algae. Unlike the blue-green algae from which they evolved, they contain true CHLOROPLASTS and so are seen as ancestors of the higher plants. Modern algae range from single-celled plants to multi-celled seaweeds. As they live in water or damp places they can survive without roots, stems or specialized VASCULAR TISSUES. Some multiply asexually; others reproduce sexually and produce free-swimming gametes.

The more complex BRYOPHYTA, which include MOSSES and LIVERWORTS, are known from Cambrian rocks. They also lack vascular tissues, but do have anchoring RHIZOIDS. Like the algae they are tied to wet or damp sites, and again free-swimming gametes are involved in their reproduction. Although bryophytes seem to represent an intermediate step in the conquest of land by plants, there is no evidence to connect them either with the algae or with more advanced plants.

Plants colonize the land

Adapting to life away from water required that plants develop roots and vascular systems to supply all their parts with food and water. The PTERIDOPHYTA and SPERMATOPHYTA managed to achieve this. Whether they evolved from a common ancestor, or at different times from different non-vascular ancestors, is not clear from the fossil record.

Despite their extra structures the pteridophytes remained associated with wet or damp places as their gametes generally only function in very moist environments. There are four kinds of pteridophytes: the LYCOPSIDA, PSILOPHYTOPSIDA, SPHENOPSIDA and FILICOPSIDA. Lycopsids appeared in the Cambrian (about 570 million years ago). They grow today as small clubmosses, yet in the Carboniferous (about 345 million years ago) they produced giant trees. Psilophytes are known from the Silurian and Devonian only (430 and 395 million years ago), and are the earliest recorded vascular plants. They may relate to the modern psilotes. Sphenopsids first appeared in the Devonian and also produced large tree-like forms in the Carboniferous. Their only living representative is the horsetail. Filicopsids, or ferns, date from the Devonian at least and are still an important group.

Above: A reconstruction of *Lepidodendron*, a lycopsid tree, is shown beside an immature specimen.

Below: A reconstruction of *Medullosa*, a pteridosperm tree about 4 metres high.

The spermatophytes have no need for moisture to reproduce, as the male gametes form POLLEN grains, and the zygote is protected in a SEED. In one sub-group, the GYMNOSPERMAE, the seeds are partly enclosed, whereas in the other, the ANGIOSPERMAE, the seeds are fully enclosed. From their beginnings in the Devonian, the gymnosperms came to dominate the world's vegetation for much of the Mesozoic, but steadily dwindled after the start of the Cretaceous. Of the various gymnosperms the PTERIDOSPERMALES or seed ferns died out, as did the BENNETTITALES, PENTOXYLALES, and CORDAITALES. Those which survived were the CYCADALES, CONIFERALES, TAXALES, GINKGOALES and GNETALES. Although they may well have an earlier, as yet undetected history, the first fossil angiosperms, or flowering plants, occur in early Cretaceous rock layers. They rapidly colonized the continents and by the

---

a long tube, called a STYLE, which supports a flat POLLEN-receiving surface known as a STIGMA.

Chloroplasts are small bodies containing chlorophyll which occur in the CYTOPLASM (*see page 13*) of a cell. Chlorophyll is a green pigment which traps sunlight and so provides the energy for photosynthesis (*see page 6*).

Coal is made up of partly carbonized vegetable matter and was first formed in swamps. The dead remains of swamp plants accumulated as peat, which on burial by later sediments was compressed into coal.

Trees fossilized in coal

Coal swamps were widespread in the northern hemisphere during the Carboniferous.

Coniferopsida are a subdivision of the GYMNOSPERMAE and comprise 4 orders. Of these the CONIFERALES, TAXALES and GINKGOALES have living examples, whereas the CORDAITALES are extinct. The earliest undoubted coniferopsid fossils are of Carboniferous age.

Conifers or Coniferales are an order of the CONIFEROPSIDA.

Cordaitales are an extinct order of the CONIFEROPSIDA. They first appeared in early Carboniferous times and died out at the end of the Permian. *Cordaites* was an imposing forest tree, at least 30 metres high, with strap-like leaves that were probably tough and leathery in texture.

Cross-fertilization occurs when sex cells or GAMETES (*see page 13*) from 2 organisms fuse to form a ZYGOTE (*see page 15*).

Cuticles consist of a waxy substance called cutin. They cover the leaves and stems of plants and so reduce water loss.

Cycadales are an order of the GYMNOSPERMAE. They first appeared in Upper Triassic times, and flourished during the Jurassic and Cretaceous, though today only 9 cycad GENERA survive. Most of the species resemble palm trees. The group as a whole displays many primitive features, and this is why cycads are often referred to as 'living fossils'.

D

Dichotomous means dividing into 2. When applied to the branching pattern of the PSILOPSIDA and some members of the LYCOP-

Above: In this reconstruction the Palaeozoic scene is dominated by lepidodendrids. *Lepidodendron* itself is shown front right, and in front of this is a fallen *Sigillaria* showing a *Stigmaria* root system. Beneath *Lepidodendron* is the small *Proto-lepidodendron*, while another, younger, unbranched specimen of *Lepidodendron* is shown front left. In the distance are several large trees of the genus *Bothodendron*. Numerous ferns are also shown.

end of the Cretaceous nearly everywhere outnumbered the gymnosperms—a position they have steadily reinforced up to the present day.

Primitive plants

After they emerged in the Lower Palaeozoic, the pteridophytes spread rapidly over the land during the Devonian to form the first forests. By now they were important as food for those animals that were beginning to leave the water. The life-cycle of all pteridophytes involves alternate SPOROPHYTE and GAMETOPHYTE generations. We have already noted how many of these plants were associated with damp habitats because of their gametes. In fact, the gametophytes themselves often only germinate in moist conditions.

Although the earliest pteridophyte fossils are of lycopsids, psilophytes have the most primitive features in the group. They are therefore often seen as the ancestors of the other three, more specialized, sub-groups. If this is true, the groups must have separated into different evolutionary lines in the Cambrian or Ordovician, for each sub-group remains distinct as far back as we can trace it. The lack of 'missing links' need not affect this theory, as plants do have a rather poor fossil record. Since they are static, plants are unlikely to be fossilized unless they are already growing in conditions where they may be preserved (such as bogs). They also lack durable hard parts, which makes preservation less likely.

The name psilophyte means 'bare plant', and this is a good description of what it looked like. It had underground structures called RHIZOMES, and from these at intervals arose slender, tapering stems up to 500 millimetres high. The stems were generally leafless and branched in a DICHOTOMOUS manner. Some carried cone-shaped SPORE capsules or SPORANGIA at the top. The stems were solid cylinders and used light to make food in the process which is called PHOTOSYNTHESIS (*see page 9*).

The lycopsids have true leaves and roots. Spore-bearing leaves, or SPOROPHYLLS, differ from the leaves that carry on photosynthesis, though some of the sporophylls may also photosynthesize. The leaves are typically small and scale-like, yet in certain fossil forms they were up to 500 millimetres long and needle-like. The primitive nature of these plants is revealed by the fact that there are no breaks or gaps in the vascular tissue at the point where the leaf bases are attached. The sporangia are often crowded together into a cone or STROBILUS.

The coal forests

Lycopsids dominated the Carboniferous COAL swamps. There were plants resembling their present-day descendants, the clubmosses, as well as the giant trees LEPIDODENDRON and SIGILLARIA. Some specimens of *Lepidodendron* grew up to 30 metres before branching, and were 2 metres across at the base. They branched dichotomously, equally at first but then more unequally. The root system had four large branches which also divided dichotomously. Fossils of these roots are named STIGMARIA. Long grass-like leaves were bunched towards the ends of the smallest branches. When these leaves dropped off, diamond-shaped scars were left, even on the oldest wood. *Sigillaria* had similar scars, but these were arranged in vertical rows and were round, hexagonal or oval in shape. The cones of *Lepidodendron* were up to 750 millimetres long and

---

SIDA, it refers to the Y-shaped forking of their stems.

Dicotyledons are 1 of the 2 classes of ANGIOSPERMAE. Their name derives from the fact that they have 2 seed leaves, or cotyledons, instead of the one in MONOCOTYLEDONS. The leaves of dicotyledons are generally broader and have a network of veins, whereas those of monocotyledons are long and thin and they have veins that run parallel to each other.

Disjunct distributions of plants or animals are those where the geographical ranges of the organisms concerned are broken up into distinct areas. These areas are separated by distance or environment (or both) and cannot be bridged by any of the organisms' methods of dispersal. The term 'disjunct' can be applied to species, GENERA or FAMILIES.

E

Endemic groups of plants or animals are those which have a very restricted geographical range. The term 'endemic' may be applied to species, GENERA or FAMILIES.

Equisetum is the only surviving genus (see *GENERA*) of the SPHENOPSIDA. It includes all the horsetails, which are plants of damp places. The stems of horsetails are jointed, and at each joint there is a ring of small branches.

F

Families are groupings used in classifying plants and animals. Related GENERA make up a family, and related families make up an order.

Fertilize is a term used when describing reproduction in organisms. It refers to

Fossil fern, Alethopteris serli

hung from the ends of some smaller branches. The air wherever these trees and their allies grew in numbers must at times have been filled with spores from these strobili. Some interesting features are found in the fossil cone known as *Lepidocarpon.* There is only one functional MEGASPORE in each sporangium, which in turn is almost completely enveloped by the sporophyll. Such an arrangement strongly resembles a true seed, and may provide a hint as to how seeds originated. *Lepidodendron* and its allies adapted to a life in swamps by having plenty of tissues for the exchange of gases, but few for conducting water. This probably explains why they apparently failed to adapt to climatic changes after the Carboniferous.

The sphenopsids also flourished in the Carboniferous coal swamps. These plants have true roots, stems and primitive leaves. Their stems are generally jointed and the leaves grow in whorls around the joints or nodes. True branch and leaf gaps seem not to occur in the vascular tissues. In many fossil sphenopsids the sporangia were developed into strobili, as they are in the living examples. Whereas the lycopsids that survive include a thousand species in many GENERA and several FAMILIES, the only surviving sphenopsid genus is EQUISETUM, with 24 or 25 species. Of the fossil groups, CALAMITES, which was closely related to *Equisetum,* included tree-like forms that grew 20–30 metres. The various types of *Calamites* carried their cones in different positions. Some were borne in clusters at the ends of the smaller branches; others hung singly from the nodes, or grew on specialized branches. *Calamites* fossils are plentiful in Carboniferous rocks, internal casts of the stem being most common. Fossils of the leaf whorls are of two types. ASTEROPHYLLITES are those in which the leaves are needle-like; those in which the leaves are more oval are called ANNULARIA.

Filicopsids are the most numerous pteridophytes. They have roots, stems, and large leaves that probably evolved from systems of branches. Apart from large leaves, filicopsids also differ from other pteridophytes as they have leaf and branch gaps that interrupt the cylinder of vascular tissues. In this they are like the gymnosperms and angiosperms. The sporangia vary, as do their positions on the leaves.

Fossil ferns are very diverse, with some huge tree-like types known from the Palaeozoic. So numerous are fossils of ferns and fern-like foliage from the Carboniferous that geologists once called it the 'Age of Ferns'. We now realize that some of these 'ferns' belonged to the seed ferns, an extinct group of gymnosperms.

Above: The Carboniferous fern-like leaves shown are: (a) *Pecopteris,* (b) *Alethopteris,* (c) *Sphenopteris,* (d) *Neuropteris,* (e) *Mariopteris,* (f) *Linopteris.* Also shown are the sporangia of living ferns, (1) *Gleichenia* and (2) *Lygodium.* Ferns are classified largely according to the structure of the sporangium.

Far left: A reconstruction of the psilophyte *Rhynia* shows the simplest vascular plant so far recorded.

Left: A reconstruction of the sphenopsid tree *Calamites*

the fusion of 2 gametes to form a ZYGOTE (*see page 15*).
Filicopsida are a sub-division of the PTERIDOPHYTA and include all living and extinct ferns. The earliest ferns are known from rocks of Devonian age.
Flora refers to all the plant species in a given area. In contrast, 'vegetation' may be defined as the kind of plant cover in an area (for example, forest or grassland).
Flower is the reproductive structure in the ANGIOSPERMAE or flowering plants. It forms a receptacle which supports 4 sets of organs. The first is an outer ring of sepals, normally green. Inside these are petals, frequently brightly coloured so as to attract insects. Within the petals occur the male and female sex organs — these are the STAMENS and CARPELS respectively.

G

Gametophyte is that stage in the life cycle of a plant when sex cells, or gametes, are produced. In BRYOPHYTA the gametophyte forms the adult plant, but in most PTERIDOPHYTA the gametophyte is only a small PROTHALLUS, unimportant compared to the SPOROPHYTE (or spore-producing) generation. In advanced pteridophytes there is no free-living prothallus. Instead spores of differing size are produced. A male prothallus develops inside the MICROSPORE and a female prothallus inside the MEGASPORE. This is taken a stage further in SPERMATOPHYTA, where the male gametophyte is the POLLEN grain and the female occurs in the OVULE.
Genera is the plural for genus. A genus is made up of related species, so *Erica cinerea* and *Erica tetralix* are both species of heather belonging to the same genus, *Erica.*

Maidenhair leaves

Ginkgoales are an order of the GYMNOSPERMAE. There is only one surviving species — *Ginkgo biloba* — the Maidenhair tree. Fossil leaves identical to those of *Ginkgo biloba* are found in Triassic rocks 200 million years old.
Gnetales are an order of the GYMNOSPERMAE. They have few fossil remains and consist of just 3 GENERA.
Gnetopsida are a sub-division of the GYMNOSPERMAE

Gymnosperms

Gymnosperms differ from pteridophytes in having a true seed, which derived from the MEGASPORANGIUM in advanced pteridophytes. To explain how, we must look at the trend from HOMOSPORY to HETEROSPORY as shown in pteridophyte fossils during the Devonian.

Homospory is the production of spores of one size. These grow into free-living gametophytes, and each gametophyte or PROTHALLUS gives rise to male and female gametes. The male gamete swims in a film of moisture to the female gamete, with which it fuses to form a zygote. The next sporophyte generation then develops from the zygote. CROSS-FERTILIZATION can only occur if there is enough moisture for the male gamete to swim from one prothallus to another. In heterospory the spores are of two sizes—MICROSPORES and megaspores—which respectively will germinate into male and female gametophytes. They grow inside the spores while these are in the sporangia, and on different prothalli. The megaspores, being heavier, fall near the parent plant and rupture to reveal the female prothallus. The microspores are produced in greater numbers and are carried away by air currents, so that they can FERTILIZE the megaspores of other plants. Heterospory therefore allows cross-fertilization to occur even in relatively dry places.

Gymnosperms are also heterosporous. But the megaspore with its female gamete is kept in the megasporangium, which stays attached to the plant. Tissue grows around the megasporangium and together they form an OVULE, which becomes a seed at maturity. The microspores contain the male gametophytes which are now called pollen. They are carried by the wind to an

Above: This reconstruction of a frond of the Permian seed fern *Emplectopteris* also shows the seeds.

Left: (**1**) A reconstruction of *Williamsonia sewordiana,* a representative of the extinct Bennettitales. (**4**) is a living cycad tree, (**5**) a cycad cone and (**2**) and (**3**) show some of the problems in reconstructing fossil plants. (**2**) is the fossil cone, *Cycadeoidea,* of the Bennettitales. It is often shown unfurled as in (**3**), but no such opened cones have ever actually been seen.

and comprise one order, the GNETALES.

Gondwana was an ancient southern continent which broke up in the Mesozoic to give South America, Africa, India, Australia and Antarctica.

Gymnospermae are a subdivision of the SPERMATOPHYTA. The OVULES of gymnosperms are carried 'naked' on cone-scales; in the ANGIOSPERMAE they are enclosed in an OVARY.

H

Heterospory occurs in advanced members of the PTERIDOPHYTA. It involves producing spores of different size — a MEGASPORE and a MICROSPORE. Microspores are carried farther from the parent plant than the heavier megaspores, so microspores of one plant FERTILIZE the spores of another. When a microspore lands on a ruptured megaspore, fertilization can take place, even in fairly dry conditions. Heterospory therefore allows CROSS-FERTILIZATION, and enables heterosporous pteridophytes to live in a wider range of habitats than homosporous types.

Homospory involves plants producing spores of the same size. In homosporous PTERIDOPHYTA, a spore develops into a GAMETOPHYTE — the PROTHALLUS — on which both the male and female sex cells are produced. The prothallus and male sex cells can only function where there is enough moisture. So homosporous pteridophytes are tied to damp places.

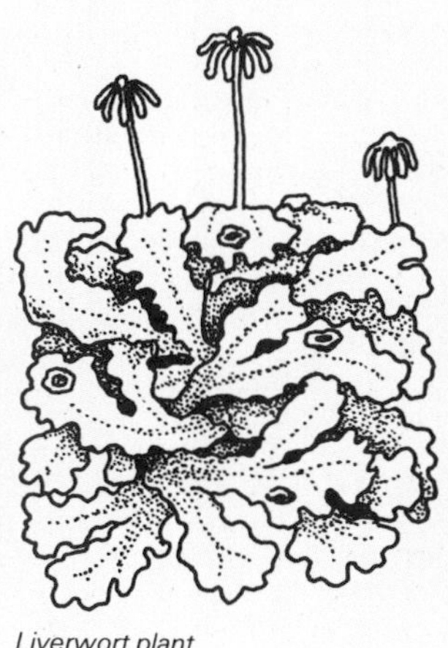

Liverwort plant

L

Laurasia was an ancient northern continent which broke up in late Mesozoic times to give North America and Eurasia.

Lepidodendron is a type of fossil LYCOPSIDA found in Carboniferous rocks. They were trees, some of which grew over 30 metres high. Fossils of the outside trunk or branches show diamond-shaped leaf-scars.

Liverworts are a class of BRYOPHYTA.

Lycopsida are a subdivision of the PTERIDOPHYTA. Living examples are the clubmosses.

M

Megasporangium is a structure which is found in advanced PTERIDOPHYTA. When ripe, it releases MEGASPORES.

opening in the ovule, and fertilization occurs inside. In effect, the seed is a protected zygote.

Although gymnosperms are known from the Devonian and were well established in the late Carboniferous, they replaced pteridophytes as the main plant types only in the Permian, after lycopsid and sphenopsid trees became extinct. We have noted already that the lycopsid trees at least may have died out owing to climatic change. Significantly, one group of gymnosperms dating from the late Carboniferous are the CONIFERS. Many of these have needle-leaves and thick CUTICLES, both adaptations for reducing moisture loss. This suggests that the climatic change was towards greater aridity.

The gymnosperms fall into three groups: the Cycadopsida, CONIFEROPSIDA and GNETOPSIDA. The last group has a limited fossil record and is made up of the Gnetales only. These are remarkable plants including trees, shrubs, lianes and turnip-like plants. Typical cycadopsids have large frond-like leaves, while the coniferopsids have needle-, fan- or paddle-shaped leaves. Both groups appear more or less at the same time in the Devonian. The earliest cycadopsids were the seed ferns, or pteridosperms, some of which grew like small trees, up to 5 metres high. Despite having seeds, the pteridosperms died out in the Cretaceous. Before they disappeared they were joined by three other types of cycadopsids: the cycads, Bennettitales and Pentoxylales. Of these only the cycads managed to survive until the present, as evolutionary relics. The Bennettitales resembled the cycads and had structures that looked more like flowers than cones.

The earliest coniferopsids were the Cordaitales — tall, slender trees over 30 metres tall, with a crown of paddle-shaped leaves. After they died out in the Permian, they were replaced by the ginkgos and conifers, two other types of coniferopsids. Just one kind of ginkgo — the maidenhair tree — now survives, and has been described as a living fossil. Conifers are still numerous, but are not so widely distributed today. The same is true of the youngest coniferopsids, the Taxales or yews.

Angiosperms

Angiosperms are the most advanced plants and as such are the equivalent of the mammals in the animal kingdom. Although they bear seeds,

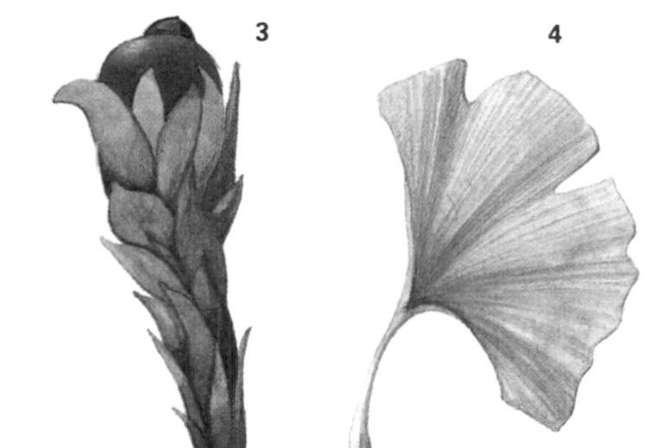

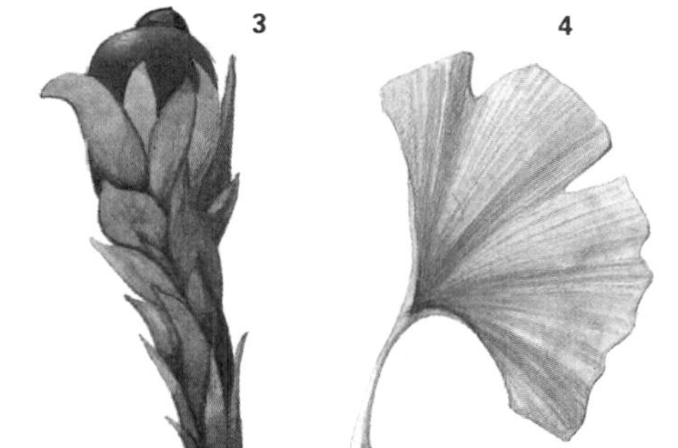

Left: (**1**) Reconstruction of a branch of *Cordaites*, an extinct genus of gymnosperm trees, showing leaves and male cones.
(**2**) Reconstruction of the top of a stem of *Lebachia piniformis*, a Lower Permian conifer.
(**3**) Reconstruction of a female shoot of the extinct yew, *Palaeotaxus rediviva*.
(**4**) Reconstruction of a leaf of an extinct species of *Ginkgo*, very similar to that of the living Maidenhair tree, *Ginkgo biloba*.

Megaspore is the spore which in higher plants divides to produce the female GAMETOPHYTE generation.
Megasporophyll is the special, modified leaf which bears the MEGASPORANGIUM.
Microspores are produced by plants belonging to the advanced PTERIDOPHYTA. A male GAMETOPHYTE develops inside the microspore, which can be carried great distances by air currents.
Monocotyledons are 1 of the 2 classes of ANGIOSPERMAE. See DICOTYLEDONS.
Mosses are a class of BRYOPHYTA.

Clubmoss

N

Niches are environmental 'slots'. In each 'slot' a population of one organism fills a specific role within its surroundings, and follows a particular way of life.

O

Ovary is the structure which contains one or more OVULES.
Ovules contain the female sex cells. A single female sex cell, or egg cell, is called an ovum.

P

Pentoxylales are an extinct order of the GYMNOSPERMAE. They lived in Jurassic times and were shrubs or small trees.
Pollen grains contain the male sex cells of the SPERMATOPHYTA. They correspond to, and evolved from, the MICROSPORES of some PTERIDOPHYTA.

Fossil pollen spore

Prothallus is another name for GAMETOPHYTE. Passing from the lowly BRYOPHYTA through the PTERIDOPHYTA to the advanced SPERMATOPHYTA, the prothallus becomes progressively more unimportant. In bryophytes the prothallus is the adult plant; in many pteridophytes it is reduced to a small green plant, independent of the larger SPOROPHYTE generation. In higher pteridophytes there are no free-living or

Left: Fossil leaves very like this leaf of the tulip tree, *Liriodendron*, are well known from rocks of the Cretaceous period. *Liriodendron* belongs to the Magnolia family, which is regarded as the most primitive of living angiosperms. By late Cretaceous times, leaf impressions of angiosperms are plentiful in the fossil record. Many of the fossil leaves found closely resemble those of living angiosperms.

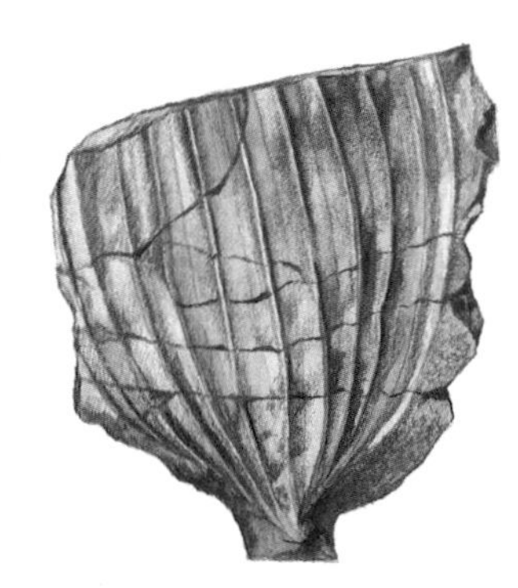

Right: This fossil of a palm-like leaf, *Sanmiguela lewisi*, has been suggested as being of a true palm. However, it is preserved in mid-Triassic rocks, and its acceptance as a fossil palm is therefore by no means widely accepted. The oldest undoubted angiosperms are known from Lower Cretaceous rocks.

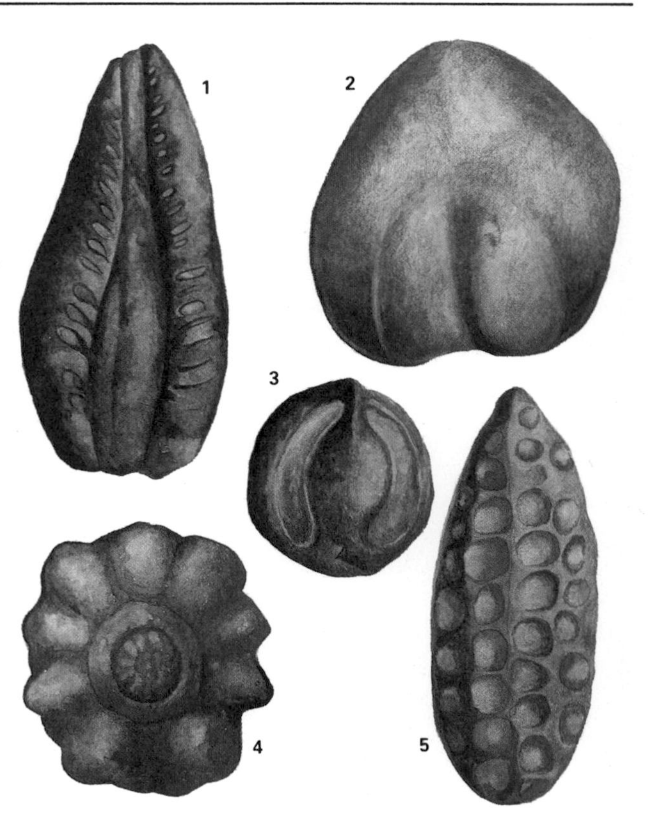

Right: A selection of fossil seeds and fruit from the Eocene London Clay: (**1**) worn fruit with seeds; (**4**) fruit; (**3**) internal cast of seed of the stemless palm *Nipa*; (**5**) internal cast of seed; and (**2**) a locule cast. Although the fruits and seeds which make up the London Clay flora were clearly carried out to sea, it is unlikely that they were conveyed any great distance by oceanic currents. In the first place the fossils are so abundant, and in the second very few of them show any structural adaptations for floating over long periods of time in ocean currents. Lastly, although modern beach drift may contain some far-travelled seeds and fruits, it is mainly of local origin.

angiosperms have several features which make them different from gymnosperms. First, the ovules are encased in an OVARY, and the seed grows inside a fruit developed from the ovary. Also, the structures bearing pollen are modified into STAMENS, and those carrying ovules into CARPELS. Both are inside a FLOWER, instead of the cone of pteridophytes and gymnosperms. Unlike the gymnosperm ovule, the carpel is closed and the pollen grains germinate on a sticky surface or STIGMA. On germination a tube extends from the pollen grain down through a cylinder called a STYLE and fuses with the female gamete in the ovule.

Efficient reproduction and seed dispersal are partly the reasons for the great success of the angiosperms. The closed carpel allows the ovule to be fertilized at a very early stage, and also to be discarded without waste if fertilization does not occur. The carpel probably began as a MEGASPOROPHYLL that remained closed, protecting the megasporangium and megaspore, and ultimately the seed. In the same way, the stamen would have been a sporophyll carrying microsporangia, and these were later covered by the tissue of an anther.

The development of colourful, scented flowers represents a further advance. The insects, birds and bats which they attract transfer pollen economically from one plant to another. Animal-pollinated plants therefore produce relatively little pollen, while wind-pollinated plants have to release clouds of it to ensure pollination. However, some angiosperms reverted to pollination by wind, apparently in places where animals could not be relied upon to perform the task. After flowers come fruits, which are adaptations that favour seed dispersal. Fruits with wings are carried by wind, pods explode and scatter seeds, while fruits such as berries or nuts, or those with fleshy coverings, are dispersed by animals.

Angiosperms throughout the world

The ancestors and precise beginnings of the angiosperms are not clearly known. When they first appear in Lower Cretaceous rocks they already show some variety and the two major angiosperm classes — DICOTYLEDONS and MONOCOTYLEDONS — are represented as well. So it seems that they must have begun earlier, in Permian or Triassic times, in tropical uplands where conditions would not have favoured

plant prothalli. Instead a male prothallus develops inside a MICROSPORE and a female inside a MEGASPORE. In spermatophytes, the male and female prothalli (or what remains of them) are found in POLLEN grains and OVULES respectively.

Psilophytopsida are an extinct sub-division of the PTERIDOPHYTA, with fossils found only in Silurian and Devonian rocks.

Psilopsida are a group of 4 plant species, native to the tropics and sub-tropics. Best known is the whisk 'fern' *Psilotum*.

Pteridophyta are a division of the plant kingdom. They include the LYCOPSIDA, SPHENOPSIDA, FILICOPSIDA, psilotopsida and the extinct PSILOPHYTOPSIDA. Pteridophytes produce SPORES.

Pteridospermales are an extinct order of GYMNOSPERMAE. They were seed ferns.

R **Rhizoids** are tiny root-like threads which attach MOSSES and LIVERWORTS to the ground.

Rhizome is a modified stem which grows horizontally underground, and serves as a food-store.

S **Seed** is a fertilized OVULE enclosed in a protective coat. A seed gives rise to a larger plant than does the SPORE of lower plants because it contains a reserve of food.

Sigillaria is a genus (see GENERA) of fossil lycopsids found in Carboniferous and Permian rocks. *Sigillaria* trees were common in the Carboniferous coal-swamps and impressions of their trunks show squarish leaf-scars arranged in vertical rows.

Spermatophyta are a division of the plant kingdom. They are seed-bearing plants which are sub-divided into the GYMNOSPERMAE and ANGIOSPERMAE, or flowering plants.

Rhizomes of water mint

Sphenopsida are a sub-division of the PTERIDOPHYTA. In Carboniferous times they were numerous, producing tree-like forms. Their only living examples are the horsetails, which are grouped into a single genus, EQUISETUM.

Sporangia are the SPORE-containing structures of the algae, BRYOPHYTA and PTERIDOPHYTA.

fossilization. But recent research on fossil pollen suggests that the amount of time required for angiosperm development in the pre-Cretaceous has probably been much exaggerated.

It is clear, however, that the angiosperms achieved near-global dominance over other plants by the end of the Cretaceous. Almost everywhere today the same four angiosperm families — daisies, grasses, peas and sedges — are among the six most numerous. From this it also follows that there is no unique or ENDEMIC angiosperm FLORA, even in the isolated southern continents of Australia and South America.

This even distribution of angiosperms could not have happened so quickly if the continents had always been in their present positions, separated as they are by huge oceans. But we know that in the Cretaceous, when the angiosperms were evolving, the landmasses were still grouped into two super-continents, LAURASIA in the north and GONDWANA in the south. They were separated by the ancient TETHYS ocean, the shrunken remnant of which is today the Mediterranean Sea. The continental fragments of Laurasia are still in contact or nearly so, but those which made up Gondwana had drifted apart by the end of the Cretaceous. Evidently many angiosperm families had spread throughout Gondwana before the break-up was complete. Some angiosperm genera must also have existed before the break-up, as they occur on several Gondwana fragments. For example, the southern beeches, *Nothofagus,* are DISJUNCT between South America, south-east Australia, Tasmania and New Zealand. And the baobab trees, *Adansonia,* are found in East Africa, Madagascar and Australia.

The angiosperms continued to evolve on their different landmasses until there are now about 225,000 species. They range in size from floating duckweeds to towering trees, and have adapted to a vast array of habitats and NICHES. As they developed isolated from each other, some angiosperms underwent convergent evolution. That is, they grew to look alike while adapting to the same basic way of life. Cacti, for instance, evolved in drier regions of the New World, while euphorbias exploited the same type of habitat in the Old World. Physical resemblances between these two groups are very striking.

Above: A fossil leaf from a flowering plant found in rocks of the Eocene period, London Clay age. It can be seen that this leaf strongly resembles one from the kind of broad-leaved, hardwood trees living today.

Below: Developing in isolation of each other, some angiosperms underwent convergent evolution. That is, they grew to look alike in the process of adapting to the same basic way of life. Cacti, for instance, evolved in the drier regions of the New World, while euphorbias exploited the same habitat in the Old World. The physical resemblances between these 2 groups are now often very striking.

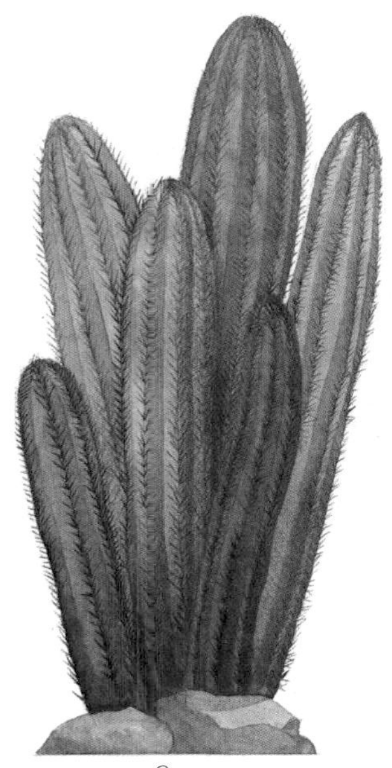
Cactus

Euphorbia

Spore is a structure involved in the reproductive processes of many plants. In some PTERIDOPHYTA the spore develops into a PROTHALLUS; in others separate spores carry the male and female sex cells.
Sporophylls carry SPORANGIA and are normally modified leaves.
Sporophyte is the SPORE-bearing generation in the life-cycle of a plant.
Stamens are filaments which support the POLLEN-sacs (or anthers) in flowering plants. They probably derived from SPOROPHYLLS.

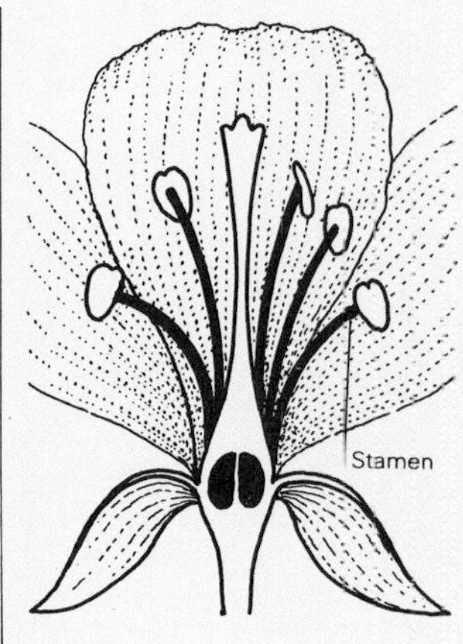

Flower stamens

Stigma is a plant's flat POLLEN-receiving surface (see CARPEL).
Stigmaria are fossil roots of the extinct LEPIDODENDRON. They grew more or less horizontally and forked into 2 (see DICHOTOMOUS). The former positions of RHIZOIDS are marked by round scars on the fossil roots.
Strobilus is another name for a cone, which is a structure made up of SPOROPHYLLS. Various PTERIDOPHYTA have strobili which carry SPORES. Cones of the GYMNOSPERMAE carry POLLEN and OVULES.
Style, see CARPEL.

T

Taxales are an order of the GYMNOSPERMAE which includes the yews. They differ from conifers in having a single OVULE, which is not on a cone-scale, and which is surrounded when ripe by a fleshy structure rather like a berry. They are the youngest of the CONIFEROFSIDA, entering the fossil record in late Cretaceous times.
Tethys was an ancient seaway connecting the Atlantic and Indian oceans, and separating the former super-continents of LAURASIA and GONDWANA. The Mediterranean Sea is its remnant.

V

Vascular tissue is organized into phloem, which conducts food and other materials up and down inside the plant, and xylem, which conducts water and minerals. Non-vascular plants include MOSSES, LIVERWORTS, algae and lichens.

The numerous basic forms of animals without backbones represent different lines of experiment in evolution. Many have survived, with varying success, to the present day.

Evolution of Invertebrates

The first animals appeared on Earth about 800 million years ago. They probably came from eukaryotic sea-living algae, but unlike their ancestors, they lacked CHLOROPLASTS (*see page 17*). The earliest animals were single-celled and both they and their living examples are grouped under the PROTOZOA. From simple beginnings the protozoans evolved many elaborate forms, and some developed skeletons for support and protection. Protozoans are the founder members of the animal family tree and the simplest of all the animals without backbones — the INVERTEBRATES.

In time, protozoans probably grouped together to form cell clumps, each type of cell specializing to perform a particular task. These clumps, or aggregates, were the first step towards multi-celled organisms and they probably looked like very simple SPONGES. Sponges are themselves the simplest multi-celled animals, each one being made up of a small variety of cells. These cells are organized into layers but are not grouped to form tissues as they are in the METAZOANS, which are higher invertebrates. Sponges are mostly FILTER-FEEDERS, drawing food into a large central body cavity through numerous tiny pores. The body is often supported by needle-like SPICULES, which may be of calcite, silica or a horny material called spongin. The spicules can be single units or may be fused together in a rigid framework. Evolutionary trends among the sponges are difficult to pick out, but there are several grades of organization which show the creatures becoming more complex. The simplest sponges (ASCON-GRADE) have a sac-like body but in others there is a folding and refolding of the

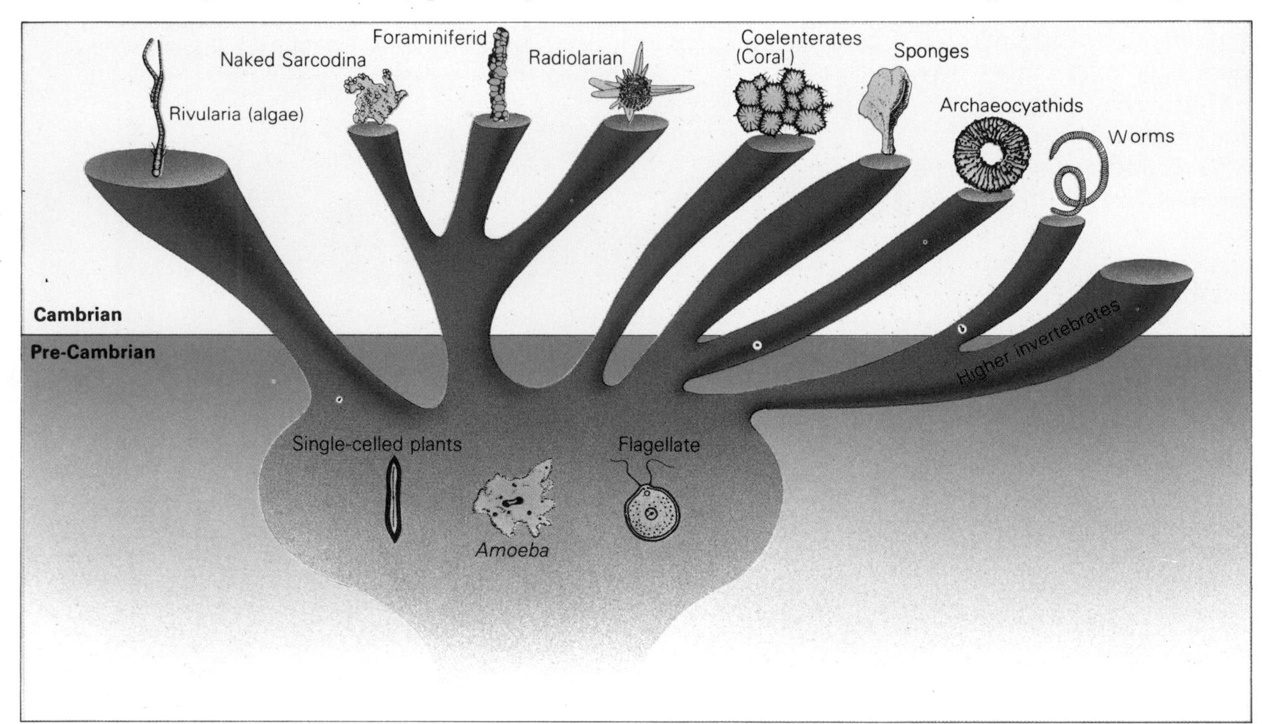

Left: Life began in the seas of the Pre-Cambrian when single-celled plants originated from non-living matter. Approximately 800 million years ago they were joined by the first single-celled animals, such as *Amoeba*, from which arose a host of different living creatures, including the sponges, corals and archaeocyathids.

Reference

A

Acorn worms are a group of HEMICHORDATES and therefore linked directly with GRAPTOLITES.

Ammonites were the most important CEPHALOPODS of the Mesozoic. Although most were PLANISPIRAL, some were either loosely or spirally coiled. Most have complex SUTURE LINES. The ammonites are important ZONE (*see page 11*) fossils for both the Jurassic and Cretaceous periods.

Ammonoids are an extinct group of CEPHALOPOD MOLLUSCS with SUTURE LINES varying from gently folded to complex. Most are PLANISPIRAL. The sub-class includes GONIATITES, CERATITES and AMMONITES.

Anisograptidae are an important family of GRAPTOLITES with characters that fall between those of the DENDROIDS and the GRAPTOLOIDS. They are known only from the Lower Ordovician.

Annelid worm is a segmented soft-bodied animal. The general term 'annelid' applies to all earthworms, sandworms and leeches.

An annelid

Anthozoa are sea-bottom dwelling COELENTERATES with POLYPOID adults. They include the TABULATE corals and the RUGOSE and SCLERACTINIAN corals.

Archaeocyathids are an extinct INVERTEBRATE group with similarities to SPONGES. They may have lived in SYMBIOSIS with some TRILOBITES.

Archaeogastropods are a primitive group of GASTROPODS with 2 gills. The common limpet, *Patella vulgata*, is a living example of this group, which first appeared in the Cambrian.

Arthropods are INVERTEBRATES with a segmented body and jointed legs. They have an EXOSKELETON of a horny material called chitin. Various water, land and aerial types are known. Fossil forms include the TRILOBITES and EURYPTERIDS, while living insects, butterflies and spiders are among the most common invertebrates.

Ascon grade describes the sac-like form which is the simplest structure among SPONGES.

B

Belemnoids, or belemnites, are an extinct

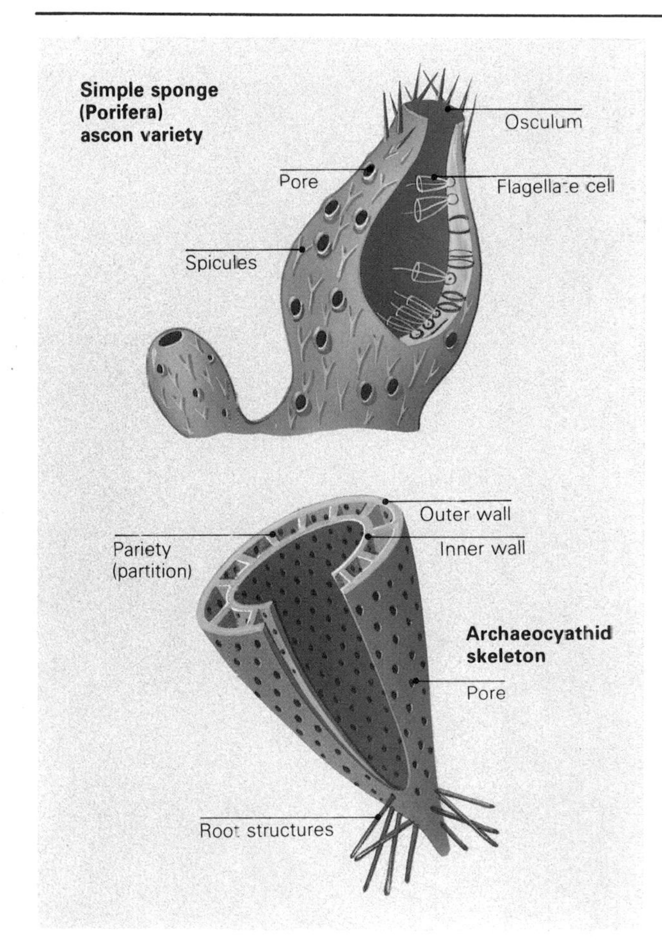

Above (top): A simple sponge showing both pores and 3-pronged spicules. The illustration is drawn in section to show the large inner cavity and upper opening. Water is taken in by the sponge through the pores and forced out again through the top opening. **(Bottom):** A sketch of an archaeocyathid. Most of these animals had a double-walled structure and pores like the sponges. Archaeocyathids were reef-forming animals, but little is known of their soft parts.

body wall which produces a much more complex structure.

Sponges have lived since the Pre-Cambrian and their long fossil history contrasts with that of their distant cousins the ARCHAEOCYATHIDS. These are known only from the Cambrian and present problems, as they have similarities to both the sponges and the corals. Like sponges they had pores, but their overall structure was more complex and some people have seen them as being more advanced (albeit short-lived) multi-celled organisms. The archaeocyathids were the first animals to form reefs and they may have lived side by side with TRILOBITES, in SYMBIOSIS. Their demise during the Middle Cambrian is one of the mysteries of fossil history, and their place as reef-builders remained vacant for tens of millions of years.

Coelenterates

The JELLYFISH and SEA ANEMONES in the seas of the world are soft-bodied creatures which show a higher level of evolution than either the sponges or the archaeocyathids. Both belong to the COELENTERATES. Jellyfish are the free-swimming MEDUSOID type and sea anemones the fixed POLYPOID type. Each has a long geological record, as the first jellyfish and the first sea-pens (ANTHOZOA-alcyonarian corals) come from rocks in Australia which are dated to about 690 million years old.

These discoveries prove that the coelenterate group is one of the most ancient metazoan lines, but only from the Middle Ordovician onwards can we follow a detailed record of important evolutionary trends. At this time appeared the TABULATE and RUGOSE CORALS (Anthozoa-Zoantharia), which had calcareous hard parts. We can compare these to the beautiful skeletons of living SCLERACTINIAN corals which are secreted by soft tissues at the base of the polyp. The tabulates were the simplest of the coral groups mentioned, as they lacked the complex inner structures of the others. They lived only in colonies and reached their peak during the Silurian and Devonian periods. The thin horizontal plates known as tabulae are their most recognizable feature, and the most important evolutionary trends they developed were pores in their connecting walls and dense tissue between the cups or corallites. Remains of rugose corals living in colonies appear later than solitary ones, and we generally think of colonial animals as being more advanced. However, both types show evolutionary trends linked with skeletal features such as the tabulae. Some trends can be linked to major phases in the evolution of the rugose corals, and a few seem to have been adopted by the scleractinian corals from the Triassic onwards. By reconstructing the soft parts of extinct tabulates and rugosans, we can tell that they were less advanced than the scleractinians. All three corals may be linked in one evolutionary line, but it is more likely that each arose independently from a soft-bodied, anemone-like ancestor.

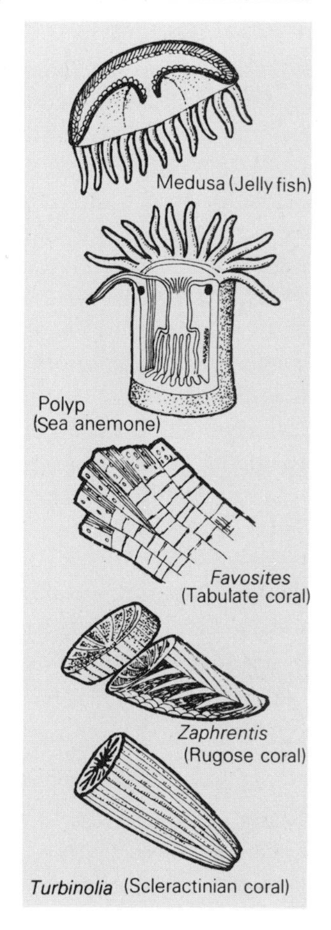

Above: The jellyfish and sea anemone are living representatives of the coelenterates. The jellyfish is a free-living animal, but polyps of the sea anemone live attached to the sea floor. Tabulate corals flourished during the Silurian and Devonian periods. All lived in colonies, with some form of connection existing between the soft parts of each individual. Tabulates died out at the end of the Permian. Rugose corals were probably the dominant coelenterates of the Upper Palaeozoic. Their skeletons were more complex than those of their tabulate cousins, and their soft parts were probably also more advanced in evolution. Scleractinian corals first appeared in the Middle Triassic, probably deriving from a rugosan ancestor. They are important in reef communities today.

Water spider, an arthropod

group of DIBRANCHIATE cephalopod MOLLUSCS. They are first recorded from the Lower Carboniferous but became really important only in the Jurassic. They were probably the ancestors of the living cuttlefish *Sepia*.
Benthic comes from *benthos*, 'bottom dwellers', and describes creatures that live on or in sea-floor sediments. They include scavengers – which consume carcasses or carrion – as well as creatures that feed by filtering organic debris from seawater or sea-floor sediments.
Bilateral symmetry is where one side or half of an animal is the mirror-image of the other.
Bivalves are soft-bodied MOLLUSCS with oval or elongated shells comprising 2 hinged valves. They first appeared during the Cambrian. Today their roles are as burrowing, boring, fixed and free-living animals.
Brachiopods are solitary INVERTEBRATES living at the sea bottom. Their soft parts are enclosed in a 2-valved shell. Superficially they resemble the bivalves but have a different size and form. The group is divided into the INARTICULATES and the articulates – both of which arose in the Cambrian.
Bryozoans are a little known but important group of COELOMATES. They live in colonies and have a skeleton made up of minute box-like units. First known from the Cambrian, they thrive today in many areas.
Burgess shales are fine-grained rocks in the Mount Field district of British Columbia, Canada, renowned for their fossils.
Byssus is a thread-like structure used by certain BIVALVES as a holdfast. It is secreted as a thick fluid which hardens on contact with seawater.

C

Centipedes are ARTHROPODS with flattened, segmented bodies, each segment having a pair of limbs. They appear in the Upper Carboniferous.
Cephalopods are close relatives of the gastropods and BIVALVES and are members of the MOLLUSC family. They are marine animals with the single-valved shell divided by septa. They range from the Cambrian to Recent periods.

Bryozoans and brachiopods

The small, often delicate moss animals, BRYOZOANS, and the sea-shells called BRACHIOPODS are usually grouped under the heading of minor COELOMATES. This means that they both have an internal cavity, or coelom, which houses the gut, and that they probably arose from the same ancestor. A likely forebear was a PHORONID WORM, a soft-bodied animal that had filaments around the mouth for feeding. This creature dwelt in the soft muds of the sea floor, and so the origin of both bryozoans and brachiopods involved them changing to a SEDIMENT SURFACE-DWELLING way of life.

The first brachiopods probably lacked hard parts, but forms with mineralized skeletons had appeared by the early Cambrian. From then on we have enough evidence to record the numerous RADIATIONS that have taken place during the last 570 million years of geological time. The first involved the least specialized brachiopods — the INARTICULATES. These forms have a phosphatic skeleton and a complex arrangement of muscles to control opening of the two valves. LINGULA is a living example of the inarticulates and the diagram shows that it also lacks an inner skeleton. The inarticulates flourished in the Cambrian but by the Ordovician they had been overtaken by forms with a calcareous shell. At first these were small and had no inner structures for support, but in time some grew to enormous sizes and developed complex skeletons to support the organ used for feeding (the lophophore). These articulate brachiopods, as they are called, flourished during the Palaeozoic and Mesozoic, occupying many niches in both shallow and deep water environments. Among the best-known articulates are RHYNCHONELLA, PRODUCTUS, TEREBRATULA and SPIRIFER.

The bryozoans are first known from the Ordovician and in contrast to their brachiopod cousins they all lived in colonies. They have undergone several great radiations during the last 500 million years and played important roles as reef-building animals. During the Palaeozoic the most important group was the TREPOSTOMES or 'stony bryozoans', several of which grew to 500 millimetres across. In the Mesozoic the CHEILOSTOMES became the most successful of all bryozoans. They developed complex front wall structures and many individuals in the colony

Right: Tens of thousands of brachiopods are known from geological records. They first appeared in the Cambrian in the form of inarticulates, which probably gave rise to a host of articulate families. Inarticulates have a rather simple shell consisting of 2 valves. The articulate shell is also made of 2 valves but many types have internal support structures. The diagram shows the relative importance of different brachiopod stocks through time.

a – Obellids
b – Paterinids
c – Kutorginids

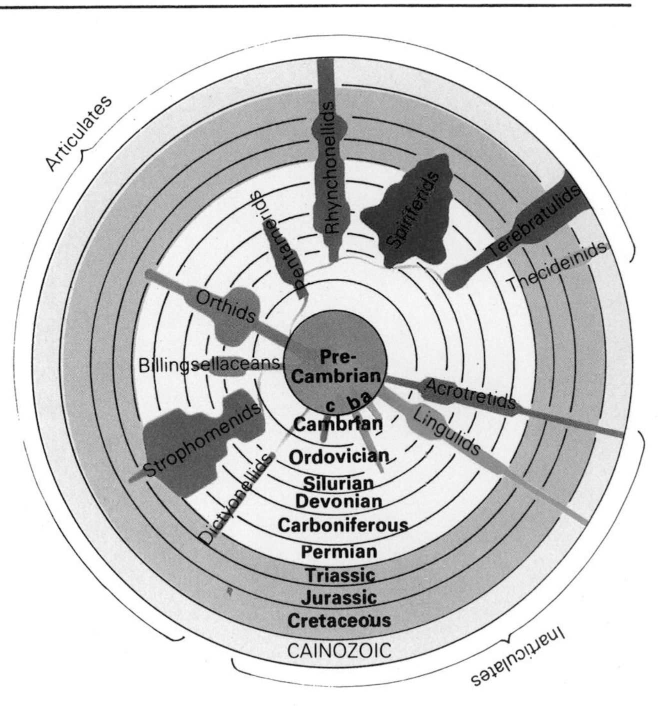

From 'Treatise on Invertebrate Paleontology', courtesy of the Geological Society of America and University of Kansas.

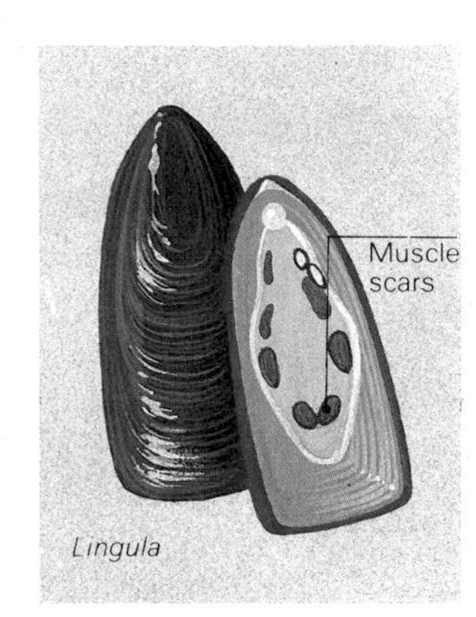

Left: *Lingula,* an inarticulate brachiopod, has survived since the Ordovician. The inside of the shell is marked by a number of well-defined muscle scars.

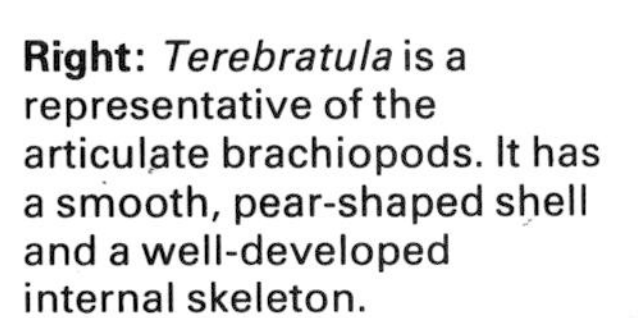

Right: *Terebratula* is a representative of the articulate brachiopods. It has a smooth, pear-shaped shell and a well-developed internal skeleton.

Terebratula

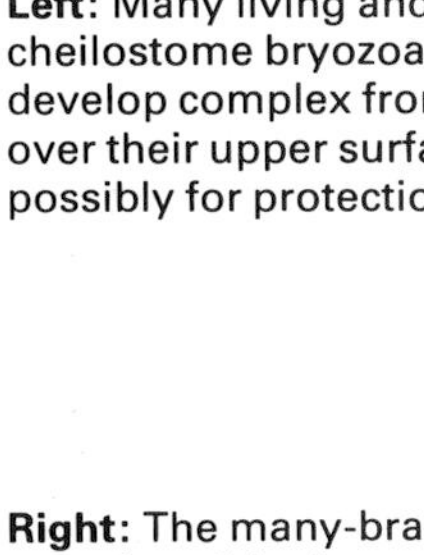

Left: Many living and fossil cheilostome bryozoans develop complex front walls over their upper surface, possibly for protection.

Front walls of living cheilostome bryozoans

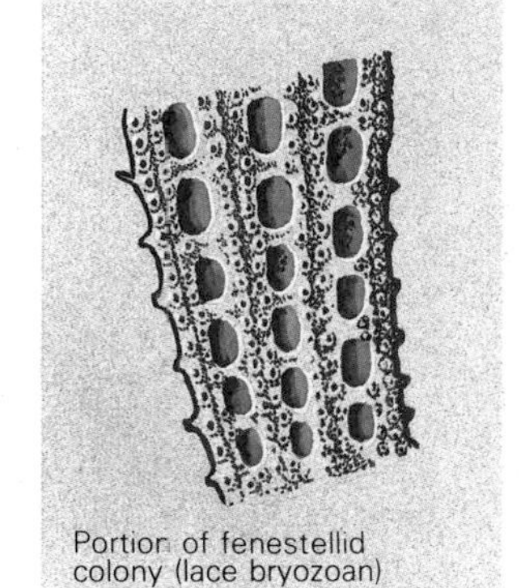

Right: The many-branched colonies of the fenestellid or 'window bryozoans' are common in Upper Palaeozoic sediments.

Ceratites are AMMONOIDS in which the backward-directed lobes of the SUTURE LINE are frilled. They are found mainly from the Triassic.
Cheilostomes are the major group of living BRYOZOANS. They first appear in the Jurassic.
Chordates are animals which have a rod of flexible tissue — the notochord — or, in more advanced forms, a backbone. The notochord was probably the first support structure to evolve in vertebrate ancestors.
Coelenterates are the simplest METAZOANS with 2 layers of cells (tissues) in the body wall. They are first known from the late Pre-Cambrian.
Coelomate animals include all those above the COELENTERATE METAZOANS. In coelomates there are 3 layers of cells (tissues) of which the outer layer forms the skin and the inner layer the gut. All higher INVERTEBRATES and vertebrates have a fluid-filled cavity — the coelom.
Corals are marine COELENTERATES which have a POLYPOID adult form. They have external skeletons which may be solitary or compound.
Crustaceans are mainly water-living ARTHROPODS which show great variation in their limb structure. They include barnacles, crabs and lobsters.
Cuttlefish are living CEPHALOPODS. They have 10 arms and their shell is a small internal structure.

D

Dendroids are an extinct group of HEMICHORDATES and an important order of the GRAPTOLITES, with many branches and 2 types of THECAL CUP on the outside of each branch. They ranged from the mid-Cambrian to the Carboniferous.
Deposit-feeders swallow up mud and organic material from the sea floor. Much of the mud they take in is deposited as casts.
Dibranchiates are those CEPHALOPOD MOLLUSCS with 2 gills, such as octopuses. Dibranchiates are first recorded from the Carboniferous.

A cuttlefish

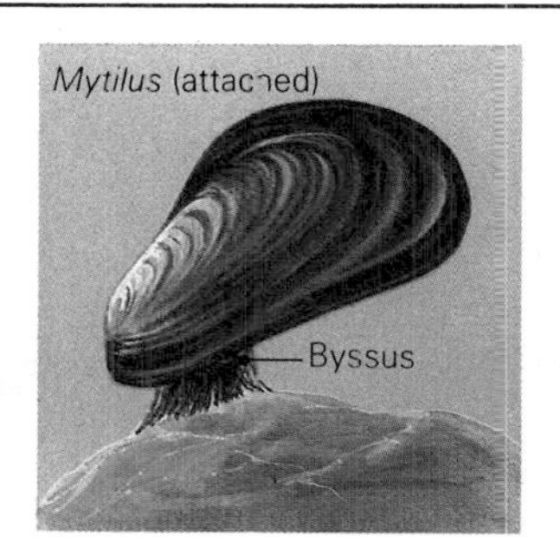

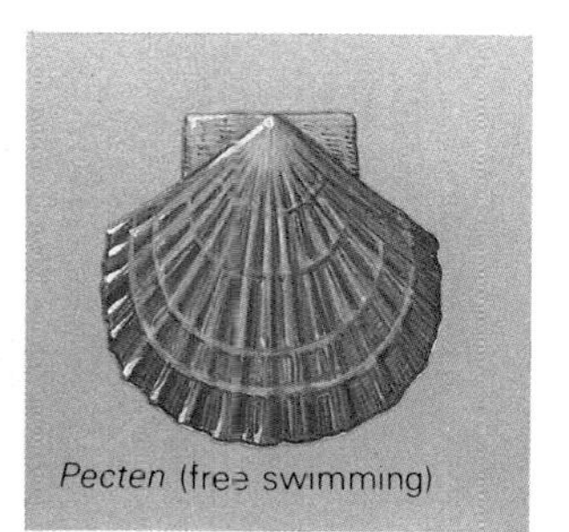

Left: Bivalve shells reflect the animal's way of life. Shallow burrowers (*Venus*) have short symmetrical valves. Deep burrowers (*Mya*) are elongate. Attached forms (*Mytilus*) are elongate with a flat lower surface for stability. Free-living forms (*Pecten*) take the shape of their muscles.

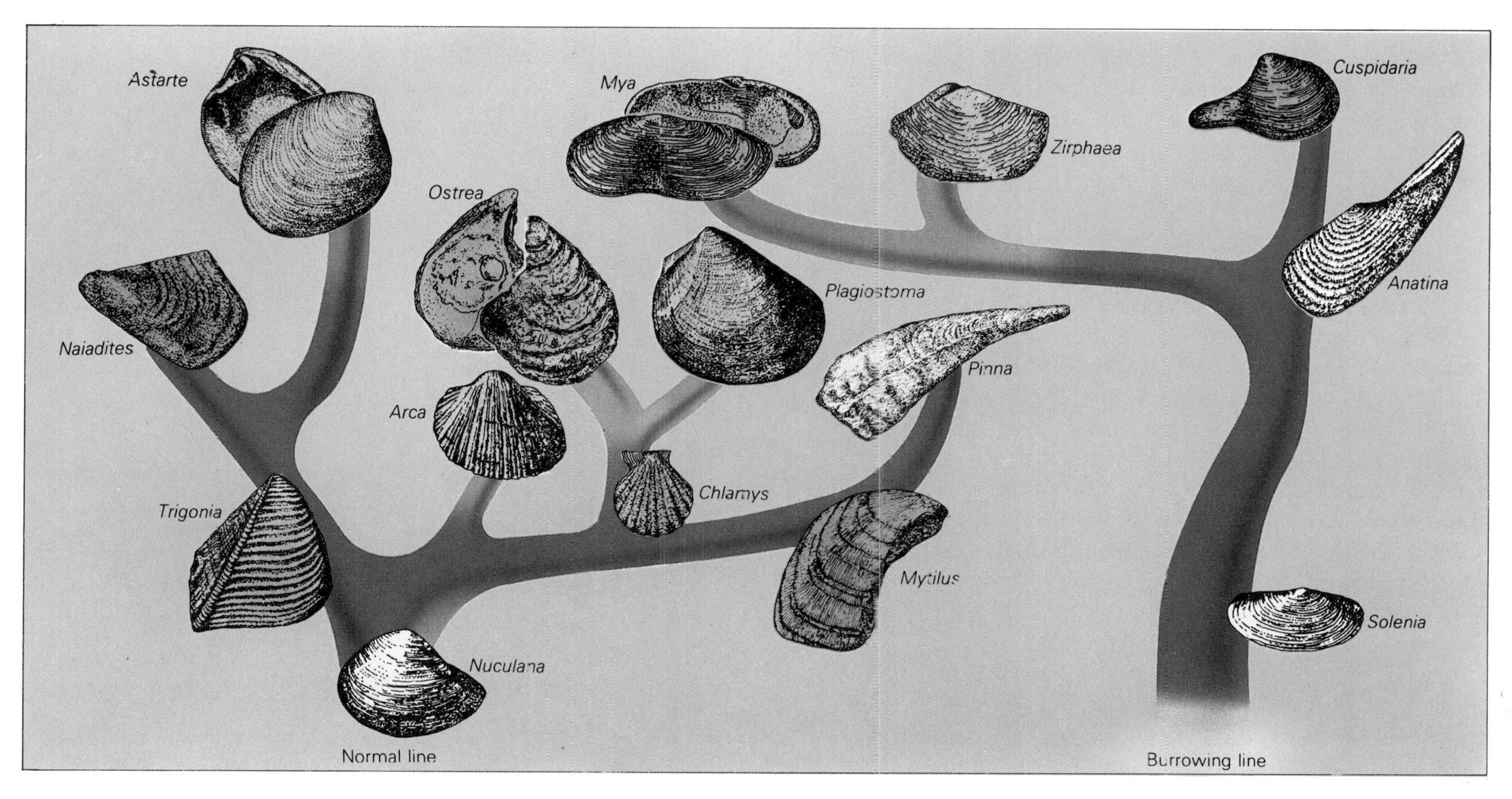

Above: This family tree of the bivalves illustrates the possible ancestry of various groupings. The branch on the *left* illustrates the probable evolutionary links between the so-called 'normal' bivalves; that on the *right* represents the evolutionary line of the burrowing types.

were specially modified to perform tasks to do with feeding or protection.

Bivalves

The millions of sea-shells found along the shoreline show how successful is an important class of MOLLUSCS known as the BIVALVES. These have a soft, unsegmented body protected on the outside by a mineralized shell. Oysters, mussels and clams are typical bivalves and they illustrate the variety of a group which can be traced back to the Cambrian. Some bivalve-like molluscs are found from the Lower and Middle Cambrian but the first undoubted bivalves come from the early Ordovician. By that time the group had become considerably varied and individuals were adapted to burrowing or to sediment surface-dwelling ways of life. DEPOSIT-FEEDERS living in shallow burrows were probably the ancestors of all Ordovician types of bivalves. Surface-dwelling filter-feeders developed only after the soft parts had been modified. The success of the surface-dwellers was also partly due to their developing a horny BYSSUS, by which many attached themselves to the sea-floor to make themselves more stable.

As various types adapted towards different ways of life, so their soft parts and shell changed. By the end of the Palaeozoic some bivalves had developed tube-like siphons. These allowed the animal to draw food into its shell while it stayed buried inside and protected by the sediment.

E **Echinoderms** are exclusively sea creatures, most having a skeleton of porous, calcareous plates. The majority have a 5-rayed or PENTAMERAL SYMMETRY. The group includes SEA URCHINS (echinoids), starfish (asterozoans), SEA CUCUMBERS (homalozoans) and SEA LILIES (crinoids). Echinoderms have tube feet that project through the skeleton and act as the animal's organs for feeding, respiration or movement.
Eocrinoids are extinct 'SEA LILIES' from the Lower Palaeozoic. Their structure is primitive, and the pores for their tube feet occur on SUTURE LINES between plate rows.
Eurypterids are extinct ARTHROPODS also known as 'water scorpions'. Their closest living relatives are the king or horseshoe crabs.
Exoskeleton is the outer skeleton of various INVERTEBRATES.

An open sea urchin with suckered feet

F **Filter-feeders** are animals that extract their food from water currents which are usually created by movements of their own feeding organs.

G **Gastropods** are MOLLUSCS. They have a true head, an unsegmented body and a large flattened foot.
Goniatites are AMMONOIDS with angular or zig-zag SUTURE LINES. They range from the Devonian to the end of the Permian.
Graptolites are an extinct group of HEMICHORDATES. They divide into DENDROIDS and GRAPTOLOIDS, and range from the Middle Cambrian to the Permian.
Graptoloids are GRAPTOLITES with a limited number of branches and one type of THECAL CUP — the autotheca.

Siphons gave the bivalves a fresh impetus and during the Mesozoic and Cainozoic various families made use of many habitats.

Gastropods

Like bivalves, GASTROPODS are members of the mollusc family. They include snails and slugs, as well as the small PTEROPODS. Whereas bivalves have a shell in two parts, the gastropod shell is a single unit, and it is always coiled. Gastropods are the only molluscs with their body organs twisted 180° so that the gills and anus are in the mantle cavity, just behind the head. This twisting is called TORSION and it enables the gastropods to draw back into their shells. It is unlikely that the ancestors of gastropods had this twisting, or coiled shells. But without doubt they were symmetrical, and their shells may have been cap-shaped. These ideas are supported by evidence from the early Cambrian gastropods *Coreospira* and *Helcionella,* which are both coiled in a simple PLANISPIRAL manner so that the shells remain symmetrical. In time, certain families developed an asymmetrical, HELICALLY-COILED shell that made them more stable. Coiling and torsion were probably closely linked in the evolution of gastropods, and it is more than likely that they gave the group distinct advantages over other BENTHIC creatures.

From the Lower Cambrian onwards the story of the gastropods has been one of great success. By the Carboniferous they lived in many niches within sea-dwelling communities and the first snails had migrated away from salt water. Many experts think that in order to migrate, gastropods had to develop a method of fertilization inside the body, and a penis. Once they had these, the gastropods could not only move to freshwater habitats but also on to land.

From living gastropods we can establish what the primitive examples were like. For instance, a number of the ARCHAEOGASTROPODS still retain two feather-like gills. More advanced forms, such as the MESOGASTROPODS, NEOGASTROPODS and OPISTHOBRANCHS have only one gill and even that has gill filament on one side only. Early in the Mesozoic the mesogastropods gave rise to an animal that had lost its gill but had changed the surface of the mantle cavity into a lung. This was the first PULMONATE gastropod, forerunner of today's successful land-dwelling forms.

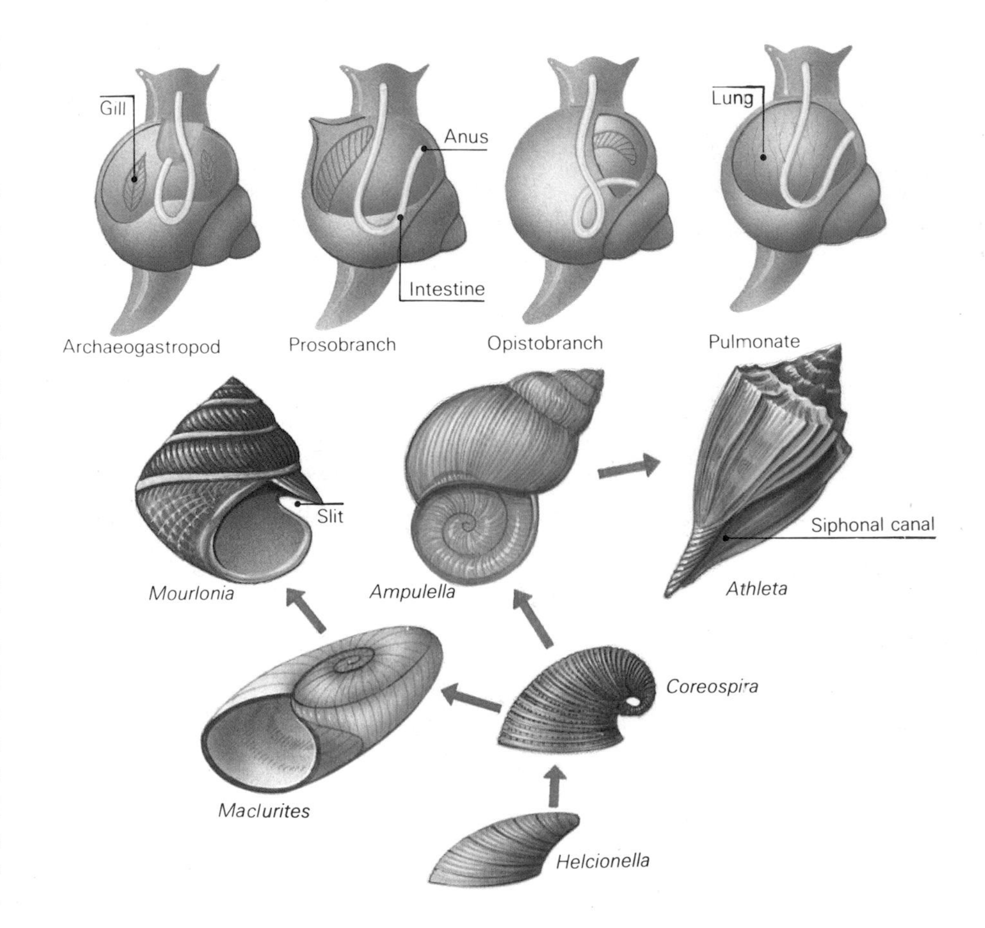

Above: The earliest ancestral gastropod probably had an uncoiled cap-like shell *(bottom)*. From this arose forms which appeared flattened and were coiled symmetrically. As the gastropods became more mobile, they needed greater stability. This they achieved by developing a conical shell. The appearance of well-defined slits and siphonal canals are linked with changes in the soft parts.

Above (top): Scientists recognize 4 major groups of gastropods, based on breathing apparatus. The 4 may represent an evolutionary sequence, with the 2-gilled archaeogastropods as the ancestors of the other groups. In turn, it is likely that the pulmonates or 'lunged-gastropods' represent the most advanced condition.

1

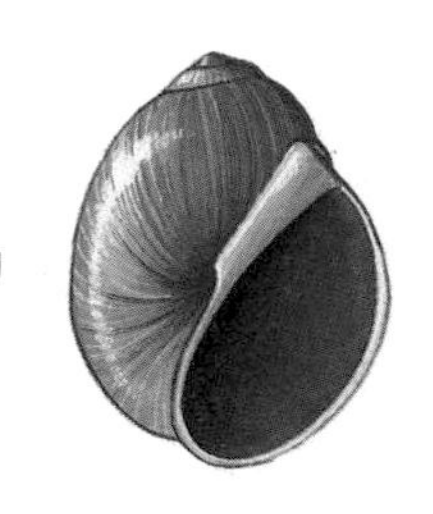

2

3

Right: During their long history the gastropods have adapted to most environmental conditions. Of the 3 gastropods illustrated, *Natica* (**1**) is a marine predator which drills through the shells of its victims; *Limnaea* (**2**) is a freshwater snail; and *Helix* (**3**) is a land-dwelling snail.

They range from the Lower Ordovician to the Devonian.

H **Helically-coiled** shells are found in most gastropods and some ammonites. The coils enlarge as they move down the vertical axis towards the animal's mouth.

Hemichordates are CHORDATES which lack bony tissues. They have a short rod of tissue — the notochord — above the mouth. This rod runs the entire length of the body in the higher chordates.

Hydrozoans are COELENTERATES which exhibit the phenomenon of 'alteration of generations'. They have an adult POLYPOID phase, and a free-swimming MEDUSOID reproductive phase.

I **Inarticulates** are BRACHIOPODS, most of which have skeletons with a high phosphate content. The 2 valves are unequal in size and the shell can be divided lengthwise into identical halves. No internal support structure exists for the feeding organ and the shells lack teeth for articulation.

Insects are a major group of ARTHROPODS. They are first recorded from the Devonian and today account for almost 1,000,000 species. These include the flies, beetles, lice, fleas, cockroaches, butterflies and bees. They have 6 walking legs and breathe air. Many insects have developed wings.

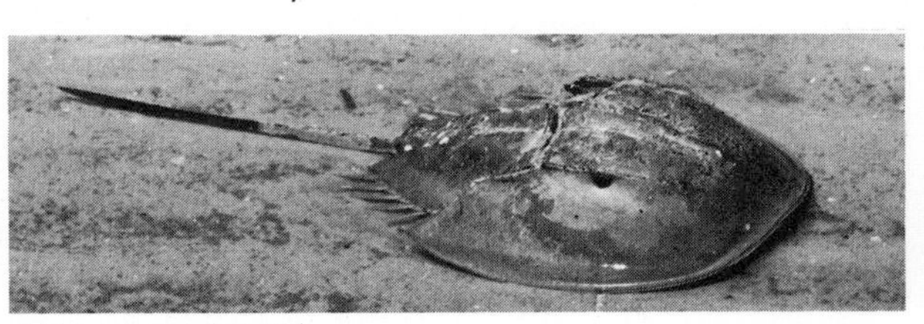

A king or horseshoe crab

Invertebrates are animals without backbones.

J **Jellyfish** are free-swimming COELENTERATES, ranging from a few millimetres up to 2 metres across.

K **King crabs** or horseshoe crabs are ARTHROPODS closely related to spiders and mites. They are sea creatures with a large hinged body and spine-like tail.

L **Lingula** is an INARTICULATE brachiopod with a phosphatic shell. Its valves are almost identical, having BILATERAL SYMMETRY. Lingula is a burrowing animal.

M **Medusoid** describes the free-living, flattened phase typical of some primitive COELENTERATES, or

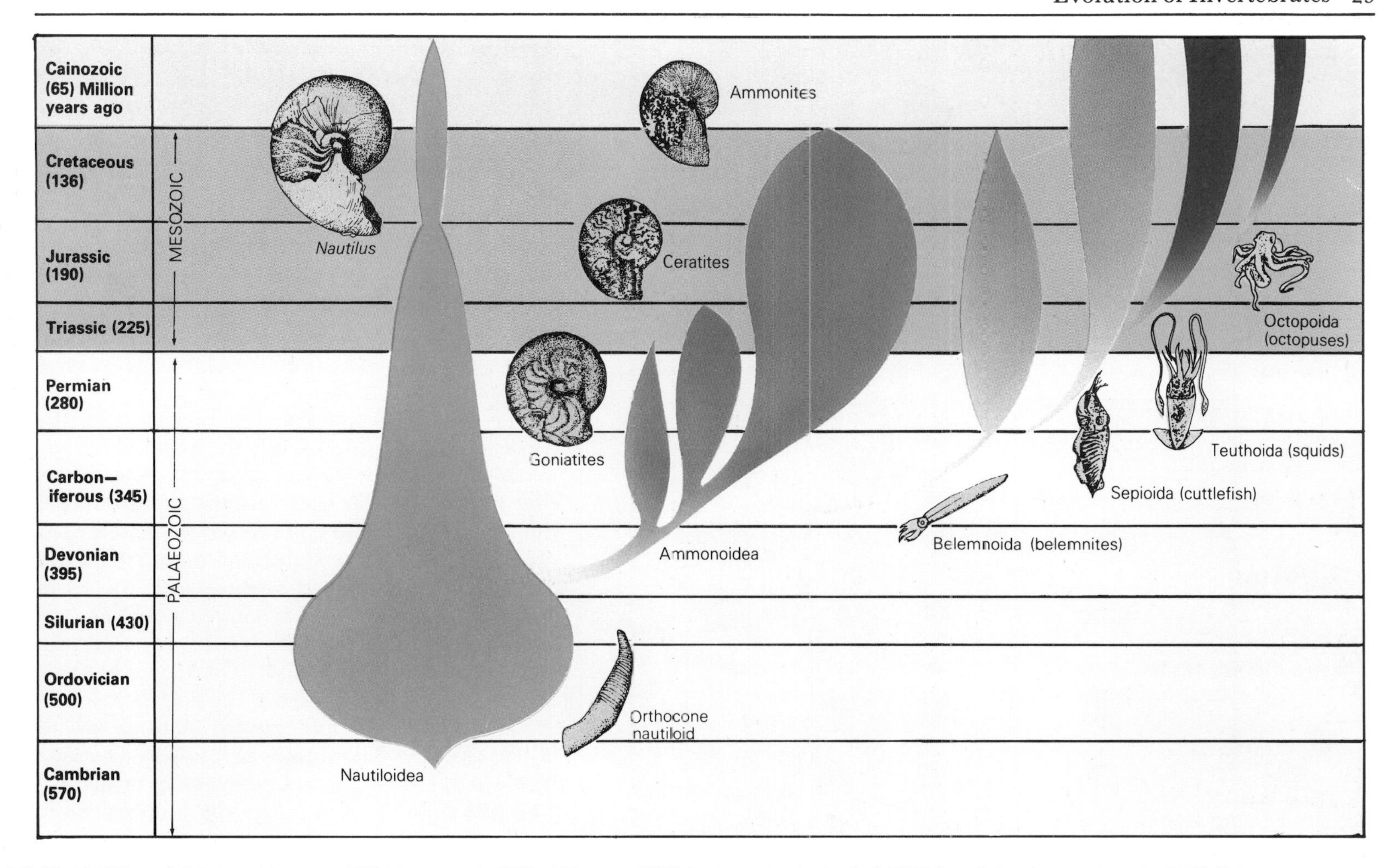

Cephalopods

Like gastropods, CEPHALOPOD molluscs such as SQUIDS, OCTOPUSES and *Nautilus* have a well-defined head with well-developed sense organs. The *Nautilus* is the sole survivor of a once large and extremely varied group known as the TETRABRANCHIATA. This word implies that *Nautilus* has four gills, whereas the squids and octopuses, which are living DIBRANCHIATES, have two.

Of these groups, the tetrabranchiates have the more important fossil history, with the earliest types recorded from the Upper Cambrian. These were also the first NAUTILOIDS and their curved outer shells suggest that their ancestor was probably a single-shelled gastropod-like animal. The nautiloids flourished in the Palaeozoic and an incredible variety of shell types, often with complex inner deposits, shows that the group had fully exploited its marine habitat. By the end of the Silurian the nautiloids, or a nautiloid-like animal, had given rise to the AMMONOIDS, which became the most successful group of cephalopods during the late Palaeozoic and Mesozoic. At first the ammonoids had rather simple SUTURE LINES. But in time these lines (which trace the junction between the inside partitions and the shell wall) became more and more complex. The trend started with the GONIATITES and continued through the CERATITES and AMMONITES. Ammonites were the peak of ammonoid evolution and their suture lines were folded into complex, rather flowery patterns.

The earliest of the dibranchiate cephalopods appeared in the Carboniferous. These belonged to the extinct squid-like BELEMNOIDS which rose to considerable importance during the Jurassic and Cretaceous. The living squids, octopuses and CUTTLEFISH probably evolved from a belemnoid ancestor some time during the Lower Cretaceous period.

Above: The family tree of the cephalopod molluscs can be traced back to the early Cambrian. The nautiloids — with simple suture lines and often with complex internal deposits — dominated the early part of the Palaeozoic era. In the Upper Palaeozoic their position was taken by the goniatites, the first of the ammonoid cephalopods. The goniatite suture line was more complex than that of the nautiloids, but simpler than that of its ceratite or ammonite cousins. Gill structure separates the nautiloids and ammonoids from the fossil belemnites, living squids and octopuses.

the adult JELLYFISH (medusa).
Mesogastropods are known from the Ordovician through to the present day. They are chiefly recognized by a single large gill on the left-hand side, and by the form of the rasping tooth or radula. Living types include *Strombus* and *Nerinea*.
Metazoans are multi-celled animals in which the cells are grouped to form tissues. This excludes SPONGES but includes COELENTERATES and all higher animals.
Molluscs are INVERTEBRATE animals with unsegmented bodies. Although most are sea creatures, a few, such as the snails and some bivalves, are successful in fresh water. PULMONATE snails include land-dwelling forms.

N
Nautiloids were the dominant CEPHALOPODS for much of the Palaeozoic.
Neogastropods are GASTROPODS with a single large gill on the left side. They are similar to MESOGASTROPODS but have a better developed nervous system and siphon. Neogastropods range from Cretaceous to Recent periods.

An octopus

O
Octopuses are living CEPHALOPODS. They have 8 tentacles and no shell.
Opisthobranchs are mostly 'naked', sea-living GASTROPODS such as the sea slugs and PTEROPODS. They range from the Cretaceous to Recent periods.

P
Pentameral symmetry describes the distinctive 5-rayed form of many ECHINODERMS.
Periderm is the translucent brown material that forms the skeleton of GRAPTOLITES.
Peripatus is an ARTHROPOD with a soft thin EXOSKELETON. It is found in tropical areas and has a muscular body, small head and numerous unjointed limbs.
Phoronid worms are a small group of minor COELOMATE animals linked with the BRYOZOANS and BRACHIOPODS. They live on or in the sediments of the sea floor. *Phoronis* is an unsegmented animal with a horseshoe-shaped organ for feeding.
Planispiral coiling is found in various molluscs. The shells are coiled in a single plane and appear disc-like. In most cases the shell opening and various coils can be

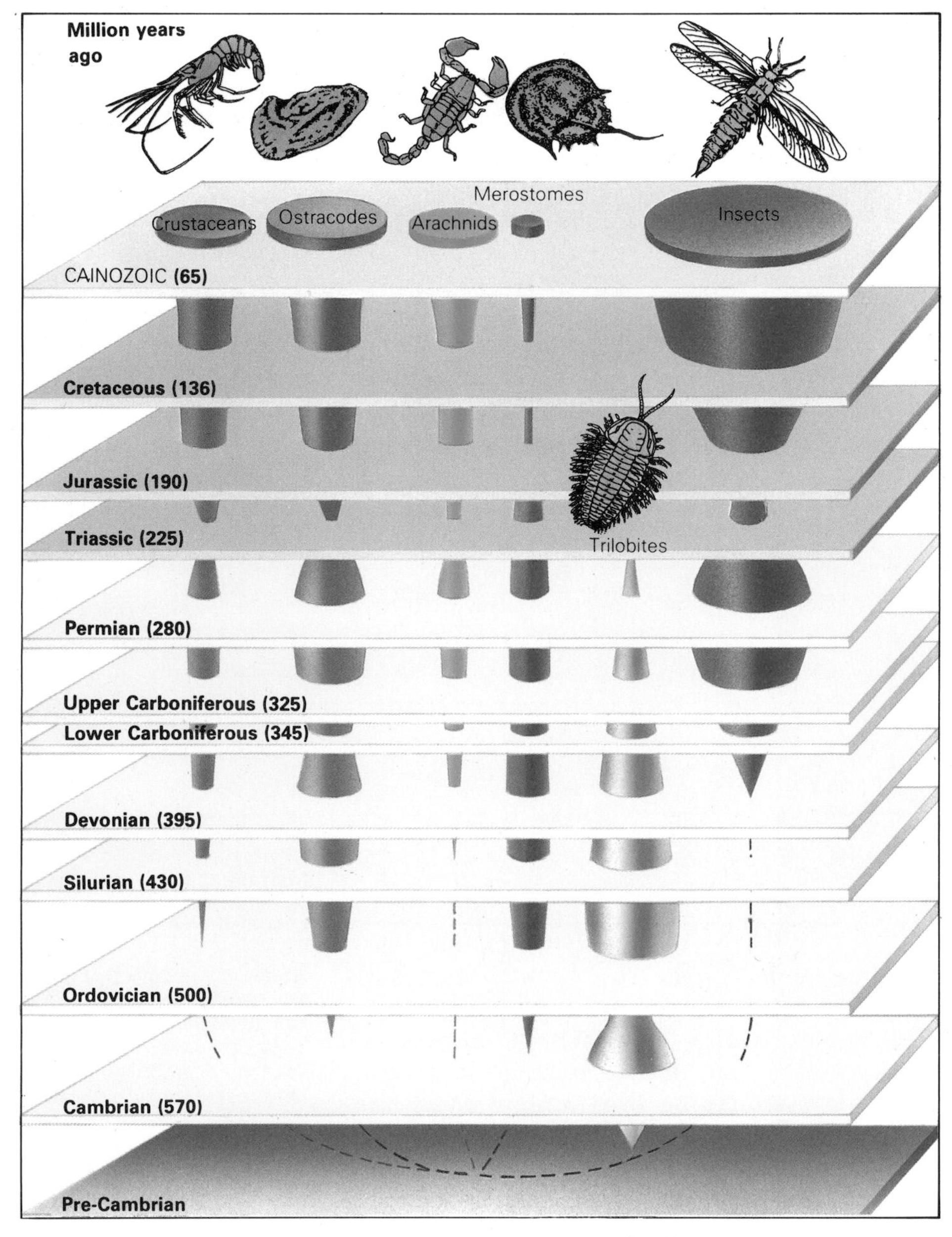

Above: The family tree of the arthropods or 'jointed-limbed invertebrates' traces their ancestry back into the Pre-Cambrian. Little or nothing is known of their ancestors, but the group was so varied by the start of the Cambrian period, 570 million years ago, that a long period of Pre-Cambrian evolution is probable. The success of the main stocks throughout recorded time is also clearly illustrated, as is the dominance of the trilobites during the Palaeozoic era. Trilobites existed on this planet for over 340 million years, while the incredibly successful insects first appeared in the Devonian. It is likely that well over 1,000,000 species of arthropods have appeared since the dawn of the Cambrian — 900,000 species exist today. Beetles, crabs, king crabs, scorpions, butterflies, flies and lice are all examples of present-day arthropods.

Arthropods

Of all the invertebrates the ARTHROPODS are probably the most successful and varied. They have a hard, segmented outer coat (EXOSKELETON) and limbs with joints. Living forms include the INSECTS, SPIDERS, SCORPIONS, CENTIPEDES and CRUSTACEANS. From fossils we find the extinct TRILOBITOMORPHS and the EURYPTERIDS, or giant 'water scorpions'. All these groups may possibly trace back to a common ancestor — an ANNELID WORM — but it is just as likely that several different groups of arthropods developed on their own from different forebears.

The first arthropods suddenly appear in the Lower Cambrian and from the beginning they make a strikingly varied group. This suggests that they extend far back into the Pre-Cambrian but that the first forms lacked a mineralized skeleton. In the early Cambrian there are several different classes of arthropods, with the main ones, the trilobites and trilobitoids, making up the Trilobitomorpha. The trilobitoids were the more varied of the two, but as their skeletons were very thin and lacked minerals, their fossils are confined to the fine-grained BURGESS SHALES of the Middle Cambrian of Canada. Typical trilobitoids were *Burgessia*, which looks rather like a minute KING CRAB, and *Marrella*, a rather exotic arthropod with large, backward-directed horns. Both *Marrella* and *Burgessia* have trilobite-like limbs, which had an upper gill branch and a lower walking leg. The trilobites themselves have a three-lobed exoskeleton, with a head (cephalon), body (thorax) and tail (pygidium). The earliest forms included spiny, small-tailed types such as *Olenellus* and the small, blind *Agnostus*. The fortunes of the trilobites waxed and waned during the Palaeozoic. Their general evolutionary trends were towards reducing spines, improving the structure of the eye and the appearance of larger-tailed species.

Of the other arthropod groups the first king crabs, crustaceans and onychophorans (*Aystriedia*) also appeared in the Cambrian. The king crabs are related to the giant eurypterids which range in time from the Middle Ordovician to the Permian. During the Silurian the first true scorpions appeared in land habitats, to be joined in the Devonian by mites, spiders and insects. The fossils of many non-marine groups are found only in sediments deposited under exceptional

divided equally by a horizontal line drawn across the front of the shell.

Plankton are the minute organisms that exist at and near the surface of seawater. Most of these organisms — plant and animal — float passively, but some swim in prevailing currents.

Polypoid describes the adult stage of some COELENTERATES, such as the SEA ANEMONE, and the soft parts of stony corals.

Porifera are mainly sea creatures characterized by numerous small pores and limited types of cell. Many have needle-like and branched SPICULES that may be fused to form a rigid skeleton. Among this group are the sponges, known since the late Pre-Cambrian.

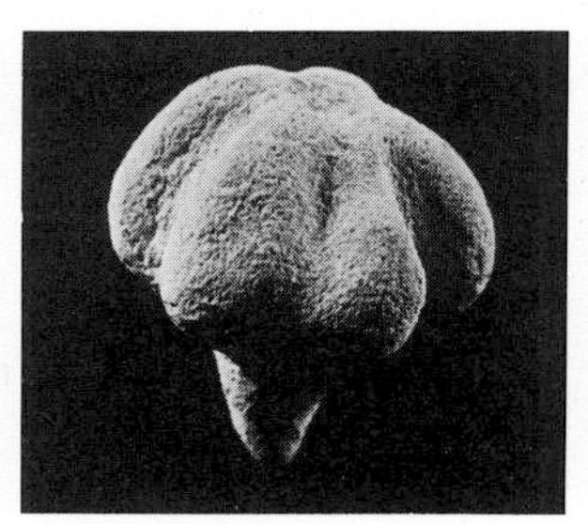

Cretaceous fossil sponge

Productus is an articulate BRACHIOPOD commonly found in rocks of the Upper Palaeozoic. In most species the lower, or pedicle, valve is much the larger of the 2.

Protozoa are single-celled animals. They are mostly sea-living and their fossil record dates from the Cambrian. Several groups develop external skeletons.

Pteropods are a group of OPISTHOBRANCH GASTROPODS. They use their foot for swimming and, unlike many other opisthobranchs, often have a shell.

Pulmonates are land- or freshwater-dwelling GASTROPODS. They have lungs, not gills, and although most retain their shell, land slugs have lost theirs.

R

Radiation is a rapid increase in the number of types in a group of organisms. It marks increased efficiency and success.

Rhabdopleura is a living HEMICHORDATE with a tube-like skeleton.

Rhynchonella is an articulate BRACHIOPOD. It has a strongly ribbed shell with a pronounced beak and poorly developed structure for its internal support.

Rugoses are a major group of 'stony corals' abundant from the Silurian to the Permian. The creatures may be solitary or live in colonies, and were important as reef builders.

S

Scleractinian corals are solitary or colonial. They are COELENTERATES with a POLYPOID adult stage and calcareous EXOSKELETONS. They are found from the Triassic to present day.

Scorpions are close relatives of the SPIDERS and EURYPTERIDS. The earliest known

conditions, but even these 'glimpses through time' give evidence of an ever-increasing variety.

Echinoderms

Unlike most invertebrates, ECHINODERMS such as the SEA URCHINS and STARFISH have an inner skeleton made up of numerous calcite plates. These are often spiny and organized so as to give the animals five rays, or PENTAMERAL SYMMETRY. This may change to BILATERAL SYMMETRY in some sea urchins but even these remain easily recognizable as spiny-skinned animals. The echinoderms live only in the sea and their fossil record spans the last 600 million years of geological time. Little or no evidence exists, however, as to their direct ancestry, but they may have come from a worm-like organism.

The first echinoderm is probably *Tribrachidium* from the late Pre-Cambrian in Australia. Little is known of it though it is unlikely to have been the forebear of the various groups that suddenly appeared in the Lower Cambrian. These included both fixed and free-living forms. Among the creatures living fixed to the sea bottom were the first EOCRINOIDS, which looked like the living and fossil SEA LILIES (crinoids). Like the first free-living echinoderms, the eocrinoids had flexible coverings in which individual plates overlapped each other. *Helicoplacus* and *Stromatocystites* are the earliest free-living forms. Their basic design is primitive but it is difficult to place them at the foot of the evolutionary line.

Many of the Cambrian echinoderm groups lived only for a short while and this suggests that they were replaced by more efficient and better protected stocks. Rigid, stronger skeletons evolved in most groups during the Cambrian and Ordovician and examples of the living sea urchins, SEA CUCUMBERS, starfish and sea lilies had all appeared by the end of the period.

Right: The 'spiny-skinned' echinoderms are and were an extremely varied group. They are represented today by the sea urchins, starfish, sea lilies and sea cucumbers, the fossil records of which can be traced back into the Palaeozoic. Several other important groups also flourished during the Palaeozoic and one, the Carpoidea, may be linked with the evolution of the vertebrates.

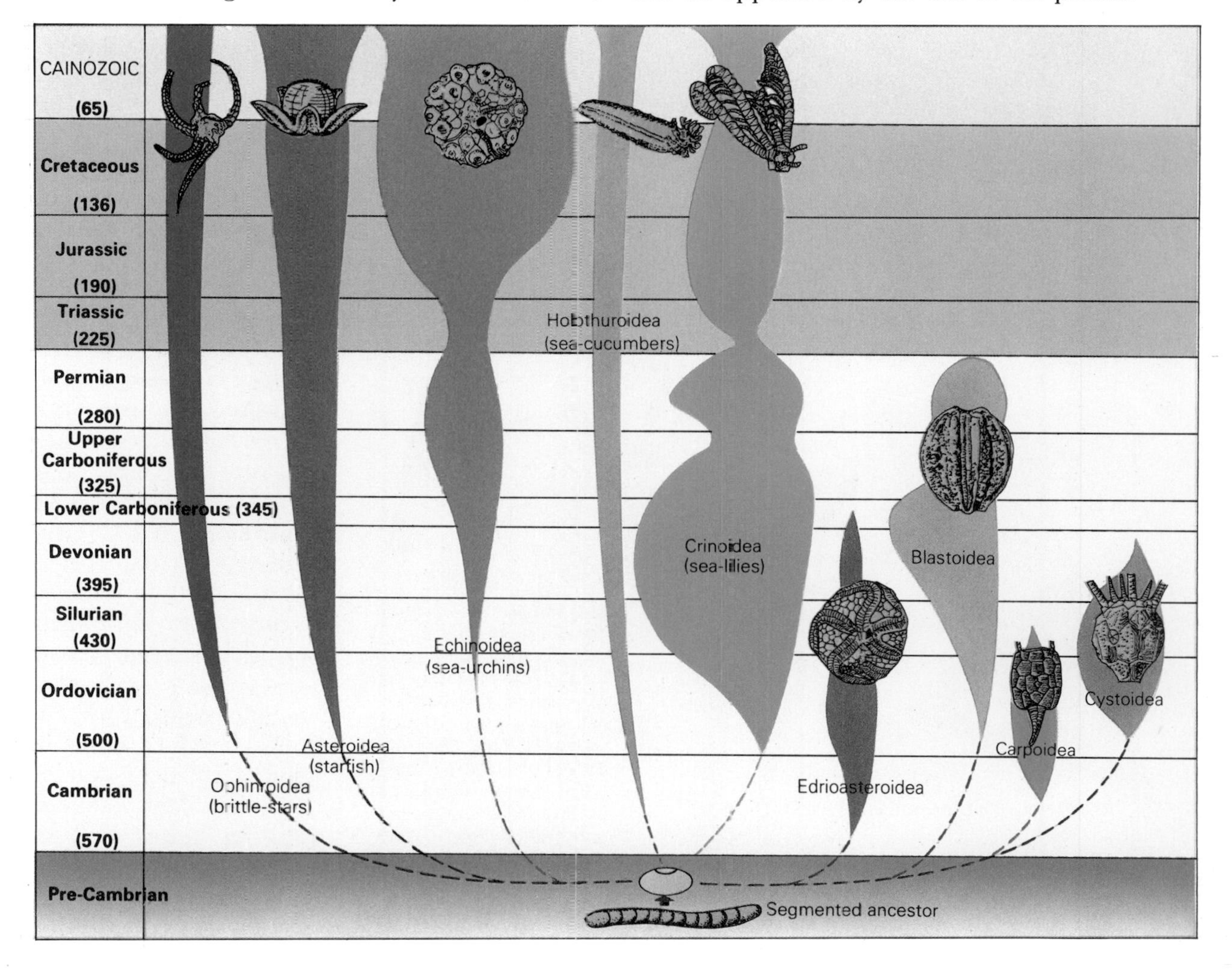

forms are from the Silurian and so they are to be regarded as the first air-breathing land-dwellers.
Sea anemones are COELENTERATES or cnidarians that lack a MEDUSOID stage in their life cycle. Their polyps are often large and the mouth is surrounded by a circle of retractable tentacles.
Sea cucumbers are ECHINODERMS which look rather worm-like. They lack rigid skeletons but do have calcareous SPICULES in their skin. They range from the Ordovician to the present.
Sea lilies, or crinoids, are SEA URCHINS with a cup-shaped body and single or paired arms. Primitive forms are on stalks while more advanced forms are free swimmers. Sea lilies are also known as the crinoids or feather stars, and are found from the Lower Cambrian to Recent periods.
Sea urchins, or echinoids, are round or heart-shaped 'spiny-skins' with a rigid shell-like skeleton. The mouth is always sited on the under surface. Sea urchins are first known from the Ordovician.
Sediment surface-dwelling is a term used to describe animals or plants that live on or within the sea floor.
Spicules are needle-like or multi-rayed siliceous or calcareous structures secreted by several groups of INVERTEBRATES. They are most commonly associated with the SPONGES but are also found in the COELENTERATES and ARCHAEOCYATHIDS.
Spiders are ARTHROPODS with 8 legs. They belong to the arachnids and are first recorded in the Devonian.
Spirifer is an articulate brachiopod characterized by a wide hinge line and a spirally-coiled structure for internal support. Spirifers range from the Middle Ordovician to the end of the Jurassic and were most abundant during the Silurian and Devonian periods.
Sponges, see PORIFERA.
Squids are living CEPHALOPOD MOLLUSCS. They have cylinder-shaped bodies and a pen-like internal shell.
Starfish are ECHINODERMS in which the body is organized into 5 distinct rays (seldom more). They are closely related to the brittle stars but appeared several million years earlier, being recorded first in the Upper Cambrian.
Suture lines seen on the outer surface of NAUTILOID and AMMONOID shells match the contact between the internal partitions, the septa, and the shell wall.

Fossil scorpion

Right: The living *Rhabdopleura* has a skeleton which is similar in structure to the extinct graptolites. *Rhabdopleura* also has a small rod of tissue above the mouth. This is the notochord found in hemichordate and chordate animals.

Zooid
Zooecium
Zooid
Rhabdopleura (Recent)
Autothecal cup
Monograptus (Silurian)
Monograptus (Silurian)

Left, right and below: Graptolites were colonial animals. Individual polyps lived in cup-like structures (thecal cups) along the edges of tubular branches (stipes).

Diplograptus (Ordovician–Silurian)
Tetragraptus (Ordovician)
Didymograptus (Ordovician)
Dichograptus (Ordovician)
Dictyonema (Cambrian – Carboniferous)

Left and above: Graptolites are known to follow a number of evolutionary trends, the most important of which was probably a reduction in the number of branches. This trend began in the Cambrian period, when species with several hundred branches were common. By the Silurian single-branched forms were dominant, and each colony was characterized by fewer, larger individuals.

Graptolites

Among the most important fossils of the Palaeozoic are the delicate, twig-like GRAPTOLITES. Their name comes from Greek and means 'stone-writings'. It also describes the way in which they are generally preserved, for most are found as white-grey carbonized films on the surface of black shale rocks. They vary greatly in form, and colonies may range from those with a single branch to those with many. Individual branches can be straight, curved or even spiral, and the THECAL CUPS, which housed the animals, may be short or long, round, triangular or hooked. For some time graptolites were grouped with the simple HYDROZOANS, but in 1938 detailed research on their skeletons revealed that they were extinct members of the HEMICHORDATES, and therefore allied to the vertebrates.

Living hemichordates comprise two classes — the ACORN WORMS and the pterobranchs; and it was because the graptolite skeletons were similar to the pterobranch RHABDOPLEURA that their relationship was confirmed. The tubes of both skeletons are made from an amino-rich material (*see page 14*) known as the PERIDERM. The inner layer of this has an open mesh-work fabric and appears as a series of rings or half rings. The association of graptolites with the hemichordates suggests that they shared a common ancestor — a phoronid worm. From the late Pre-Cambrian to the Middle Cambrian the graptolite ancestors underwent several changes in their living habits. Whereas the worms lived in sediments on the sea-floor, the first graptolites were fixed sediment surface-dwellers. These belonged to the DENDROIDS and many were shrub-like, with numerous branches and thousands of small thecal cups. During the late Cambrian a dendroid family, the ANISOGRAPTIDAE, began to produce fewer branches and cups, and it was from this stock that the 'true' GRAPTOLOIDS arose. They flourished in the Ordovician and Silurian and followed similar evolutionary trends, with successive groups having eight, four, two and in the end, one branch. More elaborate cups was another trend and it is likely that both this and the reduced number of branches were linked to changes in feeding habits and ways of life. Unlike most dendroids the majority of graptoloids formed part of the floating, or free-swimming, PLANKTON.

Symbiosis is where 2 organisms co-exist to the benefit of each other. SEA ANEMONES and certain fish provide an example. The fish are protected by the sea anemone's poisonous tentacles and in turn clean away any waste materials.

Example of symbiosis

Tabulates are an extinct group of 'stony corals'. They first appeared in the Middle Ordovician and spread rapidly throughout the world. All tabulate species lived in colonies and each individual coral was rather small. Colonies may have been loosely bound or closely packed, the individuals being polygonal in shape. Tabulates lasted until the Permian.

Terebratula is an articulate brachiopod characterized by a smooth, tear-drop shaped shell. It has a well developed opening for the passage of its stalk (pedicle) and a loop-like structure for internal support. It spans from the Lower Devonian to Recent periods.

Tetrabranchiata are CEPHALOPOD MOLLUSCS with 4 gills. They are represented today by 6 species of *Nautilus*, but were once the most abundant of all molluscs. They include NAUTILOIDS and AMMONOIDS.

Thecal cups or units occur on the outer edge of the branches of a GRAPTOLITE colony. Each cup contained an individual animal. All the animals were linked to one another by means of a common canal.

Torsion results in the internal organs of a GASTROPOD being twisted through 180° so that the mantle cavity inside the valves faces forwards.

Trepostomes are extinct BRYOZOANS characterized by massive colonies. Each animal was housed in its own elongated and progressively thicker-walled unit. Closely spaced partitions divided each unit and the construction of the skeleton earns the trepostomes the name 'stony bryozoans'. They lived from the Ordovician to the Permian.

Trilobites are extinct ARTHROPODS which lived only in the Palaeozoic. Their calcareous EXOSKELETON, or cuticle, divided both lengthways and sideways into 3 distinct lobes.

Trilobitomorphs are fossil sea-living ARTHROPODS. They include TRILOBITES and trilobitoids and are characterized by a limb which comprises a walking appendage and a gill branch.

The development of backbones meant that animals were able to evolve in size and intelligence to a degree unmatched among invertebrates. Much of their success has been due to advances in their skeletons and teeth.

Evolution of Vertebrates

The origin of animals with backbones—the VERTEBRATES—is a subject much argued about, especially as there is little direct evidence provided by fossils. Fragments of the first vertebrates come from the lowest Ordovician rocks and although this material is less than perfect, it shows that the vertebrates were established by the dawn of that period. It also shows that the search for ancestors should be among pre-Ordovician groups. In part this is true, but scientists must also look to the living soft-bodied CHORDATES (*see page 26*) for vital clues.

Forebears of the vertebrates have been sought among many invertebrate groups, including the worms and arthropods, but for various reasons these have been ruled out as true contenders. The main objections have been to their EMBRYOS, and so attention has focused on the echinoderms. The LARVAL stages of these 'spiny-skins' and the acorn worms (hemichordates) are basically similar and this may suggest that the two had a common ancestor. Recent studies support this view and point to the CALCICHORDATES—a group of specialized 'echinoderms'—as the ancestors of all the higher chordates, including the vertebrates. The evidence comes from studies of the inner structure of Cambrian and Ordovician calcichordates, the gills and nervous systems in particular. Arguments for a link between the calcichordates and vertebrates are very convincing, but many scientists still dispute it. They prefer to link the vertebrates directly to the TUNICATES, and believe that at some stage in the Cambrian a tadpole-like larva of one of these animals reproduced to give rise to a free-swimming adult. This meant that the larva did not develop into the normal sac-like adult living on the sea bed, and that a different group—similar to today's AMPHIOXUS—arose as an ancestor to the vertebrates.

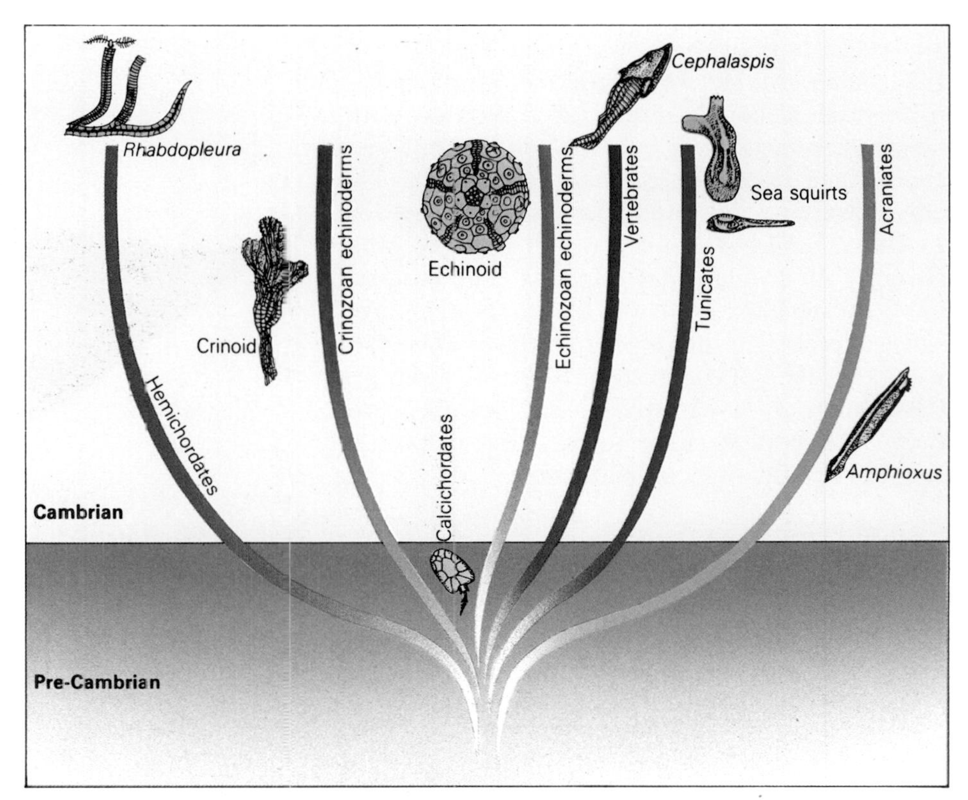

Above: The origin of animals with backbones — the vertebrates — is still one of the great unsolved problems of evolution. Of several possible ancestors, most cannot be counted as direct relatives. Many scientists believe that the calcichordates and agnathan (jawless) fishes, such as *Cephalaspis*, are directly linked.

Right: *Mitrocystella* is an example of a calcichordate. It is a flattened, rather asymmetrical animal, with a short tail. Recent reconstructions of the animal indicate that it had a complex nervous system, with a brain and single 'eye'.

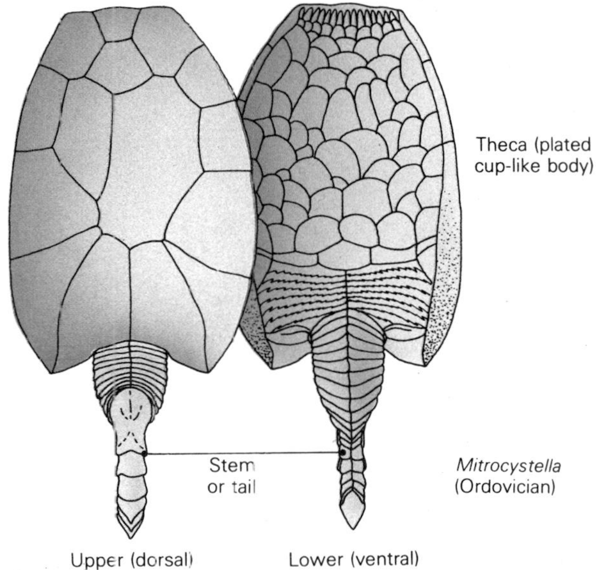

Reference

Acanthodians were the first jawed fishes. They lived during the Silurian, Devonian, Carboniferous and Permian, and are often called the 'spiny sharks'. Their bodies were covered in small, square scales, which were crowned. They also often had stout spines on both lower and upper body surfaces. The body was streamlined and the tail HETEROCERCAL. Few grew more than 200 mm.

Acheulean stone tools are commonly pointed or almond-shaped hand-axes. The Acheulean hand-axe cultures take their name from Saint-Acheul, France, but were first developed by HOMO ERECTUS in Africa.

Adaptive radiation occurs when an organism or a related group of organisms evolve into various subgroups which are adapted to a wide range of ecological NICHES (*see page 21*). For example, there were adaptive radiations of fishes in the Devonian, dinosaur-like reptiles in the Jurassic and flowering plants in the Cretaceous.

Aëtosaurs were primitive THECODONTIANS, or 'tooth in socket' reptiles. They were 4-legged, and rather like heavily-armoured crocodiles. Their armour was formed by rows of bony plates, which in some forms, such as *Desmatosuchus*, were extended sideways into large spines. The aëtosaurs were land-dwellers and some had pig-like snouts, perhaps used when rooting for food. *Desmatosuchus*, 3 metres long, was one of the largest

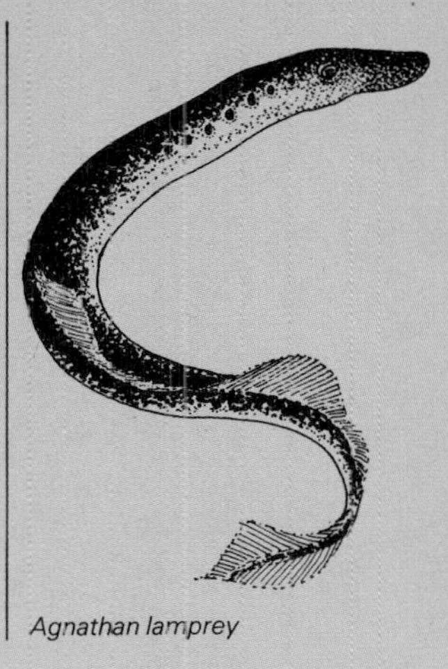
Agnathan lamprey

aëtosaurs, most of which lived only in the Triassic.

Agnathan fishes lack jaws. They have a sucker-like mouth and are represented today by the LAMPREYS and HAG-FISHES. In the Upper Palaeozoic, heavily armoured fishes such as *Cephalaspis* and *Pteraspis* represented the agnathans. Jawless fishes range from the Ordovician to Recent periods.

Amblypods are an extinct ORDER of large UNGULATES which lived in early Tertiary times. They include the Pantodonta, such as *Corypho-*

Fish

The discovery of the fish ANATOLEPIS HEINTZI in sediments of the lowest Ordovician shows that the ancestors of the vertebrates evolved during the Cambrian. *Anatolepis* was a small jawless fish (or AGNATHAN) and it is likely that it and its close relatives were MUD-GRUBBERS, feeding on the remains of living matter. The early history of the fishes is little known until Silurian and Devonian times when the larger, heavily armoured OSTRACODERMS flourished in sea and fresh waters. Like *Anatolepis* the ostracoderms were jawless fishes and although many later became quite active swimmers, it is hard to believe that they could have been hunters and PREDATORS. The only surviving jawless fishes are the eel-like LAMPREYS and HAG-FISHES, which lack the bony covering of their ancient relatives. The lamprey has a sucker-like mouth and unlike the armoured ostracoderms has adapted to a SEMI-PARASITIC way of life. MAYOMYZON from the Upper Carboniferous is like the living lamprey and these 'soft-bodied' fishes may show what the ancestors of the jawless fishes were like.

Fish develop jaws

The first jawed (or GNATHOSTOME) fishes appeared in the Upper Silurian, and the long lapse between the first jawless fishes and this event has been taken to show a direct ancestral link between them. This may be true but it is just as likely that the jawed fishes arose independently. The evolution of jaws was a major development for the vertebrates and it allowed the fishes to make use of new niches. The main difference between agnathans and gnathosts is that the latter have fewer GILL ARCHES and the first two gill bars are modified to form jaws. Unlike their distant cousins, the first jawed fishes had rounded rather than flattened bodies and paired fins. They swam with an eel-like movement of the body and probably looked for food near the water's surface. The first jawed fishes were the ACANTHODIANS. Many were rather like sharks although few were longer than 300 millimetres. During the Devonian the jawed fishes radiated dramatically and numerous examples of both bony and CARTILAGINOUS fishes appeared, as well as the heavily armoured PLACODERMS. It seems that the acanthodians and the bony fishes (OSTEICHTHYES) are closely related. But the ancestors of the cartilaginous fishes (chondrichthyes) and placoderms seem to be linked with a different, unknown, stock.

Above: *Cephalaspis* and *Pteraspis* are examples of agnathan, or jawless, fishes. They represent the 2 main families of the agnathids, both of which flourished during the late Silurian to early Devonian periods. Both fishes had a thick bony armour over the outside of the body.

Bony fishes

The osteichthyes have a bony skeleton, and the early forms also have an air sac. Typical bony fishes are cod, salmon and herring, but the coelacanth and the lungfish are perhaps of even greater evolutionary importance. The first three are typical RAY-FINNED fishes, while the last two are commonly called lobed or TASSEL-FINNED. Examples of both groups first lived during the Lower Devonian. Ray-finned fishes are less advanced in evolution, even though they now have tens of thousands of species. This exceeds the number of living tassel-finned species and may show that although ray-finned fishes were more 'primitive', they were better adapted to the fast swimming, hunter-predator role.

Among the ray-finned fishes, or actinopterygians, the general trends were linked with improvements in swimming and feeding. Heavily scaled forms were gradually replaced by fishes with thin, overlapping scales and a more flexible body. Changes to the jaws and tail took place, and a swim-bladder developed, so that during

Below: The under-surface of the head of *Cephalaspis* is characterized by a sucker-like mouth and a circle of gill openings.

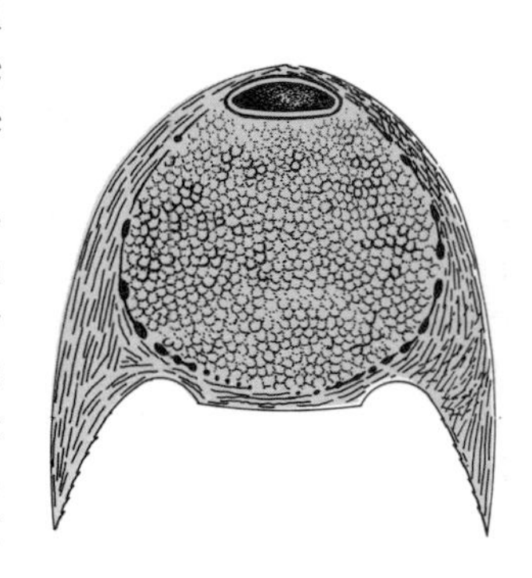

don, and the Dinocerata, which culminated in the grotesque *Uintatherium.*
Amia is a living example of an HOLOSTEAN fish. Its ancestry can be traced back to the Upper Palaeozoic, and it is from this type of fish that the TELEOSTS arose. *Amia* is also known as the freshwater bowfin. It has a long body and dorsal fin. The body is covered in thin scales and both lobes of the tail are about the same size.
Amniote egg is characteristic of the reptiles and birds. It has a shell for protection, a series of membranes which allow the developing young to be bathed in fluids and a supply of nourishment (yolk). The young reptile or bird develops in a protected environment and so there is no obvious need for a larval stage as in the amphibians. The young hatchlings are small replicas of the adult.
Amphicyonidae are extinct 'bear-dogs' which lived from Oligocene until late Pliocene times. Apart from size, they had few bear-like features.
Amphioxus is a small marine animal that looks rather like a translucent fish. It is not a VERTEBRATE, but does have a well-developed NOTOCHORD, and the presence of gill slits shows that it has a distinct relationship with the vertebrates.

Amphioxus

Anapsid describes the type of skull found in turtles and certain groups of early reptiles. The anapsid skull has no openings on the temples behind the eye.
Anatolepis heintzi is the name given to the first 'fish'. It is known from rocks of the Lower Ordovician in Spitsbergen, Norway, and is thought to be older than other remains found in the USSR and North America. No skull or fins are known, but small scales indicate the animal's link with the fishes.
Ancylopoda are an extinct sub-group of the PERISSODACTYLA, consisting of the clawed CHALICOTHERES and their ancestors. They were perhaps related to the TITANOTHERES.
Ankylosaurs were a group of heavily-armoured Upper Cretaceous dinosaurs, the 'armour' being formed from large bony plates.
Anthracotheres are extinct members of the Suina, a sub-group of the ARTIODACTYLA. They lived from Eocene until Pleistocene times, and in the late Pliocene probably gave rise to the hippopotamuses.
Anthropoids are advanced

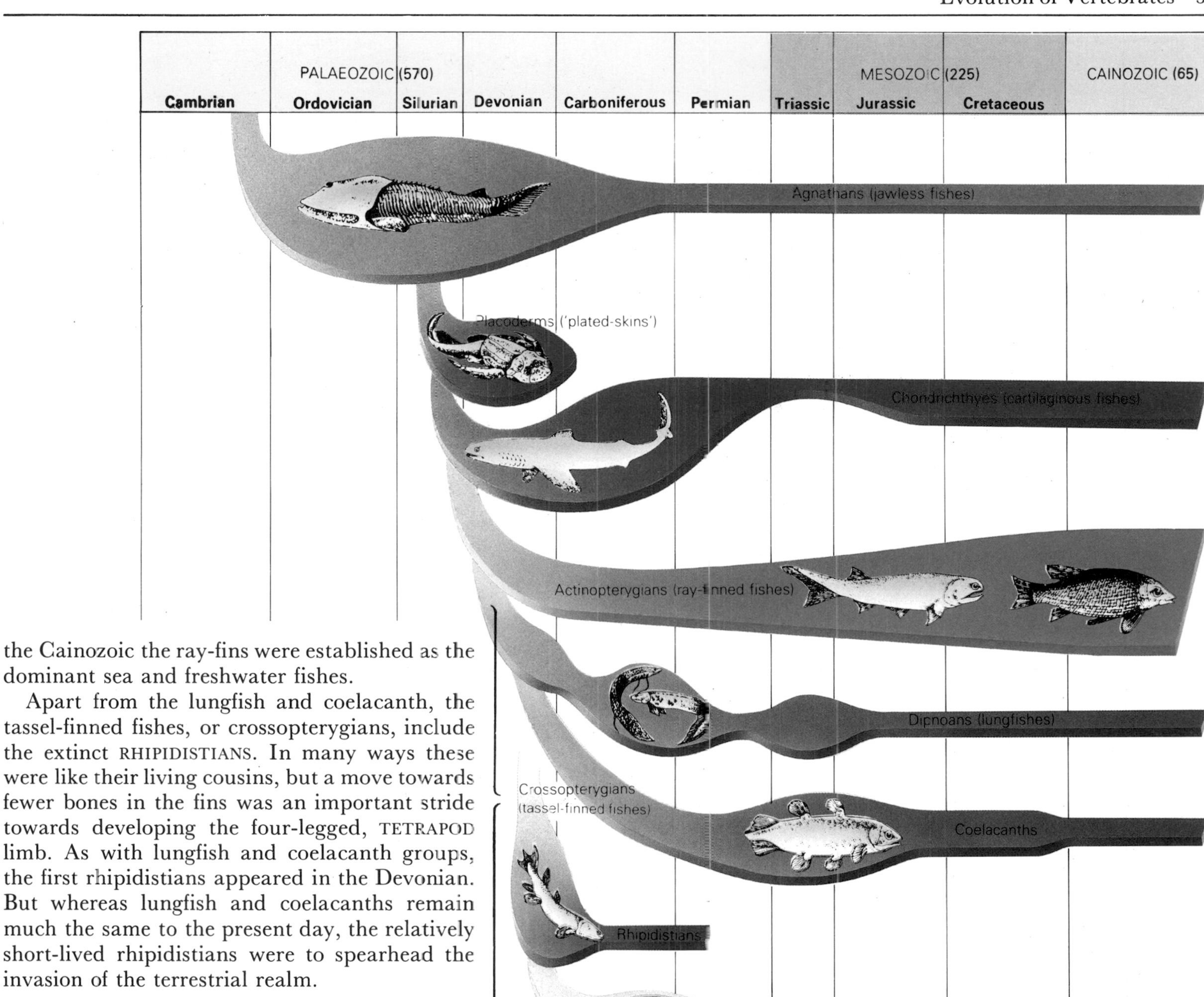

the Cainozoic the ray-fins were established as the dominant sea and freshwater fishes.

Apart from the lungfish and coelacanth, the tassel-finned fishes, or crossopterygians, include the extinct RHIPIDISTIANS. In many ways these were like their living cousins, but a move towards fewer bones in the fins was an important stride towards developing the four-legged, TETRAPOD limb. As with lungfish and coelacanth groups, the first rhipidistians appeared in the Devonian. But whereas lungfish and coelacanths remain much the same to the present day, the relatively short-lived rhipidistians were to spearhead the invasion of the terrestrial realm.

Plated and cartilaginous fishes

Of the remaining fish groups the placoderms or 'plated-skins' lived only in the Devonian (and possibly the Lower Carboniferous). There were numerous forms in both sea and freshwater niches, and a few species reached almost 9 metres in length. Unlike their close relatives the cartilaginous fish (sharks, rays and RATFISH), placoderms had heavy armour. The first sharks are known from the Middle Devonian and the first rays from the Middle Jurassic. Their early examples are similar to modern species.

Above: The first 'proto-fishes' appeared in the Cambrian period and the first jawless fish, *Anatolepis*, in the earliest Ordovician. Jawless fishes dominated the early history of the group but by the late Silurian to early Devonian, true jawed fishes were well established. The latter included the 'plated-skins', or placoderms, and cartilaginous and bony fishes. It is thought that the placoderms and cartilaginous fishes, such as the sharks and rays, are closely related and clearly separate from the ray- and tassel-finned bony fishes. Ray-finned fishes account for the vast majority of living species, but it is from the tassel-fins that the amphibians probably arose.

PRIMATES. They include the OLD WORLD MONKEYS, NEW WORLD MONKEYS, the great apes (gibbons, chimpanzees, orangutans, gorillas) and man.

Arch vertebrae are found in ancient LABYRINTHODONT amphibians. In the early development of the animal these vertebrae are formed by the hardening of several units of soft tissue.

Archaeopteryx is the first known bird. Only 5 fossils are known, 3 of which are very well preserved with excellent impressions of both tail and wing feathers. *Archaeopteryx* was probably unable to fly and had a build similar to small COELUROSAURS such as *Compsognathus*.

Archosaurs are reptiles with a DIAPSID type of skull. Unlike the snakes and lizards, archosaurs keep the bony bars between the 2 temple openings. Crocodiles, dinosaurs, PTEROSAURS and THECODONTIANS are all archosaurs.

Gibbon, an anthropoid

Artiodactyla are hoofed animals with an even number of toes, either 4 or 2, on each foot. They are the most numerous of the plant-eating MAMMALS.

Astrapotheres are an extinct order of large, possibly amphibious, South American UNGULATES, which lived from Eocene until Miocene times. They may have had a proboscis or trunk.

Australopithecus was the first undoubted HOMINID to be discovered. The name means 'Southern Ape,' but we now know that *Australopithecus* belonged to the family of man. It is not clear whether the Australopithecines were ancestors of *Homo,* or true man, or whether they and *Homo* derive from a common ancestor. The latter seems more likely.

B **Baluchitherium** was one of the giant, hornless rhinoceroses that lived in Asia during Oligocene and Miocene times. It was the largest and heaviest land mammal ever, standing over 7 metres tall, and browsed trees, much like a giraffe.

Baptornis is a fossil seabird known from rocks of the Upper Cretaceous. It was rather grebe-like in appearance and lived at the same time as HESPERORNIS and ICHTHYORNIS. Baptornis could fly, but its wings were not as well-developed as those of the 'fish-bird' *Ichthyornis.*

Binocular vision is achieved when an animal's

Evolutionary trends among the fishes

A summary of general evolutionary trends in the various fish classes must obviously include the development of jaws and a reduction in the amount and thickness of outer armour. It may be that the true jawed fishes arose more than once from different yet related ancestors. But while this idea is a theory only, the reduction of armour is a common trend in most groups. We have seen that in ray-finned fishes the reducing of armour is linked with a general improvement in swimming power and control. This is also true of other fishes. In those of the CEPHALASPID type, the development of fins and a shortening of the head shield are related trends. Thick body scales are generally seen as primitive in most groups and among the earliest jawed fishes the short-bodied CLIMATIOIDS have thick, high crowned scales. The short body is also a primitive feature and more specialized forms, such as XYLACANTHUS, have a longer body with light armour. Another trend in the earliest jawed fishes, the acanthodians, produced the jaw structure and loss of teeth in more specialized types. Again, the reduction of armour in the acanthodians has been linked with improvements in swimming. But improvements in feeding and defence also occur.

The early bony fishes (osteichthyes) had rather simple cheek structures and the most primitive PALAEONISCID fishes had to swallow their captives whole. Later forms allowed for greater movement and better methods of feeding. These adaptations were also linked with reductions in body armour and changes in the shape of the tail. They resulted in a more efficient type of fish and one which was ideally suited to a predator's life. Among ray-finned fishes the trend was towards animals with long, streamlined bodies. But several deep-bodied forms have evolved as successful adaptations. One example, *Dorypterus* from the Upper Permian, has a flattened body 'crowned' by a long dorsal fin and a rather narrow tail. It has a small mouth and no teeth, which makes scientists believe that it fed on soft plants. Many modern deep-bodied fishes are specially adapted to living in a reef habitat.

The Palaeozoic forms of ray-finned fishes are generally grouped under the title CHONDROSTEI. They represent a primitive level of evolution and present-day examples are the freshwater POLYPTERUS and the living sturgeons such as *Acipenser.*

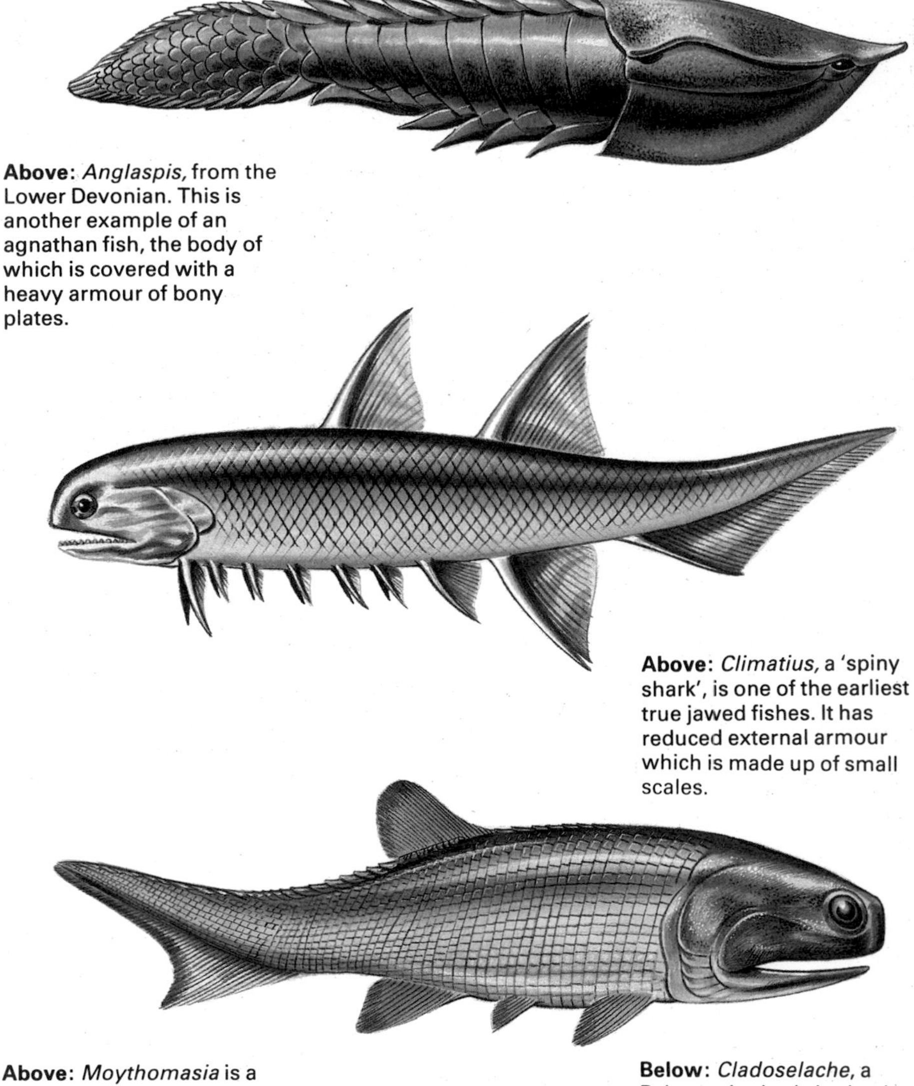

Above: *Anglaspis,* from the Lower Devonian. This is another example of an agnathan fish, the body of which is covered with a heavy armour of bony plates.

Above: *Climatius,* a 'spiny shark', is one of the earliest true jawed fishes. It has reduced external armour which is made up of small scales.

Above: *Moythomasia* is a representative of the early ray-finned bony fishes. Its body was covered by a layer of thick, overlapping scales. In later forms of such fish, these scales are often reduced, and sometimes lost altogether.

Below: *Cladoselache,* a Palaeozoic shark, had only a few scales over its body. Other Palaeozoic sharks, however, were covered in rather thick scales which seem to have thinned down to the rough skin, or shagreen, of living forms.

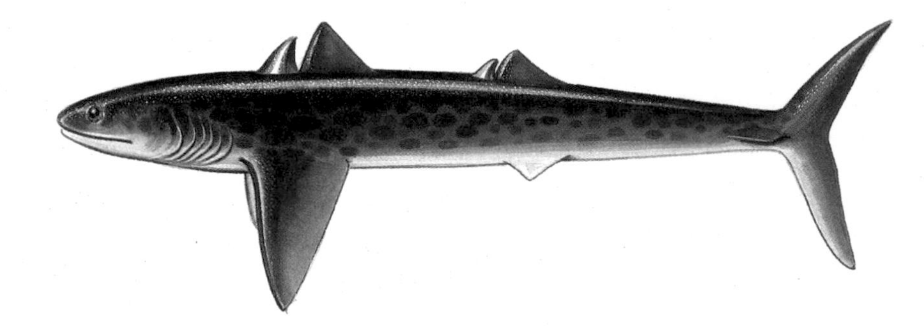

fields of vision overlap. Both eyes can then focus on the same object, and so estimate distance.

Bipedal animals walk on their hind legs. Many THECODONTIANS, dinosaurs and mammals — including man — are bipedal.

Bird-hipped dinosaurs, or ornithischians, are those in which the pubis bone has moved back to a position beneath the ischium bone. This results in a 3-pronged arrangement of the pelvis, similar to that found in birds. It is very different from the pelvis of LIZARD-HIPPED dinosaurs and other reptiles.

Bone-headed dinosaurs, or pachycephalosaurs, had a thick layer of bone over the brain case. They were bird-hipped, and seem to have lived in herds in upland regions during the Upper Cretaceous.

Borhyaena was a large, long-tailed dog- or wolf-like MARSUPIAL that inhabited South America during the Miocene.

Bovoids include the North American pronghorn (of the Antilocapridae family) and the extremely diverse range of antelopes, wild cattle, sheep and goats (of the Bovidae family).

Brachydont teeth are short or low-crowned cheek-teeth. They are characteristic of mammals which eat a mixed diet, and of those plant-eaters which consume mainly soft leaves.

Browsers are MAMMALS which eat the shoots and leaves of trees (as opposed to grazers which eat grass and other herbs). Many dinosaurs were also browsers.

Bunodont cheek-teeth have low, rounded cusps giving them a hillock-type appearance. They are typical of animals that eat a mixed diet, such as pigs and men.

Giraffes are browsers

C

Cainotheres were small, rabbit-like creatures belonging to the ARTIODACTYLA. They were RUMINANTS and were restricted to Europe. After their appearance in the Eocene, they reached their heyday in the Oligocene and became extinct in Miocene times, apparently displaced by ancestors of the true rabbit.

Calcichordates are an extinct group of echinoderms which have a definite link with the CHORDATES (*see page*

Chondrostei were replaced in the Triassic by the SUBHOLOSTEANS, which have considerably thinner scales. The subholosteans were replaced in turn by the true HOLOSTEANS (Holostei) during the Jurassic. These have even thinner scales and their jaws have been greatly modified. Holosteans thrived during both the Jurassic and Cretaceous periods, but today their only examples are the garfishes and AMIA. The downfall of the holosteans was linked to success among the TELEOSTS, the most varied group of living fishes. These simply reflect the climax of trends started in the Palaeozoic: their scales are extremely thin and their tails HOMOCERCAL.

Changes in the feeding apparatus can also be seen in the evolution of the placoderms, where several levels of organization have been recorded. These are closely linked with alterations in the shape of the body, and together they reflect important changes in ways of life. At first the placoderms were slow predators living on the sea bottom, but in time fish such as *Dunkleosteus* became active in mid-waters.

The primitive level of organization in cartilaginous fishes is shown by *Cladoselache*, the earliest shark. It grew to about 2 metres in length, and is primitive because it lacked claspers, had a large keel-like pectoral (underside) fin and a symmetrical tail. More advanced sharks develop a HETEROCERCAL tail and the organs for both feeding and movement are much changed. Most shark teeth have a high central point but during the Mesozoic some HYBODONTOID sharks developed flat teeth for crushing seashells. The fact that the cartilaginous fishes developed claspers shows that they had also developed a method of internal fertilization.

Left: *Holopteryx* is a spiny-finned teleost and an ancestor of the living squirrel fishes. Teleosts are the most advanced ray-finned fishes, and the deep-bodied *Holopteryx* is but one of the great variety of forms that evolved within the group.

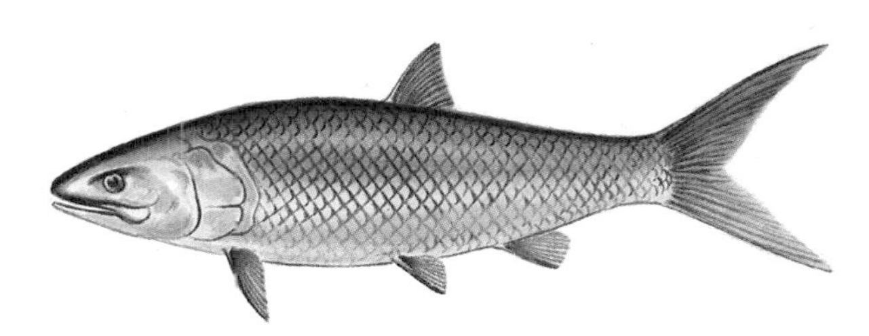

Right: *Caturus* is an extinct relative of the living bowfin *Amia*. Unlike *Palaeoniscum*, it has a small, rather symmetrical tail-fin and thinner scales. *Caturus* represents a more advanced level among the ray-fins than *Palaeoniscum*.

Left: *Palaeoniscum* is the genus after which the primitive ray-finned fishes — the palaeoniscids — are named. They were mostly meat-eating fish, with an elongate, streamlined body and a very unequally divided, or heterocercal, tail.

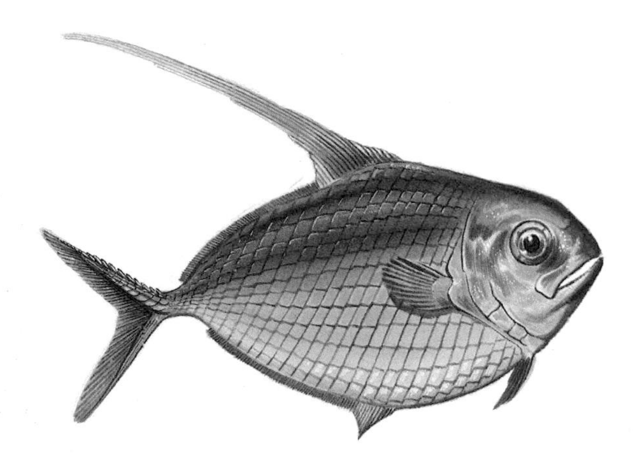

Above: *Dorypterus* is a ray-finned fish from the Upper Permian. It had a deep body and very long dorsal fin. The skull bones were small and there were no teeth. Small-mouthed, deep-bodied fishes are often found today in coral reef communities, and *Dorypterus* may have occupied a similar niche in the Permian.

From fish to amphibian

During the Middle Devonian an important radiation took place among the bony fishes. This affected ray- and tassel-finned fishes alike and for the first time forms appeared that were able to move deliberately, albeit slowly, over land. These fishes probably lived in shallow water and in times of drought they would be forced to migrate from pond to pond. They were related to the lungfish and coelacanths and called rhipidistians. The fewer number of bones in rhipidistian

Above: Living lungfishes, such as the African *Lepidosiren*, have developed means to withstand periods of drought by making a burrow in which to retreat. But this way of adapting to seasonal aridity was of limited importance in evolutionary terms.

26). They existed during the Lower Palaeozoic, and had skeletons made up of calcite plates. Most had a large 'body' and a short tail or stem. It is thought that many lay flat on the sea-floor, using their tails as 'fixing' devices.

Canidae are the family to which the modern dogs, wolves, jackals and foxes belong. Dogs have remained less specialized than other members of the CARNIVORA, which helps explain why they are so widespread, with representatives on every continent except Antarctica.

Canines are long, cone-shaped stabbing teeth which are especially well developed in the CARNIVORA. In sabre-tooth cats the upper canines were greatly elongated and used for stabbing and slicing.

Canoidea are a super-family of the CARNIVORA. According to a recent classification they include the AMPHICYONIDAE, CANIDAE, PROCYONIDAE, OTARIIDAE and URSIDAE. In this new scheme the MUSTELIDAE are grouped together with the PHOCIDAE into another super-family, the Musteloidae.

Carnassials are modified cheek-teeth which developed in both the CARNIVORA and CREODONTS. They have a serrated cutting edge and close together like scissor blades. Carnassials are therefore adapted to slicing meat and cutting tough sinews.

Walrus tusks

Carnivora are an ORDER of mainly meat-eating MAMMALS. In older classifications, land carnivores are called fissipeds, while the sea lions, walruses and seals are called pinnipeds.

Carnivore is an animal that feeds on other animals.

Carnosaurs were the major dinosaur predators, the best-known being *Tyrannosaurus rex*. They were LIZARD-HIPPED dinosaurs.

Cartilaginous fishes, such as the sharks and rays, do not have a bony skeleton. Instead it is made up of cartilage—a relatively soft, translucent tissue made up of rounded cells. Cartilage shrivels when the animal dies and therefore complete sharks or rays are rarely discovered in fossil form. As a result the study of these fishes is confined mostly to their teeth. The first cartilaginous fishes are known from the latter half of the Devonian. *Cladoselache*, the

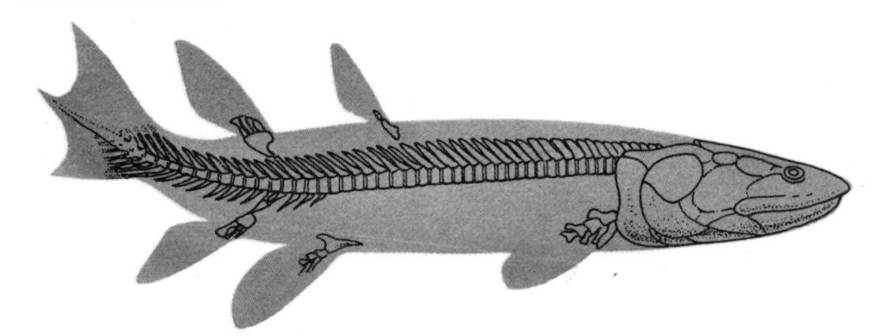

Left: The skeleton of the tassel-finned fish *Eusthenopteron,* although typically fish-like in appearance, marks an important advance in the evolution of amphibians and higher land-dwelling vertebrates.

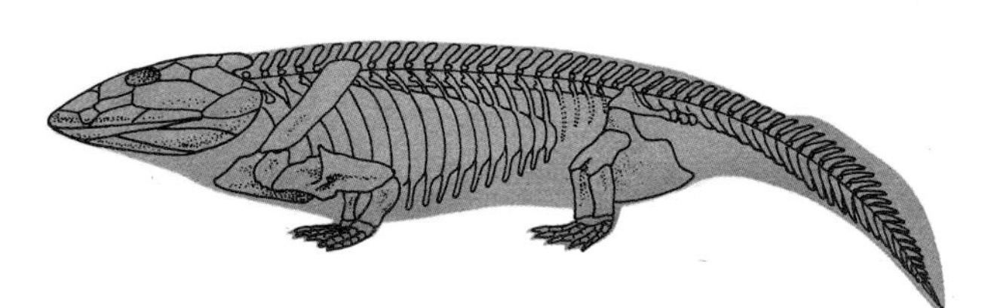

Left: The skeleton of *Ichthyostega,* the earliest amphibian, still retains a few fish characteristics, the most obvious being a bony, fin-like tail. Its short, strong limbs are a considerable advance on the tassel-fins of crossopterygian fishes.

Below: A fish has only the deep-seated apparatus of its inner ear. Without an ear drum or delicate ear bones, the fish cannot actually hear sound. Instead it picks up the vibrations from noise, and these pass along the side of the body to the brain-case. The fish ear is therefore an organ mostly used for balance and protection.

Below: In contrast to the fish ear, that of an amphibian has undergone radical changes. The ear bones are now well-developed and there is also an ear drum. Together these structures transmit vibrations to the inner ear, and hearing becomes the organ's main function, although balance is still important.

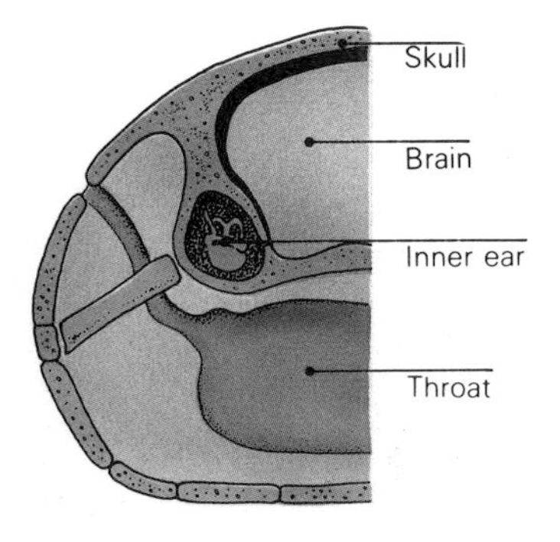

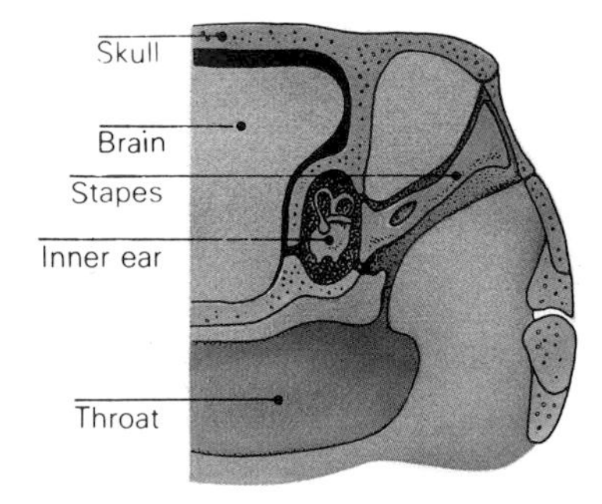

Dorsal view of the skull of *Eusthenopteron*

Dorsal view of the skull of *Ichthyostega*

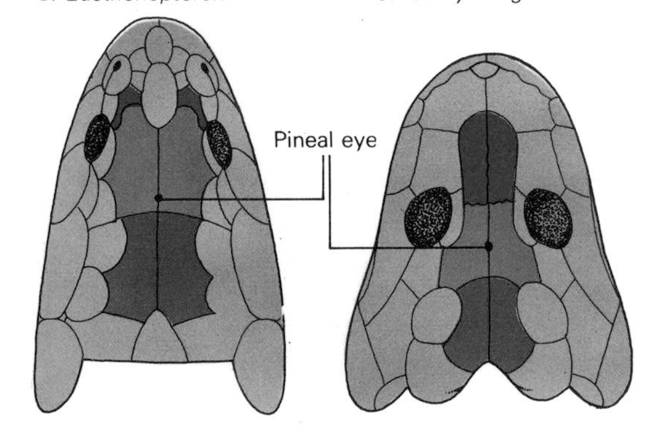

Left: A direct comparison of the skulls of *Eusthenopteron* and *Ichthyostega* shows certain similarities. Another amphibian, *Elpistostege,* appears to fall midway between, especially as regards the proportions of the skull mosaic's central bones.

fins is an obvious trend towards a four-legged creature. But other important clues to the ancestors of amphibians can be found by comparing skulls and individual teeth.

The skull roof of *Eusthenopteron,* a typical rhipidistian, is similar to that of an early amphibian. Although the *Eusthenopteron* skull has more bones, their pattern around the eye-sockets and the 'third eye' (PINEAL OPENING) is almost identical. The early amphibian's snout is longer and the area behind the eye-sockets shorter. Such changes can be expected in land-dwellers and fortunately the discovery of the 'missing link' ELPISTOSTEGE, from the Upper Devonian of Canada, proves that the changes progressed gradually. Little is known of *Elpistostege,* but the pattern of its skull bones falls between those of *Eusthenopteron* and *Ichthyostega,* the first amphibian.

Ichthyostega was a LABYRINTHODONT amphibian, a name given because their teeth appear folded, or labyrinthine, in cross section. Rhipidistians have teeth which are also labyrinthine, and such evidence obviously supports a direct descent from rhipidistian to labyrinthodont. Unfortunately not all amphibians are labyrinthodonts and it seems that a separate ancestor, or ancestors, must be found for the LEPOSPONDYLS, which are often smaller and possibly less specialized creatures.

One of the main differences between the rhipidistians and their descendants is the way in which the ear is formed. A fish ear is mainly used for balance, and its 'hearing' is limited to picking up vibrations transmitted from the body to the brain case. The inner ear is isolated. On land this would be useless, so a new device, the ear drum, was developed to pick up sound vibrations from the outside through a small, usually thin, bone called the stapes.

Relationships in the amphibian family

Remains of *Ichthyostega* have been discovered from the late Devonian sediments of east Greenland. There is no doubt that they are from a labyrinthodont amphibian, and together with *Elpistostege* and *Otocratia, Ichthyostega* forms the primitive Ichthyostegalia group. These animals are known only from the Upper Devonian and Lower Carboniferous and some PALAEONTOLOGISTS see them as the basic stock for both labyrinthodonts and lepospondyls. Others doubt

Devonian shark, is among the earliest cartilaginous fishes. The cartilaginous skeleton may be the primitive condition among the vertebrates, or it may be the result of young fishes reaching sexual maturity before their skeletons had turned to bone.

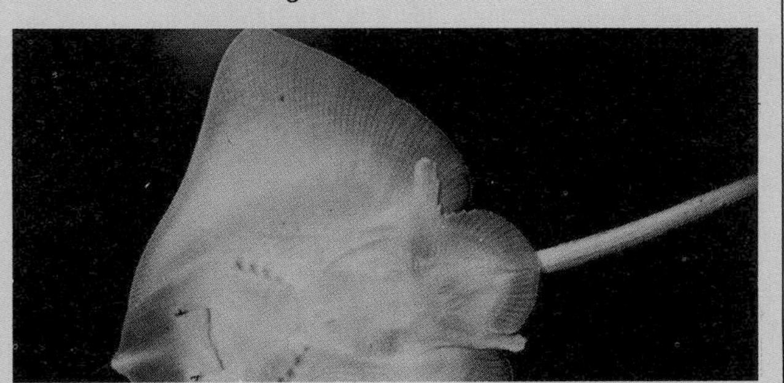

Cartilaginous fish, a ray

Cephalaspid fishes were common during the Devonian. They were jawless and had a sucker-like mouth on the under-surface of the head. The head was broad and rather flat, with two large eyes placed high on the upper surface. The tail was quite strongly developed and suggests that *Cephalaspis* was an active swimmer.

Ceratomorpha are a sub-order of the PERISSODACTYLA, and include the rhinoceroses and tapirs.

Ceratopians, or horned dinosaurs, had a large bony frill and beak-like jaws. Most of these rhinoceros-like animals had heads with a large nose-horn and 2 large, sometimes enormous, brow-horns. They lived during the Upper Cretaceous.

Chalicotheres are extinct PERISSODACTYLA, the more recent of which, such as *Moropus,* resembled clawed horses. They may have used their claws for digging up roots and tubers, or for bending down leafy branches. The group ranged from the Eocene to the Pleistocene.

Chondrostei are a group of RAY-FINNED FISHES. Today they are represented by forms such as *Polypterus,* a heavy scaled fish with lungs. Chondrostei are perhaps the most primitive ray fins, and were plentiful during the Palaeozoic and Triassic.

Climatioids were a group of 'plated-skinned' fishes — PLACODERMS. They looked more 'normal' than many of their relatives, being rather shark-like, and lived during the Upper Palaeozoic.

Coal Age is another name for the Upper Carboniferous. In North America this period

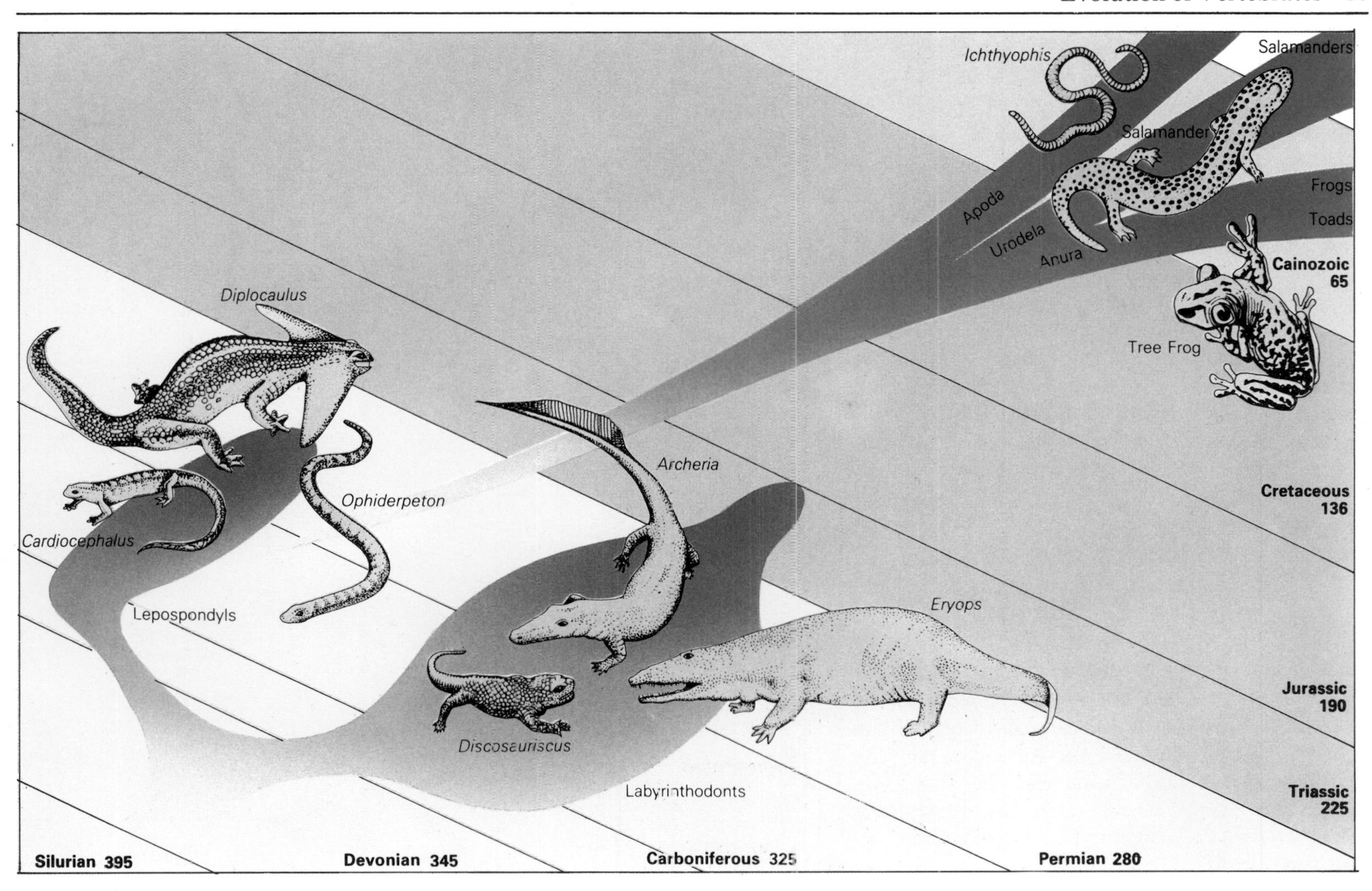

Above: The amphibian family tree clearly illustrates the 3 sub-divisions of the group. Labyrinthodonts and lepospondyls dominated the Palaeozoic era, while living frogs, toads and salamanders are important from the Jurassic onwards. The evolution of labyrinthodonts from the tassel-finned fishes is widely accepted, but the early evolution of both the lepospondyls and the recent amphibians is still a matter of discussion.

this and suggest that the two groups rose independently from the fishes. The labyrinthodont fossils are earlier, but the great variety shown by lepospondyls indicates that they too probably began during the Lower Devonian. From the Devonian to the Middle Jurassic the labyrinthodonts remained the chief amphibians, while the less important lepospondyls died out in the Permian. Some, such as SAUROPLEURA and OPHIDERPETON, were snake-like; others had small limbs and large 'horned' heads. None rivalled the labyrinthodonts in size and only a few could move beyond their ponds or lakes.

This was also true for most labyrinthodonts, for like all amphibians they had to return to water to produce young. The labyrinthodonts showed a greater variety, however, and the SEYMOURIAMORPHS especially became very well adapted to land habitats. The evolution of the labyrinthodonts involved losing the fish-like tail of *Ichthyostega,* a general flattening of the skull and the body, and a strengthening of the limbs and shoulder and hip girdles.

During the Triassic period the first modern amphibians appeared. Between these and the ancient orders there is a considerable gap, and no groups exist to bridge it and provide any direct evidence for their ancestry. Frogs, NEWTS and SALAMANDERS show some characteristics of various ancient amphibian families, but the way their backbones are constructed suggests that a lepospondyl was their ancestor.

Types of backbone

In lepospondyls and modern amphibians the backbones, or vertebrae, have a spool-shaped body called a centrum below the NEURAL ARCH. The centrum is a single structure, pierced by a hole for the NOTOCHORD to pass through. As in the labyrinthodonts, each vertebra is very bony,

of time is known as the Pennsylvanian.

Coelophysis is one of the best-known COELUROSAURS. Its name means 'hollow-form lizard'. *Coelophysis* was a small, 2-legged animal with strong hind limbs. It was a meat-eater and its long, pointed head had numerous small, serrated teeth. Both neck and tail were long, the latter serving to balance the animal while it was running. Adults grew to 3 metres long and weighed about 20 kg. *Coelophysis* was a LIZARD-HIPPED dinosaur.

Chondrosteus

Coelurosaurs were an important group among the dinosaurs. Many were meat-eaters but others became specialized as egg-stealers and nest-robbers. All coelurosaurs were BIPEDAL and it is thought that one group, the dromaeosaurids, had comparatively large brains as well as very good sight.

Condylarths were primitive hoofed animals which first appeared in the late Cretaceous and became extinct in the Miocene. They are ancestors of the modern hoofed animals or UNGULATES.

Convergent evolution occurs when organisms which are unrelated, except through distant ancestors, grow to look alike outwardly in the process of adapting to the same basic way of life.

Creodonts were primitive carnivorous MAMMALS. The earliest members of the ORDER date from the late Cretaceous, and the last representatives died out in the Pliocene. In Eocene times they were the dominant mammal predators. They had relatively small brains and were therefore poorly equipped to hunt in packs or stalk the more advanced UNGULATES that began to appear in early Tertiary times.

Crocodiles and alligators are members of the ruling reptiles or ARCHOSAURS. They are closely related to the dinosaurs and pterosaurs, and like them evolved from a

as would be expected in animals where the backbone has to support the weight of the body. But the labyrinthodonts have vertebrae made up from several bony units and their relatively complex structure can be traced back to the rhipidistians. The vertebrae of lepospondyls are often called 'HUSK VERTEBRAE' while those of the labyrinthodonts and higher vertebrates are 'ARCH VERTEBRAE'. The arch type were much more flexible for possible evolutionary change, and it appears that two lines developed from the first labyrinthodonts. The main one led to the reptiles and mammals, while the second reached its peak in the advanced STEREOSPONDYLS. These large amphibians derived from the Permian genus *Eryops*. Its descendant MASTODONTOSAURUS, the largest of all labyrinthodonts, was about 6 metres long.

Mastodontosaurus lived during the Triassic, a period which saw the labyrinthodonts rapidly decline into extinction. The chart opposite clearly illustrates this event; it also shows the times when the amphibian group undertook important radiations. The first happened during the warm, humid swampland conditions of the Upper Carboniferous, and the second during the late Cretaceous and Cainozoic. In the Carboniferous, large forms such as LOXOMMA, MEGALOCEPHALUS, *Eogyrinus* and *Diadectes* all flourished under ideal conditions. These were labyrinthodonts and they dominated both marsh and inland regions. *Eogyrinus* was adapted to water and it grew to about 5 metres long. The more heavily built *Diadectes* had strong limbs and was slightly shorter, but its reptile appearance shows a definite attempt at adapting to life on land. Both were important predators and they probably fed on smaller labyrinthodonts and lepospondyls such as *Ophiderpeton*.

Loxomma and *Megalocephalus* were also predators and they too probably lived along the edges of the Carboniferous swamps. They ranged widely throughout Europe, and related forms lived in North America. In many ways they were rather primitive and could possibly have been ancestors of the sturdily-built *Eryops* and *Cacops* which lived in the Permian and were well adapted to living on land. In this *Loxomma* and *Megalocephalus* shared something with *Diadectes*, as it was an early example of a 'truly' terrestrial, or land-living, amphibian group — the seymouriamorphs.

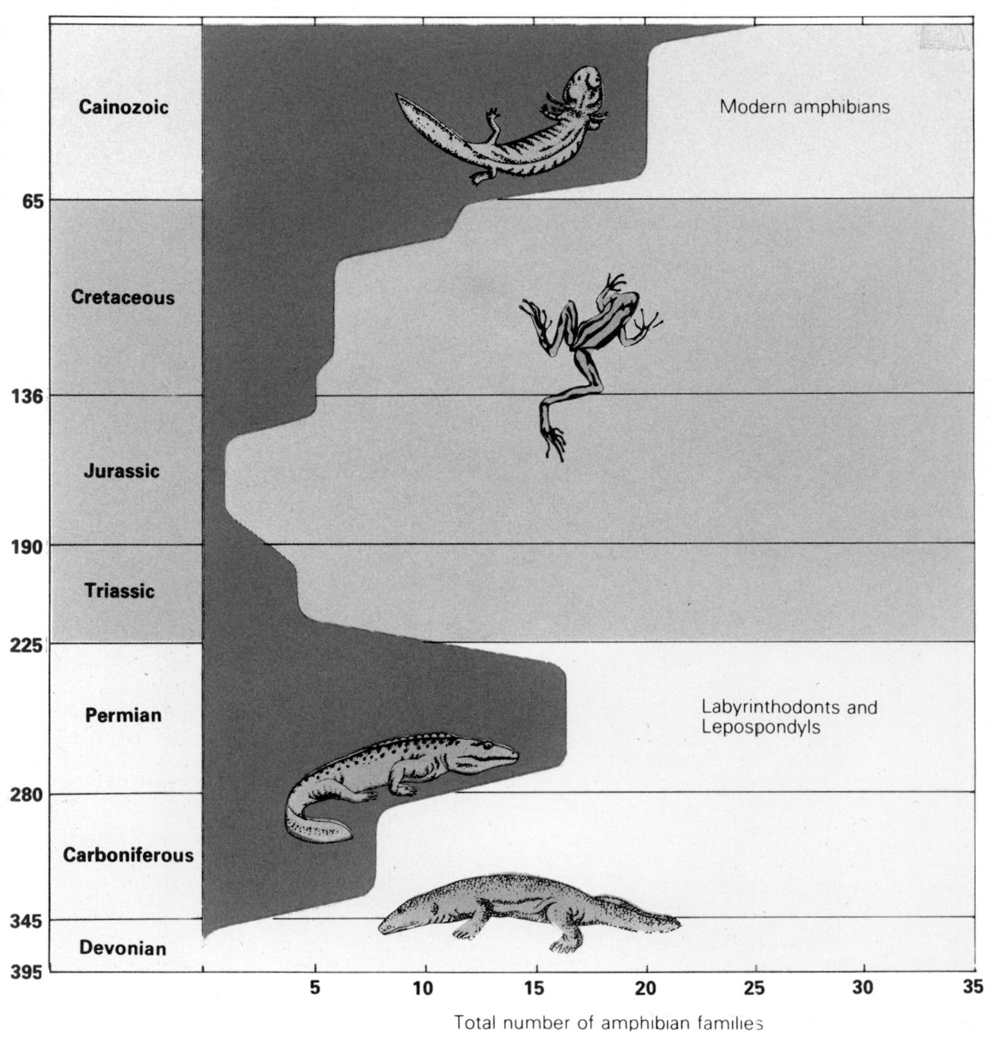

Above: This chart illustrates the varying success of the amphibians throughout the last 395 million years of geological time. During the Palaeozoic, the labyrinthodonts and lepospondyls were extremely successful, but by the end of the Triassic they had disappeared. The Jurassic and Cretaceous represent a period of gradual expansion for the modern amphibian stocks. The number of their families now exceeds that of the labyrinthodonts and lepospondyls at their peak.

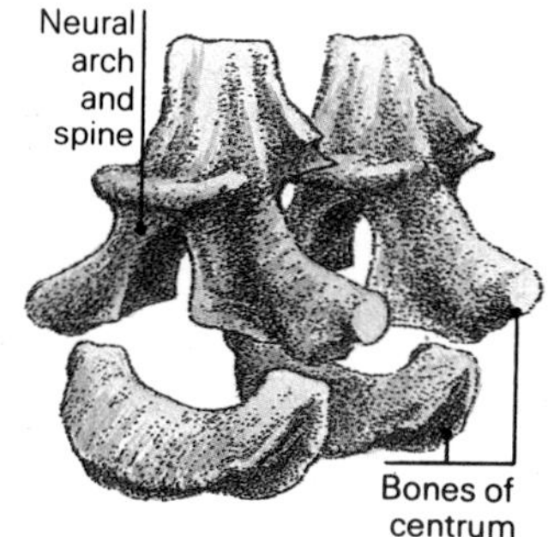

Left: 'Husk' vertebrae are found in lepospondyl amphibians. They are rather primitive and restricted in evolutionary potential. The centre of each unit is formed by the hardening, or turning to bone, of a single unit of cartilage.

Right: 'Arch' vertebrae are found in labyrinthodont amphibians, reptiles and mammals. 'Arch' describes the way in which the vertebra is formed by the hardening of several soft cartilaginous units.

THECODONTIAN ancestor. Although the crocodiles can be regarded as primitive, they are the only archosaurs to survive the 'Age of Reptiles'. Crocodiles and alligators are 4-legged, with long snouts. They live in or along the edges of rivers or swamps, and when they move on land they have a sprawling gait. Sea-going crocodiles, such as the geosaurs, are known from the fossil record. The first crocodiles are recorded from the Triassic.

D

Deinotheres were hoe-tuskers, so-called because they had powerful down-turned tusks on the lower jaws, which were presumably used for digging. They remained more or less unaltered throughout their existence, spanning the Miocene, Pliocene and much of the Pleistocene. One early palaeontologist thought that the *deinotheres* lived in rivers, and that at night they slept in the water, anchored to the bank with their tusks!

Desmostylids were large mammals that lived in the shallow waters off the shores of the northern Pacific Ocean from the late Oligocene to the Middle Pliocene. Although described as a kind of 'marine hippopotamus', their skulls were more like those of primitive elephants, while other features resemble the sea cows.

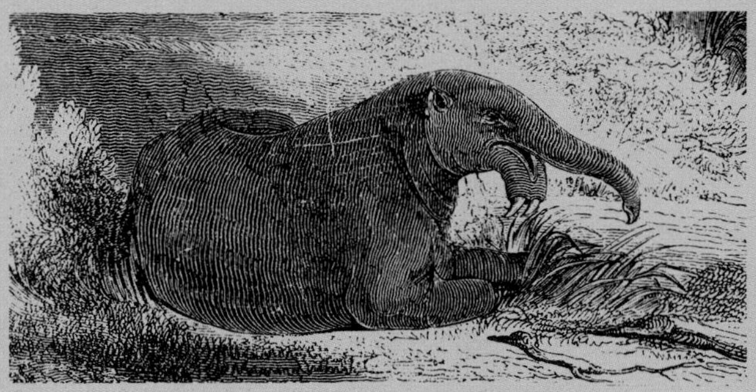

Sketch of a deinotheres

Diapsid describes the type of skull in the THECODONTIANS, dinosaurs, PTEROSAURS and crocodiles. The skull has 2 openings on the temple, behind the eye. Snakes and lizards also have a diapsid skull but unlike the ARCHOSAURS tend not to keep the bony bars between the 2 openings.

Diatrymiformes were a group of gigantic birds that existed during the Palaeocene and Eocene. They were flightless predators with huge heads and very strong legs.

Dimorphodon is a primitive

Ancestors of modern amphibians

The second peak in the evolution of amphibians is connected to the rise of modern groups and appearance of new varieties. This began in the early Jurassic and the number of different types which arose almost equalled the great radiation of the Upper Carboniferous. By the dawn of the Jurassic period frogs were firmly established and it seems that they can be linked back to the frog-like *Triadobatrachus* of the Triassic. This creature had a broad and flattened skull, and reconstructions show that the basic design for modern frogs and toads was set down over 200 million years ago. *Triadobatrachus* was rather short in the lower leg, however, and appears to have been more suited to crawling than leaping. Longer legged, true frogs appeared in the Lower Jurassic and by the early Cretaceous examples of most modern families existed in various parts of the world. These included the PIPIDS and LEIOPELMATIDS, both generally seen as being primitive forms.

Of other modern amphibians, the first salamanders and newts appeared during the Upper Jurassic. Unfortunately the fossils of this group are few and only a limited number of genera are known from the Cretaceous. But it seems that like many lepospondyls, numerous early salamanders reduced the size of their limbs and became fully adapted to living in water. This is true of certain living species and the trend to smaller limbs is usually connected with the body organ of respiration becoming longer. Other salamanders live mainly on land, often being adapted to life in upland areas.

The first reptiles

Most people accept that changes in the environment are important to evolution. The same is true for competition, and together they encourage the SURVIVAL OF THE FITTEST. By this we

Above: The illustrations of *Eryops, Diadectes, Ophiderpeton* and *Triadobatrachus* provide us with a useful insight into the variety of amphibians that has existed since the appearance of the first amphibian, *Ichthyostega*, during the Upper Devonian. *Eryops* and *Diadectes* are labyrinthodonts. *Ophiderpeton* is a lepospondyl and *Triadobatrachus* is a member of the Lissamphibia. Its general appearance shows that *Triadobatrachus* is an ancestor of the living frogs and toads. Of the animals shown, *Ophiderpeton* was probably the most specialized. It had no limbs and was specifically adapted to a life in water.

PTEROSAUR recorded from Lower Jurassic rocks in Europe. It is relatively small, with a skull about 200 mm long. It had strong teeth, a long reptilian tail, and was closely related to *Rhamphorhynchus*.

Dinosauria was the name given by Sir Richard Owen in 1841 to a group of gigantic terrestrial reptiles. The name means 'terrible lizards', from the Greek *Deinos* — terrible, and *saurus* — lizard. Unfortunately the dinosaurs are not lizards and we know that their closest living relatives are the crocodiles and alligators. Palaeontologists now divide the dinosauria into 2 groups — the ornithischians (BIRD-HIPPED) and saurischians (LIZARD-HIPPED).

Docodonts are known only from fossil teeth in North American sediments of Upper Jurassic age. They were very small primitive mammals.

Domesticated animals are kept by man as sources of food and raw materials, as beasts of burden, and as pets. Selective breeding, aimed at producing various desirable features, has greatly changed domesticated animals, so that often they look very different from their wild ancestors.

Dryopithecines were the earliest undoubted apes. They lived in Africa, Asia and Europe in Miocene times and looked something like chimpanzees. Almost certainly they were the ancestors of modern apes, and diverged from the same stock as RAMAPITHECUS about 15 million years ago. Since *Ramapithecus* is a forebear of man, it follows that the apes and man have developed along different lines from the outset.

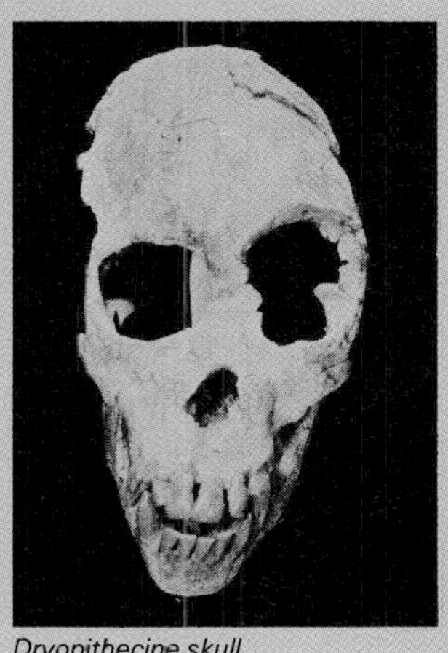
Dryopithecine skull

Ecological niches are identified by the organisms inhabiting them. They may be broad enough to cover all the animals living off an area of grassland — a grazing 'niche' — or narrow enough to include the creatures living in an animal's fur.

Elpistostege is a LABYRINTHODONT amphibian known only through the incomplete skull of one small individual. But this skull is important, as the arrangement of bones on its roof seems to be at an intermediate stage between that found in the TASSEL-

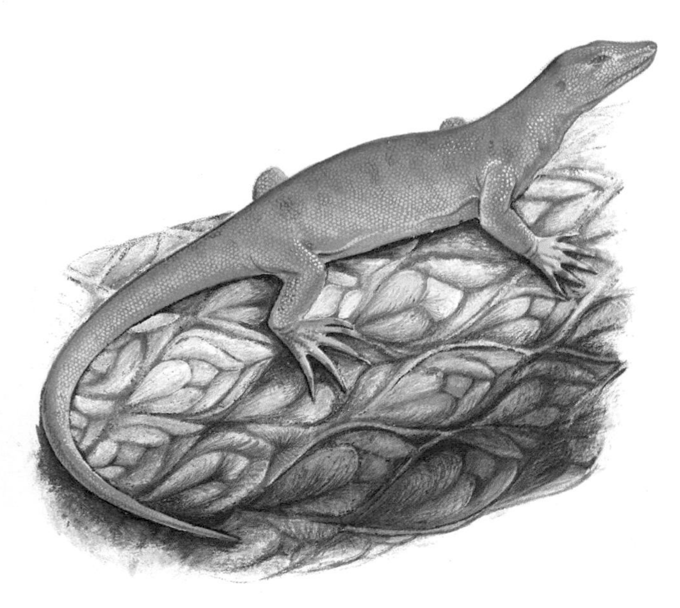

Left: Skeletons of the oldest known reptile, *Hylonomus,* are found in lower sediments of the Upper Carboniferous (Pennsylvanian) in Nova Scotia, Canada. The animal probably measured a little over 200 mm, and this small size suggests that it was an insect-eater. *Hylonomus* is found in fossil tree trunks, which were probably also the habitat of its amphibian ancestors. The structure of its skeleton, particularly that of its skull, tells us that *Hylonomus* belongs to the reptiles. *Hylonomus* is the earliest of the stem reptiles, or cotylosaurs, a group which is represented today by the turtles, tortoises and terrapins.

Below: The amniote egg is protected by an outer shell. It also has its own food reserve—the yolk—and an egg 'white', or albumen, to provide the water essential to growth. These various layers are surrounded by thin membranes which enable the reptile embryo to perform all the functions essential to its development. The amniote egg was a necessary stage in adapting to life on land.

Below: Young turtles hatching from their eggs are exact replicas of their parents. They emerge after a period of incubation during which they develop within the egg, nourished by its own valuable food supply. The eggs of the turtle, known as amniote eggs, are like those of other reptiles and the birds. Developing this type of egg allowed the tetrapods to reproduce out of water. Amniote eggs are known from fossils, and those of the dinosaurs are frequently found in nests. Most reptiles do not protect their nests, but we have evidence that certain dinosaurs cared for their young, as does the Nile crocodile today. During the incubation period the parent crocodile is known to remain close to the nest. When this is over, it will carefully remove the newly-hatched young to a safer site.

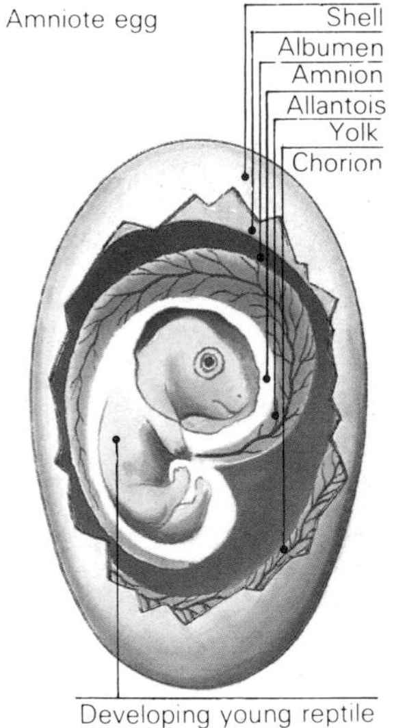

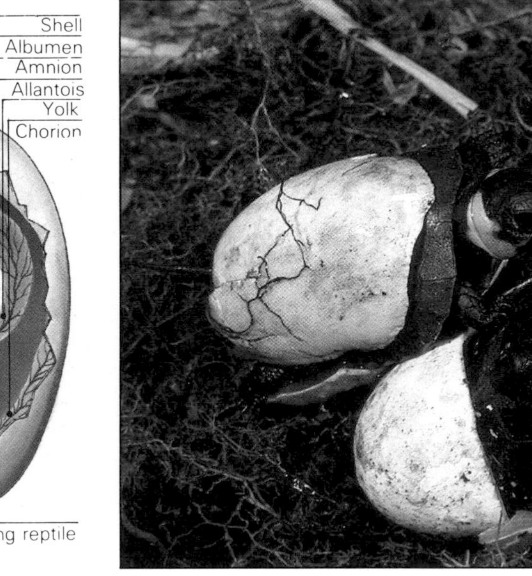

mean that some animals are better adapted than others to cope with changing conditions and then to make use of them. We have already seen how rhipidistians and amphibians appeared during the Devonian, in response to strong competition and changes in climate. A similar story unfolds during the Carboniferous, but in this case the animals in question were the first REPTILES. The swamplands of the 'COAL AGE' were ideally suited to the development of amphibians, and huge animals such as *Loxomma* and *Eogyrinus* dominated. Competition for food and territory was intense, so that smaller amphibians were forced to seek shelter and food in trees and drier areas. Many began eating insects and in time they relied less on water for protection. Their bodies changed and formed a scaly skin to help prevent them from drying up. As fertilization could take place inside the body, they were able to remain on land during reproduction and, finally, developing a membrane or shell around their eggs freed them from having to find a suitable pond in which to spawn.

It is almost impossible to answer the question: which came first, the reptile or the egg? For remains of both scaly skin and the reptilian type of egg (AMNIOTE) rarely occur in the fossil record. The first reptiles are identified by the structure of their skeleton, as important characters dividing reptile from amphibian include fewer bones in the reptile skull roof, and modifications to the limbs, shoulder and hip bones. The earliest reptiles have been found in Middle Carboniferous sediments of Nova Scotia. They include the small lizard-like *Hylonomus,* remains of which were discovered inside fossilized tree trunks.

Hylonomus is found associated with other reptiles, and together they represent two distinct lines of evolution. This suggests that the split from a common ancestor had taken place during the Lower Carboniferous. *Hylonomus* is an early STEM REPTILE, or ANAPSID, having a skull in which the bony cover is pierced only by holes for the eyes and nostrils. Some of its contemporaries, however, had an extra opening on either temple, just behind the eyes. These were the first of the SYNAPSID reptiles, which ultimately gave rise to the mammals. But synapsids are advanced reptiles, and it is to *Hylonomus* and related forms that we must look for probable links with an amphibian ancestor. As a primitive reptile

FINNED fishes and that of the first amphibians.

Embrithopods are an extinct ORDER of sub-UNGULATES, from the Lower Oligocene of Egypt. The only known representative is *Arsinoitherium,* a rhinoceros-sized creature which had 2 great nasal horns arranged side by side.

Embryo is a young animal which develops in an egg shell or inside the womb of its mother. An embryo developing inside a shell obtains nutriment from the yolk. Within the womb of a mammal, the developing embryo is supplied with nutrients through the direct umbilical link it has with its mother.

Entelodonts are extinct ARTIODACTYLA that resembled wild boars, and lived from late Eocene to Miocene times. The largest were as big as bison, which explains the description 'giant pigs'. They probably became extinct in competition with the more intelligent pigs and peccaries.

Eohippus means 'dawn horse', and is a common name for the earliest ancestor of the horse, which was about the size of a fox-terrier. But the correct name is *Hyracotherium,* for when the first fossils of this early Eocene animal were found in Europe, they were mistakenly linked with the small African hyraxes or dassies.

Epoch is a sub-division of geological time. For example, the Oligocene and Miocene epochs are sub-divisions of the Cainozoic era. An epoch is not limited to millions of years, but corresponds to a rock series, the top and bottom of which are often identified by certain fossils.

Euryapsid describes the skull type found in the PLESIOSAURS and NOTHOSAURS. Like the SYNAPSIDS, euryapsid reptiles have a single opening on the temple behind the eye socket. The opening was smaller and higher on the

Hyracotherium

Hylonomus would have kept some amphibian characters, so its solid skull roof and lack of an OTIC NOTCH are vital clues. Several groups of early four-legged animals have an otic notch, which may have marked the position of the ear drum.

In search of an ancestor

The change from amphibian to reptile is a fascinating step in the evolution of the vertebrates. Palaeontologists have searched for years among several groups of amphibians to find forms which link the two. For a long time the land-dwelling seymouriamorphs of the Upper Palaeozoic appeared to be the 'missing link'. They combined both reptilian and amphibian characters and so have been classed with both groups. Their skull roof is identical to that of some labyrinthodonts but they also have a large otic notch, which is not typical of amphibians. Modified limbs, shoulder and hip girdles also draw the seymouriamorphs closer to the reptiles, and some palaeontologists still argue that they are indeed proto-reptiles. But the discovery of large tadpole-like creatures in sediments containing SEYMOURIA suggest that it was truly an amphibian. If this is so, then the otic notch and modified limbs show that *Seymouria* and its relatives were highly specialized. As they also appear later in the geological record than the first reptiles it is unlikely that *Hylonomus* developed from such a specialized amphibian stock.

Above: The Permian amphibian *Seymouria* in many ways resembled a land-dwelling reptile, but it also retained some truly amphibian characters.

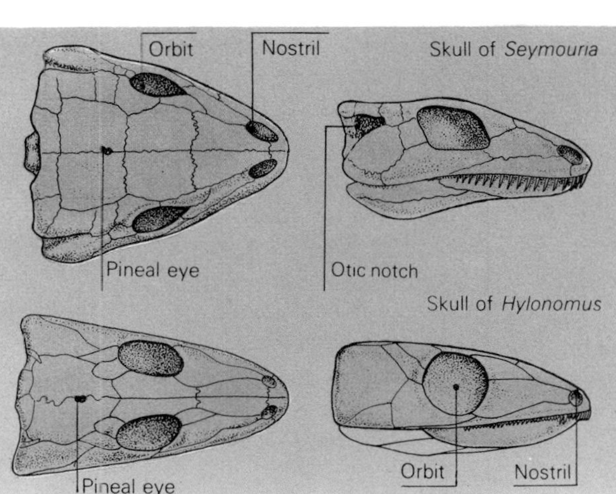

Right: *Seymouria's* skull was similar to that of most labyrinthodonts, but the large otic notch is like that found in some early reptiles. It was once thought that *Seymouria* was an ancestor of the early reptiles such as *Hylonomus*, but the otic notch eliminates it from this role.

Left: The scaly skin of the reptiles helped them in their conquest of the land. Its presence was almost as important in this respect as that of the amniote egg. Scales prevented the first reptiles from drying out, and allowed them to move away from the confines of a damp environment. Scales may be thickened to provide protection against hunters, and raised to allow the animal to lose heat when necessary.

temple in euryapsids than in synapsids.

F **Felidae** is the family to which the cats belong. Cats appeared in late Eocene times, and diversified greatly in the Oligocene.
Feloidea are a super-family of the CARNIVORA and include the Old World civets, hyaenas and cats.

G **Genetic conservation** involves preserving the GENE (*see page 13*) 'pools' of wild plants and animals and older types of domesticated plants and animals. Their genes could one day be used to improve existing strains of domesticated organisms, by cross-breeding, and there is potential for domesticating yet more plants and animals in the future. If they become extinct, however, none of this will be possible.
Gigantism describes the growth to a huge size by various, often short-lived, species.
Gill arches are well developed in most fishes. They lie behind the jaws and their bony elements help support both the jaws and gill apparatus.
Glacials occurred during the Pleistocene, when ice-sheets covered much of the continental landmasses in the northern hemisphere. On average the larger ice-sheets were roughly 2 km thick. Altogether there have been some 17 glacials, separated by warmer INTERGLACIALS, since the Pleistocene began about 1.6 million years ago.

Hyaena

Gnathostome fishes include the bony fishes, the sharks and rays, and many ancient stocks. All have jaws and are therefore easily distinguished from the AGNATHANS.
Gomphotheres were long-jawed mastodonts from which the true elephants developed, possibly as early as the end of the Miocene. The mastodonts differed from elephants in that the crowns of their cheek-teeth had simple rounded cusps, hence the name mastodont (tooth resembling the female breast).

H **Hag-fishes** are, like LAMPREYS, living jawless fishes or AGNATHANS. They feed on dead or dying fishes. The slime hag is a typical representative of this group.
Herbivores are animals that

The search for a reptile ancestor must then concentrate on other amphibians, and as both early labyrinthodonts and lepospondyls lack an otic notch, several families can be considered.

Stem reptiles

As an anapsid reptile, *Hylonomus* was the forerunner of the living turtles, tortoises and terrapins. It was also the ancestor of a more varied group of reptiles that flourished during the Permian and early Triassic. These animals are known as the stem reptiles or cotylosaurs. Many were large, cumbersome creatures, but others were comparatively small and quite agile. Among the best-known of the earliest stem reptiles is *Limnoscelis*, a medium-sized flesh-eater from the Lower Permian of North America. It was heavily built, with a long tail and rather short legs like those of an amphibian. The head was long in the snout and the front teeth sharp and rather tusk-like — ideal for gripping and stabbing prey. *Limnoscelis* probably lived in and around swamp areas, was probably SEMI-AQUATIC and fed on the fish-eating amphibians still common in the early Permian.

A close relative of *Limnoscelis* was the more specialized stem reptile *Labidosaurus*. This small creature was about 650 millimetres long, with a comparatively large head and shortened tail. It was more graceful than *Limnoscelis* and seemingly better suited to life on land. *Limnoscelis* and *Labidosaurus* were short-lived, however, and by the mid-Permian had been replaced by a reptile group known as the PROCOLOPHONIDS. These were still stem reptiles but generally had shorter jaws and better jaw movement. Early examples were less than 350 millimetres long, but with *Pareiasaurus* and SCUTOSAURUS, which appeared during the Upper Permian, came the largest of all stem reptiles. *Pareiasaurus* and its relatives were HERBIVORES, and therefore heavily built. Weight was a problem, and changes to their limbs meant that these animals supported their bodies in a more upright fashion. Their feet were also broader and perhaps they lived 'hippo-style' along the edges of swamps. *Scutosaurus* had a rather grotesque skull, with bony protuberances giving it a fearsome appearance. But this large lumbering creature was perfectly harmless. By the end of the Permian *Pareiasaurus* and its relatives had vanished, for only a few procolophonids persisted into the Triassic — a period that belonged to the more advanced descendants of the first stem reptiles.

Right: *Limnoscelis* (**1**) and *Pareiasaurus* (**2**) are examples of the stem reptiles, or cotylosaurs. They are noted for their anapsid skull, similar to that of the turtles and tortoises. *Pareiasaurus* was much the larger of the two, and rather grotesque in form. It was a semi-aquatic herbivore, whereas *Limnoscelis* was a flesh-eater. The stem reptiles flourished during the Permian. It is obvious that these rather primitive, cumbersome creatures failed to compete with their more advanced synapsid cousins, the pelycosaurs.

Most people accept that the anapsid type of skull, found in *Hylonomus* and living turtles, shows the primitive state in the evolution of the reptiles. It has no holes in the temple and the skull roof's bony shield provides more than enough protection. It is also heavy and gives only limited room for the development of important muscles. Skull types that evolved from this primitive state developed openings on the temple, making them lighter. These appeared first in the synapsid reptiles of the mid-Carboniferous, as a single opening placed low behind the eye. The later EURYAPSIDS had openings higher on the temple — such skulls are characteristic of the PLESIOSAURS and ICHTHYOSAURS. Both synapsid and euryapsid skulls are marked improvements on the anapsid type, but the most advanced design is found only in the 'ruling reptiles', the ARCHOSAURS. These include the dinosaurs and CROCODILES, the skulls of which have two temple openings and are called DIAPSID. Such holes in the skull allowed new muscles to develop, and feeding to improve.

eat plants as their sole source of food.

Hesperornis, the 'dawn bird', is, after *Archaeopteryx*, one of the earliest recorded birds. Its remains are known from Cretaceous rocks, and from these it is possible to determine that *Hesperornis* was a sea bird. It was quite large, the skull measuring about 250 mm in length. Both upper and lower jaws had teeth, although a horny sheath over the front of the upper beak is similar to that found in more advanced birds. *Hesperornis* had very small wings and breastplate, and was probably a water-loving diver.

Heterocercal tail is the type commonly found in sharks. It is noted for the upturning of the lower end of the backbone and the specialized major area of fin below and behind this region of the vertebral column.

Heterodontosaurus, or the 'different-toothed lizard', lived in southern Africa during the latter half of the Triassic. It was a fast-running biped. *Heterodontosaurus* was a BIRD-HIPPED dinosaur, noted for its different types of teeth. In many ways its dentition was similar to that of a mammal with large, tusk-like canines, and *Heterodontosaurus* probably used its tusks during territorial battles. It had muscular jaw pouches, probably used to pass plant material across the mouth during chewing.

A heterocercal tail

Hipparion was a type of lightly-built horse that lived from Upper Miocene to late Pleistocene times.

Hippomorpha are a sub-ORDER of the PERISSODACTYLA. They include the horse and the extinct TITANOTHERES and palaeotheres. The latter appeared in the Eocene and died out during the Oligocene. *Palaeotherium*, for example, was the size of a small rhinoceros and its skull was tapir-like. This animal may also have had a short trunk.

Holosteans are bony fishes represented today by the freshwater dogfish *Amia* and the garpike *Lepisosteus*. They are characterized by their scales and by the reduced number of bones in their fins. The holosteans first appeared in the Triassic, and forms such as *Lepidotes* were plentiful during the Jurassic and Cretaceous.

Hominid is a member of the family to which man belongs.

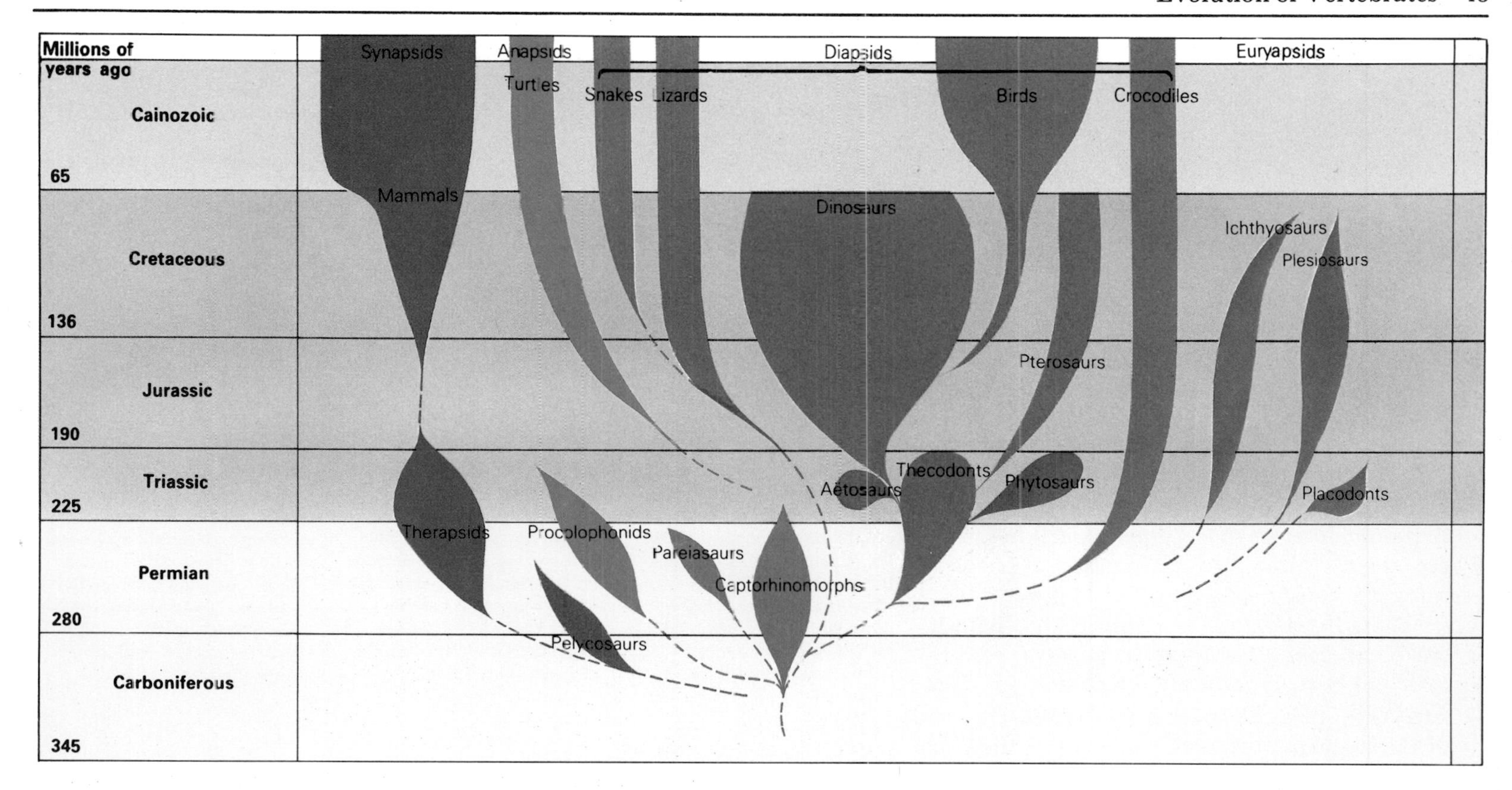

In anapsid reptiles such as the marsh turtles and land tortoises, improvements in feeding and increases in the size of the jaw muscles were made possible by the gradual erosion of the rear section of the skull roof. The turtles (or testudines) as a group have no teeth, and the front part of their jaw is covered by a horny beak or sheath. The bony shell developed by turtles and tortoises is an ideal protection against predators, and though it is often thought that these anapsids have shown few advances in evolution since the Triassic, it is noteworthy that hundreds of species today occupy many niches on land and in aquatic environments. Many testudines are herbivores, but others, like terrapins and some marine turtles, are meat-eaters. Throughout the last 100 million years, several families of huge marine turtles have lived in the oceans of our planet. In the Cretaceous the gigantic *Archelon* reached almost 4 metres, and was only slightly larger than later Cainozoic forms. Today, the leathery turtle is the largest sea-dwelling reptile. Large tortoises are known from several islands, and some individual animals have been known to survive for hundreds of years.

Above: The family tree of the reptiles traces the fortunes and relationships of these advanced tetrapods over the last 300 million years of geological time. The obvious success story is that of the diapsid reptiles. Within this group we find the thecodontians, dinosaurs, crocodiles and pterosaurs.

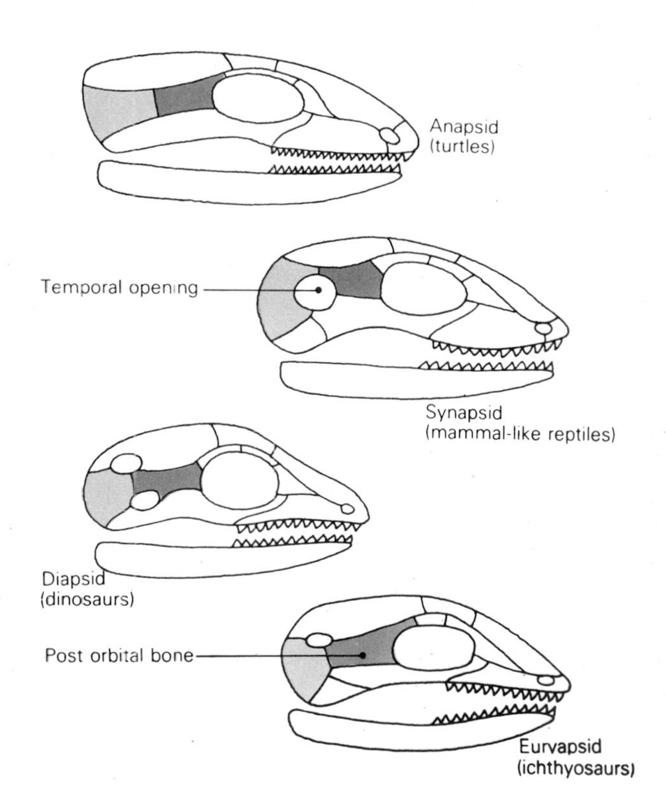

Right: Among the reptiles, zoologists and palaeontologists can recognize 4 basic types of skull. These are identified by the presence or absence of various openings on the temple, and by the pattern of the bones behind the eye. Of the 4 types the anapsid skull, without any openings, is considered the most primitive, and the diapsid type, with 2 openings, the most advanced. The synapsid skull is typical of the mammal-like reptiles and mammals, and the euryapsid is typical of the aquatic plesiosaurs and ichthyosaurs. Both of these skull types have a single temple opening.

Hominoid is a member of the super-family which includes the families of gibbons and siamangs (Hylobatidae), great apes (Pongidae) and that of man (Hominidae).

Homocercal tail is one in which both the fin parts are about the same size.

Amia, freshwater dogfish, is an holostean

Homo erectus was in many ways the first 'true' man. He appeared in Africa about 1.5 million years ago and then spread to Asia before becoming extinct about 1 million years later.

Homo habilis was an early member of the group to which modern man belongs. *Homo habilis* seems to have been an ancestor of *Homo erectus*, and lived in East Africa about 1.75 million years ago. In the early 1970s, even older fossils of *Homo* were found in East Africa, probably about 3 million years old.

Homo sapiens, or modern man, probably developed from HOMO ERECTUS somewhere between 500,000 and 100,000 years ago. Our subspecies, *Homo sapiens sapiens,* lived in Africa and Eurasia 40,000 years ago and spread to North America and Australia soon after.

Husk vertebrae are characteristic of LEPOSPONDYL amphibians. The centrum or central unit of each vertebra (backbone) is a single unit of bone pierced by a hole for the NOTOCHORD.

Hyaenidae or hyaenas are a family of the CARNIVORA, and although closely related to cats, they look very like dogs. Fossil hyaenas very similar to modern forms lived in early Pliocene times, soon after these animals first appeared in the late Miocene.

Hyaenodonts are a family of the extinct CREODONTS. Their skull and tooth row tended to be more elongated than those of the closely related OXYAENIDS.

Hybodontoids were a more progressive group of sharks that replaced the

Left: Small to medium-sized aquatic reptiles, such as *Ceresiosaurus* and *Nothosaurus,* were common during the Triassic. They belonged to the nothosaurs and were rather like the plesiosaurs in their overall shape.

Marine reptiles

Reptiles first appeared in water as anapsid MESOSAURS during the Upper Carboniferous. These were rather tiny animals, apparently adapted to eating crustaceans. However, they were short-lived, and not until the Middle Triassic did large numbers of aquatic reptiles appear. These included the NOTHOSAURS, PLACODONTS, plesiosaurs and ichthyosaurs.

Of these groups the nothosaurs were the least specialized and it seems that their ancestors came from land-based reptiles. The same is true for the placodonts, although these were much more specialized than the nothosaurs. Placodonts reached their peak in PLACOCHELYS, a turtle-like creature with a toothless beak, paddles and a bony shield. Both the placodonts and nothosaurs were short-lived groups, neither challenging as major marine predators. This role was shared by plesiosaurs and ichthyosaurs and, in the Upper Cretaceous, by MOSASAURS.

Plesiosaurs possibly came from the nothosaurs, but unlike their ancestors they grew to an enormous size and developed powerful turtle-like paddles. The ancestry of ichthyosaurs is unknown, but from the outset these fish-like reptiles were masters of the Mesozoic seas. Committed to an aquatic life, they were the only marine reptiles to produce live young.

Today the only successful marine reptiles are the turtles, the ancestors of which appeared during the Upper Triassic. MARINE TURTLES themselves first appeared in the Cretaceous.

Mammal-like reptiles

We saw in looking at the evolution of the earliest reptiles (*see page 42*) that anapsid and synapsid

Below: During the Mesozoic era many reptile groups other than the nothosaurs and placodonts adapted to an aquatic life. Some, like the mixosaurs and ichthyosaurs, were truly fish-like in character, while others retained a more reptilian appearance and returned to land to lay their eggs. Those which laid eggs on land included the plesiosaurs, turtles and mosasaurs. In contrast, the ichthyosaurs gave birth to live young, and can be described as viviparous. Of the animals illustrated, *Ichthyosaurus* and *Placodus* are known to have the euryapsid type of skull, and *Metriorhynchus* shows extreme adaptation to a sea-going life. Aquatic reptiles ruled the seas for over 130 million years, and mammals such as whales and dolphins did not appear until long after their extinction.

Cladoselache type of fish during the late Palaeozoic. They came between the primitive cladoselachians and modern sharks and were common during the late Palaeozoic and Mesozoic.

Hypsodont teeth are highly specialized cheek-teeth, adapted for living off a grass diet. These kind of teeth are found in the more advanced ARTIODACTYLA, PERISSODACTYLA and PROBOSCIDEANS.

I

Ice Age is the name commonly given to the Pleistocene epoch — which began about 1.6 million years ago — and during which there were repeated GLACIALS and inter-glacials. We now know that glaciation happened before the beginning of the Pleistocene and that the present Holocene epoch is also a typical inter-glacial.

Ichthyornis, the 'fish-bird', is well known from the Upper Cretaceous, and in particular the chalk deposits of Kansas, USA. It flew strongly and looked rather like modern seagulls or terns. *Ichthyornis* was quite small, reaching about 200 mm high. Like *Archaeopteryx,* it seems to have had teeth.

Ichthyosaur skeleton

Ichthyosaur was the most highly adapted of all water-living reptiles. Ichthyosaurs lived through most of the Mesozoic, but were especially common in the Jurassic. They were already highly specialized for living in water when they first appear in Triassic rocks. But no earlier forms are known.

Incisors are nipping teeth, though some may be developed into a chisel-type shape — as in the rodents — while in elephants they have become tusks.

Insectivorous animals live on an insect diet.

Inter-glacials, see GLACIALS and ICE AGE.

K

Kuhneosaurs were a group of ancestral lizards that had a pair of horizontal 'sails' or 'wings'. They were among the first reptiles able to glide and lived during the Triassic.

types appeared at the same time. The anapsids were primitive, while the earliest synapsids can be seen as the basis for one of the greatest evolutionary stories of all. Its probable end is with the development of man, but farther back in time it includes chapters on the evolution of the PELYCOSAURS and the mammal-like THERAPSIDS.

The first synapsids were much the same as their contemporaries, with few of the modifications in teeth and skull shown in later groups. Pelycosaurs such as *Dimetrodon* and *Edaphosaurus* are examples of the next stage in synapsid evolution. The large 'sails' on their backs were probably an attempt to regulate the temperature of their bodies. *Dimetrodon* also showed important developments in its teeth — some resembled the incisors, canines and cheek teeth of the later therapsids and mammals. Specialization of different teeth was a major evolutionary advance, enabling an animal to break its food down into smaller pieces. These could be more readily digested, allowing the creature to gain the energy it needed much more rapidly. In time some pelycosaurs were able to control the rate at which they burned their food to produce heat and energy. This proved a better system for temperature control than the 'sails' of *Dimetrodon* and *Edaphosaurus* and was adapted by their successors. These were the therapsids, and there is some evidence that certain of their advanced forms were warm-blooded. The therapsids showed improvements on the pelycosaurs, as their skull and body skeleton were adapted to a more active life. Specialization of the teeth continued, and in many forms the skull structure, coupled with larger jaw muscles, suggests that later therapsids could chew their food thoroughly. Early therapsids tended to sprawl, but in time changes in the arrangement of their limbs, hips and shoulders gave creatures such as *Lycaenops* and *Thrinaxodon* a much improved posture. According to some experts, *Thrinaxodon* had whisker pits on its snout, and if this is true we can assume that this and later therapsids were hairy. Mammal-like reptiles dominated the reptile group for over 35 million years.

The archosaurs

Crocodiles and alligators have been described as 'a mere remnant' of a once-prolific group of diapsid reptiles — the archosaurs. The word

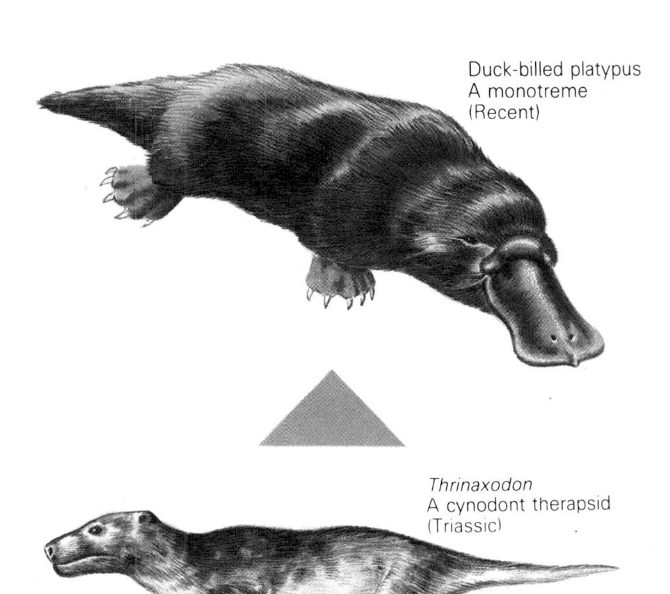

Right: The duck-billed platypus belongs to the Monotremata, a group of egg-laying mammals. Included in this group are the spiny ant-eaters, and together these 2 creatures are regarded as comprising the most primitive mammalian order. Egg-laying is a reptilian characteristic and its persistence in the monotremes may serve as a clue to their ancestry. The monotremes are warm-blooded and have many other mammalian features.

Right: *Thrinaxodon* was a cynodont or 'dog-toothed' reptile from the Lower Triassic. It was about 450 mm long and was probably warm-blooded. Many of the lower jaw bones had been fused together, and large jaw muscles had developed to increase the animal's biting power.

Right: *Lycaenops* was a mammal-like reptile (therapsid) from the Upper Permian. It grew to just 1 metre in length and was more heavily built than the later cynodonts. The jaw structure was more advanced than that of the pelycosaurs and the teeth more varied in character. *Lycaenops* was a gorgonopian therapsid and it dominated Upper Permian communities.

Pelycosaurs

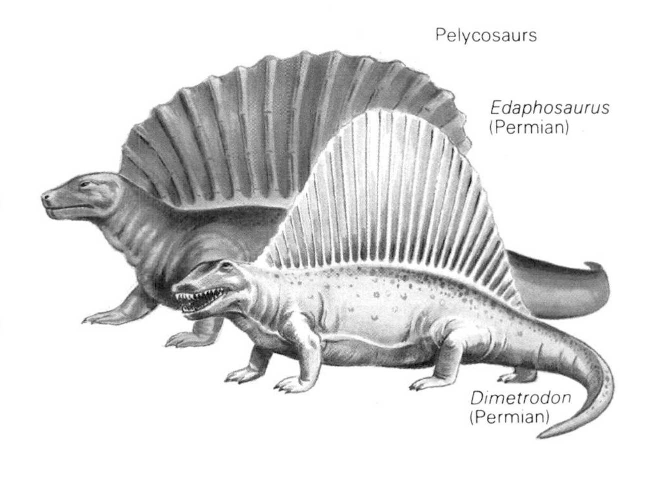

Right: *Dimetrodon* and *Edaphosaurus* are the classic examples of sail-backed pelycosaurs. They flourished during the Lower Permian, when *Dimetrodon* was the major predator. The large fin was probably a device used to regulate temperature, and these pelycosaurs can be seen as an experimental stage in the development of warm-blooded creatures. The pelycosaurs and more advanced therapsids have similar skulls and teeth.

L

Labyrinthodonts were the major amphibians during the late Palaeozoic to early Mesozoic. They were characterized by the labyrinthine structure of their teeth and by the development of ARCH VERTEBRAE. Many labyrinthodonts grew to a huge size and a number of groups adapted to a life on land. See also SEYMOURIAMORPHS.

Mole, an insectivore

Lampreys are living jawless fishes, or AGNATHANS. They have no scales and their eel-like bodies lack paired fins. Lampreys lead a SEMI-PARASITIC existence, attached to other fishes.

Larval describes a young developing animal that has to fend for itself. A typical larva is the tadpole of the frog, which has external feathery gills and a large, broad tail. Larval stages exist in many invertebrates, including the echinoderms and brachiopods. Significant changes must take place before a larva can attain the adult form.

Leiopelmatids are living frogs, generally considered as rather primitive. They have more neck and back vertebrae than other living frogs and toads. The tadpole stage is also characteristic. Leiopelmatids range from the Jurassic to Recent periods.

Lepospondyls were a group of amphibians that lived during the late Palaeozoic. Most were of modest size and many became snake-like in appearance. They are characterized by HUSK VERTEBRAE.

Lesothosaurus was a small, BIRD-HIPPED dinosaur from the Upper Triassic of southern Africa. It lived at the same time as did HETERODONTOSAURUS and was about the same size. But *Lesothosaurus* had rather simple teeth and no muscular cheeks. Its head was also smaller, although it was agile, and ran on its strong back legs.

Lithographic limestone is a fine-grained, compact sediment. By far the best-known example is that of Solnhofen in Bavaria, West Germany, which is made up of microscopic organisms and contains very well-preserved molluscs, fish and reptiles. Among the reptiles is the dinosaur *Compsognathus*, a small, agile COELUROSAUR. But most famous of all are the remains of *Archaeopteryx*, the first bird.

Litopterns are an extinct ORDER of South American

'archosaur' means 'ruling reptile' and aptly describes a group that includes the crocodiles and alligators, dinosaurs, PTEROSAURS and their common ancestors the THECODONTIANS.

The thecodontians, or 'tooth in socket reptiles', first appeared at the base of the Triassic (225 million years ago). At first the group contained clumsy 'sprawlers' such as *Chasmatosaurus*, whose legs splayed out sideways, but in time they were replaced by animals which held their bodies off the ground in what is called a 'semi-improved' posture. This involved changes in the shape and position of the limb bones and their movement with the shoulder and hip girdles. The legs were thus drawn closer to the body and thecodontians such as *Mandasuchus* and the two-legged *Euparkeria* could move over the ground in a faster, more efficient, manner. Some experts believe that a few thecodontians even attained the 'fully-improved' posture, with the limbs drawn beneath the body as in the higher mammals. Others doubt this, and claim that the 'fully-improved' stance is one of the essential differences between the thecodontians and their descendants — the dinosaurs. The 'improved' thecodontian limbs helped them to become dominant in the Middle Triassic; their explosive evolution was arrested only by the appearance of the 'terrible-lizards' (DINOSAURIA).

Competition among thecodontians themselves was intense during the Middle Triassic, and two groups, the AËTOSAURS and PHYTOSAURS successfully filled new ECOLOGICAL NICHES. The aëtosaurs grew heavy armour and specialized to a vegetarian or possibly OMNIVORE diet. They lived on land, but in common with the large crocodile-like phytosaurs they kept a primitive sprawling walk. Both groups were comparatively short-lived; they died out well before the end of the Triassic and the disappearance of their 'normal' thecodontian cousins.

SELECTION PRESSURES among competing thecodontians also led to the evolution of the pterosaurs and crocodiles, as well as the dinosaurs. Each stock inherited advantageous characters from their different ancestors, and further developments helped them to colonize new ecological niches. Crocodiles replaced the phytosaurs to become the chief flesh-eaters of rivers and river banks, with one group, the geosaurs, adapting to a sea-going life. Crocodiles survive to the present day, whereas their flying

Below: In many thecodontians the limbs are drawn close to the body. This arrangement has the advantage of lifting the animal higher and enables it to move more easily, using less energy. This 'semi-improved' posture is found today in the living crocodiles and alligators.

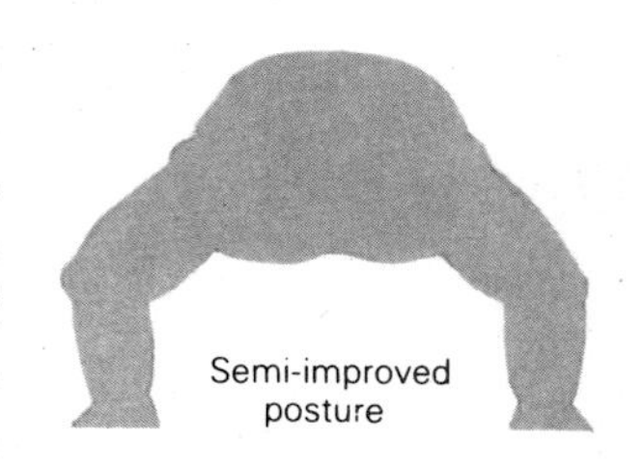

Right: *Proterosuchus* and many early reptiles were rather slow-moving creatures. The upper arm was moved sideways and the forearm held vertically. This restricted the animals to a 'sprawling' gait.

Sprawling gait

UNGULATES. Descended from the CONDYLARTHS, litopterns developed horse- and camel-like forms.

Lizard-hipped dinosaurs, or saurischians, are those in which the pubis bone points downwards and forwards and the ischium bone downwards and backwards. This results in a 4-pronged arrangement of the pelvis, similar to the condition found in many other types of reptile. See also BIRD-HIPPED.

Lophodont cheek-teeth have rows of cusps fused into ridges. They are typical of BROWSERS.

Loxomma was a primitive amphibian from the Carboniferous. Like its relative *Megalocephalus* it was distributed over large areas and was characterized by keyhole-shaped eye-holes, which possibly held a facial gland as well as the eye itself. *Loxomma* and its relatives had high yet narrow skulls and numerous large pointed teeth. These were similar in structure to those of TASSEL-FINNED fishes, while the vertebrae were more advanced in form than those of *Ichthyostega* and its relatives.

Lions, like all mammals, are warm-blooded

M **Mammals** are a class of VERTEBRATE animals. They are warm-blooded, have a protective or insulating cover of hair, and give birth to live young, which are suckled by the mother. MONOTREMES, however, lay eggs and in several other ways display similarities to reptiles.

Mammoths were elephants adapted to living in cold environments. They were protected by a layer of fat and a coat of yellow wool covered by dark-brown hair. Their great curved tusks cleared away snow covering the grass on which they fed.

Marine turtles, such as the living green turtle and leathery turtle, are sea-going representatives of the tortoises, terrapins and turtles. They have flattened shells and large paddle- or flipper-shaped limbs. Of these, the

Below: Dinosaurs, mammal-like reptiles and mammals have their limbs drawn up beneath the body. This is caused by changes in the positions of their limb and girdle bones, and in the muscles. This 'fully-improved' posture separates dinosaurs from their thecodontian ancestors.

cousins, the pterosaurs, died out at the end of the Cretaceous.

Dinosaurs appear

By the Middle Triassic dinosaurs had appeared in the southern continents. Though few in number they included both small BIPEDAL and large QUADRUPEDAL forms. They had attained the 'fully-improved' posture, and the two basic body designs seem to be adaptations enabling them to resist the pressures of the voracious thecodontians. Among the new two-legged archosaurs the BIRD-HIPPED dinosaurs, or ornithischians, were vegetarians. They were also fast runners and their appearance may have encouraged the development of similarly built meat-eaters. Like the large quadrupeds, the meat-eaters belonged to the saurischian or LIZARD-HIPPED dinosaurs and both probably shared the same ancestor.

A mammoth skeleton

forelimbs are much the larger, and pull the animal through the water with a powerful 'flying' motion. Marine turtles first appeared in the Jurassic. The largest recorded genus to live in the sea is *Archelon*, which grew over 3.5 metres long.

Marsupials are MAMMALS that give birth to very small young which either crawl into the mother's pouch or cling to the mother's fur.

Mastodontosaurus is the largest known LABYRINTHODONT amphibian. Its skull alone measured over 1 metre in length, being broad and flat and noted for several tusk-like front teeth. Various species are recorded from Triassic rocks of Germany and India. *Mastodontosaurus* is associated with a group of labyrinthodonts called STEREOSPONDYLS, characterized by a flattening of the skull and an increased hardening of the vertebrae.

Mayomyzon is the only known fossil lamprey. It is therefore related to the CEPHALASPID fishes and is grouped together with the living form *Lampetra*. *Mayomyzon* grew to about 65 mm long. Like the living lamprey it had an eel-like body with long upper and lower limbs. Its mouth was narrow and slit-like, and it probably had a long, rasping tongue. Fossils of *Mayomyzon* occur as dark stains on the surface of Carboniferous sediments, with enough detail to recognize parts of the skeleton, gill pouches, the liver and gut.

Megalocephalus, like LOXOMMA, was a LABYRINTHODONT amphibian. It was widespread during the Carboniferous, when it lived on the edges of the coal swamps. It had a large head,

This was once thought to be true for all dinosaurs, but the theory now is that ornithischians and saurischians were different types of archosaurs which evolved separately from different thecodontian lines.

Dinosaurs

During the Upper Triassic the evolution of the dinosaurs took on a fresh impetus and gradually they proved too competitive for their thecodontian ancestors. Small COELUROSAURS, large CARNOSAURS and even larger PROSAUROPODS were common and had spread over a wide area. As lizard-hipped dinosaurs they seem to be primitive types, but they were clearly more diverse than bird-hipped kinds. The coelurosaurs resembled their immediate ancestors and groups such as PROCOMPSOGNATHUS and COELOPHYSIS could easily have passed for thecodontians. Both were flesh-eaters and *Coelophysis* may even have been a cannibal. Carnosaurs were meat-eaters too, but they had already developed into large, heavily-built bipeds with sizeable dagger-like teeth. In contrast the prosauropods had four legs — a basic design which was continued by the gigantic SAUROPODS of the Jurassic and Cretaceous. The actual link between prosauropods and sauropods is in doubt, although MELANOROSAURUS from the Upper Triassic of South Africa seems an ideal ancestor.

No prosauropods survived into the Jurassic and so far as time is concerned they must be seen as one of the least successful dinosaur stocks. Increased size together with other advantages must have favoured the sauropods — for like the coelurosaurs, carnosaurs and ornithischians, they ruled the world for about 130 million years. During that time the lizard-hipped groups followed several evolutionary trends, as carnosaurs and sauropods became the largest meat-eaters and vegetarians to roam the Earth. Increased size was not important in the coelurosaurs, but the appearance of bird-like ornithomimids and large-brained dromaeosaurids shows how varied the group was.

The few examples of ornithischians from the Upper Triassic suggest that they had yet to establish themselves in secure niches. Unlike the saurischians, all ornithischians were plant-eaters and so when advancing into new habitats they may have met with a fiercer challenge. For

Right and below: Of all the reptiles, the dinosaurs were perhaps the most varied. They ranged from the size of a chicken to monsters 30 metres long. Various families adapted to different ways of life, and this is reflected in the size and form of their bodies. The different animals illustrated indicate that there were at least 19 types of dinosaur, each of which could be assigned to a different family.

Prosauropod
Pachycephalosaur
Atlantosaur
Hadrosaur
Normal coelurosaur
Camarosaur
Psittacosaur
Ornithomimid
Heterodontosaur
Stegosaur
Deinonychid
Iguanodont
Ankylosaur
Normal carnosaur
Ouranosaur
Protoceratopid
Spinosaur
Hypsilophodont
Ceratopid

with the characteristic keyhole-shaped eyes that link it with *Loxomma* at a family level. The skull was robust, with several prominent teeth. As in many primitive amphibians, its skull was high and rather narrow.
Melanorosaurus was a huge PROSAUROPOD which lived in South Africa during the latter half of the Triassic. It was 4-legged, and adults grew to almost 12 metres in length. It looked similar to *Diplodocus* or *Brachiosaurus* but differences in the skeleton separate it from the sauropods proper. According to many experts, *Melanorosaurus* may have been the ancestor of the great 'beast-footed' creatures of the Jurassic and Cretaceous periods. *Melanorosaurus* was a close relative of *Plateosaurus*, which lived in Europe at the same time.
Merychippus was a 3-toed horse that lived from mid-Miocene to Lower Pliocene times. Although its HYPSODONT teeth suggest it ate a diet of grass, the fact that *Merychippus* was much bigger than earlier horses implies that such specialized teeth would have been needed even for a diet of leaves.
Mesosaurs were a group of ANAPSID reptiles that adapted to an aquatic life during the late Carboniferous and early Permian. They are confined to South Africa and South America. Few mesosaurs grew beyond 750 mm in length, and they were all slimly-built. Their skulls were long and armed with numerous sharp, long teeth. The neck was long and powerful, and the sideways flattened tail was the main swimming organ. The hind limbs were used for movement, and the smaller front limbs for steering. Little is known of the feeding habits of mesosaurs, but they may have eaten small freshwater crustaceans, using their teeth as 'strainers'. Mesosaurs represent an early side branch from the main line of anapsid reptiles.
Miacids were early CARNIVORA, and mainly tree-dwellers.
Miohippus was a small 3-toed horse that lived in

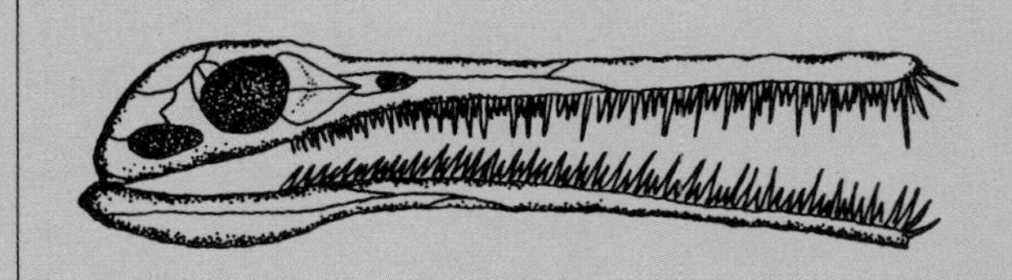

Mesosaurus

whereas the prosauropods found protection in marshy areas, small ornithischians such as LESOTHOSAURUS and HETERODONTOSAURUS lived in open, drier lands. To avoid predators they became fast runners, but during the Jurassic and Cretaceous several specialized groups evolved. These included the plated STEGOSAURS, armoured ANKYLOSAURS and horned CERATOPIANS — heavily-built and well-protected quadrupeds. The appearance of each marked periods of variation in ornithischian history. The greatest diversification happened in the Upper Cretaceous, when five major ornithischian families flourished. Among them were the ceratopians and ankylosaurs, but the two-legged hadrosaurs and PACHYCEPHALOSAURS were as important.

The evolution of the dinosaurs is therefore one of the great success stories of geological time. We can identify 19 or more different groupings and some experts say that their reign equalled 5,500,000 human generations. Why they survived for so long is difficult to answer; for instance it is hard to believe that the 'fully-improved' posture was such a major advantage. In recent years we have found evidence to suggest that the dinosaurs were warm-blooded. If proved, this would dismiss the belief that most dinosaurs were slow, cumbersome creatures. Warm blood need not have been essential for success, however, as the warm, equable Mesozoic climate was ideal for a group representing the peak of reptile evolution.

Below: The dinosaurs can be traced back into the early part of the Triassic period *(left)*. The first dinosaurs often resembled their thecodontian cousins, but within a short space of time, new and very different forms appeared throughout the world. The dinosaurs can be divided into 2 main branches by the different forms of their hip girdles *(right)*. The ornithischian (or bird-like) hip girdle, with the pubis bone extended beneath the ischium, appears more streamlined than the 4-pronged saurischian (or lizard-like) hip girdle.

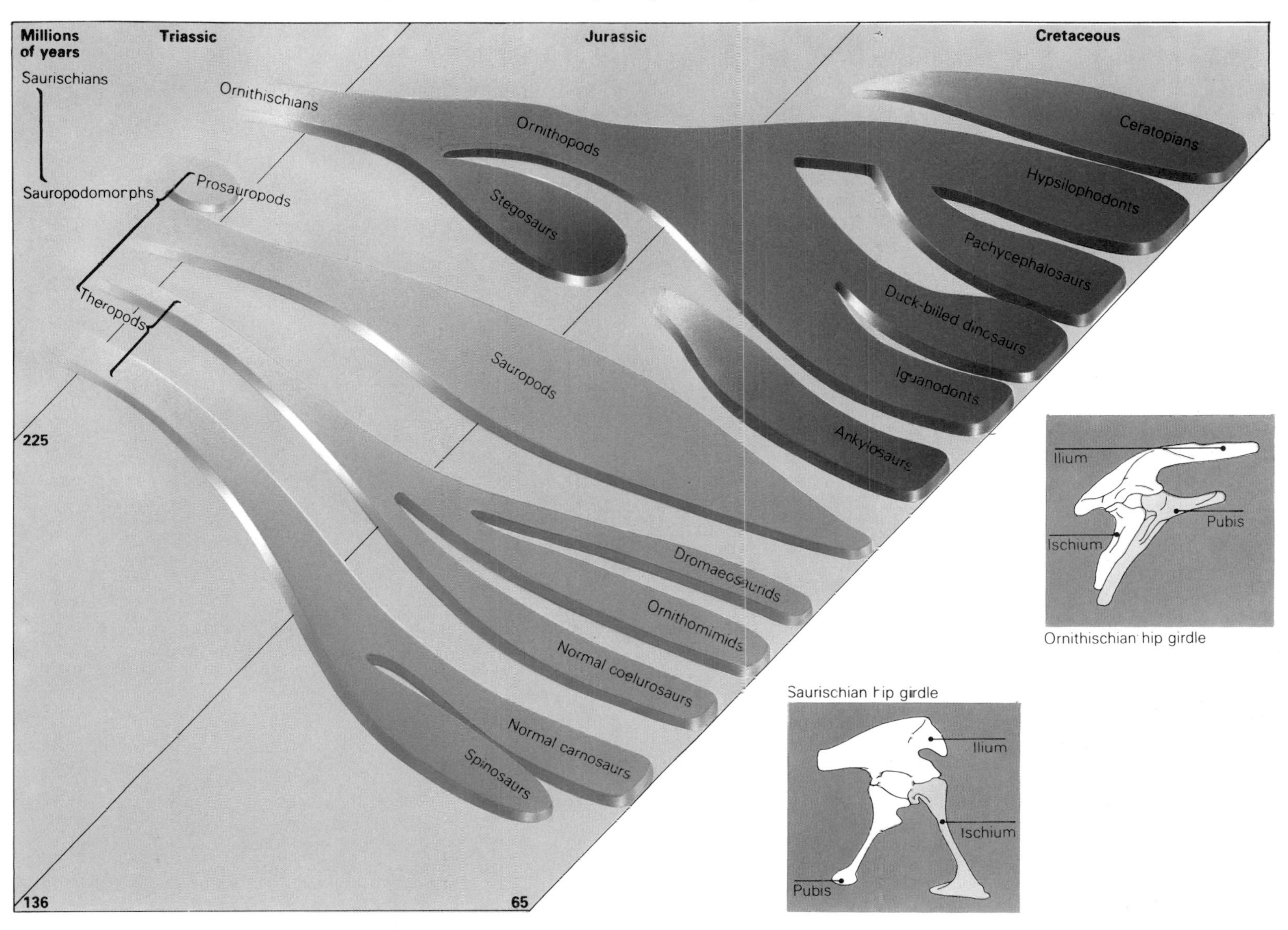

North America from mid-Oligocene to late Miocene times.

Molars are permanent cheek-teeth. HERBIVORES usually have complicated molars, whereas in the CARNIVORA they tend to be reduced.

Monotremes are an ORDER of primitive MAMMALS. They comprise the duck-billed platypus of Australia and the spiny ant-eating echidnas of Australia and New Guinea. They lay eggs, and have a body temperature which is lower than that of other mammals and also fluctuates with the environment. In these respects monotremes are in transition from the reptiles, but approach the mammals as they have hair and suckle their young.

Mosaic evolution is shown in animals such as *Archaeopteryx* where an association of truly reptile characters and truly bird characters is found.

Mosasaurs lived only in Upper Cretaceous times, but were distributed worldwide. They are particularly common in the chalk rocks of Kansas, USA. Mosasaurs swam with snake-like movements, and looked like the popular idea of a monster sea serpent.

Mud-grubbers refers to the mud-ingesting feeding habits of various animals without backbones and the ancient jawless fishes.

Mosasaurs looked like legendary sea monsters

Multituberculates were probably the first herbivorous mammals. They survived from the late Jurassic into the Eocene – a period of 100 million years – and are thus the longest-lived mammal ORDER ever.

Mustelidae are a family of the CARNIVORA which includes the weasels, skunks, otters and their kin.

N

Neanderthal man was confined to western Europe, where he lived from about 80,000 to 35,000 years ago, during the early part of the last glaciation. Because he was shorter and much stockier than men today,

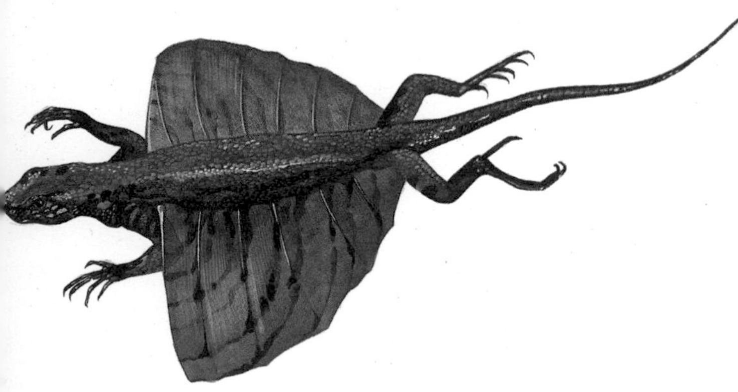

Left: *Kuhneosaurus* was one of the first flying vertebrates. It flourished during the Triassic, about 200 million years ago, in areas such as western England. In some ways it resembled the flying lizard *Draco* which lives in Asian rainforests.

Right: Primitive pterosaurs of the Jurassic, such as *Rhamphorhynchus,* had long tails and prominent, well-developed teeth.

Right: *Pterodactylus* and its close relatives lacked the long reptilian tail of the rhamphorhynchoids. Most pterodactyloids also had modified, rather slender, teeth. They lived from the Upper Jurassic to Lower Cretaceous.

Below: The skeleton of *Pteranodon* shows clearly the dramatic elongation of the fourth finger to form a wing, and the strong development of the breastplate.

Above: *Pteranodon,* of the Upper Cretaceous, was one of the largest of all pterosaurs. Adults had a wingspan of over 7 metres, and their huge, bony crests were important stabilizers during flight.

Flying reptiles

During the Upper Permian and early Triassic, competition among reptiles forced some of the smaller creatures to take to the trees for protection. Specialization took place and reptiles capable of flight appeared. The first of these were the gliding lizards or KUHNEOSAURS, which had long hollow ribs covered by a strong membrane of skin. They fed on insects and probably caught their food while gliding to earth from the tree tops. However, they were really passive fliers, and true flight developed not in these gliding lizards but in a group descended from the thecodontians — the pterosaurs — the first of which is recorded from the Lower Jurassic.

The ancestry of the pterosaurs is shrouded by time but an ideal half-way group appears to be *Podopteryx.* This small Triassic reptile was also a glider, but unlike the kuhneosaurs had no extended ribs to support its two membranes. The first membrane ran between the front and back legs, and the second stretched from the back legs to the tail. As the forelimb grew longer, so the front membrane enlarged. This new state marked the appearance of the pterosaurs, or flying reptiles. The first was DIMORPHODON, which had a large, rather primitive skull and a long reptilian tail, like that of its close relative *Rhamphorhynchus.* These made up the more primitive group of pterosaurs and from them arose the more advanced PTERODACTYLOIDS. Their tail had all but vanished and the teeth were modified or even lost. *Pterodactylus* itself was the size of a sparrow but *Pteranodon* and *Quetzalcoatlus* had wing spans of 7 and 10 metres respectively.

Evolution of the birds

The first bird, ARCHAEOPTERYX ('ancient feath-

Neanderthal man was once thought of as a separate species, but now he is widely accepted as a subspecies – *Homo sapiens neanderthalensis.*

Neural arch is the ⅄-shaped element that occurs above the central disc (centrum) of individual vertebrae (backbones). The arch is formed by 2 separate bony units and it covers the sides and upper surface of the spinal nerve cord. A prominent neural spine is found in many VERTEBRATES as an extension of the neural arch.

New World monkeys (platyrrhines) differ from the Old World monkeys (catarrhines) especially in their nostrils, which open to the side rather than down, and because most have a tail with which they can grasp branches.

New World monkey

Newts have short legs and long bodies and are closely related to the SALAMANDERS. The majority of modern species exist in Europe, where they live close to water in which they lay their eggs. During the mating season many male newts develop crests.

Nothosaurs were a group of primitive aquatic reptiles (EURYAPSIDS) that lived during the Triassic. They looked a little like small PLESIOSAURS.

Notochord is a slim rod of jelly-like material surrounded by a tough sheath found in animals such as AMPHIOXUS and a number of primitive VERTEBRATES. The notochord provides support, and is firm but flexible.

Notoungulates are an extinct and varied ORDER of mainly hoofed animals. They probably came from the CONDYLARTHS and with early exceptions were restricted to South America.

O

Old World monkeys, see NEW WORLD MONKEYS.

Omnivore is an animal that eats a diet of both plants and animals.

Ophiderpeton, like SAUROPLEURA, was a snake-like LEPOSPONDYL from the Upper Carboniferous. It grew to just under 1 metre long and all vestiges of both front and hind limbs had disappeared. *Ophiderpeton* and its relatives *Phlegethontia* and *Dolichosoma* constitute a group of specialized lepospondyls which had forked single-headed ribs. Up to 200 vertebrae have been re-

er'), is recorded from the Upper Jurassic LITHOGRAPHIC LIMESTONE of Solnhofen in Bavaria, southern Germany. Of the five known specimens, three are incredibly well preserved and various parts of their skeleton show an ancestral link with the coelurosaurs. Feathers and differences in the hip and front limb, however, divide *Archaeopteryx* from its contemporaries such as *Compsognathus*. In many ways old 'ancient feather' is the classic example of MOSAIC EVOLUTION. Some characters remain distinctly reptilian, while others are definitely bird-like.

For some time after *Archaeopteryx* the fossil history of the birds is poor. There is evidence in the Lower Cretaceous of goose-like and grebe-like birds, and a few bones to indicate that the 'fish-bird' ICHTHYORNIS had already appeared. This looked like the modern tern and in contrast to *Archaeopteryx* was an active flier. *Ichthyornis* was important among the Upper Cretaceous birds, and both it and its contemporaries BAPTORNIS and HESPERORNIS were fish-eaters with diver-like habits. *Hesperornis* was a large flightless bird, which like *Archaeopteryx* kept some reptilian characters, including teeth.

By the early Tertiary (65 million years ago) land and sea birds existed in several regions. Those living on land included ancestors of game-birds, waders, herons, and pigeons, while early relatives of the cormorants and petrels existed among sea birds. In Europe and North America a group of gigantic flightless birds, the DIATRYMIFORMES ('terror-cranes') were the chief meat-eaters on land. One species, *Diatryma steini*, stood 2 metres high and its strongly-built legs indicate that it was a powerful runner. The 'terror-cranes' were a short-lived group; during the Oligocene EPOCH their place as major predators was taken by the fast-running PHORORHACIDS.

Ichthyornis (Cretaceous)

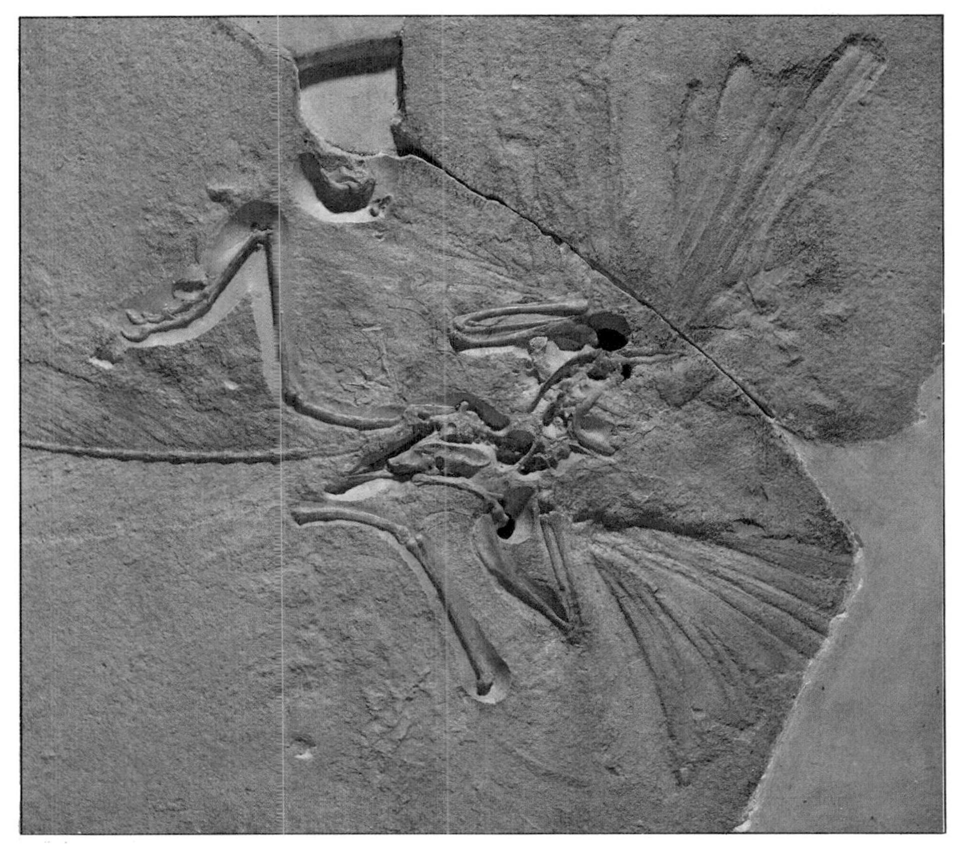

Diatryma (Eocene)

Above left and below: Two early bird forms. *Ichthyornis*, the tern-like 'fish-bird', lived during the latter half of the Cretaceous period. It flew well and probably ate fish. In the early Cainozoic the 'terror-cranes', or diatrymiformes, became the dominant bird group. They were flightless land-dwellers which grew exceptionally large.

Owl (Pleistocene)

Above: The so-called 'London *Archaeopteryx*' was found in 1861 near Pappenheim in southern Germany and was later bought by the British Museum for £700.

Left: Some experts claim that owls appeared in the Upper Cretaceous. Others suggest they began in the Cainozoic. They were common in Pleistocene bird groups.

GIGANTISM in birds was common in the Middle and Upper Tertiary; for example, *Pachydyptes*, a penguin from the Oligocene of Australia and Antarctica, stood 1.5 metres high. The first owls, hawks and primitive swifts all appeared in the Oligocene and by the end of that epoch, modern groups accounted for almost 75 per cent of the world's bird life. Most living families had appeared by the start of the Pleistocene.

The rise of mammals

The Cainozoic, which opened about 65 million years ago, is often called the 'Age of MAMMALS'.

---

corded in these snake-like creatures. Each genus exhibited differences in the number and form of teeth, and it is likely that they fed on different organisms.

Order is a category used to classify plants and animals. An order is made up of related families; related orders make up a class. So among mammals, the classification for a timber wolf would be: class, Mammalia; order, Carnivora; family, CANIDAE; genus, *Canis;* species, *Canis lupus;* subspecies, *Canis lupus griseus.*

Oreodonts are extinct North American ARTIODACTYLA that lived from late Eocene until Pliocene times. They were somewhat pig-like, though as their teeth were SELENODONT they seem to have been RUMINANTS.

A rat is omnivorous

Osteichthyes are the higher bony fishes. They include both the RAY-FINNED and TASSEL-FINNED fishes.

Ostracoderms were those early AGNATHAN, or jawless, fishes that had a thick bony skeleton.

Otariidae are the eared seals and include fur seals and sea lions. Like the PHOCIDAE they can be traced back to the Miocene.

Otic notch is found in higher vertebrates such as the amphibians and reptiles. It occurs at the back of the skull, and in early representatives of the reptiles and amphibians marked the site of the ear.

Oxyaenids were a family of the extinct CREODONTS and the most powerful predators of their times. They arose in the Palaeocene but died out at the end of the Eocene.

P

Pachycephalosaurs, see BONE-HEADED.

Pachydyptes was a giant penguin that lived during the Oligocene. Like all penguins it was a mixture of primitive and advanced features, the wings being modified to act as flippers. Flight was impossible with these, and the adaptation of the penguins to an aquatic life is also reflected in the webbed feet of its hind limbs. The penguins probably derived from strong-flying seabirds such as the albatross and petrel. *Pachydyptes* and several of its close relatives grew to the size of a man, and numerous species inhabited the coastal regions of Patagonia, Au-

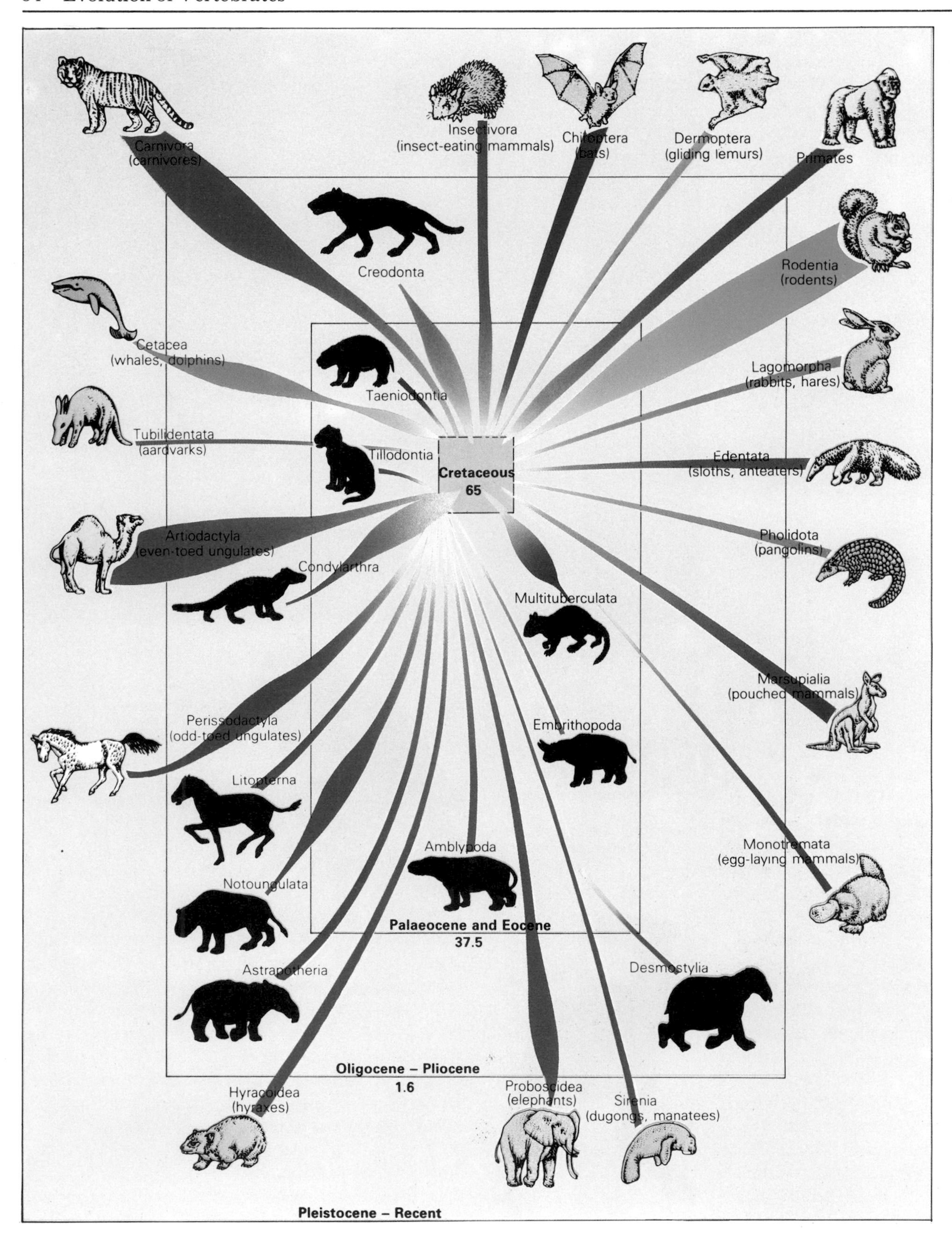

Left: The adaptive radiation of the mammals established many different orders, or groups which share certain common adaptive traits. Several of the orders were established in the Mesozoic, but the majority arose during the early Tertiary, after the extinction of the dinosaurs. Some of the less advanced groups became extinct by the end of the Eocene, although other groups lived on into later Tertiary times and some did not finally disappear until the close of the Pliocene, especially in South America. A number of the surviving orders are evidently greatly reduced in variety compared with their diversity earlier in the Cainozoic era.

stralasia and Antarctica during the Tertiary period.

Palaeoniscid fishes are a primitive group of RAY-FINNED fishes from the Palaeozoic and early Mesozoic. Most were modest in size, and many resembled the living herring. But the palaeoniscids had shiny, thick, heavy scales. Many palaeoniscids had a HETEROCERCAL tail, large eyes and an elongated mouth. A typical example was *Cheirolepis* from the Devonian.

Palaeontologists study the geological periods of the past, and the forms of life which existed within them.

Pantotheres are generally accepted as the ancestors of the higher mammals, based on the arrangement and working of their MOLARS.

Pecorans include deer, giraffes and the BOVOIDS, although sometimes the TRAGULOIDS are included as well.

Pelycosaurs were a group of early SYNAPSID reptiles characterized, in several cases, by large dorsal (back) fins. They lived during the Permian, and both meat- and plant-eaters are known.

Perissodactyla are hoofed animals with an odd number of toes. They have an excellent fossil history, which shows that they were once far more diverse.

Phocidae are earless or common seals, which first appear in the fossil record in Miocene rocks.

Phororhacids were a group of giant birds recorded from the Oligocene, Miocene and Pliocene epochs. *Phororhacos*, the best-known of these flightless animals, was long-legged and between 1.5 and 1.8 metres in height. It had a powerful beak and was possibly the major predator in parts of South America. The phororhacids' success was probably linked with the absence of PLACENTAL mammals from this region during the epochs in question.

Common seal

Phytosaurs are among the most common THECODONTIANS recorded from the Upper Triassic. They were advanced creatures whose general appearance was similar to that of living crocodiles. Like the AËTOSAURS, however, they were more heavily armoured than their contemporary thecodontians or the crocodiles. A typical phytosaur, such as *Rutiodon*, had a long skull and strong jaws armed with numerous

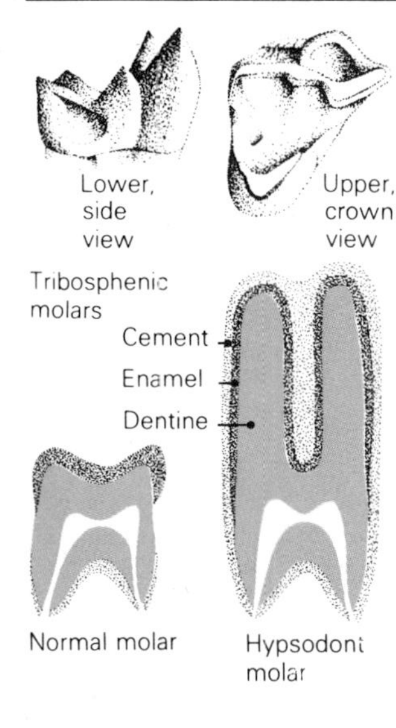

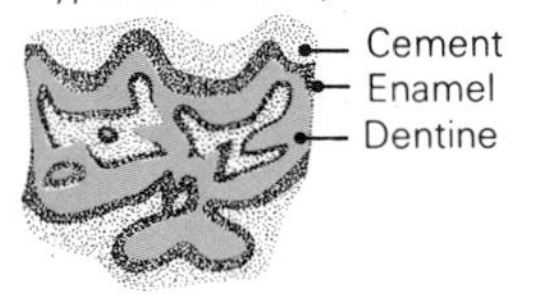

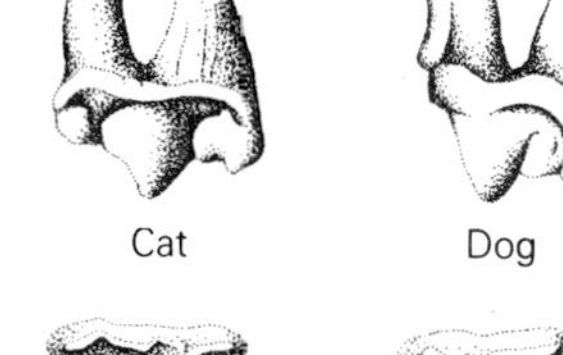

Above: Fossil teeth are important in tracing evolutionary trends in mammals. Some early species had tribosphenic molar teeth that were used to cut and crush insects. In later mammals teeth became more specialized. Certain herbivores developed high-crowned or hypsodont molars, which, as they were used, developed ridges that were ideal for grinding. Carnivores developed carnassials for cutting and slicing meat. The carnassials shown are upper ones, with roots uppermost.

Yet mammals actually appeared around 100 million years earlier, in late Triassic times. They evolved from predatory therapsid reptiles (*see page 47*), and by the Jurassic had divided into five separate ORDERS of small, relatively insignificant animals. Of these, only the MULTITUBERCULATES, a group of pseudo-rodents, survived into the Cainozoic. The TRICONODONTS, SYMMETRODONTS and DOCODONTS were probably insect- or meat-eaters, and disappeared in the Jurassic or early Cretaceous. However, it may be that the docodonts were ancestors of the MONOTREMES which live in Australia and South-East Asia. The fifth order, the PANTOTHERES, also died out in the Cretaceous. These shrew-like creatures were INSECTIVOROUS and laid eggs, and from them arose the first PLACENTAL and MARSUPIAL mammals. These two new evolutionary lines are recognized from fossils of their teeth, which even then were distinctly different.

The early marsupial *Eodelphis* was very like the living American opossum *Didelphis*, and later developed several types which flourished in the Cainozoic, especially in Australia and the Americas. Like their predecessors, the first placental mammals fed on insects. Before the Cretaceous ended they had given rise to several new orders, the most important being the CONDYLARTHS, CREODONTS and PRIMATES. Condylarths were primitive hoofed animals and seem to have been omnivorous. The creodonts, however, were meat-eaters, appearing before, and later evolving quite separately from, the true CARNIVORES. The primates, of course, include man. Despite this diversity, mammals remained unimportant in both variety and size compared with the dinosaurs of the period.

At the start of the Cainozoic mammals underwent a spectacular burst of ADAPTIVE RADIATION to fill the places of meat- and plant-eating animals left empty after the dinosaurs died out. Old orders such as the multituberculates, creodonts and condylarths continued with great success, and at the same time began many new orders. Most modern and extinct herbivores, for example, are descended from the condylarths. And, although the origins are not always so clear as in this last case, it is likely that all the orders of mammals known only from the Cainozoic in fact extend back as far as the Palaeocene or Eocene.

Deteriorating climate and more competition among the rapidly evolving mammals led to many of the older, experimental forms declining or dying out in the late Eocene and Oligocene. The multituberculates were eliminated, along with the strange TAENIODONTS, TILLODONTS, AMBLYPODS and EMBRITHOPODS. Condylarths and DESMOSTYLIDS, on the other hand, survived into the Miocene, while the creodonts finally died out only in the Pliocene. As in the Miocene the geography of the world became more as it is today, so other mammal orders developed recognizable modern forms. These were perfected in the Pliocene, when the diversity of highly specialized mammals reached an all-time peak. Further adaptation took place during the Pleistocene ICE AGE, resulting in the mammals we see today. But these are far less varied than the mammals of the Pleistocene, for they were decimated by a wave of extinctions between 60,000 and 10,000 years ago. The larger mammals were particularly badly hit, and on each continent extinctions coincided with the spread of human hunters. The 'Age of Mammals' was over and the 'Age of Man' had begun.

While the main adaptive radiation of flowering plants happened before the continents drifted far apart, that of the mammals occurred afterwards. Since communication between the three northern continents was possible for much of the Cainozoic, their mammals are very similar and are almost all placental. This was not so in the three southern continents. Australian mammals are almost entirely marsupial, presumably because Australia was cut off before the more highly evolved and competitive placental mammals could colonize it. Throughout the Tertiary in South America, marsupials also filled the flesh-eating and to a large extent the insect-eating niches. The herbivores were placental mammals, including such groups as the LITOPTERNS, NOTOUNGULATES and ASTRAPOTHERES. This situation lasted until the end of the Pliocene, when the land connection between South and North America was re-established. Advanced placental mammals were then able to cross into South America, so causing the end of the native herbivores and marsupials, apart from the opossums. Africa has been less isolated than Australia and South America. So while it has characteristic mammals, there are no marsu-

sharp teeth. *Rutiodon* grew to over 6 metres, while its close relatives reached lengths up to 10 metres. Nostrils near the top of the skull probably allowed phytosaurs to breathe while most of the body was under water. Phytosaurs lived in swamps and by rivers. They fed on fish.

Pineal opening marks the position of the 'third eye' in fish, amphibians and certain reptiles. It is usually in the centre of the skull roof.

Pipids are a group of aquatic frogs. They lived from the Jurassic to Recent periods.

Placental mammals give birth to young which are at an advanced stage of development. Inside the mother they are fed through a placenta over a lengthy gestation period.

Placochelys was the most specialized of the PLACODONTS. In many ways it resembled a small MARINE TURTLE, for its body was covered with a thick shell. This was made up of hundreds of small plates similar to that of the living leathery turtle. *Placochelys* also had well-developed paddle-like limbs, but its skull was very differ-

Mammal feeding young

ent from a turtle's and the jaws were lined with robust crushing teeth. Sea turtles and the more specialized placodonts appear to be good examples of CONVERGENT EVOLUTION.

Placoderms were one of the earliest groups of jawed fishes. Many were heavily armoured and members of the group are commonly referred to as 'plated-skins'.

Placodonts were a group of reptiles adapted to a life in water. The most advanced forms looked very much like large turtles and used their beak-like jaws to prise shell-fish from the sea floor. They lived in the Triassic.

Plesiadapis was a tree-dwelling animal which resembled a squirrel, and had rodent-like teeth. True rodents may have evolved from plesiadapids.

Plesiosaurs are common in many Jurassic and Cretaceous rocks. They first appear in deposits which mark the changeover from the Triassic to Jurassic. By Liassic times they were already well diversified.

Pliohippus was a Pliocene horse of North America, one of several types that lived in

pials. In fact, the Pleistocene extinctions exaggerated the contrasts with the northern continents, for many animals now restricted to Africa once roamed widely outside it.

Hoofed mammals

Most hoofed mammals or UNGULATES belong either to the group with odd numbers of toes — PERISSODACTYLA — or to that with even numbers of toes — ARTIODACTYLA. Both are descended from the condylarths, but early perissodactyls differed from them in several ways. Their legs were longer, while their leg joints and small foot bones were developed to concentrate the thrust of their movement on to their central toes. Consequently the number of useful toes was gradually reduced to three or even one. Their cheek teeth also evolved in a distinctive way. The PRE-MOLARS became more like MOLARS, so increasing the area of grinding surface for crushing hard plants. These and other advances made the early odd-toed ungulates more efficient BROWSERS and faster runners than the condylarths, which they eventually eclipsed.

The initial radiation of the perissodactyls established the CERATOMORPHA, HIPPOMORPHA and ANCYLOPODA. Ceratomorphs include the rhinoceroses, primitive tapirs and some extinct groups closely related to the tapirs. Rhinoceroses and tapirs were once more varied; the hornless rhinoceros BALUCHITHERIUM, for instance, was the largest land mammal ever, and probably browsed tree-tops. The hippomorphs too are now much reduced. Only the horse and its allies survive, but once there were also massive TITANOTHERES standing over 2 metres high at the shoulder, and others like *Brontotherium* with Y- or V-shaped protuberances on their noses. There are no living ancylopods. The chief ones were the CHALICOTHERES, the more recent of which, such as *Moropus,* resembled clawed horses and survived until the late Pleistocene extinctions. Their claws were perhaps used to bend down leafy branches or to unearth roots and tubers.

Although various perissodactyls had already disappeared by the end of the Eocene and early Oligocene, the group reached its peak in mid-Tertiary times when the dominant ungulates were those with odd toes. They have since been displaced by the artiodactyls and seem headed

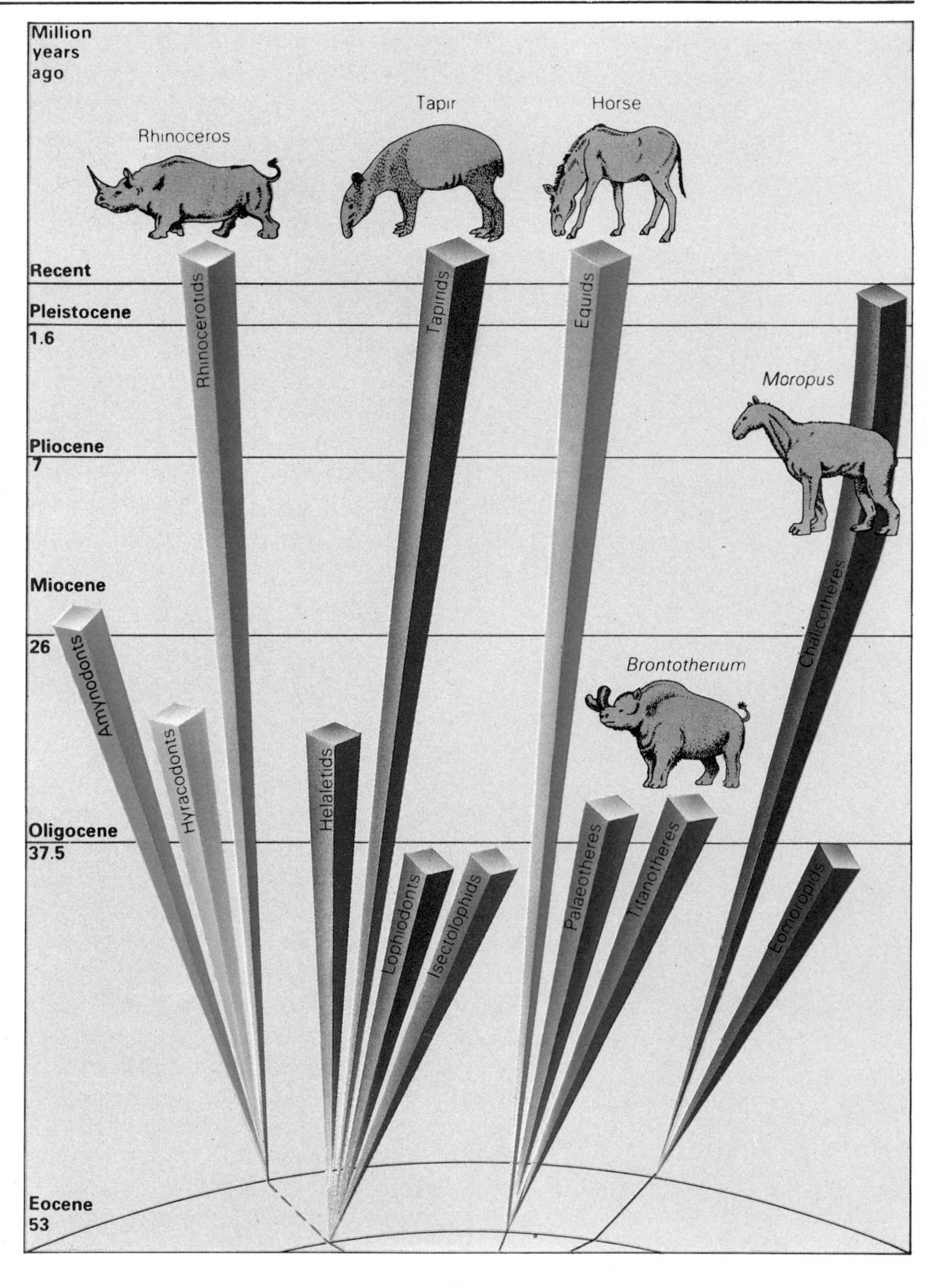

Above: The perissodactyls, or odd-toed ungulates, evolved in a way that established a variety of different families, and for a while they were the dominant ungulates. Many of the families became extinct in the Tertiary, and one was lost in the Pleistocene. The surviving families are much reduced in variety.

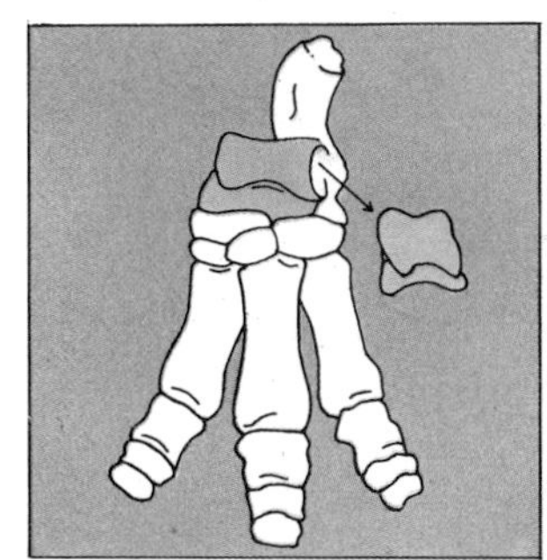

Left: These bones are from the hind foot of *Brontotherium.* A typical astragalus of a perissodactyl is also illustrated *(right)*, showing the keeled upper surface for articulation with the tibia.

North America at that time.
Polypterus is a living bony fish of the RAY-FINNED type. It lives in fresh waters of tropical Africa. The body is covered in shiny, thick scales and its dorsal scale is modified to look like a series of small sails. *Polypterus* has retained a small pair of internal lungs which are of great value during droughts.
Predator is an animal that hunts and kills for its food. A typical example was *Tyrannosaurus.*
Prehistoric overkill is a term used to describe the impact of Palaeolithic (Old Stone-age) hunters on the large mammals of the late Pleistocene. That hunting was responsible for the great Pleistocene extinctions is now widely accepted for some, if not all, of the continents.

Palaeolithic hunting tool

Pre-molars are cheek-teeth which grow in front of the MOLARS.
Primates make up the ORDER to which man belongs.
Proboscideans are members of the ORDER Proboscidea; they include elephants and the extinct mastodonts.
Procolophonids were an important group of STEM REPTILES. Some palaeontologists think they are ancestors of both the turtles and the more advanced DIAPSIDS (such as dinosaurs and crocodiles).
Procompsognathus is a small COELUROSAUR recorded from sediments of the Upper Triassic. It was a lightly-built 2-legged animal, with thin-walled bones. Its head was small, with large eyes and a pointed snout. The neck was long and slender, and a long tail acted as a counterbalance during running. Adult procompsognathids reached 1 metre in length and the animal is known only from Europe. It is found in association with *Plateosaurus* — a PROSAUROPOD — and the first turtle — *Triassochelys.*
Procyonidae are a family of the CARNIVORA, and include the raccoons, coatis and pandas. They spend much of their time in trees.
Prosauropods are a group of LIZARD-HIPPED dinosaurs from the middle and late Triassic. They were heavily-built, ate plants, and seem to be the ancestors of the giant SAUROPODS of the Jurassic and Cretaceous.
Prosimians are the least advanced PRIMATES. They include the lemurs, lorises and tarsiers. Lemurs survive

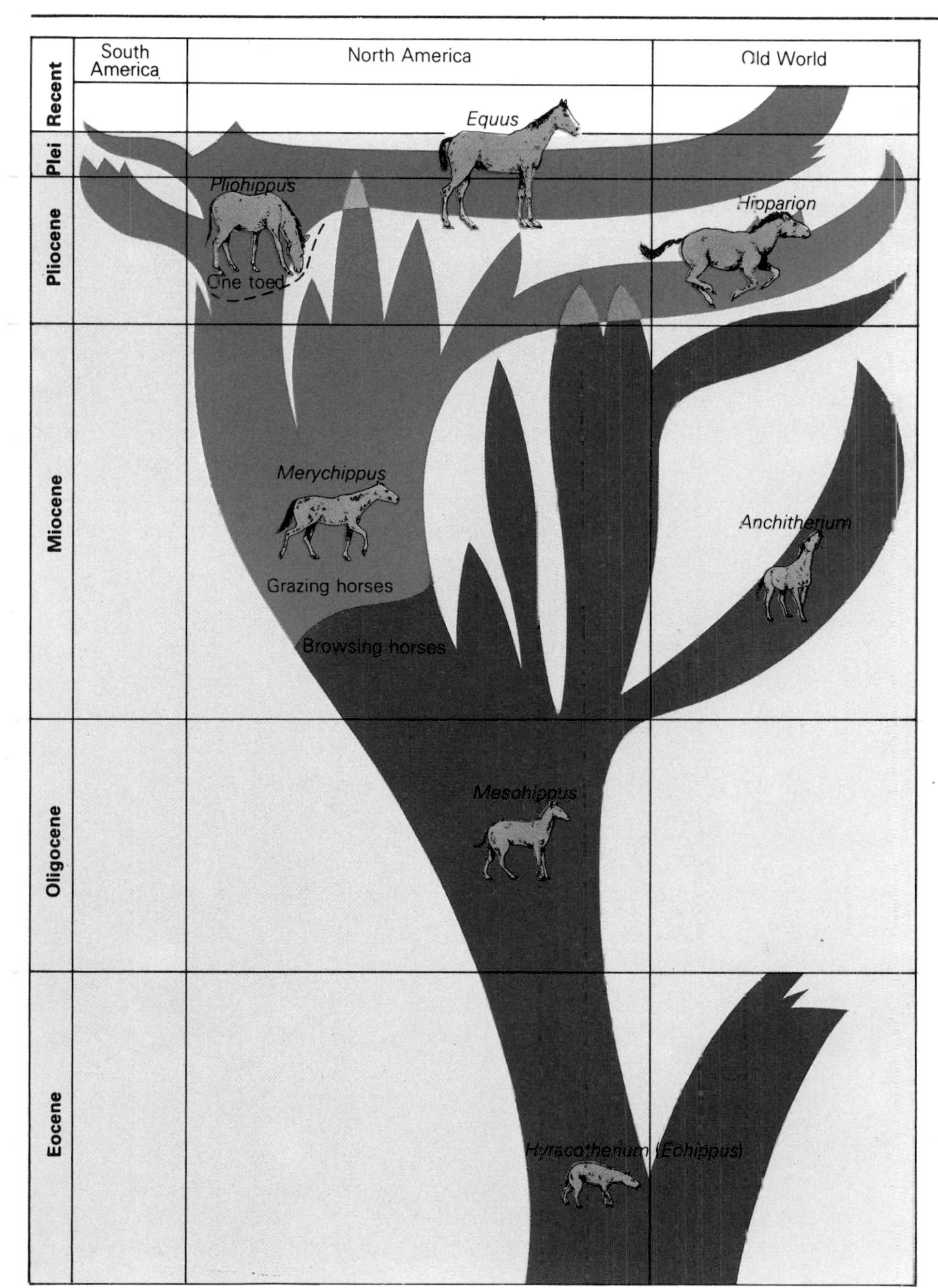

From 'Horses', Simpson (Oxford University Press)

Above: The modern family to which the horse, zebra and ass belong is the product of much evolutionary experiment. Although the majority of the advances occurred in North America, horses became extinct there in the Pleistocene and were reintroduced in the 1500s by the Spanish conquistadores. It can be seen that the modern horse is not the result of a single evolutionary development. It is instead the product of repeated trial and error. For example, the several types of browsing horses (those which lived off the leaves of trees and shrubs) became extinct in Miocene and Pliocene times. Most of the grazing horses, which lived off the grasslands of the world, disappeared in more recent times.

for extinction. All those living today are greatly reduced compared to their earlier geographical range, variety and numbers.

Adaptation in the horse

Evolutionary trends in perissodactyls can be seen in the development of the horse. The story is not of a single, progressive evolutionary line, but one of repeated trial and error. A move towards fewer toes began with the fox-sized *Hyracotherium,* or EOHIPPUS, which had miniature padded hooves. There were three toes on each hind foot and four on both front feet, although the fourth was largely useless. By the end of the Oligocene the sheep-sized MIOHIPPUS had three toes on each foot, and the central toe was further enlarged compared with that in *Hyracotherium.* Each toe was still functional and ended in a padded hoof. The first true plains horse, the pony-sized MERYCHIPPUS, also had three toes on each foot. But it walked only on the central toe, which ended in a hoof without a pad. In addition, the foot had developed a springing action. The earliest single-toed horse was PLIOHIPPUS, its side toes having been reduced to splints of bone in the upper foot. *Equus,* the modern horse, is a direct descendant of *Pliohippus.*

These adaptations for speed were accompanied by advances in horses' teeth. *Hyracotherium* had some molars with a bubbly surface on the crowns. This BUNODONT condition was well suited to an animal that browsed on the leaves of trees and bushes. Furthermore, the CANINES were smaller and a gap, or diastema, was left between them and the cheek teeth. Modern horses have large diastemas, which serve to collect food before it is passed backwards to the grinding teeth. In *Miohippus* the pre-molar teeth had become fully molar-like, with enamel ridges on the crowns. This LOPHODONT condition helped the animal to break down leaves with its teeth before digesting them. However, the crowns themselves remained low or BRACHYDONT. Cheek teeth equipped for grazing tougher grasses appeared in *Merychippus.* The crowns had increased in height to the HYPSODONT condition, were cement-covered, and the enamel ridges were folded into complex patterns. As the teeth wore down, the harder ridges stood above the softer cement and dentine in the cores of the teeth, so giving sharply crested grinding surfaces.

only in Madagascar, where there are no monkeys or apes to compete with. The lorises and tarsiers avoid such competition by being nocturnal.

Pterodactyloids were the most advanced group of PTEROSAURS. They appeared first during the Jurassic period and in contrast to the more primitive *Rhamphorhynchus* and *Dimorphodon,* had lost the long reptilian tail and possessed slender, delicate teeth. *Pterodactylus* itself was only the size of a sparrow whereas *Pteranodon* and *Quetzalcoatlus* were giants of the air. *Pteranodon* had a wingspan of 7 metres and *Quetzalcoatlus* one of 10 metres or more. In some pterodactyloids, such as *Dsungaripterus,* the jaws ended in long, sharp spikes and appear to have been used to spear fish. It is likely that *Dsungaripterus* and *Pteranodon* were ocean-going gliders whilst *Quetzalcoatlus* lived inland. There it soared over the plains like a great vulture searching for the carcass of dead animals.

Lemur, a prosimian

Pterosaurs, or flying reptiles, arose in the early Jurassic, near salt water. They glided on air currents, for it is doubtful if they could have flapped their wing-like membranes. Probably they swooped over the sea to scoop up fish from the water. Their leg bones were arranged in such a way that they could not have stood upright on land.

Purgatorius is the earliest fossil primate and takes its name from the place where it was found—Purgatory Hill, Montana, USA.

Q

Quadrupedal animals walk on 4 feet or legs.

R

Ramapithecus differed from the Miocene apes or DRYOPITHECINES in having small CANINES and INCISORS, as in man, and a flatter face. Some authorities see *Ramapithecus* as an ape with HOMINID features; others believe it is the first, albeit primitive, hominid.

Ratfish are a group of open-sea fishes which have a CARTILAGINOUS skeleton. They are therefore close relatives of the sharks and rays. Unlike their relatives they are quite rare, and their fossil record is limited. They are active swimmers, al-

Development of teeth and reduction of the toes did not always go together. HIPPARION was a contemporary of *Pliohippus,* and while its teeth were hypsodont it had three-toed feet.

Even-toed ungulates

In artiodactyls each foot generally has only four or two toes. These even-toed ungulates underwent an impressive radiation in the late Cainozoic, as the perissodactyls waned. There are various reasons for their success. For example they had, unlike the perissodactyls, an ankle-bone with grooves on the bottom as well as the top, and this is why artiodactyls are often able to make remarkable leaps. Again, many artiodactyls regurgitate their food for further chewing, after the risk of attack by predators is over. This adaptation, which permits hurried feeding but digestion at leisure, is known as rumination. The molar teeth of RUMINANTS have crescent-shaped or SELENODONT ridges, and in more advanced ruminants the upper incisors are replaced by a hard cropping pad.

The basic radiation of the artiodactyls happened in Eocene and early Oligocene times. Among the non-ruminants, the pigs and peccaries were defined at this early stage, as were the ANTHRACOTHERES — ancestors of the hippopotamus. Some early non-ruminant groups soon became extinct, however, including the ENTELODONTS, or giant pigs, the sheep-sized OREODONTS and the hare-like CAINOTHERES. Camels too appeared early, yet although these animals have a cropping pad and 'chew the cud' they are not usually classed as ruminants, because at the outset they were distinct from all other artiodactyls. The ruminants proper include the TRAGULOIDS (of which the chevrotains or mouse deer are the sole survivors) and the more advanced PECORANS. Deer evolved from the traguloids and in turn gave rise to the giraffes. BOVOIDS also branched from the traguloids, and diverged in the Pliocene into an astonishing array of animals — pronghorns, sheep, goats, musk-oxen, antelopes and cattle.

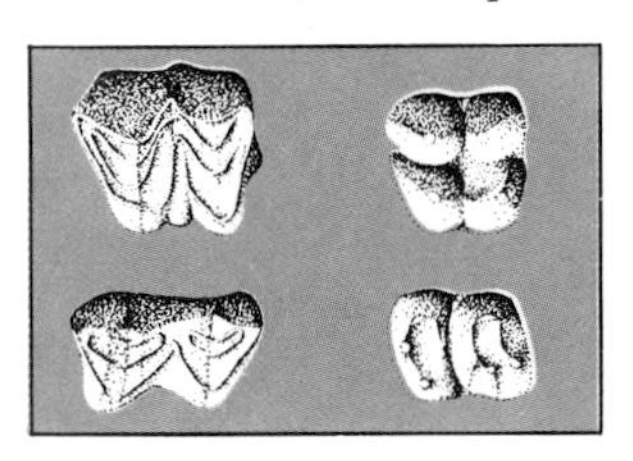

Left: Some artiodactyl teeth. Shown are those of a primitive Eocene artiodactyl (*right*) and the selenodont teeth of a Pleistocene antelope (*left*). Crown views are illustrated of worn left upper (*top*) and right lower molars (*bottom*).

Below: Hind foot bones of a hippopotamus. Also shown *(right)* is a typical artiodactyl astragalus, with a double-pulley for articulation with the tibia and with the ankle bones.

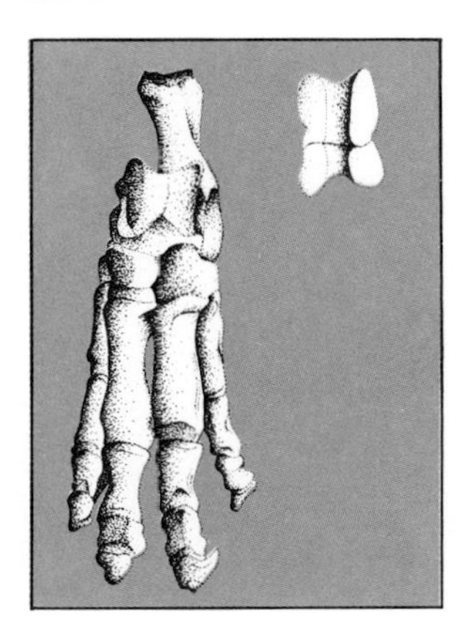

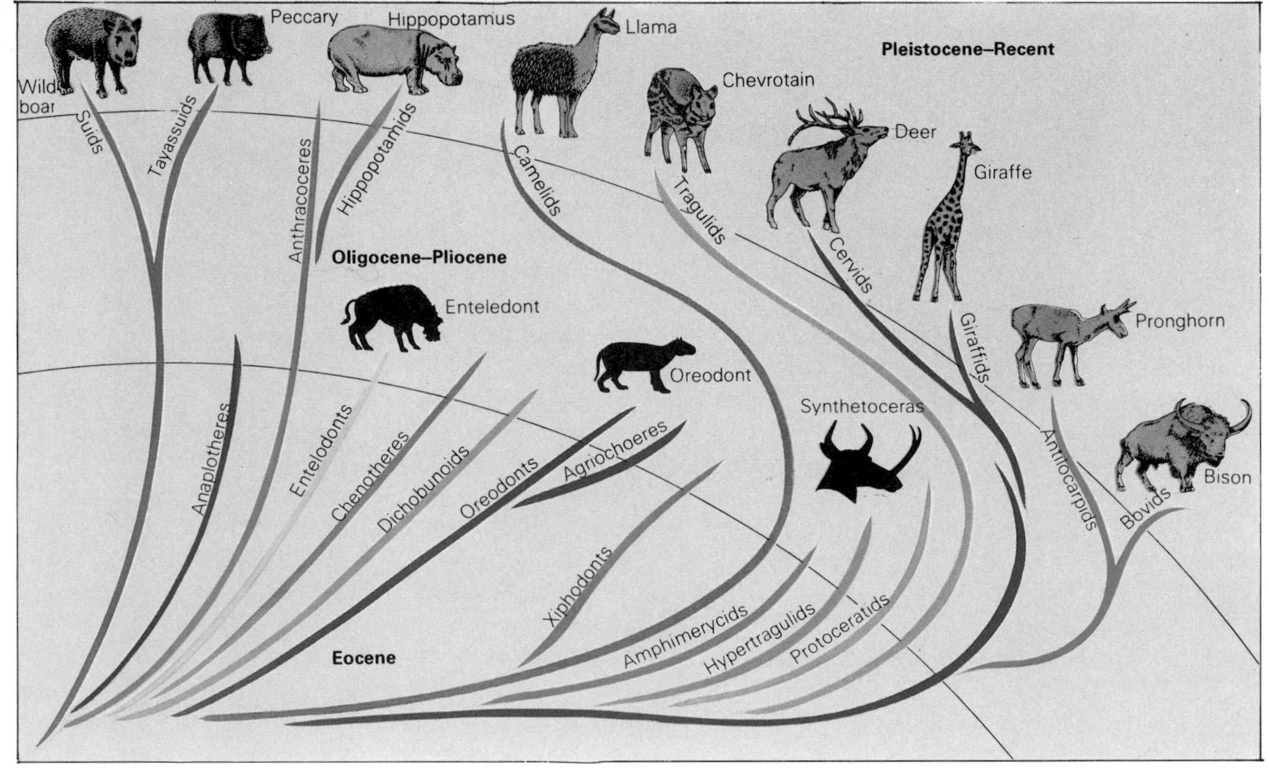

Left: The radiation of the artiodactyls, or even-toed ungulates, produced many different families, not all of which survived the Tertiary. They nonetheless remain the most varied and numerous ungulates.

though the tail is often reduced to a whip-like structure. Many forms have a long snout and a strange clasping organ is often found on the male's forehead. The ancestry of the ratfish may be traced back to the Devonian.

Ray-finned fishes constitute one of the 2 major groups of bony fishes. They are also known as the actinopterygians and are represented today by such fishes as salmon and trout. Several long-lived groups such as the palaeoniscids flourished during the Palaeozoic and Mesozoic eras.

Reptiles are higher VERTEBRATE animals which have a scaly skin and lay AMNIOTE eggs. The class is subdivided by the characteristics of the skull, and scientists recognize 4 major subgroups among reptiles:– ANAPSIDS; DIAPSIDS; EURYAPSIDS; and SYNAPSIDS.

Rhipidistians are an extinct group of TASSEL-FINNED fishes from which the amphibians diverged in Devonian times. They were hunter-killers and unique in having internal nostrils. The fins of various rhipidistians have an arrangement of larger bones similar to the walking limbs of early amphibians.

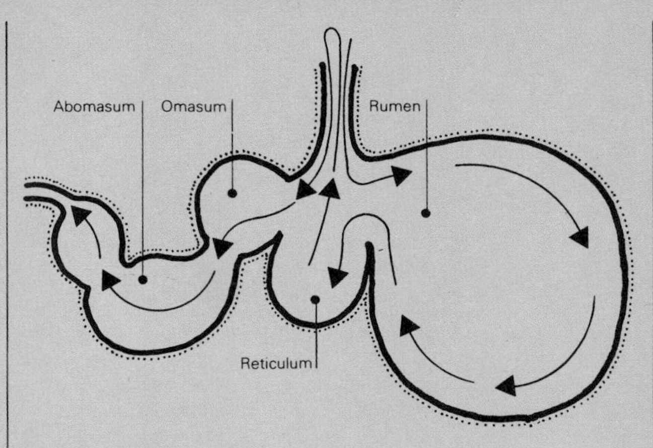

Ruminant's digestive system

Ruminants use a process whereby a pulpy mass of food is regurgitated from 2 stomach chambers — the rumen and reticulum — for chewing. After this it is swallowed again and passed into 2 other stomach chambers for further digestion.

S

Sabre-tooth cats, see CANINES.

Salamander is the name given to the long-bodied, short-limbed members of

The earliest undoubted PROBOSCIDEANS, *Palaeomastodon* and *Phiomia,* are known from the Lower Oligocene of Africa, where they probably evolved from condylarths which had migrated there. Both were elephant-like in appearance, *Phiomia,* the larger of the two, being about the size of a smallish modern elephant. By the Miocene three new groups had developed from them. The DEINOTHERES were hoe-tuskers, so called because they had powerful down-turned tusks on their lower jaws, which they presumably used for digging. Eventually the deinotheres grew to a height of almost 4 metres at the shoulder, yet otherwise they stayed remarkably unchanged until they disappeared in the widespread extinctions of large mammals at the end of the Pleistocene. The SHORT-JAWED MASTODONTS were a more varied group, essentially of browsers. They resembled modern elephants, but were shorter, stockier and had bunodont teeth. The last survived until perhaps as late as 6000 BC.

The third and last group were the GOMPHOTHERES, or long-jawed mastodonts. At first they were just a larger version of *Phiomia,* but they later branched into a number of different evolutionary lines. One ended in the curious shovel-tuskers and spoonbill mastodonts, with highly specialized lower jaws. Another led to the first true elephants. These differ from mastodonts in having higher skulls, shorter jaws, and a taller, slimmer build. The key difference, however, is that elephants have high-crowned molar teeth with numerous enamel-covered cutting plates that are dentine-filled and cemented together. Developing such molars allowed the animals to change from browsing to grazing, and several kinds of elephant therefore evolved to make use of the grasslands. During the Pleistocene, straight-tusked elephants were common in the INTER-GLACIAL periods, and alternated with MAMMOTHS in the GLACIALS. One mammoth, *Elephas trogontherii,* was the largest proboscidean of all time, reaching about 4.5 metres at the shoulder. Although the later WOOLLY MAMMOTH was smaller, it was nevertheless an animal of

Above: A selection of extinct proboscideans and the living Indian elephant.

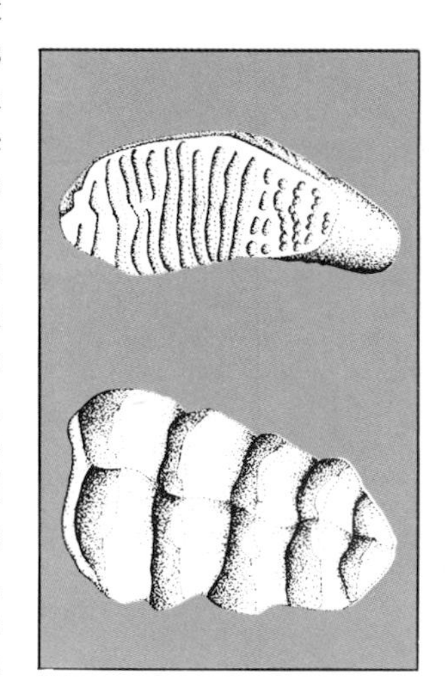

Above: The ridged upper molar tooth of a Pleistocene mammoth (*top*) is compared with the simpler upper molar of a Pleistocene mastodont (*bottom*).

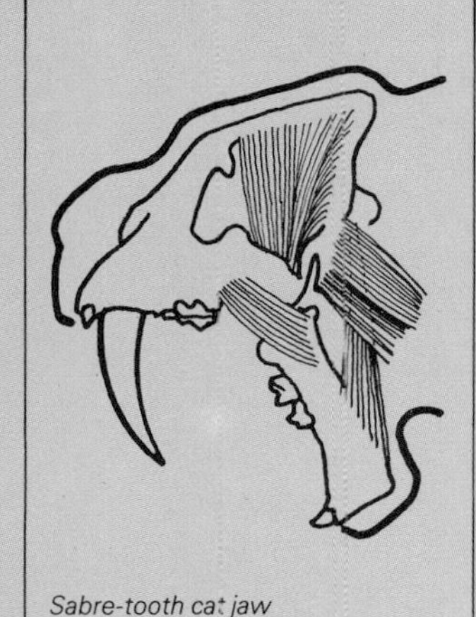

Sabre-tooth cat jaw

the order Urodela. They are closely related to NEWTS but are perhaps nearer to the primitive amphibian condition. Today, many salamanders are adapted for a life on land, and lay their eggs in warm, damp areas. Most, however, prefer a life in water and breathe through gills throughout their lives. Living forms include the Mexican axolotl and the giant salamander from Japan. It is likely that the first salamanders appeared during the early part of the Mesozoic era. The oldest known salamander from the Jurassic is similar to those of today.

Sauropleura is a snake-like LEPOSPONDYL amphibian recorded from the Carboniferous. The body is long, and apart from small vestiges the limbs have effectively disappeared. The skull is also long and pointed and appears to be adapted to an insect- or worm-eating diet. *Sauropleura* is also known as a nectridean, for its tail vertebrae have expanded fan-shaped neural spines (*see* NEURAL ARCH). *Sauropleura* and its close relative *Urocordylus,* which was also snake-like, were abundant in the coal swamps, but only 1 or 2 nectrideans survived into the Permian period.

Sauropods were a group of LIZARD-HIPPED dinosaurs that flourished during the Jurassic and Cretaceous periods. The name means 'beast-footed' and this broad, elephantine foot was characteristic of PROSAUROPODS such as *Melanorosaurus* and sauropod dinosaurs such as *Brachiosaurus* and *Diplodocus.*

Scutosaurus roamed the late Permian landscape of today's USSR. It was a STEM REPTILE and more specifically a representative of the pareiasaur family. The latter were the largest of the stem reptiles, characterized by the rotation of their limbs in towards the body. *Scutosaurus,* although not the largest pareiasaur, was almost 3 metres in length and had warty or horn-like protuberances on the face. Its limbs and backbone were massively built. *Scutosaurus* was a herbivore.

Selection pressures, such as competition for food, living space or shelter, have a considerable effect on

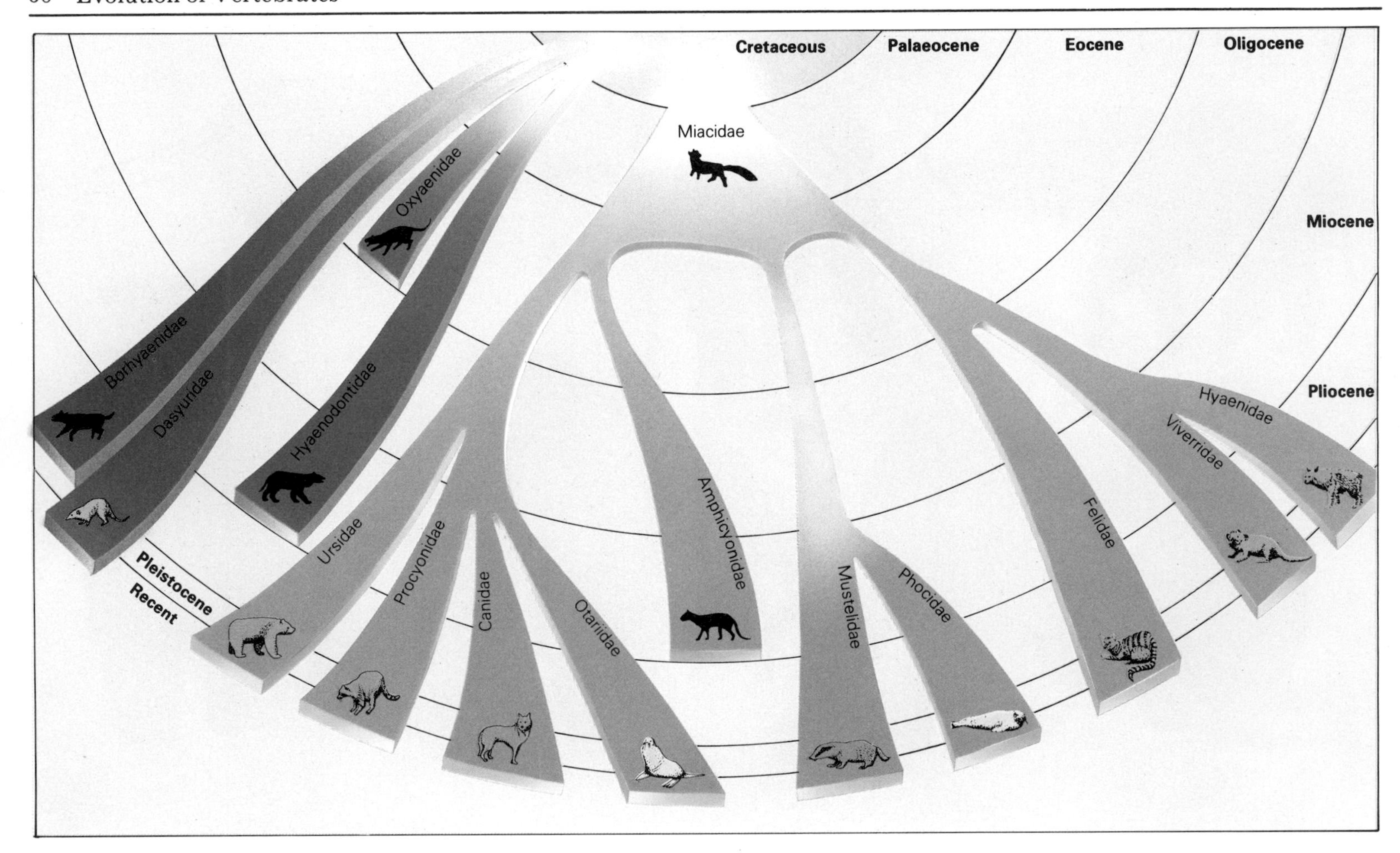

Above: Three quite separate orders of mammals have produced carnivores — the marsupials (red), the creodonts (blue) and the true Carnivora (green). The creodonts are extinct, as are the larger types of marsupial carnivores. The early Tertiary carnivorous mammals were so efficient and diverse that they prevented other lines of mammals from also becoming carnivorous.

impressive size. Only two species of elephant are living today; one in Africa and the other in India and South-East Asia. In effect, elephants, along with rhinoceroses, have been reduced to relic populations.

Flesh-eaters

Carnivorous mammals live by seeking and catching mostly vertebrate prey. They therefore evolved the senses, intelligence and the powerful, agile bodies needed for these tasks. Their teeth are also specially developed, with strong INCISORS for nipping, dagger-like canines for puncturing and stabbing, and blade-like cheek-teeth called CARNASSIALS which can be used for cutting up meat.

The earliest of the two placental types of carnivores — the creodonts — began in the Cretaceous. They later diversified into the cat-like OXYAENIDS and the HYAENODONTS. Hyaenodonts included forms similar to the sabre-tooth, dog, cat, and hyaena, and so foreshadowed many of the evolutionary lines that developed in the true CARNIVORA. Only the hyaenodonts survived the Eocene. They filled the role of scavengers until the end of the Miocene, when the ancestors of the modern hyaena displaced them. The oxyaenids died out early because the animals which formed their prey were evolving rapidly, and gradually a greater intelligence was needed to hunt them. As the Carnivora had larger brains, they succeeded where the creodonts had failed.

The carnivores living during the Palaeocene were weasel-like MIACIDS. They died out in the Eocene, but gave rise to the CANOIDEA and FELOIDEA. Of the canoids, dogs (CANIDAE) and the weasels and their allies (MUSTELIDAE) were living at the transition from the Eocene to the Oligocene. The weasel family later diversified widely and the otter part branched to give the seals (PHOCIDAE). Dogs did not become as highly

evolution. Successful competitors are obviously better adapted to the prevailing conditions and they will therefore pass on to their offspring the necessary information for success.

Selenodont teeth have highly developed crescent cusps, and are typical of RUMINANTS. So when they are found in fossil form it is assumed that the animals to which they belonged were also ruminants, but this is by no means certain (*see* OREODONTS).

Semi-aquatic animals spend much of their life in water. Usually they are quite capable of existing on land, but competition and/or the need for protection leads to their occupying habitats on the margins of swamps and lake edges.

Semi-aquatic mammal, an otter

Semi-parasitic describes the way of life of an organism that obtains part of its food directly from another living animal or plant. The blood-sucking LAMPREYS are semi-parasites.

Seymouria is a medium-sized LABYRINTHODONT from the Lower Permian of Texas, North America, the skeleton of which exhibits a number of amphibian and reptilian characteristics. Because of this, many palaeontologists believed that the animal and its close relatives were 'link fossils' which were the true ancestors of the REPTILES. *Seymouria* was 75 mm long, sturdily built, and seemingly adapted to a more terrestrial life than other amphibians.

Seymouriamorphs were a group of medium-sized LABYRINTHODONT amphibians from the Permian period. They were among the most advanced forms of amphibian to walk on Earth and were specialized towards a land-based way of life. It was once thought that they were the true ancestors of the reptiles, but this is now doubted as they appear too late in the fossil record.

Short-jawed mastodonts appeared in the Miocene, and some of them later came to resemble the great straight-tusked elephants of the Pleistocene.

Smilodon was a large sabre-tooth cat that lived in the New World from Upper Pliocene until late Pleistocene times. Although many people assume that it preyed upon slow-moving

the cats we know today — the most advanced land carnivores. Hyaenas (HYAENIDAE) are the youngest feloids, and evolved rapidly from the civets in the late Miocene.

Apart from the placental animals described above, meat-eaters also evolved among the marsupials. The wolf-like BORHYAENA roamed parts of South America in the Miocene, to be succeeded in the Pliocene by the larger sabre-tooth 'cat' THYLACOSMILUS. This animal showed a remarkable likeness to later placental American sabre-toothed cats, such as SMILODON, and provides a good example of CONVERGENT EVOLUTION. The extinct THYLACOLEO of Australia was once described as a marsupial 'lion', but we now seem to think it was a specialized herbivore! Even so, there are small native 'cats' in Australia, as well as the larger Tasmanian devil

Left: *Homotherium* and *Smilodon* were placental sabre-tooth cats. The sabres of *Homotherium* were extremely flattened and the animal preyed on young elephants. *Thylacosmilus* was a marsupial equivalent of the sabre-tooth cats, and it is possible also that *Thylacoleo* was a large lion-sized marsupial carnivore.

Below: The dog-bear *Hemicyon*, and the big dire wolf of the Pleistocene are just 2 of the many extinct relatives of the dogs. Also shown is the rather dog-like marsupial, known as *Borhyaena*, which lived in the Miocene of South America, as well as *Thylacinus*, the so-called Tasmanian 'wolf'.

specialized, which accounts for the fact that they are now the most widely-spread carnivores. But several new families broke away from the canids — the extinct dog-bears (AMPHICYONIDAE), sea lions (OTARIIDAE), raccoons and pandas (PROCYONIDAE) and, most recent of all, bears (URSIDAE). It is interesting that some of the raccoons and bears are omnivorous, while pandas are strictly vegetarian.

The Old World civets (VIVERRIDAE) are the most primitive feloids, being little-modified descendants of the Eocene miacids. By late Eocene times cats (FELIDAE) had separated from the miacids and were modern in their appearance by the early Oligocene. Two cat types then developed. First there were large, heavy SABRE-TOOTH CATS which preyed on slow-moving animals. They vanished at the end of the Pleistocene, together with the animals they hunted. The other cats were swifter and more agile, and so able to chase faster prey. These are

mammals, *Smilodon* may have been a scavenger, using its fearsome CANINES to open and divide carcasses.
Stegosaurs were a group of plated dinosaurs. They were QUADRUPEDAL plant-eaters and are known from the Upper Jurassic of North America and Africa. *Stegosaurus* may have been able to control its body temperature by regulating the flow of blood into the large, bony plates set along its back.
Stem reptiles are those, other than the turtles, that have an ANAPSID skull. They are also known as the cotylosaurs and were, with the SYNAPSIDS, the prominent reptiles of the late Palaeozoic and early Mesozoic.

Subholostean link, *Acipenser*

Stereospondyls were a group of amphibians alive during the Upper Permian and Triassic. They were represented by animals such as *Rhinesuchus*. Stereospondyls were more advanced than their *Eryops*-like ancestors. They had a flatter skull than *Eryops* and their vertebrae had a distinctive ring-shaped centre. This marks the stereospondylus type of ARCH VERTEBRAE.
Subholostean describes a group of RAY-FINNED fishes that flourished during the early Mesozoic. In many ways they resemble the most primitive ray-fins – the PALAEONISCIDS – but several features (including a modification of the tail, fewer rays within the fins and thinner scales) indicate that they were more advanced. Included in the subholosteans are the deep-bodied *Dorypterus* and *Saurichthys* which resembles the freshwater pike. *Saurichthys* had a long body and its elongate mouth was lined with sharp teeth. Subholosteans are known from the Upper Carboniferous and are probably linked with the living sturgeon *Acipenser*.
'Survival of the fittest' refers to the ability of organisms to compete against others and survive. Their success may result from some small, seemingly insignificant character which is then inherited by successive generations.
Symmetrodonts were primitive MAMMALS, and take their name from the fact that their MOLARS had 3 pointed cusps, which in the crown view are arranged in a symmetrical triangle, rather than in a straight line.

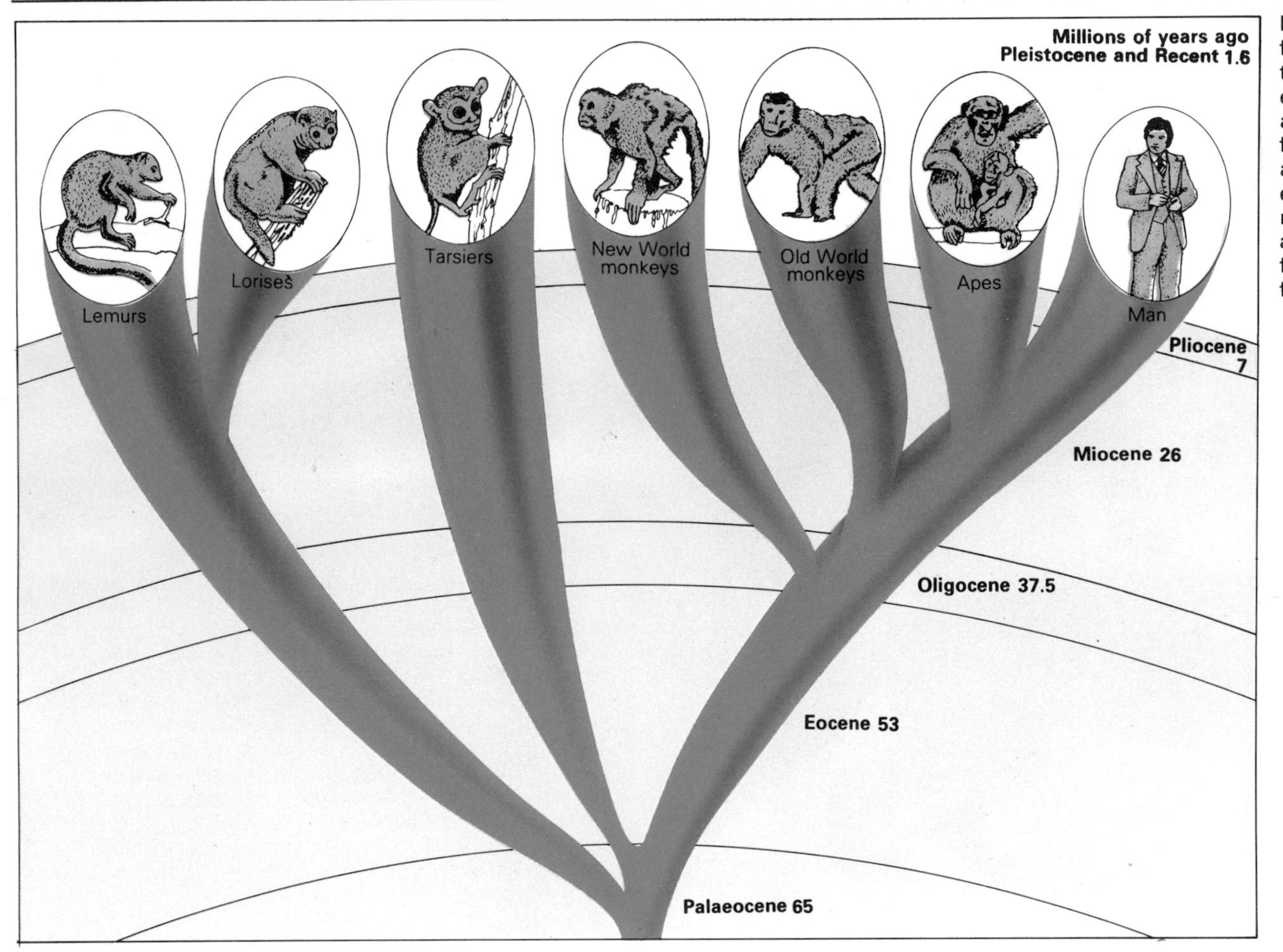

Left: The evolutionary 'tree' for the primates indicates that all the living forms have evolved separately from the ancestral stock. This means, for example, that the apes are not included in the evolutionary line that led to man. The forerunners of apes and men developed from an earlier common forebear.

and, if it still exists, the TASMANIAN WOLF or thylacine.

Primates

In the early Cainozoic primates became more fully adapted for a life in the trees. But as their bodies grew larger they could no longer walk along slender branches and twigs. Only by jumping or swinging from branch to branch could they move quickly through the tree-tops. This required longer, stronger arms, opposable first digits on the hands and feet, and nails to replace claws. Also, the eyes moved to the front of the head so as to give BINOCULAR VISION, which was vital in being able to judge distances to be jumped. Since a sense of smell was not very important to animals living in trees where they could eat insects and fruit, the primate nose and snout became smaller, resulting in a flatter face. Finally, a larger brain was also essential, for rapid co-ordination of movement and senses.

The earliest known primate, PURGATORIUS, arose from an ancestor similar to the tree-shrew in the late Cretaceous. By the mid-Palaeocene it had given rise to three new groups, typical of which was the squirrel-like PLESIADAPIS. They were in turn replaced in the Eocene by yet another three groups, which were without rodent-like characteristics and from which all modern primates descend. The PROSIMIANS, which include lemurs, lorises and tarsiers, were a separate group before the end of the Eocene. They are the most primitive primates, and lemurs, for example, still have longer legs than arms and a rather fox-like muzzle. The more advanced ANTHROPOIDS, to which monkeys, apes and men belong, appeared later. The OLD WORLD MONKEYS and NEW WORLD MONKEYS were certainly in existence by the Oligocene, and had diverged from the same stock. Forerunners of the apes appear in the Oligocene as well, apparently having a common origin with the monkeys.

Synapsid is the type of skull present in the PELYCOSAURS, mammal-like THERAPSIDS and mammals themselves. It is characterized by a single large opening on the temple at approximately the same level as the eye.

T **Taeniodonts** are an extinct North American ORDER dating from the Palaeocene and Eocene. They were an offshoot of INSECTIVOROUS animals with grinding teeth that indicate a plant-eating way of life. Some taeniodont forms were like heavy dogs.

Tasmanian wolf is probably extinct. Once common in Australia, its last traces were found in Tasmania, where some hair and footprints from this dog-like marsupial were discovered in the mid-1960s.

Tasmanian wolf

Tassel-finned fishes or crossopterygians are characterized by fleshy, lobed fins. They are represented today by the lungfishes and the coelacanth. Many palaeontologists believe that the group is closely linked with the evolution of amphibians.

Teleosts are the most successful group of living fishes. They are RAY-FINNED fishes and their internal skeleton is composed almost entirely of bone. The teleosts are very varied, the catfishes and seahorses representing lines of evolution outside those of the more typical salmon, trout and freshwater pike.

Tetrapod means '4-footed' and is a term used of the higher groups of vertebrates (amphibians, reptiles and mammals).

Thecodontians were early, primitive ARCHOSAUR reptiles which are known to be the ancestors of the dinosaurs, crocodiles and PTEROSAURS. They lived from the Upper Permian to the Upper Triassic.

Therapsids were a major order of SYNAPSID reptiles. Various families reveal a gradual evolution towards the mammals. The therapsids are also known as the mammal-like reptiles or paramammals.

The Miocene DRYOPITHECINES were undoubtedly apes. From them evolved two different HOMINOID lines. One led to today's gibbons and great apes; the other began about 14 million years ago with RAMAPITHECUS. The teeth of *Ramapithecus* show a departure from a fruit and leaf diet. Combined effects of a larger body and a reduced area of forested land resulting from changes in climate probably forced *Ramapithecus* to forage on the ground for more varied foods. Without any other form of defence, *Ramapithecus* may have used sticks and stones to ward off attacking predators. Whether the animal was itself an ape or a HOMINID is debatable, but there is little question that it was in the direct line of descent to the first true men. These appeared in Africa at least 3 million years ago. Early types like HOMO HABILIS and AUSTRALOPITHECUS gave way to HOMO ERECTUS, the forebear of modern man (HOMO SAPIENS) and his NEANDERTHAL relatives.

Left and above: While it is agreed that the family of man is linked to *Ramapithecus,* the precise evolutionary relationships between the early hominids is unclear. There seems little doubt, however, that modern men are descended from *Homo erectus.* Reconstructions of extinct groups of hominids are based mainly on fossil skulls and limb bones. From these it is often possible to estimate brain capacity, posture and movement. Evidence for the way of life of various early hominids is supplied by archaeological material found alongside their remains, and by the sediments in which they are preserved.

Thylacoleo was a lion-sized MARSUPIAL that roamed Australia during the Pleistocene. Its CARNASSIALS suggest that it was a CARNIVORE, but probably these shearing teeth were used to cut fruit.

Thylacosmilus was a South American MARSUPIAL which was as large as a tiger. It had enormously elongated, blade-like CANINES, and a deep flange of bone, the purpose of which was to protect these teeth in the lower jaw.

Tillodonts culminated in bear-sized, rodent-like animals in the Eocene and then died out.

Titanotheres were great beasts that stood over 2 metres high at the shoulder. Certain types, like *Brontotherium,* had Y- or V-shaped protuberances on their noses.

Traguloids are a superfamily of the ARTIODACTYLA and include the living tragulids, and the extinct hypertragulids, protoceratids and gelocids.

Triconodonts were primitive mammals whose fossils are identified by their MOLARS. Whereas most reptile teeth were conical or peg-like and single-rooted, early mammals had a more complex arrangement. The cheek teeth bore cusps, and the triconodonts had 3 in line, the central one being the largest.

Tunicates are marine animals that look like sponges. They have no pores, however, and the shapeless form is covered by a leathery skin. Some tunicates float, but others live in colonies on the sea-floor. Their larvae are tadpole-like, and the possession of a NOTOCHORD indicates that these animals are related to both AMPHIOXUS and the VERTEBRATES. Some experts believe that larvae of some ancient tunicates reached sexual maturity before they changed into sac-like adults, and that these larvae gave rise to a more advanced free-swimming animal which was the forerunner of the fishes.

U

Ungulates, or hoofed mammals, include almost all the larger plant-eating mammals.

Ursidae are members of the bear family. They first appeared in the Miocene and are unusual in the CARNIVORA

Panda

The influence of man

Towards the end of the last Ice Age (about 10,000 years ago), a wave of extinctions drastically reduced the variety of larger mammals on the different continents. In all roughly 200 genera disappeared. Disease and climatic change have been suggested as causes, but neither explanation is convincing. It seems most improbable that, even if stricken by disease, there were no immune individuals in the species concerned. As for possible climatic controls, it is true that there were major changes as glacial environments gave way to inter-glacial ones. Yet similar developments had happened repeatedly before in the Pleistocene without such adverse consequences. Moreover, the extinct camels and shasta sloths of North America should actually have benefited from the spread of arid lands.

An explanation which fits the facts better is that of PREHISTORIC OVERKILL. Nowhere do the main extinctions come before the spread of men with relatively advanced hunting techniques. In the scale and timing of losses, Africa and North America represent two extremes. In Africa the decline began about 60,000 years ago, with the development there of late ACHEULEAN hand-axe cultures. Around 30 per cent of Africa's mid-Pleistocene mammals vanished. In North America the decline began as recently as 11,000 years ago, and over the next 1,000 years nearly 70 per cent of North American mammals were eliminated! Again the decline coincided with the arrival in that continent of the first modern men. Extinctions on islands like Madagascar happened even later, well into historical times, for islands were the last places to be colonized by men.

Another feature which points to man's influence is that the animals which died out were without evolutionary replacements. The niches they occupied have not been filled, except by DOMESTICATED ANIMALS. Generally speaking, these are the only animals that have prospered since the Pleistocene, for the decrease in most wild animals continues. The need for GENETIC CONSERVATION is just one reason why some people view this loss with concern. Wild animals can provide genes for improving existing domesticated ones, as well as new candidates for domestication in the future.

Left and above: Some of the large mammals that were lost in the Pleistocene and Recent extinctions. *Diprotodon* has been described as a marsupial 'hippo', *Megatherium* was a giant ground sloth about 6 metres long, while the Irish 'elk' was in fact a giant deer.

Left: Domesticated animals often look quite different from their wild ancestors, both in colour, size and shape. In this case, the domesticated pig *(below)* is longer than the wild boar *(above)*, from which it is descended, and has a pinkish instead of a black-brown coat. The extra length was bred for brawn and pork, while the loss of natural colouring is not important, since a domesticated animal does not need a camouflaged coat to help it avoid predators.

---

in having a mixed or mainly plant diet. The giant panda is actually a primitive offshoot from the early bears.

V **Vertebrates** are, like graptolites and sea squirts, CHORDATE (*see page 26*) animals. Their essential characteristic is the possession of a strengthening rod of tissue, the NOTOCHORD. In the vertebrates the spinal cord is supported by a number of bony structures called vertebrae, and the notochord itself has been reduced, modified or lost.

Viverridae are a family comprising the civets, genets, mongooses and their kin. They are mainly spotted or striped forest-dwellers.

W **Woolly mammoth** ranged over all the arctic lands of the northern hemisphere in the late Pleistocene. It probably lived on the tundra during the summer, and retreated to the woodlands farther south in the winter.

X **Xylacanthus** is a RAT-FISH from the Lower Devonian. It was a long-bodied, lightly-armoured 'spiny-shark'. The body was probably covered with closely-fitting scales which had a concentric layered structure. The spines — 2 on the upper surface and several below — were probably long and pointed. The spiny-sharks ranged from the Silurian to the Carboniferous.

A mongoose

The Prehistoric World

Introduction

The Prehistoric World looks at plant and animal communities through the ages, showing how they have adapted to the surroundings in which they live. Such a study of the relationship between life and the environment is called ecology, and it stresses the way in which all living things are linked to each other and to the world about them, in habitats as different as the tropical rainforest and the arctic tundra. The fine balance of these relationships — between prey and predator, for example — can be upset by small changes in the environment or by large ones in climate or geography. **The Prehistoric World** shows that in the past such changes have had dire consequences, sometimes resulting in mass extinctions of entire species. Man's activities have added to the problems of maintaining an ecological balance, and today's concern to protect the environment goes hand in hand with our increasing knowledge of the need to preserve the variety and complexity of living species, so that this balance will not be upset beyond repair.

Plants and animals today, as in the past, belong to communities which have their own structure and web of relationships. The community will influence, and be influenced by, the course of evolution among its individual members.

Evolution of Communities

COMMUNITIES of living things function as part of an ECOSYSTEM, in which they interact among themselves and with their physical setting, or habitat. The ecosystem is organized into PRODUCERS, CONSUMERS and DECOMPOSERS. Producers are green plants, which make food by PHOTOSYNTHESIS. This involves converting light energy from the Sun into chemical energy. Some is then used by plants in RESPIRATION for their own growth and maintenance, and is lost as heat. PRIMARY CONSUMERS (plant-eating animals, or HERBIVORES) usually consume less than 20 per cent of an ecosystem's plant matter. The rest dies and decomposes, thereby releasing 'raw materials' which can be re-used by the green plants to synthesize more food. Only about 10 per cent of the energy which herbivores gain from plants is stored as new tissue, for the animal also uses much of it in respiration. The same holds for those animals which consume the herbivores (the SECONDARY CONSUMERS or meat-eating animals) and for the secondary consumers and the animals which consume them (TERTIARY CONSUMERS or top CARNIVORES). In short, there is progressively less energy available at each TROPHIC level in the ecosystem. This is why ecosystem communities have a PYRAMID STRUCTURE, with more plants than herbivores, and more herbivores than carnivores. For example, if a herbivore found enough food in 100 square metres, a carnivore of similar size would need roughly 1,000 square metres in which to live, and a top carnivore about 10,000 square metres. For this reason animals such as lions are less common than animals such as zebras.

Marine food chains

The amount and type of PRIMARY PRODUCTION in an ecosystem reflects on the nature of its animal communities. Most primary production in the world's oceans is created by single-celled green

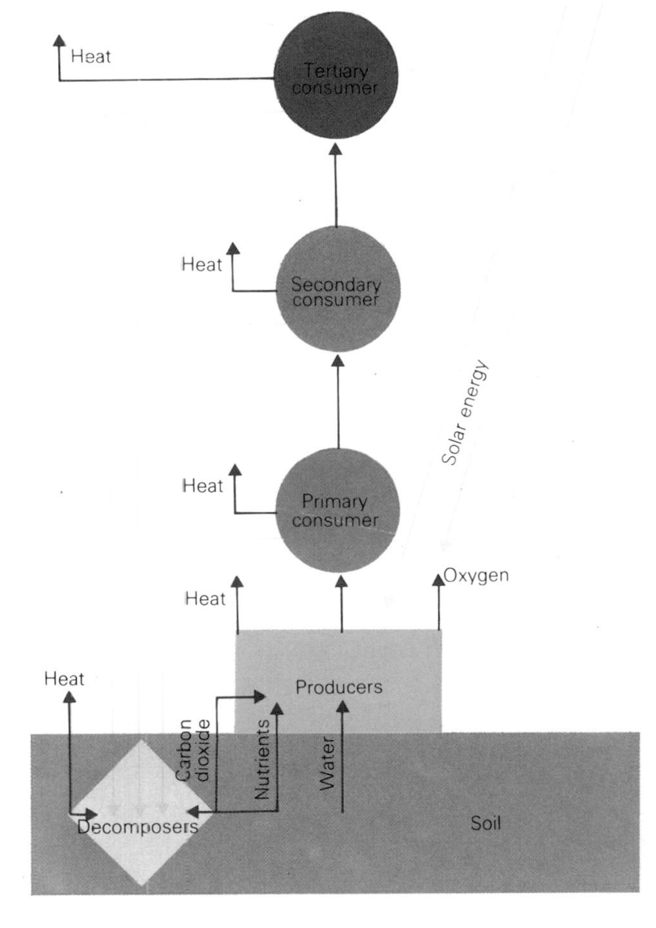

Right: In this simplified model of energy flow in an ecosystem the relationships described applied in the past as in the present. The plants or producers use solar energy to convert raw materials into food. Some of the energy captured by the plant is lost as heat, but some of it is also accounted for by the primary consumers or herbivores. Again these lose some of the energy as heat, and part of it is in turn accounted for by the secondary consumers or carnivores. Very little food energy is therefore available to the tertiary consumers or top carnivores. The remains of the plants and animals are finally decomposed, to provide the nutrients which are necessary for the producers to grow.

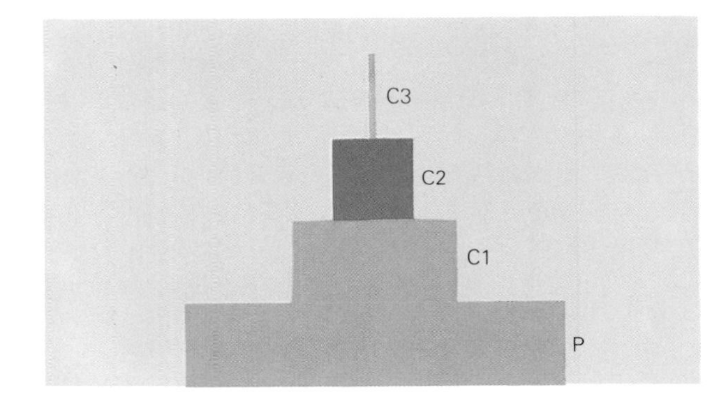

Right: From the producer to the consumer stage there is a steady loss of energy in an ecosystem. Hence there are more producers (**P**) than primary consumers or herbivores (**C1**) and more primary consumers than secondary consumers or carnivores (**C2**). Inevitably there are few top carnivores (**C3**). There will thus tend to be more herbivore than carnivore fossils.

Reference

A

Acidic peats form wherever the litter of moorland or heathland vegetation decomposes or breaks down at a slower rate than that at which it accumulates. Such vegetation contains little nutrient for the micro-organisms that bring about decomposition, and their numbers are further reduced by very wet conditions. So valley basins and moorland plateaus are ideal for their formation.

Acidic peat area

B

Benthic comes from *benthos*, 'bottom dwellers', and describes creatures that live on or in sea-floor sediments. They include scavengers — which consume carcasses or carrion — as well as creatures that feed by filtering organic debris from seawater or sea-floor sediments.

Biomass is the total weight of living matter in part of an organism, population or ECOSYSTEM. It is usually given in terms of dry matter per unit area (for example, kilograms per hectare or grams per square metre). In a mature Amazon RAINFOREST, however, there may be a plant biomass of 1,100 metric tonnes growing on every 10,000 square metres of land.

C

Carnivores are flesh-eaters.

Communities are groups of organisms living in particular areas. Each community occupies a common area, and the individual organisms are usually related by FOOD CHAINS. Often a community is named after 1 or 2 of its most obvious or numerous species, such as a spruce-fir community or a barnacle-mussel community. Or it may be named from the habitat, as in a salt-marsh community.

Consumers are organisms which satisfy their energy and food needs by eating other living organisms — plants or animals, or both.

Cretaceous is the period of geological time which lasted from 136 until 65 million years ago. Its name comes from the Latin word *creta*, which means chalk. Great thicknesses of chalk were deposited in the seas during Upper Cretaceous times.

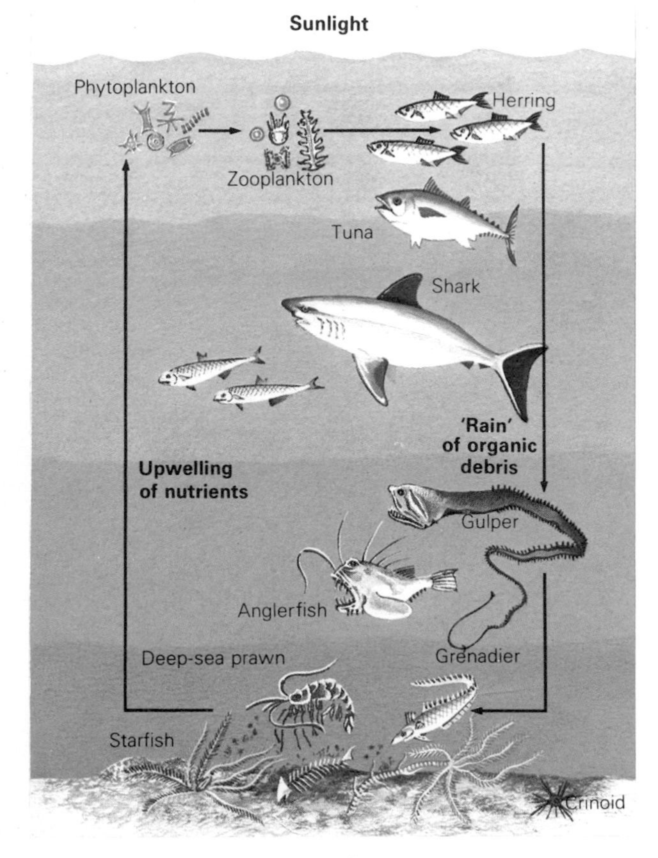

Left: In the oceans energy is produced at the primary level by the microscopic floating plants or phytoplankton. These are generally consumed by small zooplankton, which in turn form a food supply for small fish. These are preyed upon by still larger fish, such as the shark. The rain of debris from the surface waters supports a bottom-feeding food chain. Oceanic upwellings supply nutrients from the depths to the sunlit surface-waters, where they are used by the phytoplankton.

algae, or PHYTOPLANKTON, which float in the sunlit surface waters. These microscopic plants are generally too small and dispersed to be eaten directly by large animals. So there are few strictly herbivorous sea creatures equivalent to the deer, cattle or horses on land. The phytoplankton are first 'concentrated' by floating animals or ZOOPLANKTON. These extremely varied creatures include copepods — the 'insects' of the sea — the shrimp-like krill, and jellyfish. Herbivorous zooplankton are themselves mainly microscopic and are preyed upon by larger zooplankton. These in turn are consumed by smaller fish and squid which are then eaten by various larger carnivores. Such free-swimming animals form the NEKTON. As four levels of consumers often depend finally on the phytoplankton, marine FOOD CHAINS tend to be longer than their counterparts on land. But there are exceptions. For example, herrings and herring-like fish partly live directly on phytoplankton, which explains why these fish are comparatively numerous. In addition to life in the PELAGIC zone, a fine rain of organic debris and occasional carcasses falls to the ocean floor and provides food for several BENTHIC food chains. Among creatures which live on such matter are FILTER-FEEDERS (*see page 82*) like the sea lilies (crinoids), glass sponges and lamp shells (brachiopods), as well as scavenging fish. Bacteria in sediments on the ocean floor also break down organic matter, and the products released in this decomposition are carried by upwelling coastal currents into the surface waters, where they serve as nutrients for the phytoplankton.

Grasslands and forest

Of land environments, grassland resembles the marine ecosystem in that much of its primary production can be consumed. However, since grasses and other herbaceous plants are large compared with phytoplankton, they can be grazed directly by sizeable animals. Vast herds of large herbivores, together with the carnivores and scavengers dependent on them, are therefore often to be found on some of the great plainlands of the world. The greatest diversity of animals is in the SAVANNA. Here scattered trees give partial shade at ground-level, which promotes faster photosynthesis and thus a more ample food

Below: The African savanna, showing marabou storks and zebras at a waterhole. Trees dot the grassland, thus providing food for browsing animals and partial shade which helps the grasses to photosynthesize more efficiently. The presence of trees on tropical grasslands therefore permits a greater diversity of animal life.

D **Death assemblage** is a FOSSIL ASSEMBLAGE made up entirely of species that were carried from the environment in which they lived as a LIFE ASSEMBLAGE. Death assemblages may have been fossilized in the same environment as the living community, or may have accumulated in an entirely different one. It is even possible for a death assemblage of fossils to come from older rocks. Fossils of organisms that were transported after death often show signs of breakage, wear, or disarticulation, where the valves of shells, or skeleton bones, become separated. Death assemblages may also have been sorted according to size by sea or river currents.

Decomposers are organisms, such as bacteria and fungi, which obtain food by breaking down the dead remains and waste of plants and animals. The simple end-products released by such decomposition provide raw materials for new plant growth.

E **Ecological niches** may be identified by the status or position of the organisms which occupy them. For instance, we can speak of a broad 'grazing niche', although it may contain many kinds of animals living off the various herbaceous plants in any particular grassland. On the other hand, insects which live in the crevices of bark or in the fur of animals are exploiting different and 'narrower' niches.

Parasitic fly on bird

Ecological saturation is reached when the diversity of ECOLOGICAL NICHES reaches a maximum for any given environment. As new organisms evolve over time, they help create more niches for yet further new organisms to exploit. Thus ecological saturation in young ECOSYSTEMS will usually involve less diversity than in older ones.

Ecology is the study of the relationships of organisms to each other and to their physical environment. The name comes from the Greek word *oikos*, meaning 'home'. Studies are made of the ecology of single organisms, of groups of individuals (or populations) and of populations of several kinds of organisms. This third level approximately corresponds to the ECOSYSTEM. The basic relationships disco-

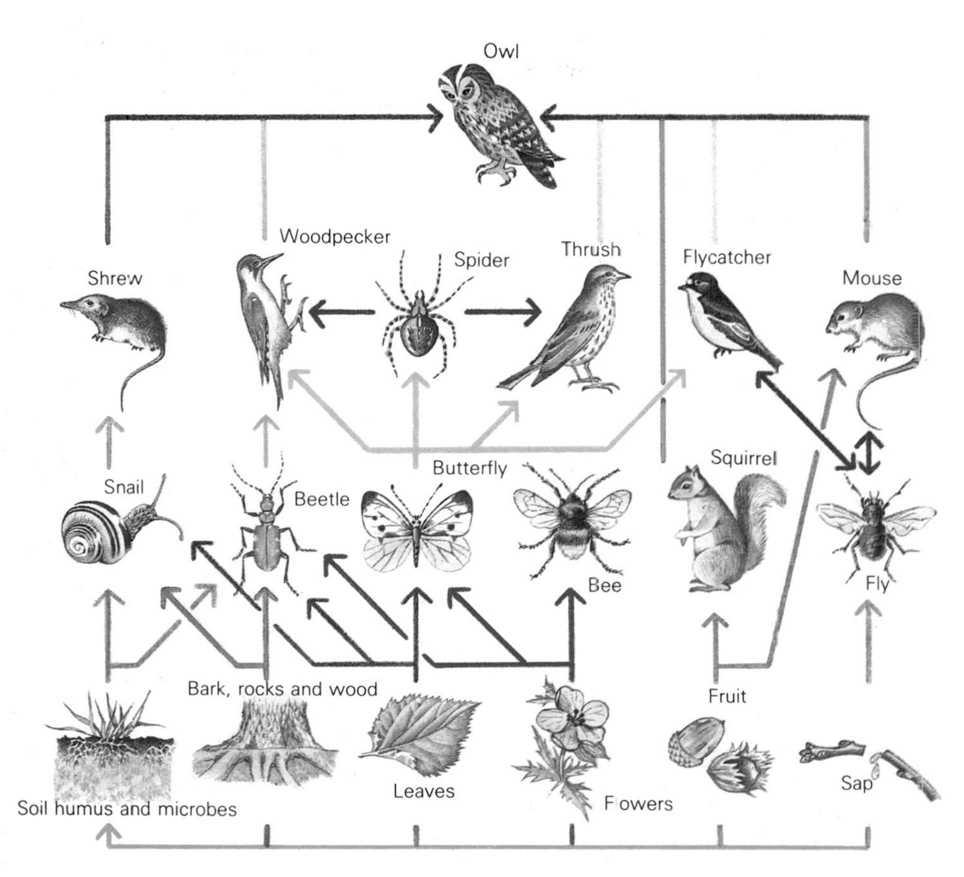

supply. The foliage of the trees, moreover, is eaten by browsing animals.

A forest ecosystem is the most productive of all, although much of its primary production is stored in forms that cannot be eaten, such as wood and bark. Consequently animal populations on the forest floor are sparse, being mainly scattered individuals or small groups. The larger the animal, the smaller the group; very large animals are therefore exceptional. Not surprisingly, perhaps, animals are more numerous in the tree-tops, where insects, birds and mammals, together with amphibians and reptiles, are usually to be found in warmer climates. Insects are the chief consumers of leaves, and so form a key link with higher levels of the food chain. But the primary production accounted for by consumers is small. Far more is eventually used by decomposers, particularly fungi and bacteria. These live mainly in the soil, in immense variety and staggering numbers. By their 'processing' of fallen leaves and dead timber, vital plant nutrients are returned to the soil.

Above: A greatly simplified food-web for a deciduous broad-leaved forest. The plants support a variety of insects, snails and small mammals like squirrels. Some of these are preyed upon by spiders and birds, while the owl represents the tertiary consumer or top carnivore.

Right: Beech woodland in the New Forest, England, during autumn. Although woodlands are the most productive and complex of all ecosystems, much of the plant matter is inedible. There are therefore no herds of large animals such as live on grasslands.

The forest ecosystem furnishes a bewildering array of ECOLOGICAL NICHES, so that while the total animal BIOMASS is relatively small, its variety is great. Indeed the food chains are connected in extremely complex FOOD WEBS. The relationships between predator and prey which make up food webs are the chief means by which plant and animal populations are naturally regulated at stable numbers. The balance is delicate, and any change in the frequency of one group of plants or animals could lead to a major change in the whole ecosystem. This often happened in the past after a species died out or a new one emerged. Man's arrival greatly speeded up the rate of such loss and addition, with corresponding effects on the delicate stable balance of nature.

Time and the ecosystem

The character of an ecosystem is influenced by climate and physical setting, but also by the length of time over which it has existed. This can best be illustrated by the RAINFOREST and the TUNDRA, respectively the oldest and youngest of the Earth's ecosystems.

Rainforests are found in the humid, tropical lowlands of Central and South America, Africa,

vered among living organisms are used to analyse fossil plant and animal COMMUNITIES in the study called palaeoecology.

Ecosystem is a functional, living unit. It is characterized by a set of organisms and their interactions, as well as the physical setting, or habitat, which the organisms influence and are influenced by. Since these essential characteristics are the same (regardless of scale) we can think of a cow's stomach or a garden pond as ecosystems. At the other extreme, an ocean — or the world itself — are perfectly good examples of ecosystems.

Ecosystem, a garden pond

Fauna is a term which describes the animals of any given area at a point in time. Sometimes it is used in a narrower sense, when referring to the fish fauna or mammalian fauna of an area. It may also apply to all (or to a particular group) of the fossil animals preserved in a sequence of rocks. For example, PALAEONTOLOGISTS may refer to the ammonite faunas of the Lower Jurassic rocks.

Food chain is the flow of energy and nutrients which passes from plants to the HERBIVORES which consume them and on to the CARNIVORES which consume the herbivores. In other words, it is a sequence or 'chain' of organisms, each of which feeds on the preceding one. In reality the picture is complicated by organisms which eat both plants and animals (omnivores) and by scavengers, which live off carrion.

Food webs are made up of interlocking FOOD CHAINS. A single food web corresponds to the predator and prey relationships found in part or all of an ECOSYSTEM. The more diverse the ecosystem, the more complex will be the food web.

Fossil assemblages are groups of fossils composed of one or more types of organisms. Members of an assemblage are found together in a layer or layers of rock. The assemblage will have either the same mix of species throughout, or will vary uniformly in the species from which it is composed. Above, below and sideways, an assemblage will give way to rocks without fossils or to other fossil assemblages. One assemblage therefore records a specific history of ECOLOGY and preservation.

Right: The great diversity of life in the rainforest is demonstrated by the fact that in the Asiatic rainforest there are 6 different types of gliding animals. Among them are the colugo, giant flying squirrel, flying gecko, flying frog and flying snake. The gecko is a flying lizard, as is the flying draco. The latter is not shown.

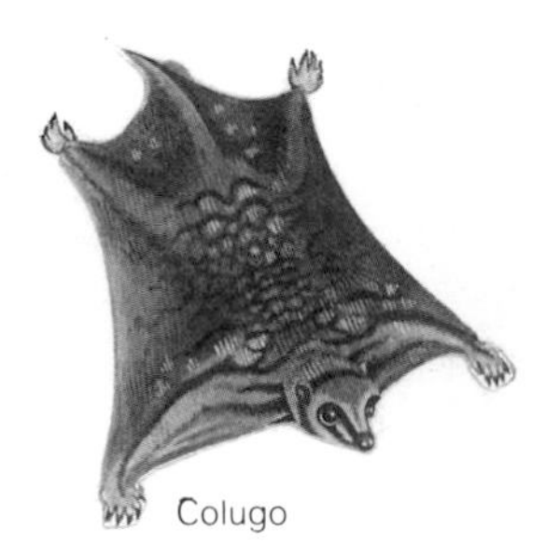

Left: Rainforest in Sarawak, eastern Malaysia, is a 'living museum'. Partly through climate and partly because of a long history of environmental stability, the rainforest is the most productive and diverse of all the Earth's ecosystem types.

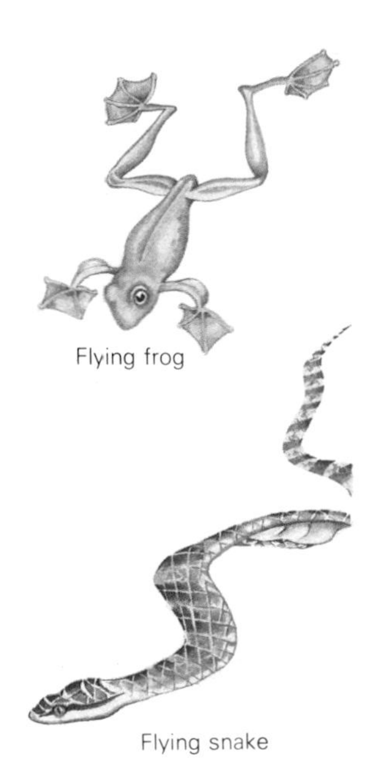

South-East Asia and the Indonesian islands. The climate is typically warm and moist, without marked seasonal contrasts. From fossil evidence we know that in general appearance and character the rainforest has existed since CRETACEOUS times, which ended 65 million years ago. Its spectacular variety of plants and animals makes it the most complex ecosystem on Earth. An estimated 30,000 different species of flowering plants grow in Indonesia alone, of which 3,000 are trees. (About 2,000 plant species overall grow in Britain.) Similarly there are nearly 300 species of land mammals in Tanzania, compared with nearly 50 in Britain.

One reason for this great diversity of life is that the rainforest is evergreen, with continual flowering and fruiting. Nor is animal reproduction restricted to a particular season, since the supply of plant food is constant. More generations can therefore be produced each year than in areas with less tolerant climates. All other things being equal, this means that new species can evolve at a faster rate in the rainforest than elsewhere. Just as important, perhaps, is the fact that the rainforest environment has been more or less stable for well over 60 million years. No dramatic change and no serious 'weeding out' of older evolutionary lines have meant that species tend to accumulate. Over the millennia they have become more specialized as they adapted to ever-narrower niches. The rainforest has been described as a 'living museum' and in some respects this description is apt.

The tundra

Tundra lies to the north of the coniferous forests of North America and Eurasia. It is an area of arctic climates, with marked seasonal contrasts. Because of the climatic rigours, vegetation is dominated by sedges, rushes, grasses, mosses and lichens, and is often very sparse. As the amount and variety of plant foods are limited, animals are correspondingly fewer and less diverse. Many animals actually leave the tundra in winter, when food is most scarce. Some animal populations also undergo marked fluctuations. The lemming, for instance, has a population 'boom', followed by a 'crash', every fourth year,

---

H **Herbivores** live entirely or almost entirely on a diet of plant food.

I **Isotopes** of the same element have the same number of protons (positively charged particles) but a different number of neutrons (particles neither positively nor negatively charged).

Cows are herbivores

L **Lake muds** accumulate at the bottom of lakes. They are composed of particles washed into lakes by rivers and streams, as well as organic debris from plants and animals that live in and around the lakes. Lake muds can thus provide an historical record of an individual lake and its surrounding area over thousands of years.

Life assemblages of fossils are composed entirely of species that belonged to a single COMMUNITY, preserved in the environment where they lived. Life assemblages are identified by such clues as fossils of organisms still in their life positions, or those which show no signs of damage or wear. Fossil coral reefs or traces of an animal's track are especially useful in this respect. Life assemblages often occur following the rapid burial of a community by a blanket of sediment.

M **Mesozoic** is an era of geological time which lasted from 225 to 65 million years ago. It is otherwise known as the 'Age of Reptiles' or the 'Age of Middle Life' and includes the Triassic (which began about 225 million years ago), Jurassic (which started about 190 million years ago) and finally the Cretaceous (which started about 136 million years ago) periods.

Mixed death assemblages are death assemblages of fossil organisms which lived in 2 or more different environments. In effect, the remains of organisms which came from various habitats were brought together (by the action of sea currents, for example) before they became fossilized.

as to some extent do the foxes and owls that prey upon it. Such fluctuations partly reflect the few species and resulting simple food chains.

Yet the harsh climate may not entirely explain the simple, unstable nature of the tundra ecosystem. Some species have adapted successfully to this environment, and before the late PLEISTOCENE the arctic FAUNA was much richer, with animals such as the woolly mammoth and woolly rhinoceros. If some species have succeeded in colonizing the tundra, why not more? Perhaps the answer is that the tundra ecosystem is very young. It has suffered recurrent glaciation in the 1,600,000 years since the Pleistocene Ice Age began, the last continental ice-sheet having disappeared just 10,000 years ago. It seems likely that this has not been long enough for ECOLOGICAL SATURATION to occur. Some experts even argue that the growth of ecological diversity in the tundra ecosystem is in its infancy.

Clues to the past

We are able to interpret what PALAEOENVIRONMENTS and their associated plant and animal communities were like from studying their FOSSIL ASSEMBLAGES and the rocks in which these are found. Great care is needed when interpreting traces of preserved organisms, partly because the fossil record is incomplete and often misleading, and partly because we can never know the precise ECOLOGY of organisms which are now extinct. Fossils are only a sample of former populations, and it is sometimes difficult to tell if they belong to different populations, or whether they are variations within the same one.

The interpretation has to start with individual fossils. Where a fossilized animal or plant has a close relative living today, we have some idea of the environment in which the ancestor lived. Obvious examples are provided by the sea urchins, brachiopods, corals and cephalopods. They are all marine creatures, and so it is reasonable to accept that the area where their fossils are found was once under water. Even where there are no living representatives, or where the relationship between fossil and living

Above: Caribou on the tundra around Prudhoe Bay, Alaska. Although it looks similar to grassland, the tundra has less primary production and so supports fewer animals. Because the arctic weather is so severe, plants can photosynthesize for only a short period. The tundra is the youngest of the world's ecosystems.

Left: Trumpeter swans and caribou (in Eurasia, the caribou are called reindeer) return to the tundra in the summer, though the lynx is a winter visitor. The wolf preys in packs on the caribou. The lemming lives all year round on the tundra, and is a prime source of food for the snowy owl.

N **Nekton** are marine animals which move by swimming. Herrings, sharks and whales all belong to the nekton. Since they live in water above the sea-floor sediments, nektonic organisms are also PELAGIC.

O **Old Red Sandstone** is a rock laid down in the Devonian period, in large rivers and lakes. However, much of it is neither red nor sandstone.

P **Palaeoenvironments** are ancient environments, those that existed in the geological past. Many are recorded in successions of rock strata, and may be reconstructed from the nature of the rocks themselves, and from any fossils they contain. Reconstructions of this kind are based on an understanding of present-day environments. But it should be stressed that numerous past environments cannot be closely matched with any modern ones, so their real character will always be the subject of speculation.

Mackerel-shark, a nektonic animal

Palaeontologist is a geologist who studies the remains – or fossils – of prehistoric plants and animals found in sedimentary rocks (rocks comprised of ancient sediments). Such studies reveal a great deal about evolutionary changes in organisms through time. They are also helpful in identifying rock formations, particularly those in which fossil fuels such as oil and coal occur. Lastly, they tell as much about the environments in which the rocks themselves were laid down.

Palaeozoic is an era of geological time between 570 and 225 million years ago. It was the era of 'ancient' life, and included 6 geological periods: the Cambrian (570 million years ago); Ordovician (500 million years ago); Silurian (430 million years ago); Devonian (395 million years ago); Carboniferous (345 million years ago) and Permian (280 million years ago).

Pelagic describes the organisms that live in sea water, as opposed to those

Above: From the fossils found at Olduvai Gorge, Tanzania, we can reconstruct this scene. *Homo erectus* (**1**) approaches the lake. Hoe-tuskers *Deinotherium* (**7**), hippopotamuses (**8**) and giant baboons (**6**) are by the lake edge. A short-antlered giraffe *Libytherium* (**2**) and large relative of the bush pig *Tapinochoerus* (**5**) are in the foreground, with 3-toed horses *Hipparion* (**4**) and zebra-like animals (**3**) behind. Most of these animals are now extinct.

Left: Bed I at Olduvai Gorge, Tanzania. The Gorge's stratified sediments are about 90 metres thick, and formed in and around an ancient lake. The river which cut the Gorge revealed these sediments. Bed I is the oldest and in 1959 a hominid skull, together with pebble tools of the 'Oldowan industry', was discovered there. The skull was that of a robust australopithecine, but the tools were made by *Homo habilis.*

creature is remote, fossils may still denote a particular environment. For example, TRILOBITES (*see page 95*) died out at the end of the PALAEOZOIC, yet the fossils with which they are found are always of marine organisms, so there is little doubt that they too were sea creatures. Of course, we can make mistakes in drawing conclusions of this kind, for the remains of many organisms will have been carried away from their original habitats before being fossilized. Many land plants, for instance, are carried to the sea by rivers and become fossilized in marine sediments. Recognizing the importance of such redistribution, PALAEONTOLOGISTS divide fossilized remains into LIFE ASSEMBLAGES, DEATH ASSEMBLAGES and MIXED DEATH ASSEMBLAGES.

To make more detailed reconstructions of ancient communities we need to understand more about the ecology of fossils. Again we can largely assume this from the known ecology of their living descendants. Further information generally comes from studying the SEDIMENTOLOGY of rocks in which fossils occur, and in some cases from the composition and structure of the fossils themselves. A number of examples will illustrate these points.

which live on or in the sediments on the sea floor. They include the swimming NEKTON, and the PLANKTON (*see page 89*) organisms that are mainly transported by waves and currents.

Photosynthesis is a process powered by sunlight. With the aid of their green pigment – chlorophyll – plants produce foods such as glucose from simple raw materials such as carbon dioxide and water.

Phytoplankton are floating plants, most of which are microscopic and single-celled ALGAE (*see page 75*). Macroscopic phytoplankton are restricted to the seaweeds, some of which, like the Sargasso weed, are quite large. To resist sinking, many of the microscopic plankton contain air bubbles or droplets of oil, while others have developed long spines or similar projections. The name plankton comes from a Greek word meaning 'wanderer'.

Pleistocene is the geological epoch which began about 1.6 million years ago and finished about 8000 BC. It coincided with cycles of glacial and inter-glacial climates. Indeed, the 'post-glacial' epoch in which we live is also a typical inter-glacial. Our post-glacial epoch is referred to as the Holocene or Recent, and together with the Pleistocene makes up the Quaternary period.

Pollen analysis is also known as palynology, and involves sampling, identifying and counting fossil pollen grains. The information gained is used to reconstruct past vegetation, focusing especially on changes through time. Many sub-divisions of the PLEISTOCENE in north-west Europe are based on palynological evidence. However, at least some of these sub-divisions are now thought to be wrong, not through any error of identification, but through problems in interpreting the information.

Primary consumers obtain their food directly from green plants. They are also known as HERBIVORES.

Primary production results from plants converting light energy into chemical energy, or food. Such production can be measured as dry weights of organic matter per unit area of ground per unit of time. An example is grams per square metre per year.

Producer is an organism capable of PRIMARY PRODUCTION; in other words, a plant.

Plants are primary producers

Modern coral reefs are found only in relatively shallow water in warm seas, and as they resemble MESOZOIC and TERTIARY reefs so closely, we presume that fossil reefs of these ages developed in similar conditions. More subtle records of water temperature are found in the calcite shells of some marine creatures. As the shell grows, two ISOTOPES of oxygen (0^{16} and 0^{18}) are incorporated into the calcite. The ratio of 0^{16} to 0^{18} depends on temperature, there being more 0^{18} as the temperature rises. By measuring the amounts of both isotopes in fossil shells we can estimate sea temperatures in ancient times fairly accurately. However, this cannot be done if the calcite has been altered by chemical change, which is often the case in very old rocks.

To show how the structure of fossils is used in reconstructing palaeoenvironments, we may mention the lack of growth-rings in *Cordaites*, an extinct Palaeozoic tree. Tree-rings develop through seasonal alterations of fast and slow growth, and the fact that *Cordaites* has none suggests that it grew in uniformly warm, humid conditions. Studying sedimentology is especially helpful where fossil groups which had considerably varied ecological requirements have living descendants. Fish fall into this category, for they may live in the sea, in fresh water, or in both. Hence many OLD RED SANDSTONE fish of the Devonian period (395–345 million years ago) are regarded as freshwater types, from the characteristics of the sandstone and because they are never found together with fossils that are undoubtedly marine.

Studying pollen

At certain times of the year plants produce a veritable rain of pollen and spores. These can be preserved in ACIDIC PEATS and LAKE MUDS, so that pollen and spores fossilized at different levels in such deposits give a fairly full record of the vegetation growing at the time when those levels were forming. For POLLEN ANALYSIS samples of peat and lake muds are taken at various depths. The fossil pollen and spores are then extracted by chemical treatments which destroy the material in which they are preserved. The grains are mounted on slides and inspected under powerful microscopes where it is usually possible for the scientist to identify the genus or species of the plant.

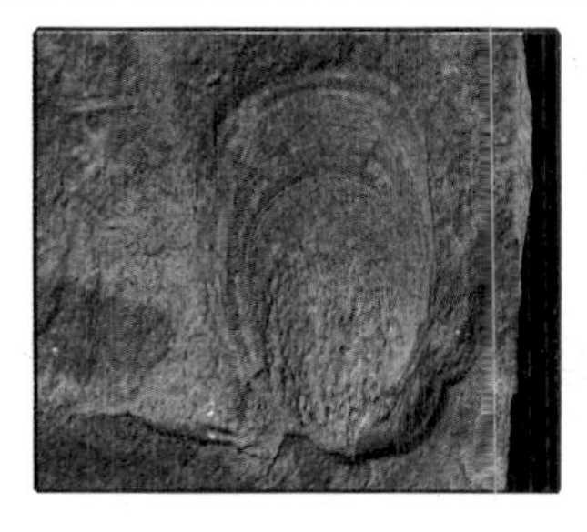

Above: *Lingulella* lived from the Cambrian to the Middle Ordovician. It appears similar to the modern *Lingula* (**below**).

Pollen diagrams are used to show the results. Every major species is represented by a graph which traces its importance at the depths sampled, and so changes in vegetation through time are revealed. Pollen diagrams from the northern hemisphere show that during the glacial stages of the Pleistocene, treeless tundras extended much farther south than at present. Between glacial periods, however, the diagrams reveal a succession of vegetation types. In north-west Europe, for example, each inter-glacial period opened with the spread of birch and pine woodland, which was in turn replaced by a forest

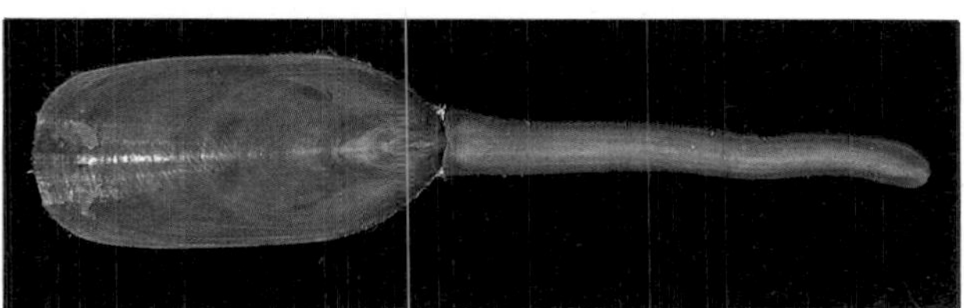

Left: Today the primitive inarticulate brachiopod *Lingula* is found in Japanese waters where it burrows in sands and muds, anchored by its worm-like pedicle (stalk). The earliest types are found in Silurian rocks.

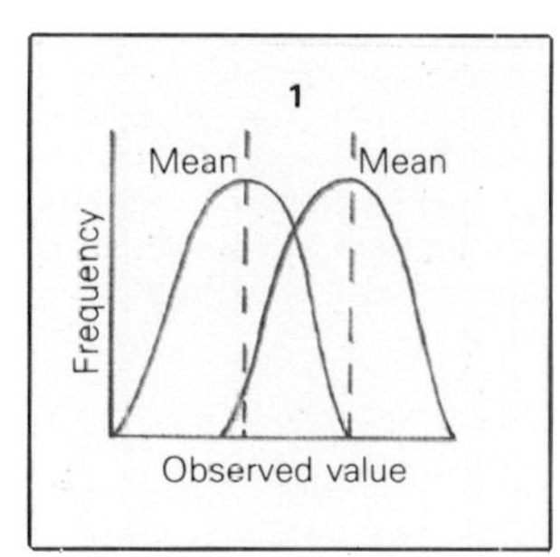

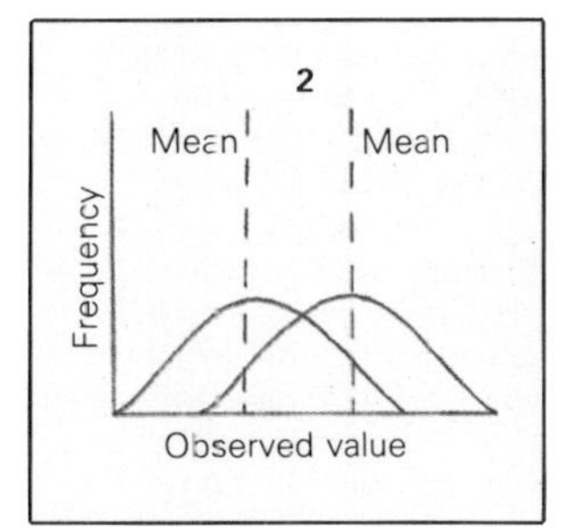

Left: Data plotted on a graph gives information and shows how accurate it is likely to be. Here, the shell lengths of 4 samples have been plotted 2 in **1** and 2 in **2**. The large scatter of values shown in **2** indicates that the difficulty in mean length may be due to chance, whereas **1** may reflect a true difference in mean length.

Left: Articulated shells of the bivalve *Donax vittatus*.

Right: Wave action eventually disarticulates and breaks up the shells of dead marine organisms to produce the kind of debris shown here. This assortment of shelly material, gravel and sand is found on beaches at high-tide marks.

Pyramid structure describes the relationship between organisms in a FOOD CHAIN. The 'pyramid of numbers' describes the normal pattern where in a given area there are many more plants than HERBIVORES, and many more herbivores than CARNIVORES, especially TOP CARNIVORES. The 'pyramid of BIOMASS' has a similar pattern, but is based on the dry weights of the organisms concerned, instead of their numbers.

R **Rainforest** accounts for about 16% of the world's broad-leaved forest vegetation, although in parts of the tropics it is being cleared at an increasing rate. So dependent on each other are many of its plants and animals that even minute disturbance or disruption can have significant effects.

Respiration occurs in all living cells. It is the process by which organic molecules — carbohydrates, fats and proteins — are broken down to yield energy. When oxygen is used to bring about the breakdown, chemical energy and heat are released. This is aerobic respiration, in which the waste products are carbon dioxide and water. Anaerobic respiration or fermentation is less efficient and yields less energy, giving alcohol and carbon dioxide as waste.

S **Savanna** is tropical grassland which typically has varying amounts of open woody vegetation and a scatter of trees. In recent years many of the large savanna HERBIVORES and their dependent CARNIVORES have been greatly, sometimes catastrophically, reduced in numbers.

Secondary consumers gain their food indirectly from green plants by eating other animals. They are also known as CARNIVORES.

Weasel, a secondary consumer

Sedimentology is the study of rocks which have formed from deposits of sediment, although the term is also used when referring to characteristics of such rocks. These include grain size and shape, their minerals, small-scale fabric and larger-scale structures. Properties of this sort provide important clues for establishing the PALAEOENVIRONMENTS in which a rock was laid down. Indeed if a rock has no fossils, sedimentological analysis may be the only way to establish the environment in which it was laid down.

Above: Great clouds of pollen and spores are often produced by plants, and these fall like rain from the atmosphere. Most of the grains decompose in the soil, but where they fall into lakes, marshes or bogs they are often preserved in sediment. The environment shown here is typical of one which would preserve pollen.

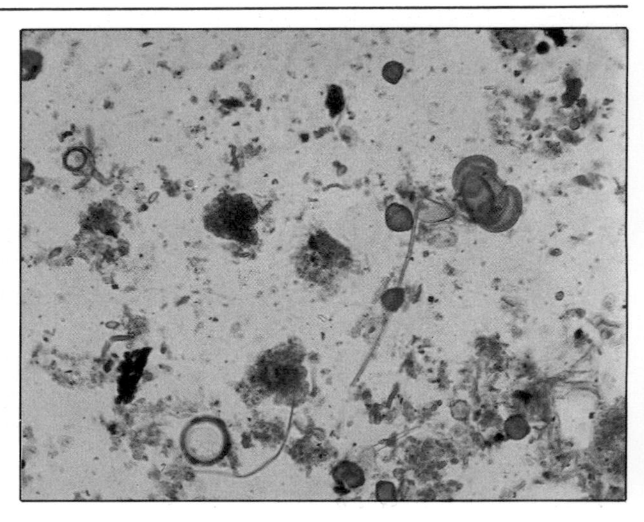

Above right: Grains of fossil pollen, stained with a red dye, as seen under the microscope. The large grain at the top right is that of a Scots pine; the others are mainly of birch. The brownish material in the slide is the remains of the peat in which the pollen grains were preserved.

Below: Diagrams of tree pollen taken from Ice Age and post-glacial sediments of a lake in upland Britain. The sediments were sampled at different depths, and the tree pollen identified at each depth is shown as a percentage of all the tree pollen present. In the late glacial and early post-glacial periods, birch and pine were the dominant trees. But as the present inter-glacial developed, elm and oak began to replace them. About 5500 BC the climate was warm and moist and this is reflected by the spread of alder and lime into the woods of upland Britain. The arrival of Neolithic farmers coincides with a decline in elm pollen, as this tree was lopped for fodder, and felled to cultivate the fertile soils on which it grew. As the clearings were abandoned, trees with wind-blown seeds quickly colonized them, and this accounts for the appearance of significant amounts of ash pollen and the increase in birch pollen figuring in the diagrams.

Birch Pine Elm Oak Lime Alder Ash
Water
Coarse lake mud
Fine lake mud
Fine lake mud
Clay
Silty mud
0 20 40 60 100 0 20 40 0 20 0 20 40 5 0 20 40 60 5

of mixed deciduous hardwood trees. As the climate and soil deteriorated, forest gave way to coniferous woodland once more, and then eventually changed to heathland as the next glaciation approached.

Even so, the vegetation of the inter-glacial periods of north-west Europe can be distinguished by pollen. Indeed, the relative dating of Pleistocene rocks in the East Anglian region of England is largely based on fossil pollen. There are possible sources of error in reconstructing past climates and plant communities from pollen diagrams, but these can be allowed for. For instance, some pollen types (such as oak) are prone to decay, whereas others (such as pine) are more resistant to decomposition. Again, certain pollen grains, particularly those of conifers, are carried farther than others by the wind, and so are more likely to be preserved over a wide area. Wind-pollinated plants in general also produce much more pollen than those which are pollinated by insects. This is an additional reason why such plants are again over-represented in pollen rain.

A second source of error arises from the fact that plant communities may not always respond to small or short-lived climate alterations with changes in the composition of their species. Even where the climate shift was large or long-lasting, there may have been a considerable time-lag before the composition of vegetation at any one site was affected. Studies of fossil insects from the later Pleistocene have revealed that the rate of climate change was more dramatic than the fossil pollen suggests.

T

Tertiary is the geological period which lasted from 65 to 1.6 million years ago. It is sub-divided into 5 epochs: the Palaeocene, Eocene, Oligocene, Miocene and Pliocene. The Tertiary and Quaternary periods together make up the Cainozoic era — the era of 'new' life.

Tertiary consumers are top CARNIVORES which eat SECONDARY CONSUMERS and PRIMARY CONSUMERS. Tertiary consumers are the dominant carnivorous animals in an ECOSYSTEM, and include birds of prey, the big cats, wolves and hunting dogs. They have always been seen as a threat to man, either directly or through competition for the same food supply, and have therefore been relentlessly hunted and exterminated by him.

Tertiary consumer, an eagle

Top carnivores, see TERTIARY CONSUMERS.

Trophic levels are defined according to the food sources used by the organisms in an ECOSYSTEM. Thus organisms which obtain their food from the breakdown of dead matter are said to belong to the DECOMPOSER level.

Tundra of the arctic variety is extensive in North America and Eurasia. It is sometimes called cold desert, and the low PRIMARY PRODUCTION of these northern tundras makes the comparison with desert a meaningful one. The tundra ECOSYSTEM is very fragile, and now that the tundra is being opened up for mineral exploitation and tourism the risk of major environmental damage is considerable. Fossil tundra soils are common in many mid-latitude areas of the northern hemisphere. They indicate that during the glacial stages of the PLEISTOCENE the vegetation belts were pushed much farther south of their present positions.

Z

Zooplankton are floating animals ranging in size from microscopic creatures to jellyfish. Particularly important members of the zooplankton are the copepods — the 'insects' of the sea — and the shrimp-like krill.

From its beginnings in the Pre-Cambrian era until the end of the Palaeozoic (about 225 million years ago) life became more varied. The dominant creatures were marine invertebrates and early animals with backbones.

Palaeozoic Communities

The oldest undoubted traces of life are fossils from the ONVERWACHT SERIES of rocks in South Africa. They are tiny MICRO-FOSSILS of simple single-celled organisms (probably BLUE-GREEN ALGAE), preserved in CHERTS and other fine-grained sediments thought to be about 3,200 million years old. Similar micro-fossils and those of rod-like BACTERIA occur in the FIG TREE SERIES of rocks in South Africa, which are slightly younger at around 3,100 million years old. STROMATOLITE communities of blue-green algae and bacteria are also found in rocks over 3,000 million years old in Zimbabwe, and are relatively common in rocks laid down around 2,300 million years ago. All these organisms were PROKARYOTES, which reproduce by ASEXUAL means. Therefore MUTATIONS — which may lead to evolutionary change and variety—would not easily spread throughout prokaryote populations. This is possibly why such early PRE-CAMBRIAN micro-fossils and stromatolite communities resemble their modern descendants.

Increasing amounts of oxygen in the atmosphere brought about by the blue-green algae allowed the first EUKARYOTE cells to evolve. The earliest eukaryote fossils are known from rocks in north Australia dated at roughly 1,500 million years old. They resemble green ALGAE and apparently reproduced asexually. In rocks about 1,000 million years old a variety of fossil eukaryotes are found, which suggests that by then sexual reproduction had developed. Consequently EVOLUTION could proceed more rapidly, and over the next 400 million years eukaryote organisms diversified and gave rise to the first multi-celled forms of life.

Multi-celled organisms first appear in rocks somewhat less than 700 million years old in Australia and some other continents. The Australian fossils are all of soft-bodied animals — collectively referred to as the EDIACARA FAUNA — several of which cannot be matched with any animals living today. Others, however, belong to or look like annelid worms, jellyfish and other COELENTERATES, and ECHINODERMS. The stage was then set for the appearance of animals with hard parts. Their fossils mark the end of the Pre-Cambrian era and the opening of the PALAEOZOIC, a transition which occurred about 570 million years ago.

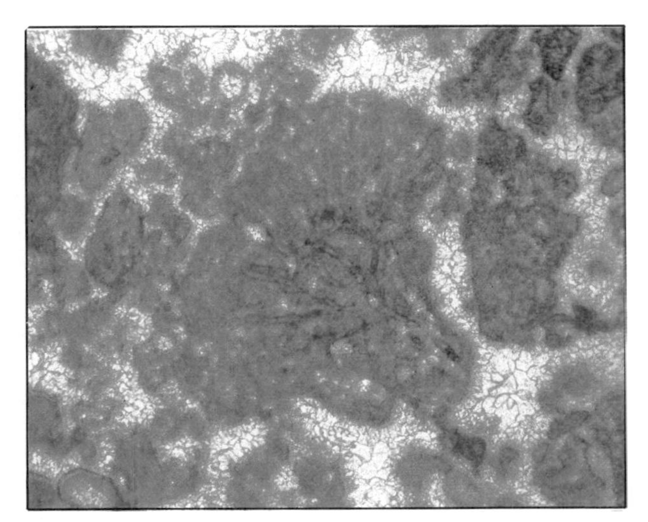

Right: *Medusina dawsoni* has been interpreted as a fossil Pre-Cambrian jellyfish. It forms part of the Ediacara fauna, from the Ediacara Hills, Australia.

Left: Fossil micro-organisms from the Pre-Cambrian gunflint cherts of Ontario, Canada. These micro-organisms were probably blue-green algae.

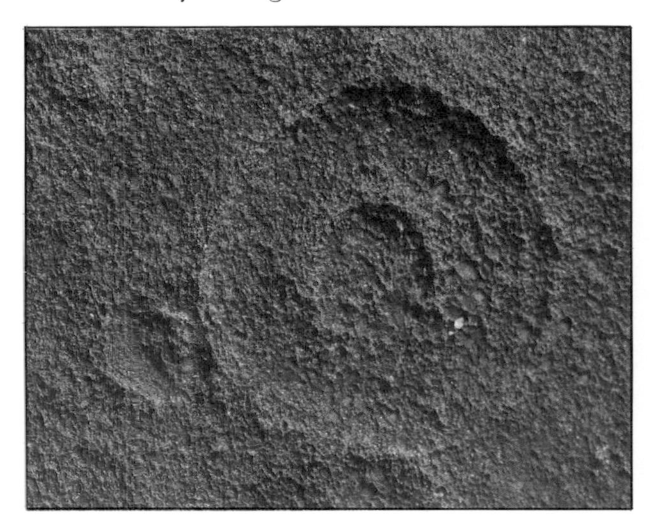

Reference

A **Acaste** is a well-known TRILOBITE from the Silurian of Europe and North America. Its head shield is larger than its tail and has 2 large concentric eyes. The facial SUTURE LINES (*see page 114*) run from the front of the head shield around the back of the eye and then sideways to cut the edge of the shield. *Acaste* had 11 body segments and a comparatively small, well-rounded tail made up of several fused segments. The best-known species is *Acaste downingiae* from the Wenlock Limestone of Dudley, England.

Algae are simple plants that live permanently in water. They may be single- or many-celled and although most are soft, several families have deposits of calcium carbonate in or around their cell walls. In some forms, such as *Chara*, a calcium carbonate deposit in the outer layers of the cell has helped to preserve these delicate structures in various freshwater sediments.

Ammonoids are an extinct group of CEPHALOPOD molluscs with gently folded to complex suture lines. The majority are coiled in a plane, but straight, turreted and exotic forms are also known. The sub-class Ammonoidea includes the GONIATITES, ceratites and ammonites, of which the goniatites are the most primitive. The last ammonoid lived in the Upper Cretaceous

Algal seaweed

Amphibians are a major group of VERTEBRATES, characterized by a so-called 'double life'. Most amphibians lay their eggs in water. These develop into a tadpole larval stage, which in turn changes into an adult amphibian.

Anapsids are reptiles with skulls that have no openings on the temples behind the eyes. The turtles and the COTYLOSAURS are anapsids. It is thought that the anapsid skull represents the primitive condition among the reptiles and that it is inherited directly from amphibian ancestors. In some turtles the back of the skull has been modified, related to the development of large muscles, and a large area of the skull roof is effectively missing.

Anthracosaurs were a major group of LABYRINTHODONT amphibians. They in-

Cambrian sea life

The Cambrian is the earliest of the six periods that comprise the Palaeozoic era. It lasted about 70 million years and in many parts of the world its base SEDIMENTS reveal the spread of shallow seas over continental platforms. The beginning of the period is also marked by the sudden appearance of many new animal groups, particularly those with hard parts. Their appearance is one of the great mysteries of the fossil record, and numerous theories have tried to account for it. Climatic change and the increased activity of predators have been favoured, but it is just as likely that animals developed hard, outer skeletons in response to the vast number of new ECOLOGICAL NICHES (*see page 68*) that had become available. This may have involved some deep-water species adapting to the rigours of shallow-water habitats, as well as the evolution of new forms to exploit untapped food sources.

The first TRILOBITES, BRACHIOPODS, MOLLUSCS, CRINOZOANS and ARCHAEOCYATHIDS all appear at the beginning of the Cambrian. They made a significant increase to the number of known families, and altered the composition of communities living on the sea bottom. Of the various groups, trilobites were the most important newcomers, for even in the earliest Cambrian they showed considerable diversity. Their jointed limbs were unique and represented a major advance in animal movement. They were to be the dominant INVERTEBRATES (*see page 105*) of the period. In many areas their remains and distinctive tracks and trails are associated with shallow-water environments, but in others they are found in the fine sediments typical of deeper water. Forms such as *Paradoxides* and the tiny agnostids are often found with INARTICULATE brachiopods and small cone-shaped molluscs. The brachiopods, such as *Lingulella,* were SUSPENSION-FEEDERS (*see page 114*). They procured their food by vibrating a fringed feeding organ, so creating water currents which carried the food to them. Trilobites and molluscs scavenged for their food, and also took in sediment to extract nutrients.

Below: Communities living in Cambrian shallow seas were dominated by trilobites and inarticulate brachiopods. This reconstruction shows one such community. *Paradoxides* is the representative trilobite and *Lingulella* an early burrowing inarticulate brachiopod. Gastropods, such as *Bellerophon,* also lived in many areas.

Trilobite provinces

In the Middle Cambrian trilobites were often associated with archaeocyathid REEFS. Archaeocyathids were creatures like SPONGES, with a double-walled skeleton. Their garden-like

cluded fish-eating forms such as *Eogyrinus* and were characterized by the structure of their skulls and backbone.

Archaeocyathids are an extinct group of INVERTEBRATES (*see page 105*) with affinities to sponges and corals. Most have a skeleton consisting of a cone within a cone, the 2 walls being linked by radial and horizontal partitions. Both walls are pierced by numerous pores. Many archaeocyathids have a well-developed 'rooting' structure. They lived during the Lower and Middle Cambrian and are known to have formed reef 'gardens'. It is believed that they had a SYMBIOTIC RELATIONSHIP with certain trilobites.

Archegosaurus was a long-snouted amphibian from the early Permian. It lived in Europe and southern Asia, but related forms occurred worldwide. *Archegosaurus* had the typical teeth of a LABYRINTHODONT amphibian. Most remains of these creatures are found in sediments deposited in the sea, and so it seems that they had adapted to a sea-going, fish-eating life.

Arthrodires were a group of ancient fishes. They were representatives of the PLACODERM ('plated-skin') stock and were common in both fresh and sea-water during the Devonian.

Arthropods have no backbone, but do have a segmented body and jointed legs. Their outer protective covering is a horny material called chitin. Fossil forms include the TRILOBITES and EURYPTERIDS, while among living groups are the insects, butterflies and spiders.

Asexual refers to the method of reproduction in certain animals and plants. It does not involve sex cells and often takes the form of a simple splitting or division of the contents of an individual cell. In this way the new organisms inherit all their characteristics from one parent.

Aysheia is one of the few known fossil ONYCHOPHORANS. It has a thin segmented exoskeleton and numerous unjointed legs. The caterpillar-like appearance is similar to that of the velvet worm PERIPATUS. *Aysheia* is recorded from the marine Burgess Shales of British Columbia, Canada. It is of Middle Cambrian age.

B

Bacteria, like the BLUE-GREEN ALGAE, are prokary-

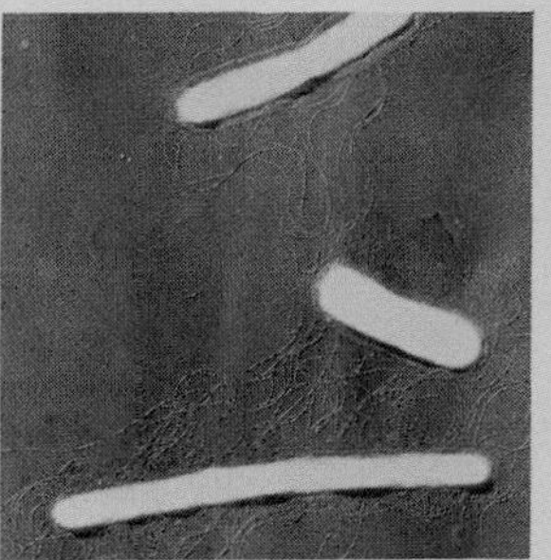

Rod-shaped bacteria

communities are known to have covered vast areas, and perhaps, like certain living fish and corals, the archaeocyathids and trilobites may have developed a SYMBIOTIC RELATIONSHIP. Throughout the Cambrian, trilobites are valuable ZONE FOSSILS, and as guides to the FAUNAL PROVINCES existing then.

During the Cambrian the trilobites of North America were quite distinct from those of most of northern Europe. Although what is today south Greenland was land, the northern part of the British Isles and eastern North America were covered by a shallow shelf sea. The same marine conditions prevailed over Wales, southern England and much of northern Europe. But between the two was the deep IAPETUS OCEAN, forming a natural barrier to migration. The faunas of the two areas therefore existed in comparative isolation, with OLENELLID trilobites characteristic of North America and north-west Scotland, and REDLICHIIDS typical of northern Europe.

Apart from trilobites, other ARTHROPODS are also recorded from Cambrian communities. Unfortunately, these animals had thin outer skeletons, and their remains are found only where conditions for preservation were exceptionally good. These arthropods were the TRILOBITOIDS and ONYCHOPHORANS. Their remains are best known from the Middle Cambrian Burgess Shales of British Columbia, sediments which seem to have been deposited under relatively deep water. Among the best-known of the trilobitoids were MARRELLA and *Burgessia.* The former has an apt TRIVIAL OR SPECIFIC NAME *(Marrella splendens)* for its unique, wedge-shaped head has four splendid, long, backwardly-directed horns. *Burgessia* is staid in comparison, and looks something like the living HORSESHOE CRABS. Onychophorans are represented in the Burgess Shales by AYSHEIA, a caterpillar-like creature that may be an ancestor of the main arthropod line. It resembles the living ony-

Left: *Peripatus* is a modern onychophoran, the form of which falls between the worms and the arthropods. Its eye is like a worm's, while the body cavity is like that of a typical arthropod. *Peripatus* lives in the tropical forests of Brazil.

Left: A delicate impression left by the onychophoran *Aysheia.* In many ways this creature closely resembles *Peripatus,* having a caterpillar-like shape and paired, jointed limbs. But unlike *Peripatus,* it was a marine animal. *Aysheia* is found in the Burgess Shales of the Middle Cambrian.

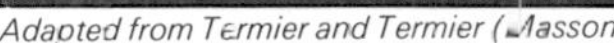

Adapted from Termier and Termier (Masson)

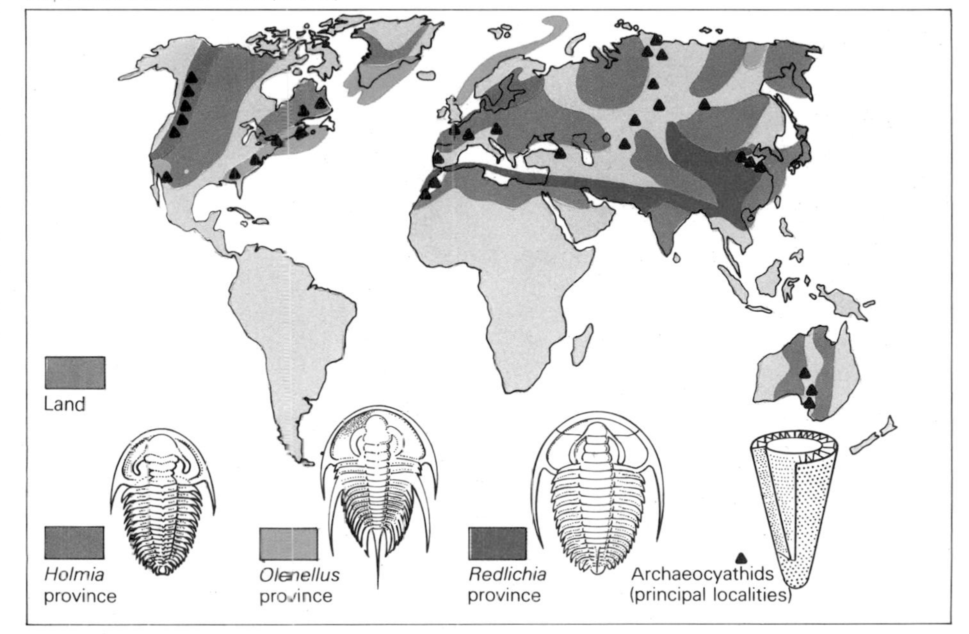

Right: During the Cambrian period, sea covered many areas that are now land. Among the sediments deposited were the remains of many trilobites, and from the distribution of these remains palaeontologists can recognize that several distinct faunal provinces existed (as shown opposite). Today evidence of these provinces is found on different continents. During the Cambrian they formed distinct entities, each having their own individual types of trilobites.

otes. This means that their cells do not have a well-defined nucleus. They are single-celled organisms but, unlike the blue-green algae, lack chlorophyll. They obtain their energy from a variety of sources.

Bedding planes lie parallel to the surface of deposited rocks. Successive bedding planes may be picked out by colour changes, or by changes in the size of the materials deposited. Fossil clusters often denote a bedding plane which is not necessarily horizontal.

Bivalves are soft-bodied MOLLUSCS with oval or elongated shells comprising 2 hinged valves. They first appeared during the Cambrian period. Today their roles are as burrowing, boring, fixed and free-living animals.

Blue-green algae are the simplest and oldest group of all plants. They occur as single cells or in chains, and have no well-defined nucleus. Living blue-green algae occur in many environments on land and in the sea, and will grow on snowfields or across hot thermal springs. The first blue-green algae in the form of single cells are recorded from rocks 3,300 million years old. Approximately 2,500 million years ago, dome-shaped structures called stromatolites appeared world-wide. These exist today along the tidal beaches of the Bahamas and Australia, consisting of sheets of blue-green algae and limy sediment.

Brachiopods are solitary invertebrates (animals without backbones) living at the sea bottom. Their soft parts are enclosed in a shell with 2 valves. The group is divided into 2 classes — the INARTICULATES and the articulates — both of which arose in the Cambrian.

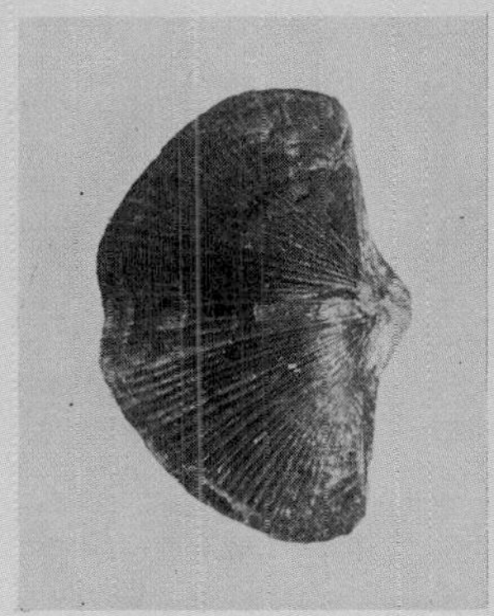

A brachiopod

Brackish water is partly fresh and partly salt. Stretches of such water occur behind coastal spits and banks. They restrict the amount of tidal water that can replenish the standing lagoon, which receives a fairly constant influx of fresh water.

Bryozoans are a little known but important group of animals. They live in colonies and have a skeleton made up of minute box-like units. Bryozoans are first known from the Cambrian, and still thrive today in many areas.

chophoran PERIPATUS, but while *Aysheia* was a sea creature, *Peripatus* lives on land.

Life in the Ordovician

During the Ordovician the Iapetus Ocean still separated northern Europe from North America and Greenland, so that distinct faunal provinces persisted in those areas. Once again the provinces can be identified by their trilobites, but in many areas deep-water sediments also contain characteristic GRAPTOLITES. The trilobites are often found with brachiopods, and the term 'SHELLY FACIES' describes the sediments in which they are found. By the beginning of the Ordovician, brachiopods and graptolites were significant members of various marine communities. Their importance increased gradually during the period until they surpassed the trilobites as the dominant invertebrates. Ordovician communities became much more complex than their Cambrian counterparts, and apart from new families of trilobites, brachiopods and graptolites, a whole host of BRYOZOANS, corals and NAUTILOIDS appeared during the period. Some of these filled niches left vacant following the late Cambrian extinctions, which included the archaeocyathids. Their place was eventually occupied by the corals, which with the bryozoans took part in a major period of reef-building during the Middle Ordovician. Among the echinoderms, more advanced groups such as the sea urchins and starfish evolved. Stalked crinozoans were common in several shallow-water communities, different species forming distinct 'CRINOID gardens'.

Modes of feeding

Crinoids are among the most important

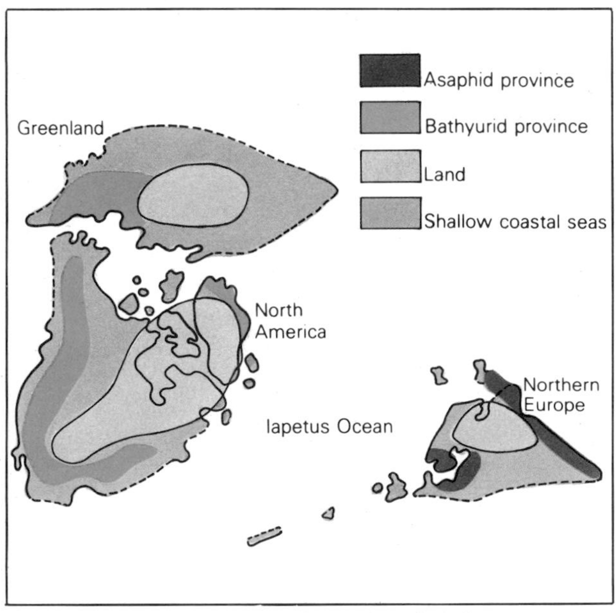

From 'The Ecology of Fossils', McKerrow (Duckworth and Co. Ltd.)

Left: The Ordovician world was very different from that of today. A deep ocean — Iapetus — separated North America from northern Europe, and the shallow seas that surrounded the isolated areas of land had their own characteristic types of trilobites. These animals were restricted to certain seas by either geographical or ecological controls. The area to which they were restricted may be termed a 'province'. For example, Bathyurid and Asaphid provinces existed in the Ordovician.

Below: Orthid brachiopods, sea snails, crinoids and nautiloids provide evidence of the varied animal groupings that existed in some flat-bottom Ordovician environments. In some places these groupings are dominated by trilobites; in others by brachiopods. The brachiopods were mostly flattened, broad forms with a pronounced ribbed ornament. In these environments, trilobite trails mark the wandering of these animals over the surface in search of food. The rather delicate nature of the animals in certain Ordovician environments, especially those where black shales were deposited, may indicate a shortage of food. Invertebrate animals such as the brachiopods and crinoids lived mainly in shallow water during the Ordovician. Some communities included numerous orthid brachiopods. Many of the trilobites of the Ordovician, particularly the trinucleids, were blind. This suggests that they were bottom-dwellers and that they possibly burrowed into the sediment. Long spines from the sides of the head, extending backwards, were used to steady these animals, which could also tuck their tails underneath their bodies to protect their softer surfaces. The nautiloids were the larger scavengers and hunters of these times.

C **Calamites** is a large HORSETAIL plant recorded from the Upper Carboniferous. It lived along the edges of swampland waters and consisted of an underground rhizome, or rooting portion, and an upright stem. The stem was typically jointed and bore whorls of prominent, long leaves. *Calamites* was a giant among horsetails. Plants 18 metres high with trunks 400 mm wide have been discovered.

Carbonates are rocks composed of carbonate minerals. Limestones are typical examples. They may form from the accumulation of animal skeletons, or from solutions containing calcium carbonate.

Fossils in limestone

Cartilaginous fishes such as the sharks and rays do not have a bony skeleton. Instead it is made up of cartilage — a relatively soft translucent tissue — consisting of rounded cells. Cartilage shrivels up when the animal dies and therefore it is rare for complete sharks or rays to be discovered as fossils. The first cartilaginous fishes, or chondrichthyes, are known from the latter half of the Devonian period. *Cladoselache,* the Devonian shark, is among the earliest. It is possible that the cartilaginous skeleton is the primitive condition among the vertebrates, or that it resulted from young embryonic fishes reaching sexual maturity before their skeletons had turned to bone.

Cephalopods are a class of MOLLUSCS known from the Cambrian to the present day. They are entirely marine in habitat and are divided into 2 groups by the number of their gills. Tetrabranchiata have 4 gills and are represented in the fossil record by nautiloids and ammonoids. Dibranchiates have 2 gills and are represented today by the squids, cuttlefish and octopuses. The majority fossil group of dibranchiates are the belemnites.

Chert is a form of silica in rocks which originated as sediments.

Chonetoids were small articulate BRACHIOPODS with flattened shells. Most were characterized by prominent spines arranged along the outer edge of the lower (pedicle) valve.

Cladoselache was an early shark known from the late Devonian. Individual animals ranged from 400 mm to 1.2 metres in length.

echinoderms, and during the Palaeozoic all forms had stems or stalks. The bodies of these animals were globular and plated, with long arms arranged symmetrically around the mouth. During feeding small, sticky TUBE FEET trapped food particles which were then passed along food tracts to the mouth. The crinoids were therefore FILTER-FEEDERS, and many were adapted to living in currents of water from which they could, through the fan-like arrangement of their arms, obtain food very efficiently. In the 'crinoid gardens' several levels of creatures existed, each exploiting a different food zone.

Many Ordovician trilobites were adapted to mud-grubbing. These included TRINUCLEUS and its close relatives — blind trilobites with large head shields. They lived directly in line with the prevailing currents, using the deep pits that border the head shield as sensory organs.

The role of SCAVENGER in many Ordovician communities was occupied by the nautiloids. During the Ordovician these distant relatives of the squid and octopus had many diverse forms, commonly being straight, curved or coiled. A few may have grazed plants on the sea bottom but others, like the living *Nautilus,* were active CARNIVORES (*see page 67*). Nautiloids showed many evolutionary trends during this period, modifying the shell and internal deposits according to their way of life. These animals may have occupied some niches which in later periods were dominated by the fishes.

Modifications to their outer skeleton also occurred among the graptolites during the Ordovician. In the early part of the period, shrub-like creatures fixed to the sea floor were common, but throughout most of the Ordovician the free-swimming PLANKTON graptoloids were

Below: Numerous trilobites are to be found in the muddy, deeper-water sediments of the Ordovician. The most common types are *Lonchodomus, Remopleurides* and *Tretaspis.*

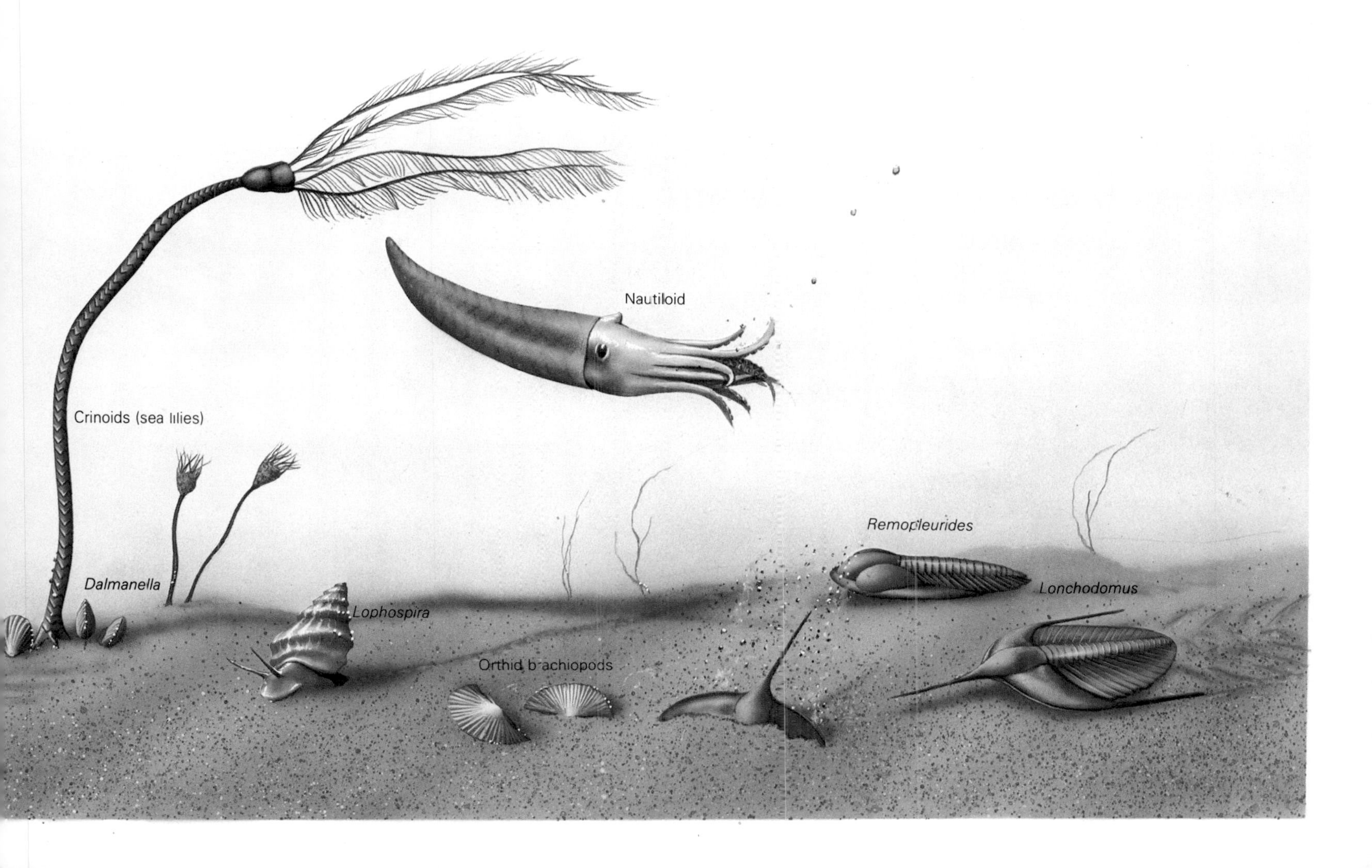

Coelacanth is the common name given to the living form *Latimeria* and its fossil relatives. Coelacanths are grouped with the RHIPIDISTIANS and lungfishes as TASSEL-FINNED bony fishes.

Coelenterates are multi-celled animals which have 2 layers of cells (tissues) in the body wall. They include the sea anemones, jellyfish and corals, and are first known from the late Pre-Cambrian.

Continental shelves are the gently sloping areas of sea floor around the continents. Nowhere are they more than 200 metres deep. Marine life is concentrated on the continental shelves rather than the open oceans, because nutrients for PHYTOPLANKTON (*see page 72*) are

Coelenterates, sea anemones

supplied to the sea in vast quantities by rivers draining off the landmasses. At the edges of continental shelves there is a sharp descent into the OCEAN BASINS. These edges are where the continents were once joined together.

Corallites are the individual skeletons deposited by coral polyps and may vary considerably in shape and size. The term is usually used when referring to solitary corals. When describing a colonial coral, the individual corallites are known collectively as the corallum. Corallites occur in TABULATE, RUGOSE and scleractinian corals.

Cosmopolitan is a term used to describe the widespread, global distribution of a given group of plants or animals.

Cotylosaurs, or the stem reptiles, are the most primitive group of ANAPSID reptiles. They are a very varied group, containing animals such as *Hylonomus* and *Scutosaurus.* They were, with the PELYCOSAURS, the prominent reptiles of the Upper Permian and early Triassic.

Crinoids are a group of ECHINODERMS. Most have stalks and live on the sea bottom. They are a varied group and were particularly important in Palaeozoic communities. The crinoid body has a round THECAL CUP, topped by long, plated arms. In many species there is a stem, or stalk, beneath it. The cup is made up of thick plates of calcite and a 5-fold, or pentameral, symmetry is normal. The first crinoids appeared in the Lower Cambrian. They are frequently called 'sea lilies' and are represented today by

the dominant group. These forms had fewer branches, and reducing the number of branches within the graptoloids was a significant trend. By the end of the period the number of branches had been reduced from many to one, with a corresponding reduction in the number of individual THECAL CUPS. The cups also increased in size and it is likely that this made the colony much more efficient in feeding.

The Silurian

The northern Iapetus Ocean became less important as a barrier to migration during the Silurian period. As a result the separate faunal provinces of the Cambrian and Ordovician became less distinct and ultimately merged. Various groups of organisms became truly COSMOPOLITAN in their distribution, most communities being dominated by either brachiopods or graptolites. Although still common, trilobites were decreasing. As in the Ordovician various forms, such as *Dalmanites,* adapted to reef environments, while others, such as ACASTE and *Calymene* persisted on soft SUBSTRATES.

Shelly facies

Once again we can identify both 'shelly' and 'GRAPTOLITIC FACIES'. The 'shelly facies' had numerous brachiopods, with different groupings or associations occurring regularly in various regions. Groupings were determined by such factors as the depth of water, the type of sediment on the sea floor and SALINITY. Palaeontologists can now plot the distribution of these communities with some accuracy and record the changes in types of animals that occurred from coastal to deep-water environments. In shallow water, the persistent LINGULA lived among thin-shelled bivalves and small brachiopods. All were filter-feeders, while the gastropods that crawled on the sea bed, such as POLEUMITA, grazed plants. A limited variety of animals existed within the community that *Lingula* dominated, but farther away from the shoreline there was a greater diversity, mainly of larger brachiopods and solitary corals.

In contrast to the Ordovician, the Silurian TABULATE corals were quite varied. Numerous species flourished in reefs, and different families were represented — *Favosites,* SYRINGOPORA, *Halysites* and HELIOLITES being the best-known

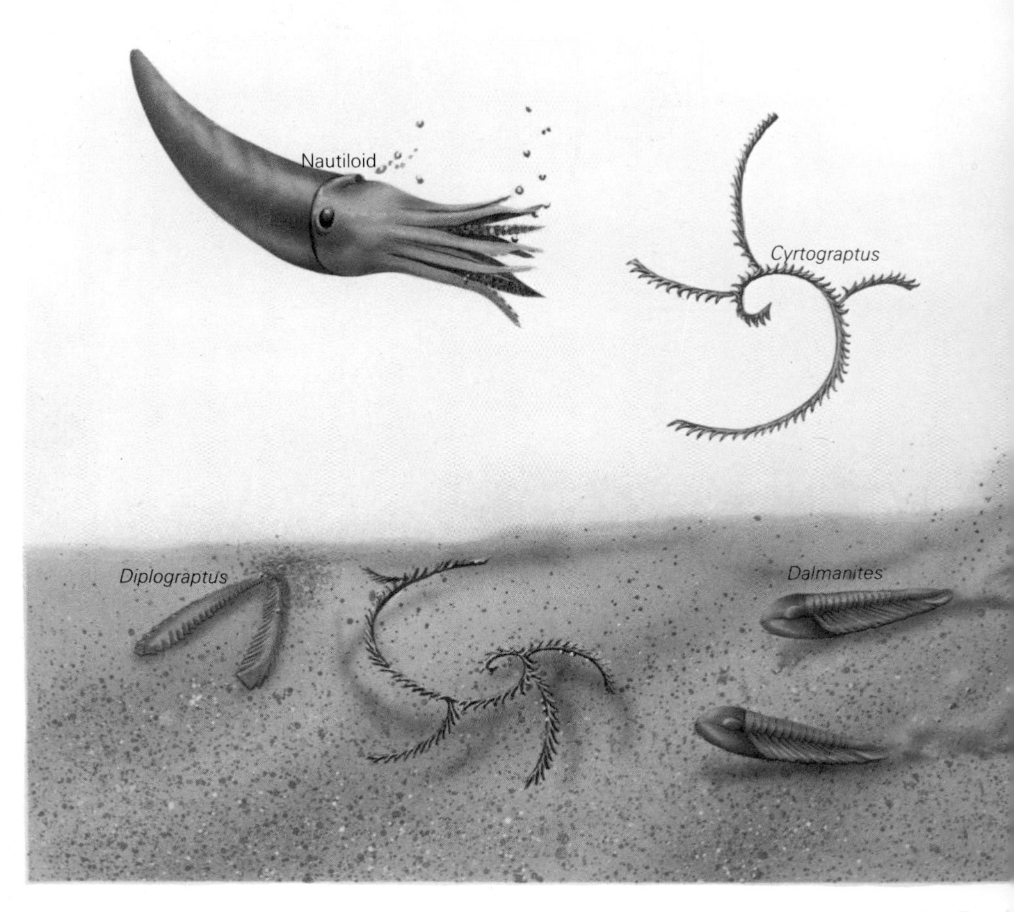

Right: During the Silurian period a number of distinct communities existed on the sea floor. Their composition and distribution were controlled by various ecological factors, such as water depth and sediment type. We can therefore recognize a succession of communities, from shallow-water sandstones to deep-water shales. Brachiopods were the most common form of life on the Silurian sea floor, although many other animals were present at different depths. Graptolites were relatively numerous in offshore environments and, as planktonic creatures, were widespread in their distribution. *Cyrtograptus* and *Diplograptus* were common in the Lower Silurian. In coastal communities there were many bivalves and *Lingula.* Farther out to sea brachiopods, such as the strophomenids and pentamerids, became more common. Tabulate corals and massive bryozoans such as *Hallopora* are commonly found in Silurian limestone deposits. They are associated with brachiopods and trilobites, including *Dalmanites.* Although trilobites were less significant than during the Cambrian or Ordovician, forms such as *Dalmanites* were still common in deeper-water Silurian communities.

both stalked and unstalked free-living forms.

Crinozoans are ECHINODERMS, mostly living fixed to the sea floor. They have an obvious 5-part form and usually have arms which deliver food to the mouth. Some crinozoans — the cystoids and blastoids — had no stems to fix them to the floor and probably lived crawling on the sea bottom. Other crinozoans adapted to a free-swimming life.

Crustaceans are mainly aquatic ARTHROPODS which show great variation in the structure of their limbs. Included within the Crustacea are the barnacles, OSTRACODES, crabs and lobsters. In the most primitive crustaceans, food is brought to the mouth on currents set up by the limbs. But in the crabs and lobsters, food is lifted to the mouth by means of well-developed limbs. The first crustaceans are recorded from the Cambrian period.

Sea lily, an echinoderm

D

Diapsids are reptiles with skulls that have 2 openings on the temple behind the eye. The thecodontians, dinosaurs, pterosaurs and crocodiles are diapsid reptiles. Snakes and lizards also have a diapsid type of skull, but unlike the archosaurs tend not to keep the bony bars between the 2 openings. The first diapsids probably appeared in the late Palaeozoic.

Diplocaulus was a 'horned' amphibian from the Upper Carboniferous and Lower Permian of North America. It lived in ponds, and its broad head and body suggest that it never ventured on to dry land. Its main features were the 2 horn-like extensions at the back of the skull. Adult animals grew to just over 500 mm in length. *Diplocaulus* was a typical LEPOSPONDYL amphibian.

Diploceraspis was a strange 'horned' amphibian from the early Permian. It was a LEPOSPONDYL and therefore had vertebrae in which the centrum was a spool-shaped bony cylinder. *Diploceraspis* had a flat body and a rather grotesque head which was extended backwards on either side. Like its relative DIPLOCAULUS it was a pond-dweller which never ventured on to land.

Diplograptids are an extinct group of GRAPTOLITES recorded from the Upper Ordovician and Lower Silurian. They had a single branch, or stipe, with THECAL CUPS on both sides. The dip-

types. The solitary corals are RUGOSE, and their limited variety, compared with that of the Devonian and Carboniferous, suggests that they were at an early stage in their evolution. All corals — large and small, solitary or living in colonies — resembled living forms, their soft parts bearing comparison with sea anemones. They trapped food with the STINGING CELLS on their tentacles, and most lived in warm waters.

These waters were rich in the minerals (CARBONATES) that form limestone, and the sediments of the sea floor were often muddy. Inshore from the reefs, corals were often associated with the large brachiopod *Pentamerus*, the strong shell of which was ideally suited to shallow water. This animal lived in an upright position with the thicker, weighted part of its shell fixed in the sediment to keep it stable. In deeper waters the brachiopods were generally thinner and perhaps flatter. A decrease in size

Below: *Pentamerus*, a medium to large-sized brachiopod, was common in moderately shallow water during the Silurian. It had a strongly-built shell and was very efficient in filtering water to gain food.

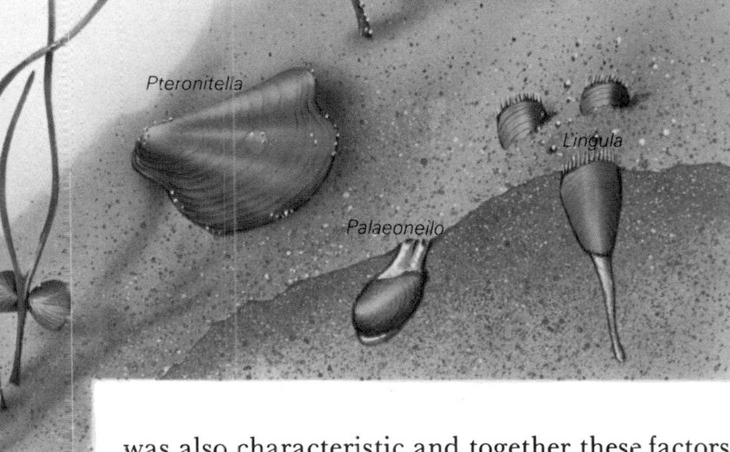

Streptelasma
Halysites
Pentamerus
Hallopora
Atrypa

was also characteristic and together these factors suggest a falling-off in food supply. Trilobites were quite common in deeper water, where they scoured the sea bed for food.

Graptolitic facies

In the 'graptolitic facies', single-branched MONOGRAPTIDS thrived throughout the world. These were the pinnacle of graptolite evolution and their large individual cups obviously held larger, more efficient individual organisms. At the beginning of the Silurian, monograptids were just appearing, while the DIPLOGRAPTIDS that had persisted since the Ordovician flourished in many areas. Diplograptids were probably planktonic and there is firm evidence to support the idea that many branches hung down from their one complex float structure. No such evidence exists for the monograptids, although many palaeontologists think that they too were

lograptids were probably PLANKTON organisms and evidence shows that they were attached to large floating structures. Diplograptids were worldwide in their distribution.

Dunkleosteus was a gigantic fish from the late Devonian of Germany. Its head was covered in large bony plates and the armoured head and neck region was about 3 metres long.

E

Echinoderms are a group of marine animals which usually have a 5-fold, or pentamerous, form. Most have a skeleton composed of calcareous plates and they are often called 'spiny-skins'. Some echinoderms are free-living; others have stems and live fixed to the sea floor. They range from the Pre-Cambrian to Recent periods.

Ediacara fauna are a group of fossil animals found in a rock known as the Pound Quartzite, at Ediacara in south Australia. There are annelid worms and what seem to be jellyfish, as well as other animals of uncertain type. They are younger than rocks which have been dated at 700 million years old, and older than those in which fossils of the first known trilobites are found. Elements of the Ediacara fauna have also been discovered in other continents.

Eryops is one of the best-known of the Permian LABYRINTHODONT amphibians. Like *Loxomma* it is a RHACHITOME, a rather primitive type of amphibian with a particular type of vertebral structure. *Eryops* was a heavily-built creature which measured approximately 1.8 metres in length. It had a large head and numerous sharply pointed teeth. Its limbs were well-developed, and although it spent much of its time in swamps it was capable of walking on land. *Eryops* is known from Texas, North America.

Eukaryotes are organisms which have definite nuclei (membrane-bound bodies) in their cells. All plants, animals and fungi are eukaryotes.

Eurypterids are an extinct group of ARTHROPODS. They are also known as 'water scorpions', and their closest living relatives are the king crabs or HORSESHOE crabs.

Evolution means 'unfolding'. It is the theory describing the process by which all forms of life have evolved from organisms which lived

Fungus, a eukaryote

planktonic. In the case of *Monograptus turriculatus,* a spiral form, the skeleton suggests that the colony rotated frequently in search of food. The same theory may be put forward for *Cyrtograptus,* a representative of a short-lived, Middle Silurian family. Several important graptolite families vanished at the end of the Silurian, and the distribution and numbers of these hitherto important HEMICHORDATE creatures were to become extremely limited during the succeeding Devonian period.

Silurian reef environment

As we have noted, tabulate and rugose stony corals flourished in the warm, lime-rich seas of the Silurian. Today we can find the remains of these animals in several limestones, among them the rich BEDDING PLANES of the Wenlock Limestone, which provide a considerable amount of data on ancient reef communities. Bedding planes represent the position of the ancient sea floor, and in the Wenlock Limestone corals are found with bryozoans, brachiopods, crinoids and trilobites. The sediment in which those fossils were entombed is a fine mud, which was deposited under quiet, undisturbed conditions. Tabulate corals such as *Favosites* and *Halysites* — the 'chain coral' — were, together with bryozoans, the main reef-building and binding animals. In life they were probably variously coloured, with masses of small POLYPS forming a distinctive, patchy cover. The conditions under which they flourished were probably similar to those of modern reef corals, where the shallow, well-oxygenated waters range between 22 and 28°C. Tabulates were simple in structure and exhibit only a few evolutionary trends. Among these was the development of small packing tubes between the main CORALLITES. The trend reached its peak in the heliolitids, of which *Heliolites* is well-known in the Wenlock Limestone.

Below: From blocks of limestone which contain fossils (such as the one shown on the page opposite) palaeontologists can reconstruct the community that existed in a given area millions of years ago. The reconstruction below is of a Silurian reef community, and is based on beautiful fossils collected from the Wenlock Limestone in England. The relationships between various creatures within the community can be compared by scientists with those living in reef populations today.

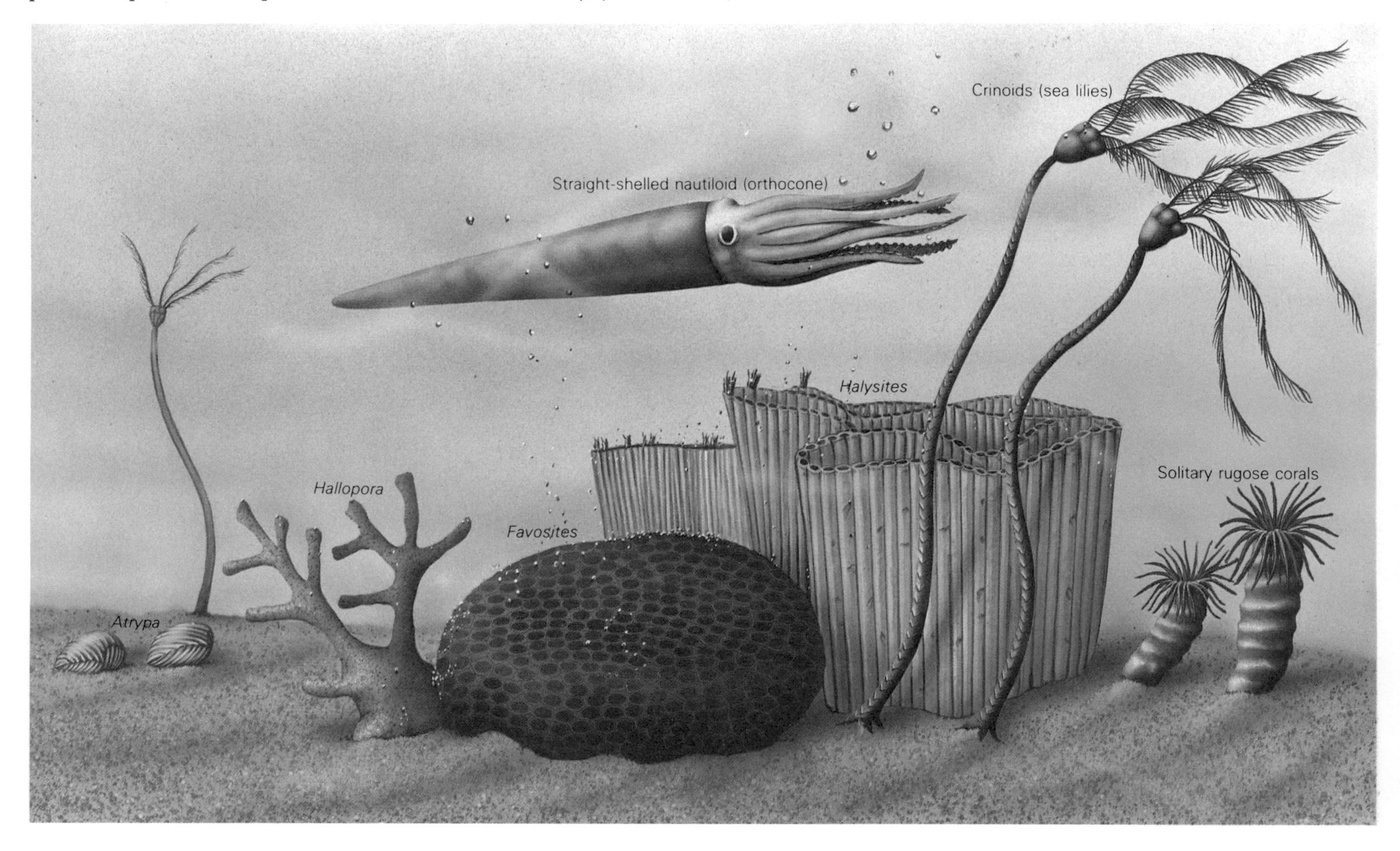

many millions of years ago. Charles Darwin (1809–82) and Gregor Mendel (1822 – 84) are considered by many to be the fathers of evolutionary theory. A period of chemical evolution preceded that of living organisms.

F Faunal provinces are, or were, specific areas of the world inhabited by a number of associated plant and animal populations. The areas are isolated from each other by physical or ecological barriers (*see* ECOLOGY, *page 68*) which prevent migration.

Fenestellids were a group of delicate lacy BRYOZOANS common during the Silurian, Devonian and Carboniferous periods. A *Fenestella* colony was rather vase-like in shape, while that of *Archimedes* had a spiral arrangement. In both colonies the arrangement of the individual animals governed the direction of feeding currents through the 'window'-like spaces of the colony.

Fig Tree Series is a group of rocks in the Barberton Mountain Land of the eastern Transvaal, South Africa. They have a maximum thickness of over 2,000 metres, and comprise rocks of slate, clayey grits or greywackes, together with layers of banded CHERT and banded ironstone. Together with the ONVERWACHT SERIES, they include some of the oldest little-altered sediments in the world.

Filter-feeders are animals that extract their food from water currents which are usually created by their own feeding organs (*see* LOPHOPHORE).

Flora is the general term applied to all the species of plant life growing in a particular area. It is used in the same way as is 'fauna' when speaking of animals.

Fusulinid foraminiferids. Foraminiferids are single-celled aquatic organisms, often less than 1 mm in diameter, surrounded by a shell. Fusulinids were shaped like wheat grains and had calcareous shells. On ocean floors, where little debris accumulates, the remains of calcareous foraminiferids may build up oozes — and these fossils make up the great bulk of certain limestones.

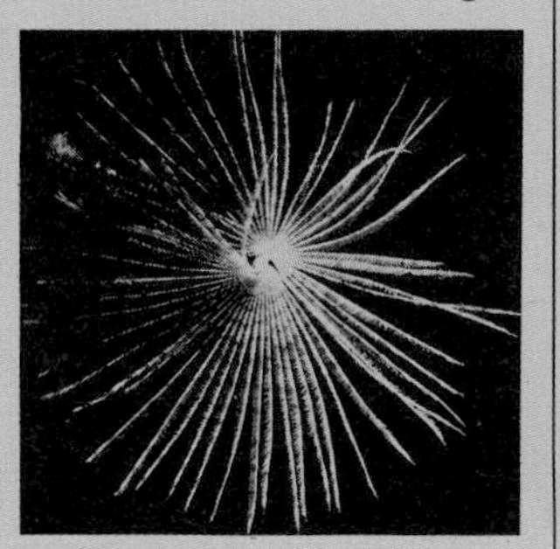
Peacock worm filter-feeding

G Gondwanaland, or Gondwana, is the name given to the southern supercontinent that existed during the Palaeozoic and early

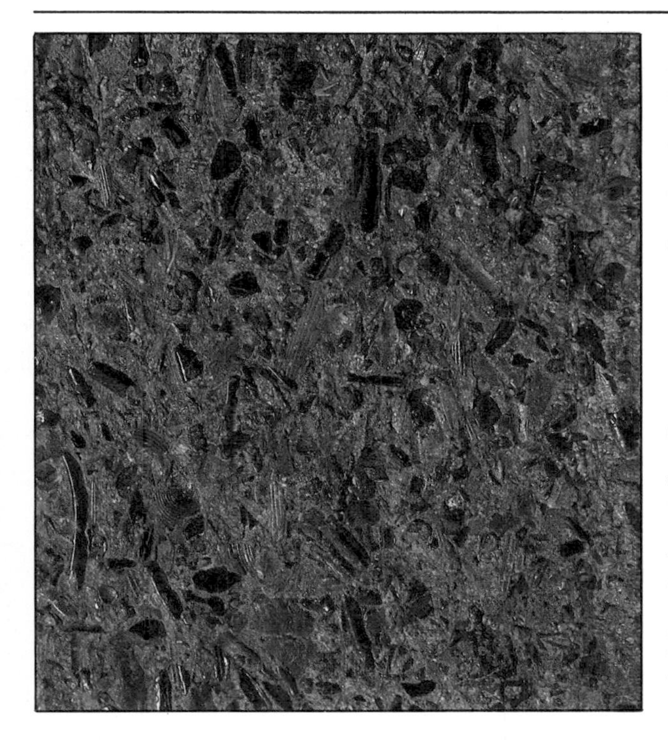

Left: Accumulations of bone on a bedding plane, or concentrated within a limited thickness of rock, are called bone beds. These may represent the sudden death of many vertebrates, or reflect the slow rate of sediment deposit in a particular area.

Below: A fossil-containing rock surface which reveals what life was like on the Silurian sea-floor. The rock is a limestone, and the various fossils — including crinoid ossicles, bryozoans, brachiopods and corals — show that the deposits which formed it gathered at the bottom of a warm, shallow sea.

Bryozoans associated with the tabulates in the main reef framework included robust forms such as *Hallopora,* as well as delicate encrusting types. *Hallopora* was a 'STONY BRYOZOAN' and the structure of its individual tubes bore some resemblance to those of the tabulate corals. Stony bryozoans reached their evolutionary peak during the Silurian. They probably had a ring of tentacles around the mouth and fed on microscopic organisms, as do living species. Bryozoans shared the role of reef-binders with the STROMATOPOROIDS and calcareous algae.

Within the reef a number of specialized niches were occupied by various brachiopods, molluscs and arthropods. One of the most common brachiopods was *Atrypa*, a small to medium-sized animal which often occurred in 'nests' or clusters within the main body of the reef. It was one of the earliest SPIRIFERIDS (*see page 113*) and its spirally-arranged feeding organ was very efficient. *Leptaena* was also a reef-dwelling brachiopod. It lived on the edges of the main reef complex, and its strongly-curved shell appears to be adapted to life on a soft substrate. When seen in cross section the shell of *Leptaena* is L-shaped, and it seems likely that this helped to raise the shell opening well above the sediment surface. As a result, *Leptaena* could filter-feed without taking in unnecessary sediment.

Among other organisms found associated with the reef, trilobites such as *Dalmanites* and 'PHACOPS' were robust and could see well. They were active creatures, and scavenged on the sea bottom. Certain species of *Dalmanites* had long tail spines, possibly used by the animal to stabilize itself or to correct its direction of movement. Other scavengers in the reef community included nautiloids and gastropods. Crinoids occupied the higher feeding levels.

Bone beds

Evidence for the increasing importance of fishes during the Lower Palaeozoic is preserved in the Ludlow Bone Bed. The unit itself is rather thin and the actual material fragmentary. The bones and scales belong mostly to JAWLESS FISHES, and this exceptional concentration may reflect an environment where a limited deposit of sediment took place. Bone beds occur at rare intervals throughout the post-Silurian strata, and such high concentrations of VERTEBRATE remains offer

Mesozoic. It was formed from the present continents of Africa, South America, Australia, Antarctica and India.

Goniatites are a group of ammonoid CEPHALOPODS with angular or zig-zag SUTURE LINES (*see page 114*). They are usually small and most have rather tightly coiled shells. The first goniatites appear in the Lower Devonian and it seems that they arose from a straight-shelled group of MOLLUSCS known as the Bactritoidea.

Graptolites are an extinct group of HEMICHORDATES. They are divided into 2 major groups, the Dendroidea and the Graptoloidea. The former have many branches and 3 types of THECAL CUP, while the graptoloids have less than 32 branches and 1 type of cup only. Dendroids first appeared in the Cambrian and died out in the Carboniferous. The graptoloids were shorter-lived and existed from the lowest Ordovician to the end of the Devonian.

Graptolitic facies is the term used to describe those sediments, with their GRAPTOLITE animals, that were deposited in deep water during the Palaeozoic era.

H **Heliolites** is one of the best-known TABULATE corals. Like *Halysites* and SYRINGOPORA it lived in colonies, but the form of its skeleton is unique. The colony consists of large CORALLITES bounded by a number of small tube-like structures. Every corallite has its own thin walls and is surrounded by more than 12 of the smaller tubes. *Heliolites* was a prominent member of Silurian and early Devonian shallow-water communities. It is found world-wide.

Hemichordates are chordate animals which lack

Hemichordate, acorn worm

bony tissues. They have a short rod of tissue — the notochord — above the mouth. *Rhabdopleura* and the acorn worms are living hemichordates. The former is a colonial organism that lives on the sea floor. It has a tube-like skeleton which bears some resemblance to that of the GRAPTOLITES. *Rhabdopleura* collects its food by means of tentacled arms placed above and behind the mouth. The acorn worms, such as *Balanoglossus,* are free-living animals which look rather like earthworms. *Balanoglossus,* however,

an opportunity to study the vertebrate faunas of the time. Often the bones are associated with fossilized droppings, or coprolites, and the bed is usually rich in phosphate.

On to land

We have evidence to show that during the Silurian, both plants (PSILOPSIDS) and animals (scorpions) had evolved sufficiently to venture on to land. Both groups of organisms had solved problems of adapting to life out of water, such as developing new methods of breathing and preventing their bodies from drying out. They can therefore be considered the founder members of true land-living communities.

Marine communities in the Devonian

Evidence exists in many regions for reef communities during the Devonian. Once again the reefs are characteristic of limestone deposits, and corals, bryozoans, stromatoporoids and algae were the main building and binding agents. Shallower- and deeper-water marine communities are also recognizable, and many new groups of animals appeared to occupy various niches. Among the most important of these were the GONIATITES and the 'true' spiriferids. Goniatites were the first AMMONOID CEPHALOPODS and their appearance marks a progressive decline in the importance of the nautiloids. Most goniatites were small, coiled animals which lacked the internal deposits of their nautiloid cousins. The material separating the internal chambers of a goniatite was more strongly folded than in a nautiloid, and we think that this both increased the strength of the shell and allowed the animal to swim at greater depths.

In spiriferids, the characteristic sideways expansion of the shell is marked by a broad HINGE-LINE and two distinct 'wings' or 'ears'.

Above right: Fossilized remains of one of the most fearsome of all Devonian animals — the eurypterids. These were distant cousins of the trilobites, and some grew up to 3 metres long.

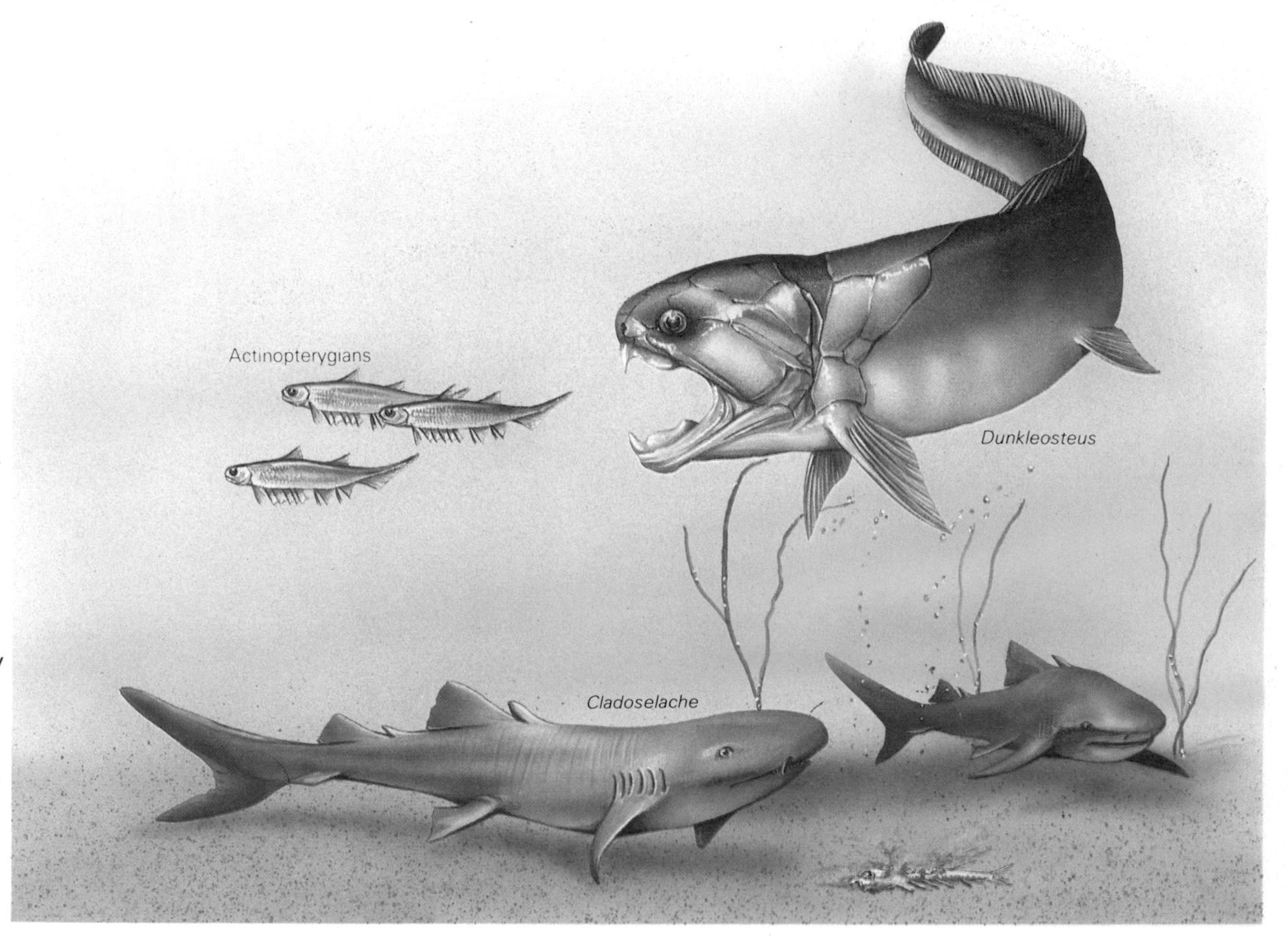

Right: Fishes underwent an incredible increase in variety and numbers during the Devonian. In the absence of any higher vertebrates they dominated most freshwater and marine communities. In the seas of Europe and North America, *Dunkleosteus* and its relatives were the major predators, along with the shark *Cladoselache*.

has numerous gill slits on the underside of its trunk.
Hinge-line is the area of articulation that exists in BIVALVES, BRACHIOPODS and OSTRACODES. The bivalve hinge-line is characterized by a number of teeth and sockets. Brachiopods also have teeth and sockets but they are less well-developed. Brachiopods with hinge-lines are grouped as the Articulata.
Horseshoe or king crabs are not crabs at all. They are ARTHROPODS, which are closely related to the spiders, scorpions and EURYPTERIDS. The first horseshoe crabs appeared in the Lower Palaeozoic.
Horsetails are a group of PSILOPSID plants which today are represented by the genus *Equisetum*. This plant typically has a stiff, upright stem which is divided at joints into several units. The stem also bears a number of scale-like leaves which are arranged in distinct whorls. The jointed stem and leaf whorls are characteristic of the horsetails through time, the same features being found in the tree-like *Calamites* of the Carboniferous. This plant grew to 18 metres in height and shows the former success of these rather primitive plants. The first horsetails appeared in the Middle Devonian.

Hydra feeding

Hydrozoans are COELENTERATES which show the phenomenon of 'alteration of generations'. They have an adult stage, and a free-swimming reproductive stage. The group includes *Hydra* and colonial corals.

Iapetus Ocean was an area of deep water which separated much of North America and Scotland from the rest of Europe and Newfoundland during the Lower Palaeozoic.
Inarticulates are BRACHIOPODS with shells which have 2 valves of unequal size but which can be divided lengthwise into identical halves. They lack internal support for the feeding organ and teeth for articulation. Their skeletons mostly have a high phosphate content.

Jawless fishes, or agnathans, are represented today by the lampreys and hag-fishes. These have CARTILAGINOUS skeletons and sucker-like mouths. The lampreys are semi-parasites, while the hag-fishes feed on dead and decaying matter. In the Palaeozoic, agnathans

Inside, a spiral support structure is very well developed. In life this was covered by the soft tissues of the feeding organ (LOPHOPHORE) and strong currents brought water in towards the centre of the shell. The spiriferids were efficient filter-feeders and this allowed them to flourish in deeper water than most other medium-sized brachiopods. In deeper waters they were associated with the delicate 'lace bryozoans' such as the FENESTELLIDS and several types of small corals.

Shallow reef communities

In shallower reef communities the corals were larger, and although tabulates were still common, large colonial rugose corals were also now plentiful. Their skeletons were much more complex than those of the tabulates and their larger polyps were probably more efficient in feeding. There were still fewer rugose than tabulate corals, algae and bryozoans, but their appearance represents the first major colonization of the reef habitat by members of Rugosa. In many reefs these corals were found with massive stromatoporoids, which often formed distinct mound-like structures. There are still doubts about the stromatoporoids, although many people believe that they are related to the living HYDROZOANS. They reached their evolutionary peak during the Devonian and provide valuable indications about the environment. Atrypid brachiopods and trilobites again filled their specialized niches in the Devonian reefs. It is impossible to tell whether or not the reef-dwelling corals of the Devonian were hermatypic. Hermatypic refers to the presence of microscopic algae within the soft tissues of the animal, and indirectly to the symbiotic relationship that exists between the two organisms. Such a relationship is common in modern reef communities. Deep-water corals are often referred to as ahermatypic. It is unlikely that any of the small solitary Devonian corals were truly ahermatypic, but forms such as *Calceola* and *Goniophyllum* show interesting adaptations to living in soft sediments. Both have 'lid-like' covers for protection or to prevent sediment from covering the polyp, but whereas *Goniophyllum* is angular and lived partly embedded in sediment, *Calceola* was slipper-like and rested with its flat surface on the sea floor.

Right: *Calceola sandalina*, the 'slipper coral', is one of the most common Devonian corals. Its overall shape and lid-like operculum are thought to be adaptations to a life spent resting on the muddy sea-floor.

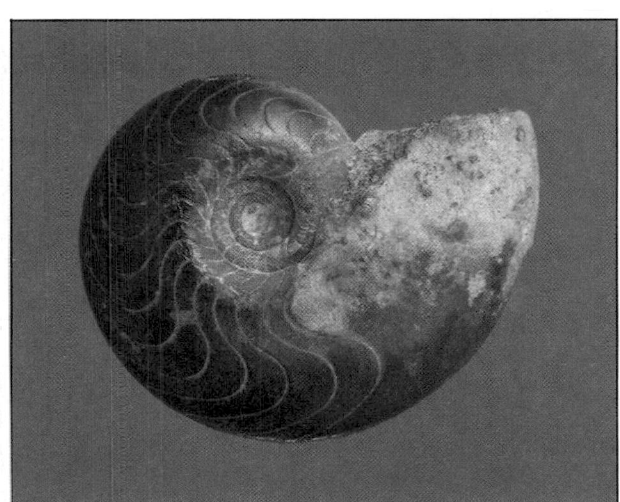

Right: During the Devonian, the first ammonoid molluscs appeared in the seas. They were mostly small to medium-sized, were coiled and had fairly simple suture lines. They were called goniatites and *Manticoceras*, shown here, is a typical example.

Right: Spiriferids were among the more common Devonian brachiopods. They were advanced creatures which had complex spiralled internal skeletons to support the feeding organ. Food was drawn into the shell from both sides and waste materials expelled from the central region.

such as *Cephalaspis* and *Pteraspis* were heavily-armoured. Jawless fishes range from the Ordovician to Recent periods.

L Labyrinthodonts were the major amphibians of the late Palaeozoic to early Mesozoic. Many grew to a huge size and a number of groups adapted to a life mainly on land.
Laurasia was a huge land-mass formed by the fusion of North America, Europe and much of Asia. During the late Palaeozoic to early Mesozoic it formed the northern part of the super-continent called PANGAEA.
Lepospondyls were a group of amphibians that lived during the Upper Palaeozoic. Most were of modest size and many became snake- or even worm-like in appearance. They were characterized by husk-type vertebrae, in which the lower unit — the centrum — was a single, spool-shaped structure with a central hole for the passage of the notochord.
Lingula is the classic case of a 'living-fossil'. It is an INARTICULATE brachiopod characterized by a shell in which the 2 valves are almost mirror-images of each other. The valves are elongate and lack a HINGE-LINE of any significance. The outside of the shell is marked by distinct growth lines and inside there is a complex arrangement of muscles. These are used to open and close the valves. *Lingula* is a burrower and is attached to the base of its burrow by a thick stalk. A shallow water-dwelling animal, it seems to occupy the same niche now as it did some 500 million years ago.
Lophophore is the tentacled feeding organ of both the BRYOZOANS and the BRACHIOPODS. Movements of the tentacles set up currents from which the animal obtains food and oxygen.
Loxomma was a primitive RHACHITOME amphibian from the Carboniferous, and was distributed over large areas. It had large, keyhole-shaped eye-holes, possibly holding a facial gland as well as the eye itself. *Loxomma* and its relatives had high, narrow skulls and pointed teeth.
Lungfishes are represented today by 3 tropical types which live in areas of sea-

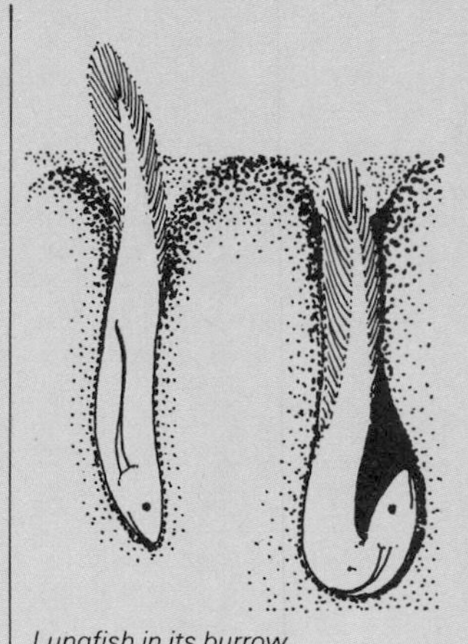

Lungfish in its burrow

Giant water scorpions and fishes

Great arthropods or 'water scorpions' — the EURYPTERIDS — flourished during the Devonian. Unlike their early Palaeozoic counterparts they probably lived in BRACKISH WATERS, perhaps driven out of their original marine habitat by the rapidly-evolving fishes. Eurypterids grew to over 1.8 metres in length, but even they were no match for creatures such as DUNKLEOSTEUS, a huge PLACODERM fish from the Devonian. Its skull alone measured several metres in length and its huge jaws made it a formidable predator. Other fish predators included the shark CLADOSELACHE, an early CARTILAGINOUS fish. The Devonian saw the peak of placoderm evolution, for unlike the sharks and rays these 'plated skins' were a short-lived group.

Movement on to land

Dunkleosteus and *Cladoselache* represent only a part of the amazing success story of fishes during the Devonian. They ruled the sea, but related forms, and a host of other fishes, flourished in freshwater lakes and rivers. There the competition for food and territory was fierce, particularly among the carnivorous ARTHRODIRES and bony fishes. The latter included ray- and TASSEL-FINNED forms, both of which show considerable diversity. Ray-finned fishes (actinopterygians) are still represented by hundreds of species, but the tassel-finned fishes (crossopterygians) are restricted to a few species of LUNGFISHES and the COELACANTH *Latimeria.* During the Devonian there was much more variety among crossopterygians, various forms exhibiting several interesting developments. Obvious among these was the strong fin, the general form of which ultimately bears direct comparison with the walking limb of land animals. The development of the rounded fin coincided with that of the lung and together they enabled the crossopterygians to occupy niches in shallow water.

Crossopterygians moved into shallow waters during a time of climatic change, when long arid spells resulted in ponds and lakes drying up. To counter this, lungfishes built protective burrows, while the coelacanths eventually sought refuge in the depths of the oceans. A third group of crossopterygians — the RHIPIDISTIANS — did neither, but relied on their strong fins to struggle from one pond to another. From this group emerged the first of the land-dwelling TETRAPODS — *Ichthyostega.*

The first amphibian

The pattern of its skull roof and complex structure of its teeth indicate that *Ichthyostega* derived from a rhipidistian ancestor. It also retains a strong fish-like tail and the limbs are outspread as to allow only a slow SPRAWLING

Below: During the Devonian, tassel-finned rhipidistian fishes lived as predators in shallow, freshwater environments. One of the most important was *Eusthenopteron,* a medium-sized animal with many features that make it an ideal ancestor for the amphibians. *Eusthenopteron* probably used its fins for support, while waiting in hiding for its prey. In times of drought the sturdy fins may have been used as primitive 'legs' when the fish 'waggled' its way from a drying pond towards safety.

sonal drought. When water is scarce they live in shallow burrows to avoid drying up. During the Devonian lungfishes were more common, and burrowing was an ideal adaptation to cope with the aridity then common in many areas.

Lycopsids are represented today by the clubmosses, spikemosses and rush-like quillworts. These are rather inconspicuous herbaceous plants, but in the past clubmosses were represented by massive trees. The first lycopsids were small, but during the Carboniferous huge trees such as *Lepidodendron* flourished in the coal measure forests. *Lepidodendron* grew to 30 metres in height and had a girth of 1 metre; the tall, straight stem was capped by a thick crown of branches. Lycopsids have lived from the Devonian to Recent periods.

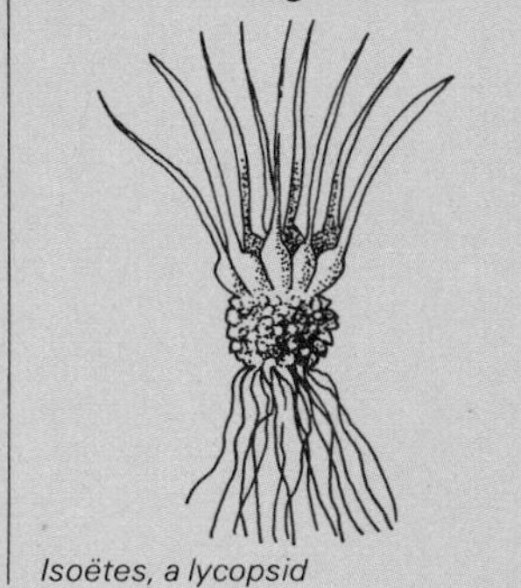

Isoëtes, a lycopsid

Lysorophus was a small amphibian from the early Permian of North America. It measured only a few millimetres in length and lived in ponds. It had small limbs and some scientists believe that it breathed through gills all its life. It looked worm-like, although the skull had numerous sharply-pointed teeth. *Lysorophus* was a LEPOSPONDYL.

M

Marrella is a TRILOBITOID from the Middle Cambrian of British Columbia. It has a large, horned head shield and 2 pairs of antennae. Like the TRILOBITES its limbs consist of a jointed walking leg and a feathery gill branch.

Mass extinction is the relatively sudden disappearance (that is, in a few tens of millions of years or less) of important groups of organisms which had previously been dominant and diverse in various habitats. They disappear without trace from the fossil record, while new groups of organisms rapidly evolve to take their place. Major extinctions of land plants have preceded extinctions of land animals, and the extinctions always affect groups which are related, rather than similar ecological types. Mass extinctions in the sea brought the Palaeozoic era to a close, and mass extinctions on land and sea ended the Mesozoic era.

Megalocephalus, like LOXOMMA, is a LABYRINTHODONT amphibian of the RHACHITOME type. It was widespread during the Carboniferous,

Above: *Ichthyostega*, the first amphibian, appeared in the Upper Devonian. It had strongly-developed legs and a long, fish-like tail. *Ichthyostega* was therefore a fully-developed tetrapod, but it also retained some primitive characteristics. Like the rhipidistian fishes, *Ichthyostega* had a labyrinthine tooth structure and arch type vertebrae. Because it was an amphibian, *Ichthyostega* had to return to water to lay its eggs. It lived in a landscape which was rather inhospitable, with early vascular plants growing only in damp areas.

GAIT. This animal's appearance marks the conquest of land by the vertebrates. It is unlikely that *Ichthyostega* moved far beyond the banks of lakes or rivers, and like all AMPHIBIANS it had to return to water to reproduce. Although it probably ate fish, *Ichthyostega*'s arrival may have been linked with the diversification of insects and other arthropods on land. This first amphibian was quite modest in size, but its uncontested claim on a new niche ensured its success. By the end of the Devonian amphibians were established in the northern hemisphere and the Carboniferous is aptly named the 'Age of Amphibians'.

Devonian plants

The evolution of both *Ichthyostega* and the arthropods is no doubt closely tied to the emergence of VASCULAR PLANTS. The first of these had, as we know, appeared in the late Silurian and by the Devonian both the primitive psilopsids and LYCOPSIDS were firmly established. They grew in swampland areas and although their roots were still anchored in water-sodden sediments, other features show that they too were gradually conquering the problems of a life on land. Both psilopsids and lycopsids protected their spores in terminal SPORANGIA , and relied on the wind to disperse them. The sporangia prevented the spores from drying out, and when transported to a damp environment, they would develop into a unit called the PROTHALLUS. Once mature, this produced both male and female sex cells which then united to give rise to the adult plant. By the end of the Devonian, plants had evolved in which the sporangia were no longer terminal. The evolution of land plants was essential to the development of FOOD CHAINS (*see page 69*). They were the primary producers of food and so supported all other organisms living

living along the edges of coal swamps. It had a large head, and, like *Loxomma*, had keyhole-shaped eyes. As in many primitive amphibians, the skull was high and narrow.

Micro-fossil is a general name given to any organism of very small or microscopic proportions. Protozoans, ostracodes, spores and pollen are all regarded as micro-fossils and are studied in micro-palaeontology.

Mississippian is the lower of the 2 divisions of the Carboniferous period in North America.

Molluscs are invertebrates which have unsegmented bodies. They include bivalves, snails and octopuses. Most are sea creatures.

Monograptids are a group of GRAPTOLITES which have a single branch with the THECAL CUPS arranged only on one side. They are the most advanced of the graptolites and mark the climax of their 2 major evolutionary trends. These were a reduction in the number of branches, or stipes, and an overall increase in the size of thecal cups. Monograptids may have been free-swimming organisms. They first appeared in the early Silurian and died out in the Devonian. Their remains are found world-wide.

Mutations are errors which occur in the duplication of cells. If mutations occur in an organism's sex cells, they can be passed on to the next generation, so perpetuating an alteration to the organism.

N **Nautiloids** were the dominant group of CEPHALOPODS for much of the Palaeozoic era. They show a great variety in shell type and deposited a range of internal deposits to help control their buoyancy. The shell of the living *Nautilus* is made of aragonite and is divided by simple transverse septa. The first nautiloids appeared in the Upper Cambrian. Shells over 4.5 metres long have been recorded from the Ordovician.

Neoptera, a stonefly

Neoptera are those winged insects able to flex and also fold their wings backwards. They evolved from the PALAEOPTERA and many living forms have no secondary wings.

O **Ocean basins** occur beyond the edges of the CONTINENTAL SHELVES and are on average about 3,800 metres deep.

on land. Some insects had already adopted a parasitic relationship with swampland plants.

Lower Carboniferous marine life

The Carboniferous is renowned for the thick limestone rock sequences that characterize the early (Lower) part of the period, and the deltaic and coal swamp deposits of the Upper part. As in earlier periods, limestones indicate warm, shallow seas, and some deposits were obviously laid down under conditions similar to those in the West Indies today. Corals and brachiopods were the dominant invertebrates of the Lower Carboniferous, with various families showing important evolutionary trends. During this sub-period (MISSISSIPPIAN) algae, bryozoans, echinoids and molluscs were important members of several communities.

Corals

Rugose corals now far out-numbered the tabulates, which were mainly represented by *Favosites* and *Syringopora.* Of the rugose forms large, single corals often lived in shallow waters and on reef slopes, while colonial species abounded in reef communities. *Caninia* is one of the largest recorded solitary corals and seems to have preferred well-oxygenated waters, which had a limited deposit of sediment. In contrast, the much smaller ZAPHRENTIDS appear to have enjoyed the muddy substrates of deeper water, rich in decaying organic matter. *Caninia* may have grown rapidly to adult size in order to gain a stable feeding position as soon as possible. Rapid growth may also have been a feature of the colonial form *Lithostrotion.* In this case the stimulus was perhaps competition for food in the reef community, the need for a strong skeleton being less important in a zone of densely-packed organisms. In some species of *Lithostrotion* the individual polyps became closely packed and probably improved the efficiency of the whole colony. This was certainly true for the most advanced species, in which the polyps were linked within the colony.

During the Carboniferous several rugose families developed a strong, rock-like structure in the centre of their skeletons. This was called the 'axial boss', and its development was probably linked with a general improvement in the fixing

Below: Solitary corals, crinoids, bivalves and brachiopods colonized the seaward slopes of Lower Carboniferous reefs. Small ammonoids are also found in this community. Although complete remains of sea cucumbers are rarely found, tiny spicules reveal their former presence in deeper-water environments. Lace bryozoans such as *Fenestella* were common in communities living on muddy sea bottoms during the Carboniferous. They were delicate filter-feeders, obtaining food particles from the surrounding sea water, and are found in association with small solitary corals, burrowing bivalves and small brachiopods.

Olenellid is the common name to describe TRILOBITES. It refers to the earliest group – the Olenellina. In general they have large semi-circular head shields and many spiny body segments (as in *Olenellus*).

Onverwacht Series is a group of rocks which underlies the FIG TREE SERIES, and is about 15,000 metres thick. It comprises various volcanic materials, and sediments which contain fossils.

Onychophorans are represented today by the living velvet worm *Peripatus.* Their bodies are segmented and they have unjointed limbs that can be inflated with blood for walking. *Peripatus* lives in tropical forests, but the fossil form *Aysheia* (Middle Cambrian) was undoubtedly marine.

Ophiderpeton was a snake-like LEPOSPONDYL from the Upper Carboniferous. It grew just under a metre long and all signs of front and hind limbs had disappeared. *Ophiderpeton* belonged to a group of specialized lepospondyls which had forked single-headed ribs. Some appear to have had up to 200 vertebrae.

Ostracodes are small CRUSTACEANS with a 2-valved shell or carapace. The valves are held together along a distinct upper HINGE-LINE and the soft parts are inside. Like other ARTHROPODS and crustaceans, they have well-developed limbs. The ostracode body has only a few segments. Ostracodes live in freshwater or marine communities and most live on the sea-floor. The first ostracodes are recorded from the Cambrian period.

P

Palaeoptera were the earliest group of winged insects. They appeared in the Upper Carboniferous and were characterized at first by 2 pairs of equal-sized wings.

Palaeozoic is the era of ancient life. It began with the dawn of the Cambrian period, approximately 570 million years ago, and ended with the passing of the Permian, 345 million years later. The periods comprising the Palaeozoic were the Cambrian, Ordovician, Silurian, Devonian, Carboniferous and Permian. At the beginning of the era, trilobites and brachiopods were the dominant forms of life. In the Ordovician the graptolites and nautiloids flourished. By the Devonian and Carboniferous the corals were abundant, and the fishes,

Palaeozoic plant

of the polyp to its skeleton. Unlike modern corals, the Rugosa were generally unable to fix themselves to the sea floor. This must have presented problems in colonizing some habitats, although it did not prevent the group from reaching a peak during the Carboniferous.

Brachiopods

In many communities the rugose corals are found associated with brachiopods, of which the spiriferids and PRODUCTID BRACHIOPODS show the most significant developments. Spiriferids are by no means as common as during the Devonian, but their efficient feeding method allowed them to persist in the deeper waters around the reefs. Variety among the productids was spectacular; a few massively-built species measured over 300 millimetres across the hinge-line. In some reef limestones, productids accounted for over 80 per cent of the shell animals. They represent a major burst in brachiopod evolution, and their success was probably the result of living partially buried in the sediment of the sea floor. This was a new way of life within the group, the stability of various individuals being improved by their developing long spines. Most forms had a large, convex lower valve and a lid-like upper one. Other brachiopods to develop spines included *Chonetes* and related groups. These were comparatively small forms, first recorded from the early Silurian. As in productids, the spines were used for stability and enabled CHONETOIDS to inhabit soft substrates.

In many Lower Carboniferous communities, stalked crinoids occupied the higher feeding levels. Most species were common to the reef slopes and only a few lived in deep waters. In contrast the 'lace-bryozoans', such as *Fenestella*, flourished in less lime-rich seas where they are found with small corals, trilobites and bivalves.

Left: The rugose coral *Caninia* was extremely large compared to many of its contemporaries. Individuals 200 mm long are common. *Caninia* shared its shallow reef environment with numerous brachiopods, bivalves and trilobites. Brachiopods and corals (such as *Cyathaxonia*) are typical of Lower Carboniferous reef environments. Algae and bryozoans were also very common in binding and building the reef framework. The dome-like growths of stromatolitic algae identify tidal flat communities of the Lower Carboniferous.

amphibians, reptiles and land plants had all appeared. The era's end was marked by the mass extinction of numerous groups.

Pangaea means 'all lands', and was first used in the 1920s by the German meteorologist Alfred Wegener to describe the single super-continent thought to have existed in Permian times. This super-continent would have had an irregular outline and been surrounded by the universal ocean of Panthalassa — the ancestor of the Pacific. The present continents are fragments of Pangaea which have drifted apart.

Pelycosaurs were a major group of SYNAPSID reptiles that flourished during the Permian period. They are perhaps best-known for the great sail-backed reptiles *Dimetrodon* and *Edaphosaurus,* but other less spectacular species are of equal importance. The pelycosaurs are the oldest synapsids and although comparatively primitive when compared with the THERAPSIDS, they mark a major advance over the ANAPSID stem reptiles.

Peripatus is an ARTHROPOD with a soft, thin outer skeleton. It is a velvet worm, or ONYCHOPHORAN, and is related to the Cambrian form AYSHEIA. *Peripatus* has a muscular body, a small head and numerous unjointed limbs. It is found today in damp tropical forests.

Phacops is a TRILOBITE commonly found in rocks of the Silurian and Devonian. Its external skeleton is compact, with the head shield dominated by a large central region. *Phacops* has large eyes and it is easy to identify the individual lenses that gave the animal a mosaic-type vision. The head shield and body segments are well-rounded and the tail is comparatively small. *Phacops* could roll itself into a tight ball for protection.

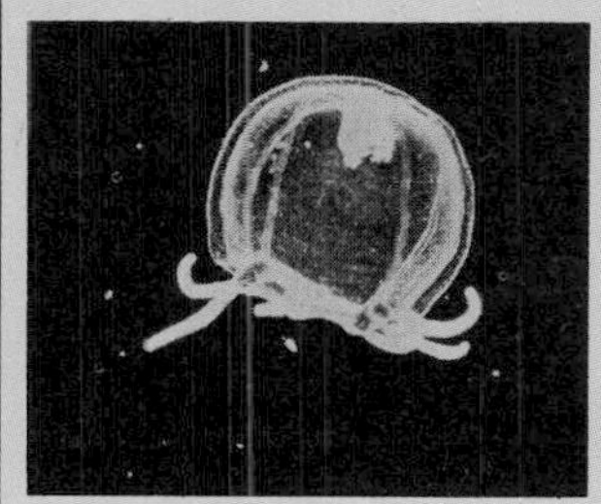

Bell plankton

Placoderms were one of the earliest groups of jawed fishes. Many were heavily armoured and members of the group are commonly called 'plated-skins'.

Plankton are the minute, even microscopic, organisms that exist at and near the surface of seawater. Most plant and animal organisms float passively, but others may swim in the prevailing currents.

Poleumita is a gastropod from the Lower Silurian rocks of Europe and North America. Its shell is coiled in a plane, with deep SUTURE

In such communities, goniatites and nautiloids shared the role of free-swimming invertebrate scavenger, while on the sea floor, SEA CUCUMBERS fed on decaying organic matter.

Coal measure swamps

In contrast to the limestones of the Lower Carboniferous (or Mississippian), sediments of the Upper Carboniferous (or Pennsylvanian) are frequently without fossils. The general exception to this are the coal measures, in which a profusion of plant fossils reveals former densely-vegetated swampland areas. Occasionally these swamplands were flooded by sea, so that marine organisms such as goniatites and productid brachiopods characterize specific layers. Flooding by fresh water also occurred, and under these conditions communities of freshwater BIVALVES flourished for short periods of time. Swamps covered vast areas of Europe and North America, and their warm, humid conditions suited the developing amphibians and insects.

The coal forests mostly developed around open waterways, with different plants occupying various levels and zones. Along the water's edge the dominant plant was CALAMITES. This is related to the living HORSETAILS and its stem was similarly divided into vertical units. Some species of *Calamites* were shaped rather like ornamental firs, and their large trunks are known to have littered

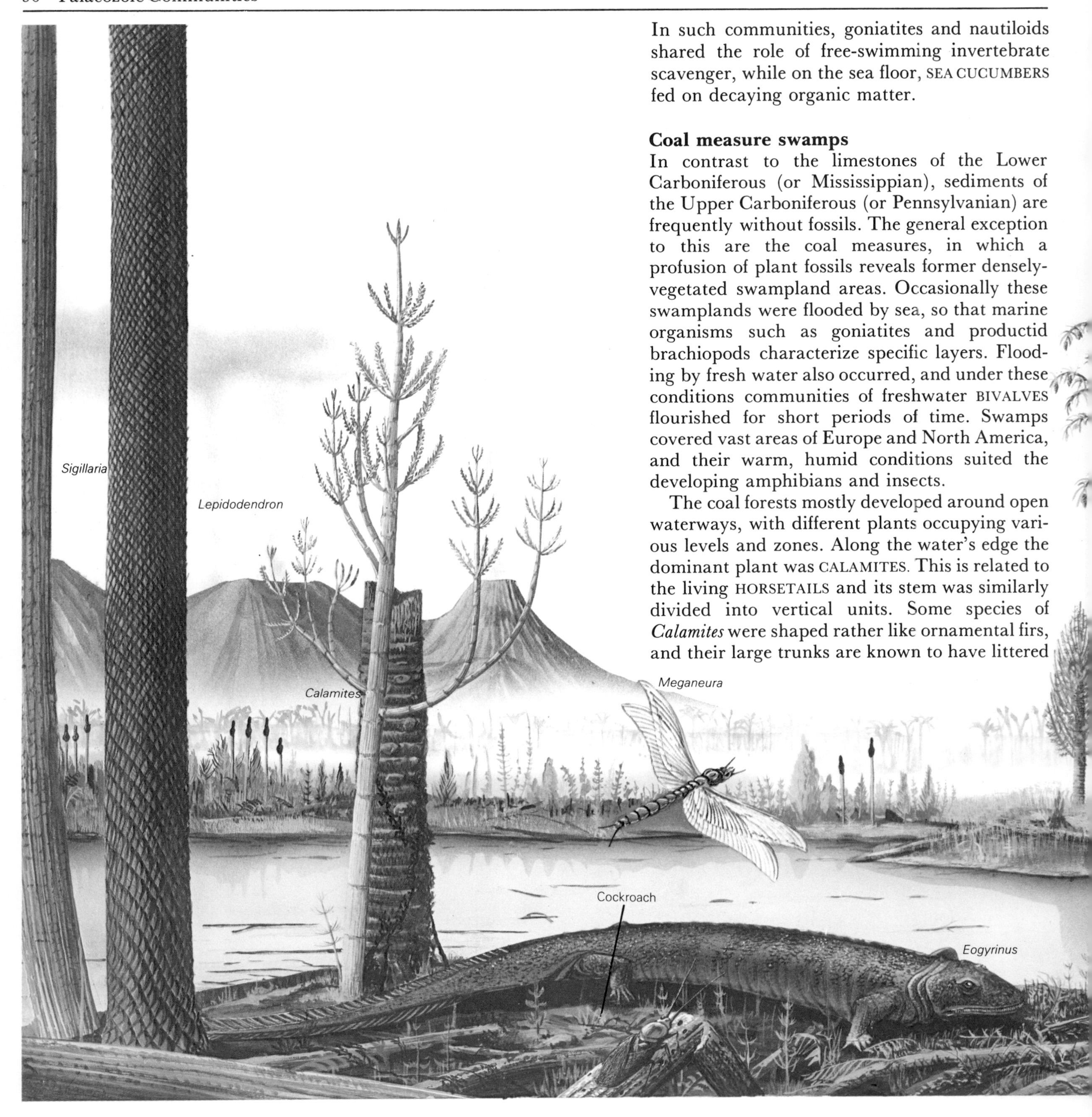

LINES (*see page 114*) between each of the whorls or coils. *Poleumita* has strong growth lines and a raised angular ridge on the upper surface. It grazed plants, moving slowly over the sea floor.

Polyps are the fixed individuals of corals and sea anemones. They have a cylindrical body and a ring of tentacles around the mouth.

Pre-Cambrian is the name of the era which preceded the Palaeozoic and ended about 570 million years ago. It lasted for about 4,000 million years and therefore accounts for about 85% of the Earth's history. For a long time Pre-Cambrian rocks were thought to contain no fossils, but over the last 20 years or so they have been discovered in increasing numbers.

Productid brachiopods were very common during the Upper Palaeozoic. Their upper valves were usually flat and the lower ones strongly convex. Some groups were bizarre and coral-like in appearance; others were adorned with long spines. Productid brachiopods ranged from the Lower Devonian to the Upper Permian.

Prokaryotes are organisms which have no compact nucleus in their cells, as the nuclear material is dispersed in the protoplasm. Bacteria, blue-green ALGAE and the actinomycetes make up the prokaryotes.

Prothallus is a small, flat, often heart-shaped plant. It represents the stage that produces sex cells in mosses and liverworts.

Provincial communities are largely made up of organisms restricted to a limited area of land or sea. They are usually isolated by barriers which prevent them from migrating and mixing with other communities. When in the past barriers to migration between continents or oceans were few, communities were more uniform or cosmopolitan.

Fern prothallus

Psilopsids are a group of 4 plant species, the best-known of which is the whisk 'fern' *Psilotum*. All species belong to the tropics or subtropics.

R

Redlichiid trilobites are a major group restricted in time to the Lower and Middle Cambrian. Most have a large head shield, large eyes and a small, spine-like tail.

Reefs may be either ac-

the flood plains that characterized the Upper Carboniferous. Other well-known lowland plants were *Lepidodendron* and *Sigillaria* (lycopods) and *Neuropteris* and *Alethopteris* (pteridosperms). *Lepidodendron* and *Sigillaria* grew to approximately 35 metres in height, and although they were sparsely distributed they dominated the surrounding vegetation. Both plants are noted for the unique leaf scars on their trunks, as *Neuropteris* and *Alethopteris* are known by their leafy, fern-like fronds.

Away from the floodplains, plants further upland were dominated by *Cordaites* and emerging closely-related conifers. Not all forms of *Cordaites* were confined to drier areas, however; some seem to have existed, like living MANGROVES (*see page 106*) in brackish-water areas.

In the swamp forests amphibians, which had first appeared in the Upper Devonian, now ruled. ANTHRACOSAURS such as *Diplovertebron* and *Eogyrinus* (*Pteroplax*) were common, the former representing the primitive, ancestral line, and *Eogyrinus* becoming specialized towards living in water. *Diplovertebron* measured about 150 millimetres, while *Eogyrinus* reached 4 to 4.5 metres long. *Eogyrinus* had a round, rather snake-like body, and used its flattened tail to propel itself.

Other large amphibians of the Upper Carboniferous swamp forests include LOXOMMA and MEGALOCEPHALUS. Unlike *Eogyrinus* these were heavily built with strong outspread limbs. Their heads were broad and flattened, and overall their general build seems suited to a more terrestrial way of life. During the Upper Carboniferous this probably meant an existence along the edges of the swamp, where both animals fed on small amphibians and possibly insects. Among these small amphibians were the snake-like OPHIDERPETON and *Dolichosoma,* and the long-bodied SAUROPLEURA, and *Microbrachis.* All these were LEPOSPONDYLS, probably adapted to eating insects. *Sauropleura* was, like *Ophiderpeton,* rather snake-like and the drastic reduction of its limbs suggests that it spent much of its time in water. *Microbrachis* was shorter-bodied and, although much reduced, its limbs were still used for movement. At 100 millimetres long, *Microbrachis* was among the smallest of the amphibians. It was less than half the size of the first reptile — *Hylonomus* — also from the Upper Carboniferous, and so may have fallen prey to it.

Insect remains from the coal measures are not uncommon, and both winged and wingless species have been found. Most winged forms belonged to the PALAEOPTERA and were able to move their wings only upwards and downwards. Typical of these were *Mischoptera* and *Meganeura,* two large dragonfly-like insects. Cockroaches were also numerous at this time, while the earliest forms of the more advanced NEOPTERA

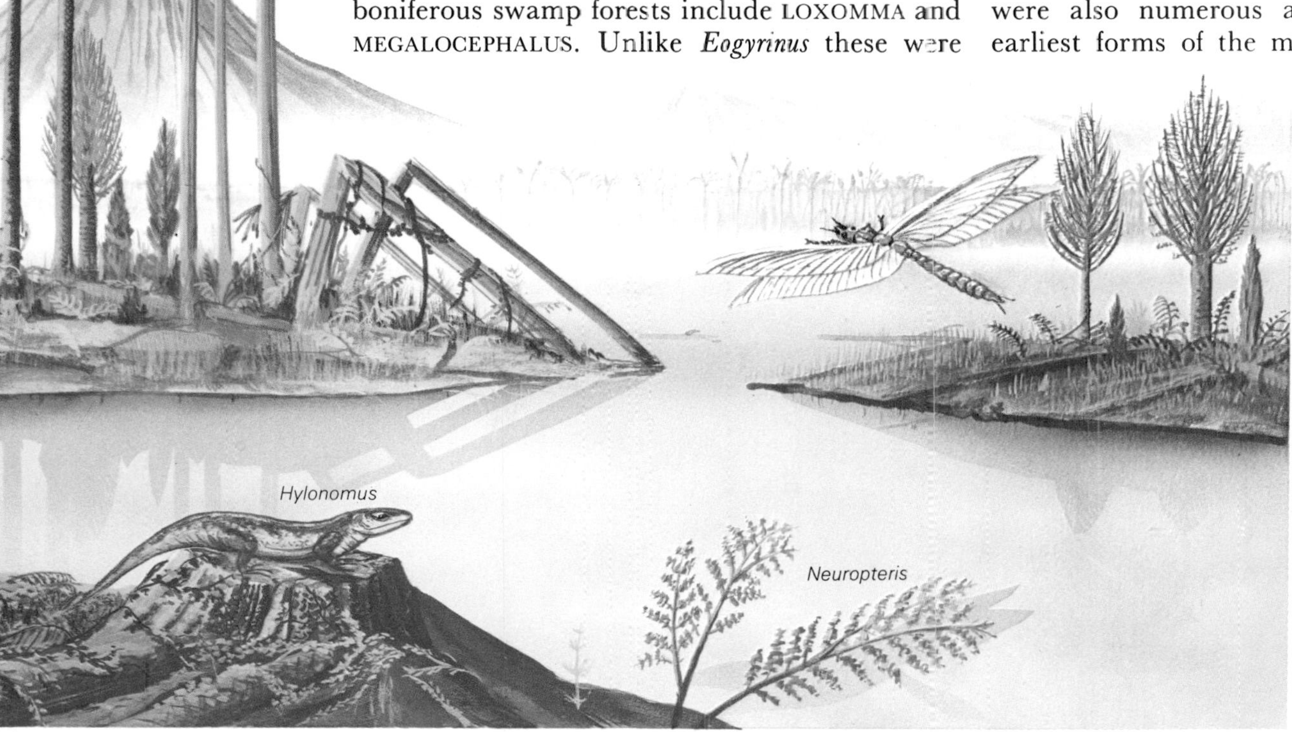

Left: The Upper Carboniferous is the first period of geological time noted for forests, when huge tree ferns and sphenopsids (distant relatives of the horsetails) were common. Amphibians such as *Eogyrinus* flourished in the swampland regions. Other vertebrates, including the first reptile *Hylonomus,* also lived in this forest environment, where numerous insects occupied different niches. The coal-forming swamp forests of the Upper Carboniferous covered vast regions of several continents.

cumulations of organic remains or simply ridges of rock on the sea floor. To most palaeontologists it means the former, and represents the site where the accumulated organisms once lived. This means that in most cases the animals are still in their living position, or have not been transported far by currents. The first 'reefs', built solely by plants, occurred in the Pre-Cambrian, whereas the first animal reefs, built by the ARCHAEOCYATHIDS, are found in Cambrian rocks.

Reptiles are higher vertebrates which have a scaly skin and lay amniote eggs. Four major types comprise the group: ANAPSIDS, DIAPSIDS, euryapsids and SYNAPSIDS.

The crocodile is a reptile

Rhachitome describes the structure of the vertebrae (backbone) in the tassel-finned RHIPIDISTIANS and some primitive amphibians.

Rhichtofenids are a group of rather exotic, oddly-shaped BRACHIOPODS that flourished during the Permian period. They were articulate brachiopods, with valves of unequal size. The lower, or pedicle, valve was coral-like in shape, and the upper valve was lid-like. Many rhichtofenids developed root-like spines to fix in the sediments of the sea floor.

Rhipidistians are an extinct group of TASSEL-FINNED fishes from which amphibians diverged in Devonian times. The fins of various rhipidistians have larger bones arranged in a similar way to the walking limbs of the early amphibians.

Rugose means 'rough', and the word is used to name and describe certain Palaeozoic corals. These are in fact termed the Rugosa and one of their characteristics is the rough external surface of their skeletons. Rugose corals may be single or colonial in form and are characterized by radial partitions (septa) and small horseshoe-shaped plates

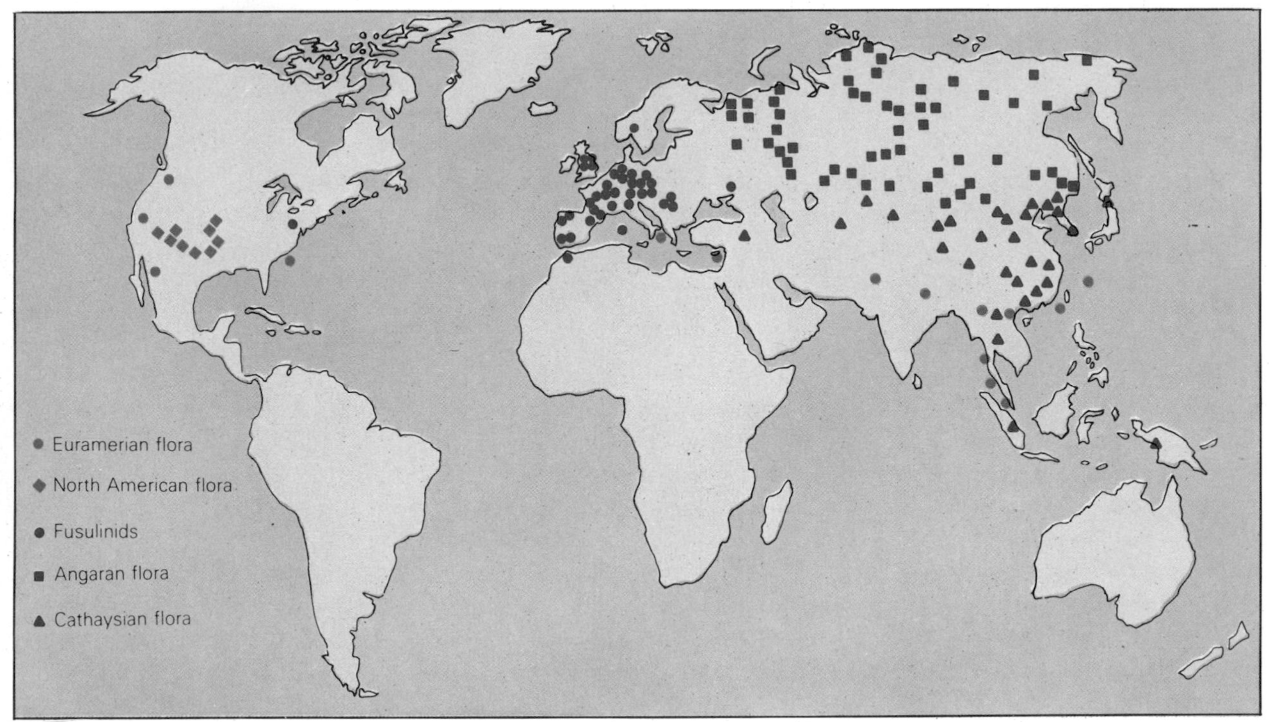

From 'Atlas of Palaeobiogeography', A. Hallam (Elsevier)

Left: A map of the world as it is today. During the Permian, however, the landmasses were arranged very differently, and geologists recognize that a single super-continent — Pangaea — existed for most of the period. Great ice sheets covered large areas of South America, Africa, India and Australasia. To the north of the ice sheets the plant life, or flora, was acclimatized to wet, cold conditions. It was known as the *Glossopteris* flora, and its tolerance of a cold, wet climate was shared by the Angaran flora of Siberia. In Europe and North America the floras enjoyed warmer, drier conditions. During the Permian there was an east-west seaway from China to Spain, while sea covered large areas of western America. Fusulinids flourished in these seas.

began to appear. Unlike palaeopterans these insects can flex their wings backwards.

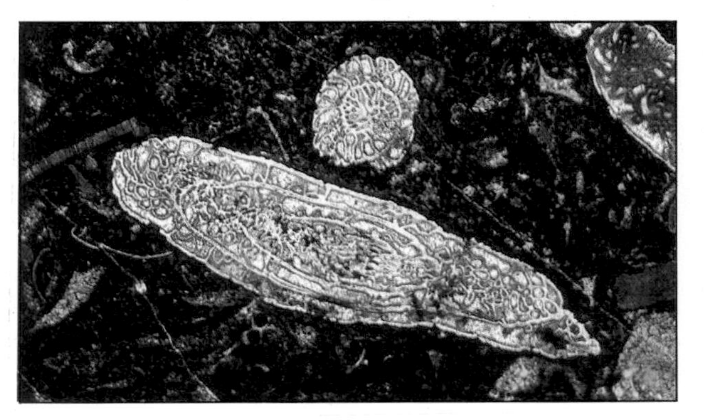

Left: The fusulinids are a very important group of micro-fossils. During the Carboniferous and Permian periods they were distributed throughout the world and they evolved rapidly. The sections through the outer covering, shown here, reveal that fusulinids had chambered and complex skeletons. These were rounded in cross section and cigar-shaped in lengthways section.

Permian life

The Permian period lasted approximately 55 million years, from 280 to 225 million years ago. At its beginning, the continental masses of GONDWANALAND and LAURASIA collided, and the seas of the world retreated from the shores of the new super-continent of PANGAEA. In the southern continents huge ice sheets marked the dawn of the new period, while to the north forest lands covered vast areas of North America, Europe and Asia. Plant remains indicate that three separate FLORAS existed in the north, and to the south, areas of South America and Africa were covered by the *Glossopteris* flora. The plants of this flora grew in wet-lands, similar to the Angaran flora of Siberia, and sharp differentiation in their growth rings reveals that both were adapted to cold environments. In contrast, the plants of American and European floras had a more regular growth-ring pattern, indicating that they were adapted to warmer, more equable climates.

Climatic conditions naturally affected the distribution of most organisms. Among vertebrates the sail-backed PELYCOSAURS, COTYLOSAURS and amphibians flourished around the equator, while WARM-BLOODED mammal-like REPTILES dominated the colder southern lands. In the equatorial region, limestone deposits mark the presence of warm shelf seas. These were rich in organic debris and in some areas great barrier reefs fringed the coastline. To some extent the communities living in these areas were a continuation of those that existed during the Carboniferous, although invertebrates such as the productid brachiopods and the crinoids had diversified further. Some of the productids were similar to their Carboniferous relatives, but others developed elongated spines or adopted a coral-like form. The last are known as the RHICHTOFENIDS and they were well adapted to colonize reef environments. Their elongated

called dissepiments. The rugose corals range from the Middle Ordovician to the end of the Palaeozoic era.

S **Salinity** is one of the basic properties of seawater and varies according to the amount of salts dissolved in it. Normal seawater has a salinity of about 3.433% (or 34.33 g of salt per 1,000 g of water).

Sauropleura is a snake-like LEPOSPONDYL amphibian recorded from the Carboniferous. The body is long and apart from small vestiges, the limbs have disappeared. The skull is long and pointed and appears adapted to an insect- or worm-eating diet. *Sauropleura* was numerous in coal swamps.

Gull feeding on fish remains

Scavengers feed on the remains of other animals.

Sea cucumbers, or holothurians, are free-living ECHINODERMS with a rather fat, worm-like appearance. Their bodies are not plated and only small calcareous remains indicate their presence in the fossil record. They range from the Ordovician to Recent periods.

Sediments are rocks formed from minerals that have either been carried to the site by water, wind or ice, or been deposited in their original place through chemical action.

Seymouria is a medium-sized LABYRINTHODONT from the Lower Permian of Texas, USA. Its skeleton is well-known and shows a number of reptile and amphibian characters. Because of this it was once thought that *Seymouria* and its close relatives were link fossils which were the true ancestors of the reptiles. *Seymouria*, which was 750 mm long, was sturdily-built and seems to have been adapted to a more land-based life than other amphibians.

Seymouriamorphs were a group of medium-sized LABYRINTHODONT amphibians from the Permian period. They were among the most advanced amphibians to walk on the Earth and were specialized towards a land-based life. It was once thought that they were the true ancestors of the reptiles, but this is now doubted as they appear too late in the fossil record. Unlike many of the earliest reptiles, seymouriamorphs have a prominent notch at the ear drum. This also suggests that they were already too specialized to be ancestors of the reptiles.

lower valve gave them height which helped in their search for food, while the lid-like upper valve protected their soft parts from attack. Unlike most brachiopods, it seems that rhichtofenids had developed means to create a rhythmic current flow in order to bring food to their mouths. This replaced the pumping action of other productids. In the Permian reefs of western Texas, USA, rhichtofenids are found together with siliceous sponges, nautiloids, gastropods and rugose corals.

Fusulinids

Warm water environments also encouraged the continued expansion of FUSULINID FORAMINIFERIDS. These small, spindle-shaped forms first appeared in the late Carboniferous, but during the Permian their increased numbers are marked by fusulinid limestones. Although only single-celled, and therefore rather simple organisms, fusulinids had shells of very complex structure. In fact successive types of fusulinids, widely distributed, became more and more complex. Most of these existed for only limited periods of time and therefore can be used as zone fossils in many areas. Certain types also appear to mark distinct faunal provinces.

Lagoons and basins

Inland from the barrier reefs and limestone-rich seas, the Permian coastlines featured LAGOONAL areas (*see page 105*) and land-locked basins. Both were subject to high evaporation and their waters were highly salt. In the lagoons, however, constant replenishment by fresh sea water kept the overall salinity lower than in the inland basins, and so lagoon communities were more diverse. Calcareous algae flourished there and their remains contributed to the accumulating sediment. Brachiopods, bivalves and gastropods thrived under these conditions, although free-swimming organisms were restricted to a few nautiloids. In the land-locked basins there was less individual variety and the communities were dominated by bivalves such as *Bakevellia* and *Schizodus*, gastropods and OSTRACODES. These last are small, two-valved CRUSTACEANS in which the shell, or carapace, is hinged along the upper margin. They are common to both marine and freshwater environments and seem to flourish

Below: During the Permian, the fusing together of the continents resulted in significant climatic and geographical changes. In many areas the coastline was dotted with land-locked basins (*right*). In these the water was very salty, so that only a few animals could survive. The animal life is aptly described as 'impoverished'. In the lagoons that bordered the seaward side of the Permian coastline, the variety of animals was significantly greater (*left*), although several of the forms found in the land-locked lagoons are tolerant of less saline conditions. Beyond the lagoons a more normal marine fauna existed. From the few Permian marine outcrops known throughout the world, it is obvious that many groups of vertebrates were less important than they had been earlier in the Palaeozoic.

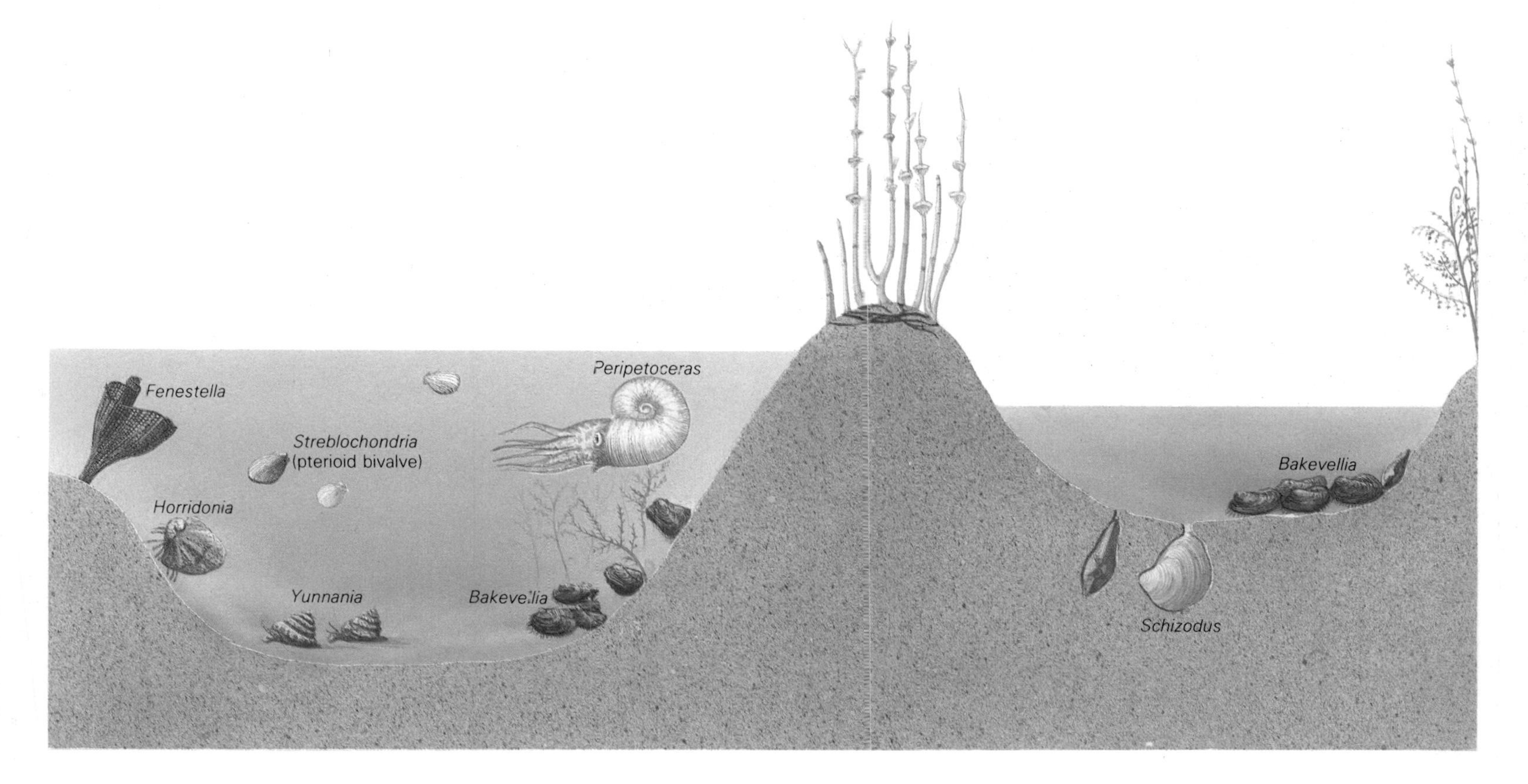

Shelly facies describes certain sediments and their enclosed animals which were deposited in shallow water. They are also called shelf facies.
Specific name, see TRIVIAL NAME.
Sponges are mainly marine organisms, characterized by numerous pores and a limited number of cell types. Many secrete needle-like and branched spicules that may be fused to form a rigid skeleton. The first sponges appeared in the late Pre-Cambrian. Zoologists recognize different grades of complexity in these animals, as the body wall is effectively folded into smaller chamberlets. Sponges are also known as Porifera.
Sporangia are the spore-containing structures of ferns.
Sprawling gait describes the awkward side-to-side movement of the more primitive 4-legged animals. It can be seen in the living salamanders and results from the outspread arrangement of limbs from the shoulder and hip girdles.
Stinging cells, or nematocysts, are characteristic of the jellyfish, sea anemones and corals. The cells occur on the surface of the tentacles and consist of a sac-like body and an elongate thread. The thread may be whip-like, barbed or adhesive. Stinging cells are used to catch and hold the small organisms on which the animals feed.

Fire salamander

Stony bryozoans, or trepostomes, were the dominant group of BRYOZOANS during the Lower Palaeozoic. Their colonies were often stick-like, although massive globular structures were also common. The trepostomes died out during the Triassic.
Stromatolites are reef-like communities of ALGAE and bacteria. Living examples have only recently been recognized, as sea creatures feed on them and stop them from developing into large structures. However, such creatures had not evolved in the Pre-Cambrian era, and large stromatolite colonies were therefore quite common then.
Stromatoporoids were important reef-building creatures of the Palaeozoic. They had layered skeletons and their soft parts were probably similar to those of living HYDROZOANS. They ranged from the Cambrian to the Cretaceous.

under fetid conditions, such as those on the floors of the inland basins.

Permian land animals

The welding together of the world's continents during the late Carboniferous and earliest Permian periods brought with it major changes in the Earth's climate. Huge glaciers covered Antarctica and large areas of South America, Africa, India and Australia. Deserts prevailed in equatorial regions and dense forests covered vast tracts of what are now the USSR and China. These conditions affected the distribution of animal populations, and as yet no large vertebrates have been recorded from the early Permian rocks of ice-bound Gondwanaland.

From the limited evidence we have, it appears that the two reptile stocks of the Upper Carboniferous — the ANAPSIDS and the SYNAPSIDS — were firmly established by the dawn of the Permian. Possibly the first DIAPSID reptiles had also appeared, but they remained insignificant until the end of the period. Amphibians still made up a large part of several vertebrate communities, and most of the families common in the Carboniferous were also to be found in the early Permian. Of the two major groups, however, the lepospondyls were greatly reduced in numbers. The survivors included DIPLOCAULUS and DIPLOCERASPIS (two rather grotesque 'horned' forms) and the highly specialized LYSOROPHUS, a water-dwelling amphibian with reduced limbs and a rather worm-like body.

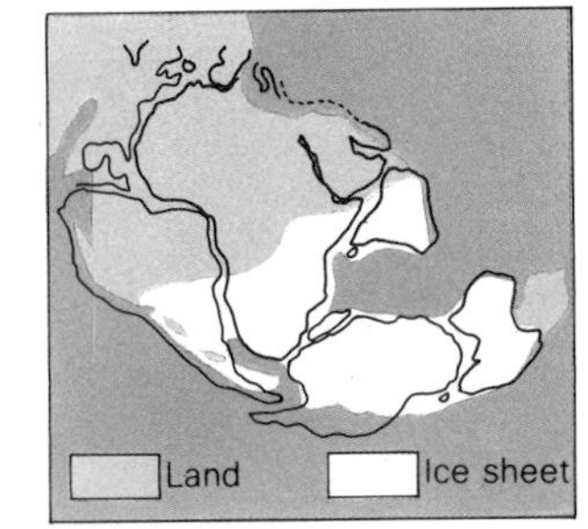

Gondwanaland
Permo-Carboniferous ice sheet

Above: Polished rock surfaces and thick deposits of glacial debris provide evidence of a late Palaeozoic glaciation over large areas of southern Gondwanaland. This glaciation spanned the Carboniferous-Permian boundary and is itself evidence of the former fusion of the southern continents.

For the second major group — the LABYRINTHODONTS — we have much more impressive evidence. Some labyrinthodonts still lived in water or were semi-aquatic in their habits; others had adapted to a more terrestrial way of life. Of water-dwelling forms, ARCHEGOSAURUS, a long-snouted RHACHITOME, emerged as a specialized fish-eater. Other rhachitomes, such as ERYOPS, also ate fish, but their bodies were heavily built and their skulls much flattened. It appears that *Eryops* waded rather than swam, and was a major predator in shallow swampland areas. On land the dominant amphibians were the SEYMOURIAMORPHS, a group with a rather 'pseudo-reptilian' appearance. SEYMOURIA was moderately sized with strong limbs and a short head and tail. It

Substrate is the term usually used to describe the sediments on the surface of the sea floor. It is possible to have both soft and hard substrates, and the fauna and flora will vary accordingly. On a soft substrate live bottom crawlers and animals that burrow into the sediment. On a firm substrate, fixed and cemented forms, as well as boring animals, would be more common.

Symbiotic relationship describes an intimate association of 2 organisms which benefits them both.

Synapsids are reptiles with skulls that have a single large opening on the temple at approximately the same level as the eye. This type of skull is present in the PELYCOSAURS, mammal-like THERAPSIDS and mammals themselves. In many therapsids and mammals the back of the skull is much modified, related to the increase in size of the jaw muscles.

Syringopora is an extinct TABULATE coral which existed from the Silurian to the Carboniferous. It formed rather massive colonies characterized by long cylindrical CORALLITES. Inside the corallites were a few spinose septa and numerous cross-partitions — the tabulae. *Syringopora* was worldwide in its distribution.

Tabulate corals are an extinct group of stony corals. They first appeared in the Middle Ordovician and quickly spread throughout the world. All known tabulates are colonial organisms, the CORALLITES of each individual being very small. Colonies may be loosely associated or closely packed. In the case of *Halysites*, the 'chain coral', the colony looks rather organ-like, whereas the corallites of *Favosites* touch on all sides and are polygonal. The tabulates range from the Ordovician to the Permian periods.

Tassel-finned fishes, or crossopterygians, have fleshy, lobed fins. They are represented today by lungfishes and the coelacanth. Many people believe that the group is closely linked to the evolution of amphibians.

Tetrapod means '4-footed' and is a word used of the higher groups of vertebrates. Amphibians, reptiles and mammals are all tetrapods, although some species modify their stance

Hippopotamus, a tetrapod

lived alongside its cousin *Diadectes* and these two appear to be the nearest the amphibians ever came to becoming truly terrestrial. But like all amphibians, *Seymouria* and *Diadectes* were forced to return to water to reproduce.

Permian reptiles

Reptiles were the true masters of the early Permian world, however, and considerable diversity had taken place in the group since the Carboniferous. Among the 'stem reptiles' or cotylosaurs (anapsids) several different stocks appeared. These included both plant- and flesh-eaters and a few groups that had adapted to a semi-aquatic life. *Limnoscelis* was such an animal. It grew about two metres in length, and its long tail and snout suggests that it was rather crocodile-like in its habits. *Labidosaurus* was much smaller than *Limnoscelis,* with strong limbs and specialized teeth which indicate that it lived on land. Although important, such 'stem reptiles' were overshadowed during the early Permian by the 'sail-backed' reptiles and related pelycosaurs. These were synapsids, and of the two major groups, *Edaphosaurus* lived on plants and *Dimetrodon* was a flesh-eater.

Edaphosaurus was heavily built, with a maximum length of about 3.5 metres. Its skull was short and rather flattened, but it had a deep body and a back dominated by a series of strong, greatly elongated spines. In life a strong membrane was stretched across these spines and the two together formed a distinctive 'sail'. The 'sail' was also a feature of *Dimetrodon.* A large-skulled predator, *Dimetrodon* was similarly proportioned to *Edaphosaurus* with adult forms reaching 3.5 metres in length. The teeth of the two animals were quite different, however. Whereas those of *Edaphosaurus* showed little variation, those of *Dimetrodon* bear some comparison with mammal teeth. *Edaphosaurus* also had several tooth-studded plates which were used to crush plants. *Dimetrodon's* teeth may be seen as a vital clue in the evolution of synapsid reptiles, and most people accept that pelycosaurs are ancestors of the mammal-like reptiles of the Upper Permian and Triassic. The 'sails' of *Dimetrodon* and *Edaphosaurus* are also thought to be the first stages towards controlling body temperatures. By the Upper Permian, truly warm-blooded creatures

Below: This reconstructed scene is set around a swamp in a generally arid Permian landscape. The vegetation is sparse and the vertebrate animals include several reptiles and amphibians. *Dimetrodon* and *Edaphosaurus,* the sail-backed lizards, are the most advanced members of the community. *Dimetrodon,* the flesh-eater, is the dominant animal, feeding on most of the other creatures. *Edaphosaurus* was a herbivore and usually avoided predators by spending much of its life partly immersed in the waters of the swamp. Of the amphibians, *Eryops* was a water-dwelling form, whereas *Diadectes* was more suited to life on land

to become bipedal, or 2-legged.

Thecal cups, or units, are situated on the outside edge of the branches on a GRAPTOLITE colony. In each individual cup was an animal, and the animals were all linked together by a common canal.

Therapsids were a major order of SYNAPSID reptiles. Various families reveal a gradual evolution towards the mammals, so that the therapsids are also known as the mammal-like reptiles or para-mammals. They arose from the PELYCOSAURS during the early Permian. The main evolutionary trends shown by therapsids are concerned with changes in the number and variety of teeth, modifications of the skull and limbs and probably the development of hair. It is now thought that certain therapsids were warm-blooded. They were very successful during the early Triassic but failed to compete with the rapidly-evolving THECODONTIANS *(see page 115).*

Trilobites are an extinct group of ARTHROPODS which lived only in the Palaeozoic era. They had a calcareous covering, or cuticle, divided both lengthways and sideways into 3 distinct lobes.

A trilobite

Trilobitoids are relatives of the TRILOBITES. Most fossil groups are known from the Middle Cambrian Burgess Shales of British Columbia, Canada.

Trinucleus belongs to a family of blind TRILOBITES characterized by a broad, pitted head shield. The head shield is divided into 3 large lobes, and 2 long, backwardly-directed spines arise from the rear corners. *Trinucleus* has only 6 body segments, all of which are fairly well rounded. The tail is small and triangular and composed of several fused segments. *Trinucleus* is recorded from the Lower and Middle Ordovician.

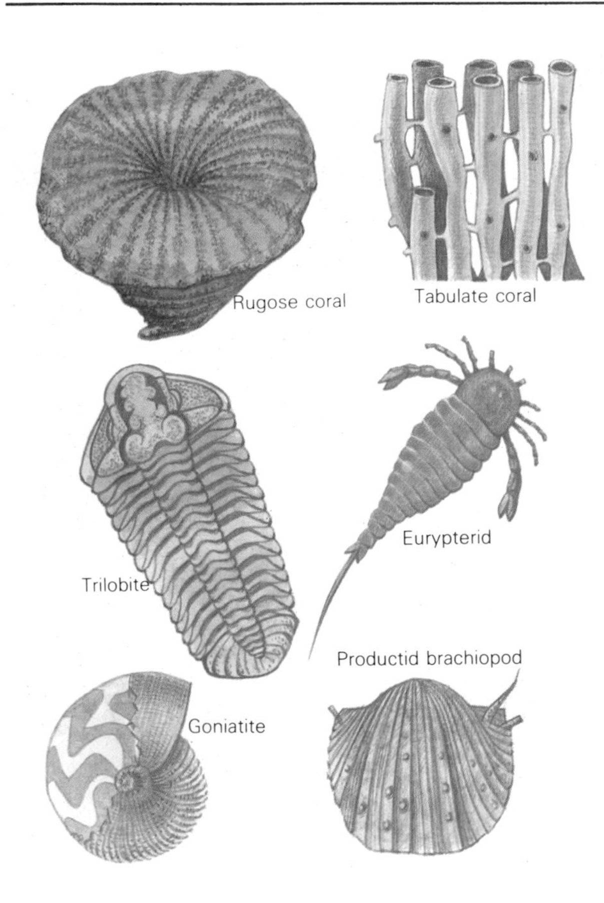

Left: Representatives of some of the marine organisms which became extinct at the end of the Permian.

Oyster
Ostreacea (bivalve molluscs)
Cardites
Carditacea (bivalve molluscs)
Periwinkle
Littorinacea (gastropods)
Limpet
Patellacea (gastropods)
Phylloceras
Phylloceratina (cephalopods)

Right: The opening of the Mesozoic witnessed the emergence of many new groups of marine organisms. Representatives of some are shown here.

had appeared. These were the mammal-like THERAPSIDS, which replaced their ancestors as both the major plant- and meat-eating animals. They had also spread into areas from which the southern ice sheets had retreated.

Changing landmasses

The MASS EXTINCTIONS which brought to a close the Palaeozoic era were largely confined to the sea, although on land the pelycosaur reptiles also disappeared. Marine organisms lost included fusulinid foraminiferids, some corals, trilobites and other arthropods, various gastropods and ammonites, bryozoans, brachiopods and stalked echinoderms.

Many theories have been presented to find a single cause for these dramatic extinctions, but none is wholly satisfactory. A more detailed explanation involves the former positions of the continents. Today there are several separate landmasses in different climatic zones — hot, temperate and cold. Surrounding the landmasses are CONTINENTAL SHELVES, separated from each other by deep OCEAN BASINS. Variations in climate, and isolation imposed by the ocean basins, have led to highly PROVINCIAL COMMUNITIES developing among marine organisms. In these communities, the greatest diversity exists off the shores of smaller landmasses. This is because seasonal effects increase with the size of the landmass, and so the supply of nutrients carried from land to the sea by rivers fluctuates more. An unstable food supply for marine organisms results, and reduces their diversity.

But at the end of the Permian, climates were more uniform and the landmasses had come together to form the vast continent of Pangaea. The continental shelf area was therefore reduced and there were few barriers to prevent migration. Moreover, food in the seas around this continent must have been seasonally unstable. In short, there was less potential for diverse animal communities in the late Permian seas, far less than that of today. This was the basic reason for the extinctions, and for the fact that few of the surviving species were widespread ones.

Trivial name (or specific name) is the second of the 2 names used to define a species (e.g. *Homo sapiens)*. Both names are always printed in italics and the specific name is usually followed by the name of the author who first described the species.

Tube feet extend from the complex apparatus of fluid-filled tubes and bladders inside ECHINODERMS. They stretch through pores in the skeleton and help the animal with such activities as movement, respiration and food-gathering.

V

Vascular plants have water-conducting tissue in the form of elongate, dead tubular cells. This is called the xylem. They also have tissues capable of transporting food — the phloem. Flowering plants such as the rose or oak, as well as the ferns and horsetails, are examples of living vascular plants. The simplest of these are *Psilotum* and *Tmesipterus,* members of the Psilotales. Both have an underground rooting structure — the rhizome — an upright vascular stem and branches that occur in equal-sized pairs. They are closely related to the earliest vascular plant *Cooksonia,* which is known from rocks 400 million years old.

Vertebrates, like the graptolites, lampreys and tunicates, are chordate animals. The essential character of all these groups is the possession of a strengthening rod of tissue called the notochord. The vertebrates' spinal cord is supported by a number of bony structures called vertebrae, and as a consequence the notochord itself has been reduced, modified or lost completely.

W

Warm-blooded describes those animals that produce their own heat by burning up food within the muscles of their body. All mammals are warm-blooded.

An okapi, one of the vertebrates

Z

Zaphrentids are small, solitary, horn-shaped corals from the Carboniferous. They are rather robust, with strongly-developed radiating septa. Unlike many other RUGOSE corals, they lack the small horseshoe-shaped plates called dissepiments.

Zone fossils have a wide geographical distribution and a short life span. They are important in identifying sedimentary rocks from different areas.

The extinction of many sea-living creatures brought the Palaeozoic era to a close, but life forms continued to diversify in the Mesozoic. The first dinosaurs, mammals, birds and flowering plants appeared.

Mesozoic Communities

The great continent of PANGAEA (*see page 89*) began to break up at the start of the Mesozoic (about 225 million years ago). It first divided into the northern super-continent of Laurasia and the southern super-continent of Gondwana, separated by the TETHYS Sea. By the close of the Mesozoic (65 million years ago) Gondwana itself had split to give today's southern continents and India, while North America had become detached from Eurasia. As the Mesozoic advanced, therefore, the world's environments became ever more separate and provincial, in the sea and on land. Organisms adapted to these changing environments, so that although there were PERIODIC EXTINCTIONS, the Mesozoic saw progressive DIVERSIFICATION among the various plants and animals.

Among the INVERTEBRATE sea creatures of the early Mesozoic were several new groups of BIVALVES (*see page 77*) and GASTROPODS. AMMONITES with complex SUTURE LINES replaced the earlier types with simple sutures, and more modern kinds of corals appeared. Squid-like BELEMNITES were also present for the first time.

The transition from Palaeozoic to Mesozoic made little impact on land animals. Amphibians had given way to reptiles by the Middle Permian and some of the reptiles persisted into the Triassic (225 million years ago). Before the end of this period, however, a range of new reptile lines had begun, including lizards and DINOSAURS and swimming forms such as ICHTHYOSAURS, PLESIOSAURS and TURTLES. The MAMMALS (*see page 120*) existed by late Triassic times, having diverged from an older reptile stock.

There were important developments in the early Mesozoic plants as well. In particular a number of GYMNOSPERM families spread widely, at the expense of the older LYCOPSID (*see page 86*) and SPHENOPSID trees. Of the dominant Permian plants only the ferns remained plentiful.

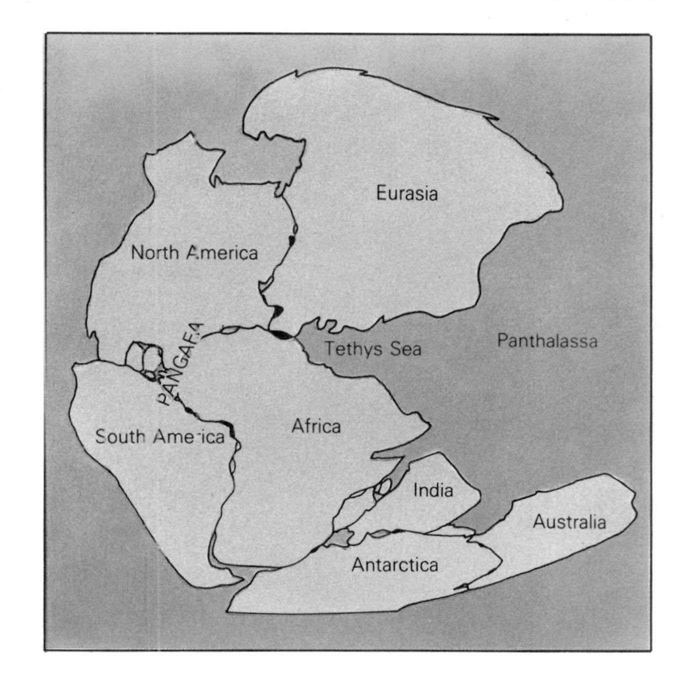

Right: The super-continent of Pangaea persisted for millions of years during the Triassic. Land 'bridge' connections existed between most continents, and these aided the rapid radiation of the dinosaurs.

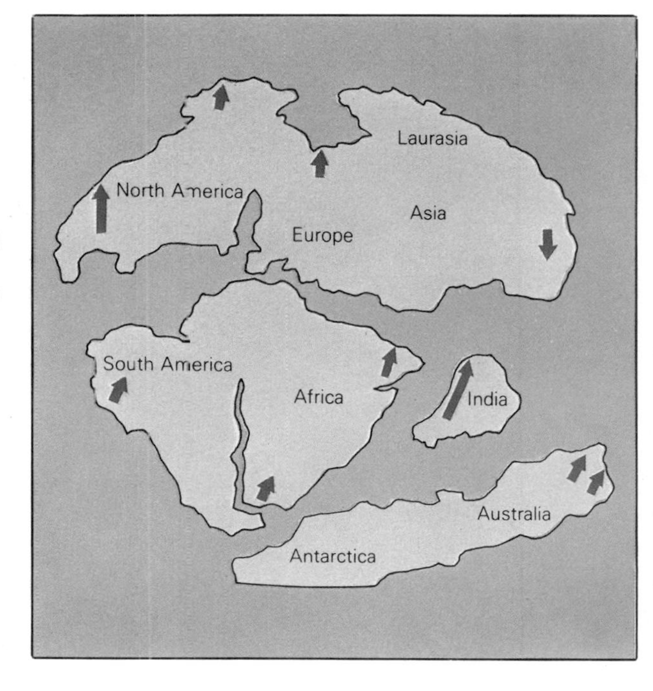

Right: During the late Triassic, the super-continent of Pangaea began to drift apart, with different landmasses moving in different directions. The arrows indicate the general direction of movement taken by each individual landmass. In time, continued movement of the various continental plates resulted in the geographic arrangement we know today.

Reference

A

Acanthopholids were an important group of armoured ANKYLOSAURS. Unlike their sister-group the NODOSAURS, they kept a more flexible body armour and failed to develop a heavy head covering.

Aëtosaurs are a heavily-armoured group of THECODONTIANS recorded from the Triassic period.

Allosaurus, the 'strange-lizard', lived during the Upper Jurassic. It was a large, meat-eating dinosaur which grew to an incredible 11 metres in length. Like its close relatives *Megalosaurus* and *Tyrannosaurus* it was 2-legged, with a short neck, small arms, and long tail to serve as a counter-balance when the animal was running. The teeth of *Allosaurus* measured 80 to 100 mm in height and their serrated edges would have provided sharp cutting surfaces.

Ammonites were the most important cephalopod MOLLUSCS of the Mesozoic, and are identified by the coils of their shell. They are important ZONE FOSSILS (*see page 96*) for the Jurassic and Cretaceous periods.

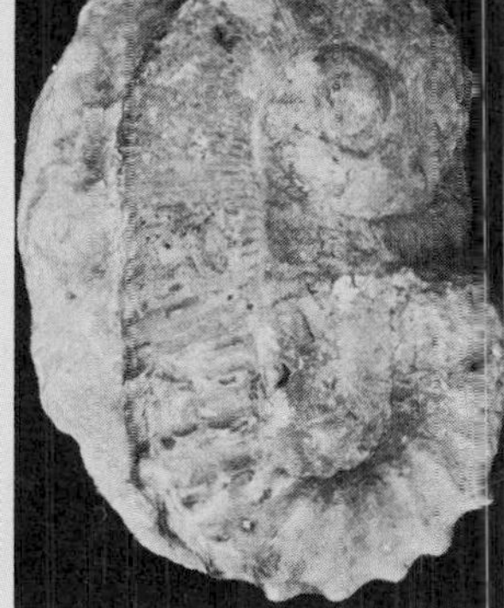

Ammonite

Angiosperms are flowering plants and are first known from early Cretaceous rocks.

Ankylosaurs were a group of heavily-armoured Upper Cretaceous dinosaurs. See also ACANTHOPHOLIDS and NODOSAURS.

Archaeopteryx is the first known bird. Only 5 fossils are known, 3 of which are very well preserved with excellent impressions of both tail and wing feathers. *Archaeopteryx* was probably unable to fly and was built like a small COELUROSAUR.

Archosaurs are reptiles with a diapsid type of skull, which has 2 openings on the temple behind the eye. Unlike the snakes and lizards, archosaurs retain the bony bars between the openings on the temple. Crocodiles, dinosaurs, PTEROSAURS and THECODONTIANS are all archosaurs.

B

Belemnites are an extinct group of cephalopods which had 2 gills and are therefore related to the living squids and cuttlefish. Their soft parts were squid-like but their 3-

Triassic vertebrate communities

The dawn of the Triassic period was marked by the disappearance of the anapsid PAREIASAURS and the sail-backed PELYCOSAURS (*see page 89*). At first, reptiles were dominated by the mammal-like DICYNODONTS. Some of these grew to the size of small rhinoceroses and probably lived in herds on the edges of swampland. They were preyed upon by their close cousins the CYNOGNATHIDS and lived alongside the first mammals, ARCHOSAURS and lizard ancestors. By the Middle Triassic dicynodonts had been replaced as the major herbivores (or plant-eaters) by the RHYNCHOSAURS — a group usually associated with modern lizards — and by the TRITYLODONTS, another group of mammal-like reptiles. As before, the cynognathids were the chief predators, but they were being challenged by the rapidly emerging THECODONTIANS.

The passing of the Middle Triassic saw the dicynodonts' continued decline, while most of the cynognathids, tritylodonts and rhynchosaurs disappeared. Thecodontians now ruled, their rapid evolution probably closely linked with the dying out of their contemporaries. But thecodontians were not the only archosaurs; also emerging were the dinosaurs.

Early dinosaurs

The first dinosaurs are recorded from the Middle Triassic. They have been found in South Africa and Argentina, and this widespread distribution suggests that they split from the thecodontians at the end of the Lower Triassic. By the late Triassic the COELUROSAURS and ORNITHOPODS had been joined by PROSAUROPODS and CARNOSAURS. Well-established communities of these existed in south Germany and South Africa.

The largest dinosaur of the community in South Africa was the plant-eating prosauropod MELANOROSAURUS — a four-legged animal which grew to over 12 metres and weighed several tonnes. In contrast, the ornithopods LESOTHOSAURUS and HETERODONTOSAURUS were lightly-built and BIPEDAL. Both lived on plants, but *Heterodontosaurus* (the 'different-toothed lizard') had special teeth, with tusks that were probably used during fighting. *Lesothosaurus* was about the same size as *Heterodontosaurus*, but its teeth were rather primitive and it lacked the muscular cheek pouches of its fellow ornithopod.

As yet no late Triassic ornithopods have been found in Europe or North America. This suggests

Below: During the second half of the Triassic various types of dinosaurs flourished in southern Africa. Most lived beside lakes and swamps, and both lizard- and bird-hipped dinosaurs were common. Inland the countryside was dry and barren. Of the bird-hipped dinosaurs, *Heterodontosaurus* and *Lesothosaurus* were the most common. They were agile animals which were able to outrun the meat-eaters which lived at the same time. In contrast, *Melanorosaurus*, a lizard-hipped prosauropod, relied on its huge size to deter predators.

part shells were quite distinct. They consisted mainly of a bullet-shaped guard, the remains of which are frequently discovered in Jurassic and Cretaceous sediments. The first belemnites are recorded from the Carboniferous and the last from the Tertiary.

Belly River is the first of 3 very important geological formations, rich in dinosaur remains, from the Upper Cretaceous of North America.

Bennettitales were palm-like members of the GYMNOSPERMS and are found as fossils in rocks ranging from the Triassic to the Cretaceous. They reached their peak in the Jurassic.

Bering land bridge is thought to have linked Asia with North America during the Cretaceous and Cainozoic. The 'bridge' was probably a stretch of dry land that allowed various animals to migrate from one continent to the other.

Bernissart is a town in Belgium made famous by the discovery of 31 associated *Iguanodon* skeletons in 1877. The skeletons were found in a fissure some 300 metres below ground level.

Iguanodon skeleton

Bioturbation is the disturbance of sediments by burrowing animals, whose action causes the BEDDING PLANES (*see page 77*) in sediments to become distorted or obscure. Sediment layers of differing grain-size or texture may be so mixed that they result in a single layer of more or less uniform texture. With sediment layers similar in grain-size and colour, mixing as a result of bioturbation is more difficult to detect.

Bipedal refers to animals that walk on their hind legs. Many THECODONTIANS, dinosaurs and mammals — including man — can be so described.

Bird-hipped dinosaurs, or ornithischians, are those in which the pubis bone has moved back to a position beneath the ischium bone. This results in a 3-pronged arrangement of the pelvis, similar to that found in birds. It is markedly different from the pelvis of LIZARD-HIPPED dinosaurs and other reptiles.

Bituminous shales are rocks made up of mostly clay-size particles. They are hardened into layers which

that the southern continents were originally the centre of their evolution and that their migration northwards was slow but steady. The coelurosaurs, on the other hand, spread rapidly across the huge Pangaean landmass. In North America COELOPHYSIS belonged to this group, while in south Germany PROCOMPSOGNATHUS filled the role of a small meat-eater and scavenger. During the Upper Triassic, the present German area was lowland, with large stretches of barren land bordering swamp. *Procompsognathus* hunted on the edges of these regions, probably for small amphibians, reptiles and possibly eggs.

The lush vegetation along the water's edge provided good food for the prosauropods in the community, with *Plateosaurus* and *Plateosauriscus* occupying the ECOLOGICAL NICHE (*see page 68*) held by *Melanorosaurus* in South Africa. Of the two, *Plateosaurus* is the best known. Barely half the size of *Melanorosaurus*, its small head and relatively slender forelimbs gave it a rather awkward appearance. Its body's basic design was for that of a four-legged animal, but it seems likely that *Plateosaurus* spent at least some time on two legs. As with most animals that live on plants, its body was bulky. Even so, the hind limbs could support the animal as it reached upwards to feed. Its flat teeth show that *Plateosaurus* fed on soft, succulent vegetation.

In contrast, the surviving rhynchosaurs used their strong beaks and crushing teeth to feed on roots, shoots and tough seeds. These squat, powerfully-built animals sought protection in the shallow waters of swamps, where they and their young were relatively safe from attack by coelurosaurs or carnosaurs. The shallow waters

Right: Many regions suffered arid conditions during the Triassic. Ponds and lakes frequently dried up during hot, dry spells, and the footprints of various animals were preserved in drying muds. Sometimes it is possible to identify the animal that left its prints.

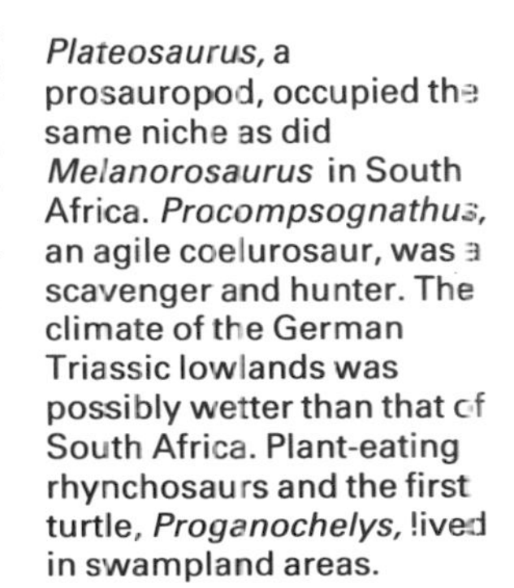

Plateosaurus, a prosauropod, occupied the same niche as did *Melanorosaurus* in South Africa. *Procompsognathus,* an agile coelurosaur, was a scavenger and hunter. The climate of the German Triassic lowlands was possibly wetter than that of South Africa. Plant-eating rhynchosaurs and the first turtle, *Proganochelys,* lived in swampland areas.

Below: By the Upper Triassic, dinosaurs had spread to many parts of the world. From southern Germany we have found evidence that a diverse variety of animals existed, including both bird- and lizard-hipped dinosaurs. In this German region,

readily split with the 'grain', and which contain bitumen (hydrocarbons) or other carbon matter. Such rocks gather as muds rich in organic matter from partly decomposed plant and animal remains. The partial decomposition results from a lack of oxygen on the sea-floor. This may be due to LAGOONAL conditions which are partly isolated from the sea, or to stagnant water in the deeper parts of marine basins.

Bone-headed dinosaurs, or pachycephalosaurs, had a thick layer of bone over the brain case. They were ORNITHOPODS and seem to have lived in herds in upland regions during the Upper Cretaceous.

A concretion

Browser is an animal that feeds or grazes on plants.

C **Calcareous concretions** are masses of material, rich in calcium carbonate, within a less resistant rock. Such masses are normally concentrated around a nucleus, which may often be a fossil. The calcium carbonate will already have been present in the rock.

Camptosaurus was a large ORNITHOPOD dinosaur that lived during the late Jurassic. It measured 5 metres long and weighed about 3.5 tonnes. *Camptosaurus* was a 2-legged herbivore, and many scientists believe that it roamed in herds over the North American landscape. It was the forerunner of *Iguanodon* and, like its descendants, had 3 main toes on each foot. *Camptosaurus* is found with *Apatosaurus,* the huge SAUROPOD, and the CARNOSAUR *Allosaurus.*

Caprina is an exotically-shaped RUDIST BIVALVE recorded in sediments from the Cretaceous period. The 2 valves are unequal in size, the lower or right valve being horn-shaped and the upper or left valve strongly coiled. The outer wall of the caprinid shell is relatively smooth, marked only by fine growth lines. *Caprina* lived on the upper slopes of rudist reefs. It is known from Europe, North Africa and North America.

Carnosaurs were the major predators of the 'Age of Dinosaurs'. Best known of these LIZARD-HIPPED dinosaurs was *Tyrannosaurus rex,* 'king of the tyrant lizards'.

also provided homes for several kinds of amphibian and for the first turtle — TRIASSOCHELYS. The largest amphibian was a huge labyrinthodont — MASTODONTOSAURUS — with a flat skull well over a metre in length. It fed on fish, and its considerable bulk contrasted with the strange, flat form of the PLAGIOSAUR amphibian *Gerrothorax*. This also had small limbs, and probably spent most of its life in the water.

Changes in the Jurassic

The Jurassic, beginning about 190 million years ago, saw major influxes (or TRANSGRESSIONS) of the sea on to the world's landmasses, which were then in the early stages of separating from each other. In the Lower Jurassic the diversity of sea life was still increasing after the great Permian extinctions. Among the common animals living on the sea bed and undergoing important developments in evolution were the bivalves, gastropods and crustaceans. And the BENTHIC communities (*see page 67*) to which they belonged were becoming more closely related to the different sediment types on the sea floor. The NEKTON (*see page 71*) were not so tied. Some ammonites, for example, were worldwide in their distribution, suggesting that climates generally were equable. Fish and sea-going reptiles were present as well.

In Britain the Lower Jurassic or LIAS rocks are mainly shales which have frequent layers of silt or sand, impure limestones or ironstones and, occasionally, BITUMINOUS SHALES. Apart from ammonites, bivalves are plentiful. They include oysters and gryphaeas, various other creatures that could swim through the water by clapping their valves together, and several animals that lived in the sediments on the sea floor. These sediment-dwellers filtered organic debris from the sea water or extracted it from surrounding sediments. In addition, there are nests or colonies of RHYNCHONELLID, TEREBRATULID and SPIRIFERID brachiopods. These animals were also FILTER-FEEDERS, but they lived on, rather than in,

Below: Reconstruction of a scene from the Lower Jurassic seas of Britain. Going from right to left, the sea-floor passes from hard ground to sand, and then to muddy sand and clay, with stagnant mud in the deeper water. While nektonic (free-swimming) animals like the ammonites and belemnites were not restricted by the character of the sea-floor, the benthic animals were. The benthic (bottom-dwelling) animals shown here are detritus-feeders and suspension-feeders. Remains of these animals or of their burrows (trace-fossils) are common in Lower Jurassic rocks.

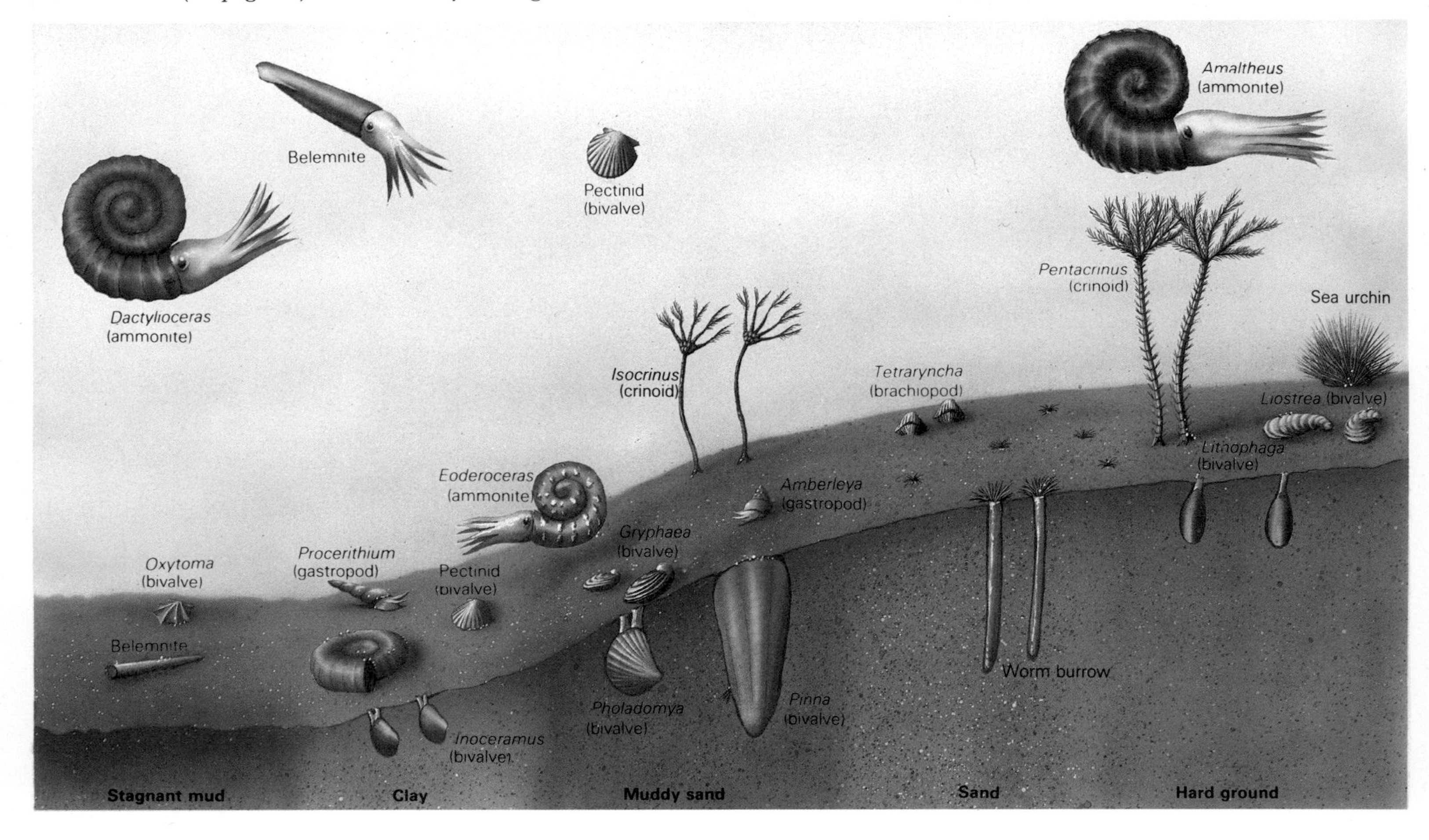

Ceratopians, or horned dinosaurs, had a large bony frill and beak-like jaws. Most of these rhinoceros-like animals had heads with a large nosehorn and 2 large, sometimes enormous, browhorns. They lived during the Upper Cretaceous.

Chalk was deposited in seas generally around 300 metres deep, but ranging to as little as 50 metres in depth. Measurements taken from fossil shells in the chalk suggest water temperatures between 13.5 and 28.5°C. Salinity (the amount of salt) was probably normal.

Claosaurus was one of the earliest DUCK-BILLED dinosaurs. It is known only from

Chalk fossil

North America, where it lived approximately 90 million years ago. It was smaller than later HADROSAURS and its rather simple teeth and feet indicate that it was a primitive representative of the family.

Climatic change involves a permanent shift in temperature and/or rainfall patterns in an area. The causes are complex. Long-term changes may result from continents drifting into warmer or cooler latitudes; from changes in the distribution of land and sea; and from the building of new mountain chains or the erosion of old ones. More rapid changes and variations can be triggered by fluctuations in solar radiation.

Coccoliths are minute oval structures made up of elaborate patterns of calcite platelets which surround a single cell.

Coelophysis is one of the best-known of the COELUROSAURS. Its name means 'hollow-form lizard'. *Coelophysis* was a small 2-legged reptile with powerful hind limbs. It was a meat-eater and its long pointed head was armed with numerous small serrated teeth. Both neck and tail were long, the latter serving as a balancing organ while the animal was running. Adult coelophysids grew up to 3 metres long and weighed a little over 20 kg. Like *Tyrannosaurus* and *Brachiosaurus, Coelophysis* was a LIZARD-HIPPED dinosaur. In times of food shortage *Coelophysis* probably became cannibalistic and ate its young.

Coelurosaurs were an important group of THEROPOD dinosaurs. Many were meat-eaters but others became

sediments on the sea floor. Remains of gastropods are frequently found, and a range of grazers, scavengers and DETRITUS-FEEDERS are represented. Crinoids, or sea lilies, are another group of SUSPENSION-FEEDERS which are often encountered. Their remains are usually found in small fragments, the result of wave-action in stormy Jurassic seas. Many TRACE FOSSILS can also be seen in Liassic rocks.

Communities living in muddy sand contained the most diverse range of creatures. Clays and silts provide a rather unstable foundation for animals on the sea floor, while sands are usually associated with comparatively shallow water, where wave-action may cause great disturbance and rapid burial. Muddy sands give a firm anchorage, yet the water is usually shallow enough for the mud to be stirred up and so provide a food source for filter-feeders.

During the Middle Jurassic, marine environments in north and east England were replaced by FLUVIATILE, DELTAIC and LAGOONAL conditions. Farther south, in the area of the Cotswold Hills, shallow seas still prevailed, and deposits of limestone and clay were laid down. Even so, few ammonites or belemnites are to be found in them. These animals had to live in water containing a certain degree of salt and so were confined to truly open seas. Despite the closeness of land, the surrounding seawater was nevertheless clear, so that bottom-living animals were quite varied and included many corals, as well as the usual bivalves, gastropods, brachiopods and echinoderms. Open sea environments lay to the south, across southern England and northern France.

Towards the end of Middle Jurassic times, sea extended once again over much of north-west Europe. A varied sequence of clays, limestones and calcareous sandstones was laid down, with numbers of ammonites and belemnites reappearing in some of the clays and limestones. Towards the end of the Jurassic there was a REGRESSION of the sea, and as it retreated, a

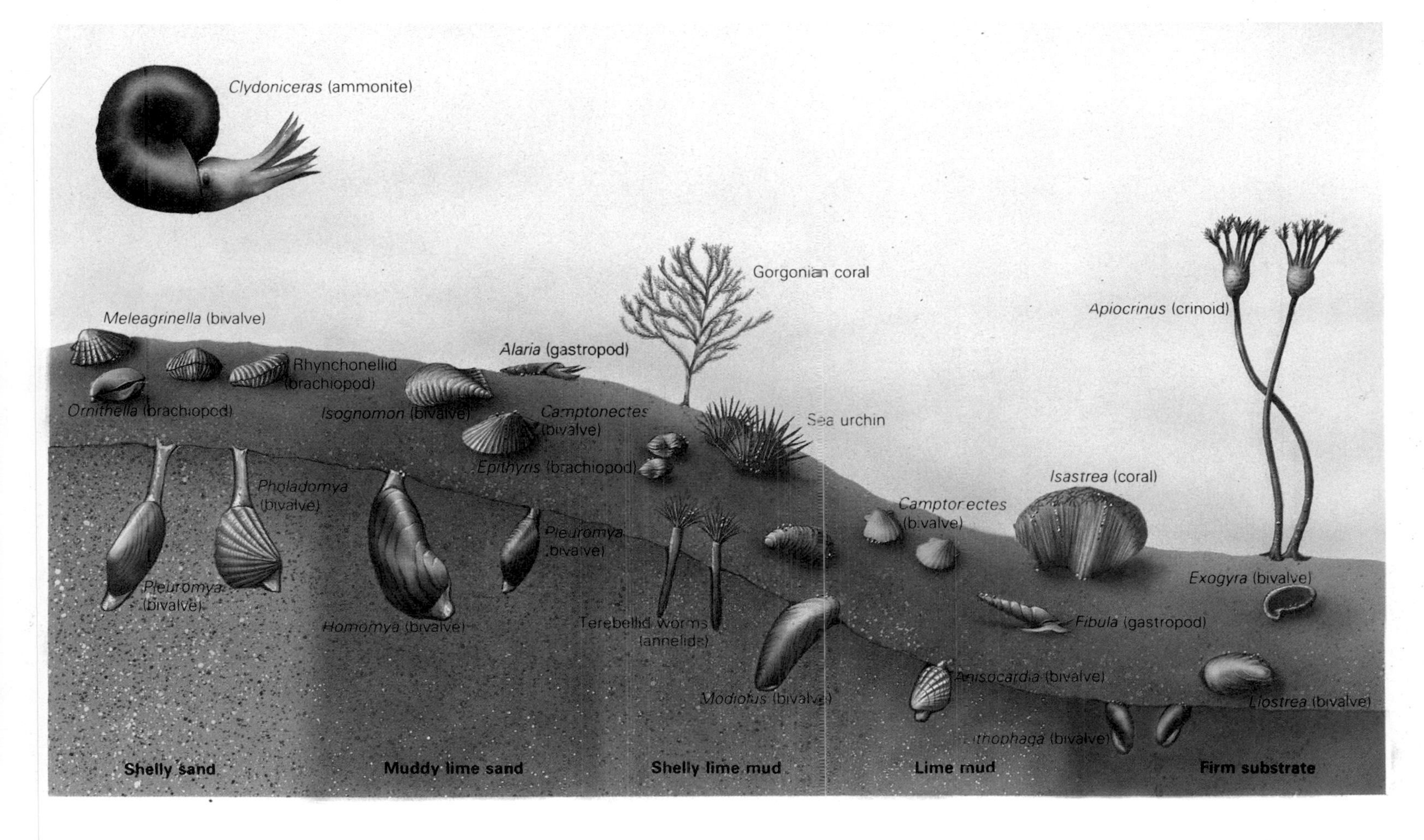

Below: Reconstruction of a British mid-Jurassic marine environment. The shallowest part of the sea-floor is largely shell sand, passing in the deeper water into muddy lime sand, and then into shelly lime mud, with a firm bottom in the deepest water. Because of the variable salinities, ammonites were infrequent. However, the water was clear and so corals thrived, together with a wide range of detritus-feeders and suspension-feeders.

specialized as egg-stealers and nest-robbers. All coelurosaurs were BIPEDAL and some palaeontologists think that one group, the dromaeosaurids, had comparatively large brains and very good sight. They lived from the Middle Triassic to the Upper Cretaceous.

Convergent evolution results in organisms which, though not closely related, look alike. Organisms that follow the same way of life often evolve similar physical adaptations.

Cycads are a group of GYMNOSPERMS with leaves like feather-palms. They were plentiful during the Jurassic

A cycad

and Cretaceous, but only 9 groups remain today.

Cynognathids lived during the Triassic. They were mammal-like reptiles, lightly built but with the limbs drawn beneath the body. They were active meat-eaters, with powerful jaws and sharp teeth.

D

Deinonychosaurs were a group of THEROPOD dinosaurs whose name derived from the 'terrible-claw' *Deinonychus*.

Deltaic is the name for fan-shaped alluvial environments which form at river mouths. Deltaic sediments gradually become coarser as they go upwards. This is because the oldest (lowest) sediments are the fine particles which were originally carried farthest from the river mouth. As the delta builds up it advances, so that coarse shallow-water sediments come to rest on the older deep-water types.

Dental batteries are rows of densely-packed teeth found inside the mouth of DUCK-BILLED dinosaurs such as *Corythosaurus*. These teeth are found at the back of the jaws, where hundreds are arranged in a very complicated manner. Each tooth is leaf-like in shape, with a central ridge. Together they provided the animal with an extensive grinding and crushing surface. As the upper teeth wore down, so new ones grew to replace them. The stomach remains of duck-billed dinosaurs show that they ate pine-needles, twigs and seeds.

Detritus-feeders are creatures that live off the organic matter in the sediments on the sea-floor. The organic matter may be coatings around the sediment grains,

mosaic of lagoons, freshwater lakes and low-lying land developed. This landscape persisted into the WEALDEN phase of the Lower Cretaceous.

Jurassic land animals

To most palaeontologists the Jurassic period is characterized by marine and ESTUARINE sediments. As we have seen, invertebrates and vertebrates then flourished in many regions of the world, and most sea environments were of the tropical–warm, temperate kind. True land deposits are quite rare, so the record of land-dwelling communities is rather patchy. In the Lower Jurassic the number of areas with evidence of land-living vertebrates is particularly poor, although some signs do exist for the continued presence of mammal-like therapsids and the diversification of early mammals. Marine deposits yield further vital clues, and the skeleton of the first PTEROSAUR—*Dimorphodon*—is known from the Lower Jurassic of Germany. SCELIDOSAURUS, the earliest QUADRUPEDAL ORNITHISCHIAN, is also known from the corresponding rock in England (Lias) and shows the continuing diversity of the ornithischians.

Scelidosaurus, the 'limb lizard', was a rather strange creature. It was fairly large and heavily built, with a small head and weak jaws. Its back was studded with bony plates arranged in rows from the back of the head to the tip of the tail. The hind limbs were rather larger than the front, and it seems that the animal grazed in a 'head-down' position. *Scelidosaurus* was a short-lived type, but its design makes it a likely ancestor for the STEGOSAURS and ANKYLOSAURS.

The stegosaurs

Stegosaurs lived only in the Upper Jurassic, and most discoveries of them have been made in East Africa and North America. In East Africa the stegosaur example was *Kentrosaurus,* while in the western USA, *Stegosaurus* filled the niche of low-level BROWSER. Both animals looked something like their scelidosaur ancestor, for both were heavily built and had small heads. *Kentrosaurus*

Below: *Kentrosaurus* occupied the same niche in East Africa as did *Stegosaurus* in North America. Both animals were slow-moving plant-eaters that gained protection against potential attackers from their bony spines or plates. *Brachiosaurus,* the 'arm-lizard', was the largest animal (of which we have certain proof) ever to walk on Earth. It is known from East Africa and North America.

or particles in the spaces between the grains. The smaller the particles the greater amount of organic matter they contain. Fine-grained sediments can therefore support more detritus-feeders.

Dicynodonts were a successful group of mammal-like reptiles during the Permian and Triassic periods. They were plant-eating, and had a toothless beak covered by a horny bill. Many dicynodonts had 2 large canine tusks in the upper jaw. One of the best known dicynodonts is *Lystrosaurus,* a marsh-loving animal from various parts of GONDWANALAND (*see page 82*).

Dinosaurs were a group of reptiles characterized by a 'fully improved posture', in which the limbs were drawn beneath the body. The dinosaurs are divided into 2 separate groups – the LIZARD-HIPPED saurischians, and the BIRD-HIPPED ornithischians. They were the dominant animals for 140 million years, from the Triassic to Upper Cretaceous.

Diversification refers to the number and variety of species within a community.

Duck-billed describes the broad, flattened snout of the hadrosaur dinosaurs. Consequently the animals are often called 'duck-billed dinosaurs'.

E

Estuarine conditions exist or existed at the mouth, or estuary, of a river. The word can describe a semi-enclosed coastal body of water with tidal flats and barrier islands.

Everglades cover a large area of Florida in the south-eastern region of the USA. They are swamplands, noted for their snake- and crocodile-infested waters and their humid sub-tropical climate. The Everglades were formed about 5,000 years ago, when waters from the great Okeechobee lake flowed southwards towards the Gulf of Mexico. According to scientists the waters were only a few millimetres deep but covered an area 64 km wide. Their flow kept the water-table at the surface.

Dinosaur National Monument, Utah, USA

grew over 5 metres long and weighed about a tonne. Behind the head were two distinct rows of plates, and above the hip were eight pairs of elongate spines. *Stegosaurus* weighed almost twice as much and grew to over 6 metres in length. It, too, had a small head and weak teeth, but the bony plates along its back were very much larger. The purpose of these plates is something of a mystery, but their zig-zag arrangement and overall structure point to them being a simple type of temperature control. The difference in ornamentation may indicate that the two were adapted to different climates.

The presence of stegosaurs in both East African and North American communities is significant. But it is not the only connection between the areas, for SAUROPODS, carnosaurs, coelurosaurs and ornithopods have also been discovered in both regions. Perhaps of all such animals the most important is *Brachiosaurus*, one of the largest animals ever to live on Earth. In both communities *Brachiosaurus*, the 'arm lizard', filled the role of a high-level browser, alongside several other types of sauropod. At 26 metres long, 12.6 metres high and weighing 80 tonnes, *Brachiosaurus* was a record-breaker, although its position as the largest dinosaur has now been challenged by the discovery of 'SUPERSAURUS', a monster judged to be 30 metres long and about 100 tonnes in weight. The equable Jurassic climate seems to have suited giant sauropods and encouraged their widespread distribution. The same was probably true for the plant-eating ornithopods, coelurosaurs and carnosaurs.

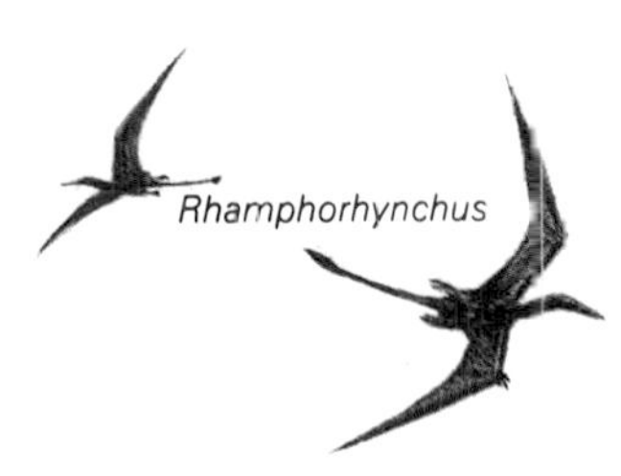

The Lower Cretaceous

At the beginning of the Cretaceous, 136 million years ago, the continental masses were arranged

Below: The Morrison Formation community of North America is one of the best-known of all vertebrate communities. It is characterized by the presence of *Brachiosaurus* and *Stegosaurus*, as well as coelurosaurs, carnosaurs and ornithopods.

Filter-feeders are creatures that obtain their food by filtering sea water for suspended particles of organic matter. Filter-feeders living on sea-floor sediments need a stable anchor, and are therefore less common on muds than on stable sands and silts. Too much mud can also choke the filter-feeding mechanisms of these creatures.

Flowering plants, see ANGIOSPERMS.

Fluviatile sediments are those which are deposited in a river.

Gastropods belong to the MOLLUSCS. They have a true head, an unsegmented body and a large flattened foot on which they crawl about.

Gault Clay is a dark, stiff, clinging clay which was deposited in a Cretaceous sea, at a maximum depth of about 180 metres. It contains numerous fossils. In the London area, the Gault arrests the downward movement of water through the overlying CHALK. Since the chalk is folded into a vast saucer-like structure, the Gault acts as the floor and sides of a great underground reservoir, from which London gets much of its water.

Ginkgos are members of the coniferophytes — a group of naked seed plants. The living Maidenhair tree *Ginkgo biloba* is the only survivor of a family of plants that once flourished in many parts of the world. Ginkgos were deciduous trees with broad, sub-divided leaves. Their reproductive structures are borne on separate plants, the male pollen-bearing organs carried on catkin-like structures. The ginkgos are essentially primitive plants which flourished during the Mesozoic era. They are the oldest living species of tree.

Gymnosperms are seed-bearing plants, like the ANGIOSPERMS. However, they lack flowers, and their seeds are not enclosed within a fruit. They include the conifers and cycads, and dominated the world's vegetation through most of the Mesozoic.

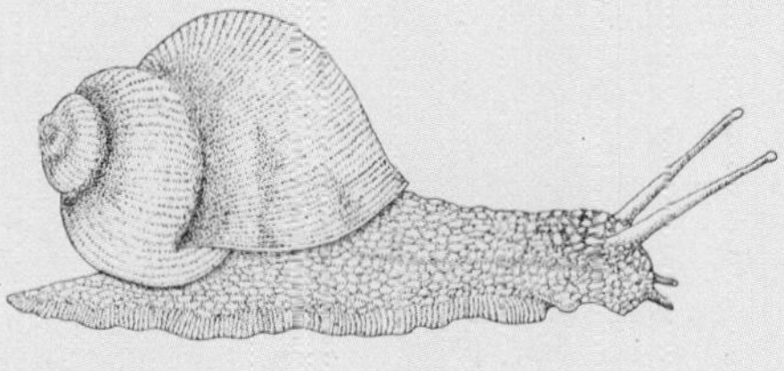

The snail is a gastropod

Left: *Hippurites* is a representative of a specialized group of bivalves known as the rudists. These have valves very unequal in size. The right valve is large and coral-like; the left is lid-like. The valves are articulated by means of large teeth and sockets. *Hippurites* has a very thick wall to the right valve. It is among the largest known bivalves and has been discovered in many areas of southern Europe, North Africa, North America and Asia. Its distribution during the Upper Cretaceous follows the coastline of the ancient Tethys Sea.

in much the same way as in the Jurassic. As the period continued, however, the Atlantic opened and gradually separated South America from Africa and the British Isles and Greenland from North America. SEA-FLOOR SPREADING also led to the break-up of the Australasian, Indian and Antarctic block. These changes resulted in many land-living communities becoming isolated, and they can also be directly linked with a gradual onset of climatic seasonality in many lands. Desert covered large tracts of what are today Mongolia and China, while dense coal-forming forests grew in Siberia and areas of the southern hemisphere. On land the Cretaceous was the period of dinosaurs and pterosaurs; in the sea, huge reptiles, as well as ammonites, bivalves and echinoderms, were most common.

Rudist colonies

Throughout the Cretaceous the important ocean

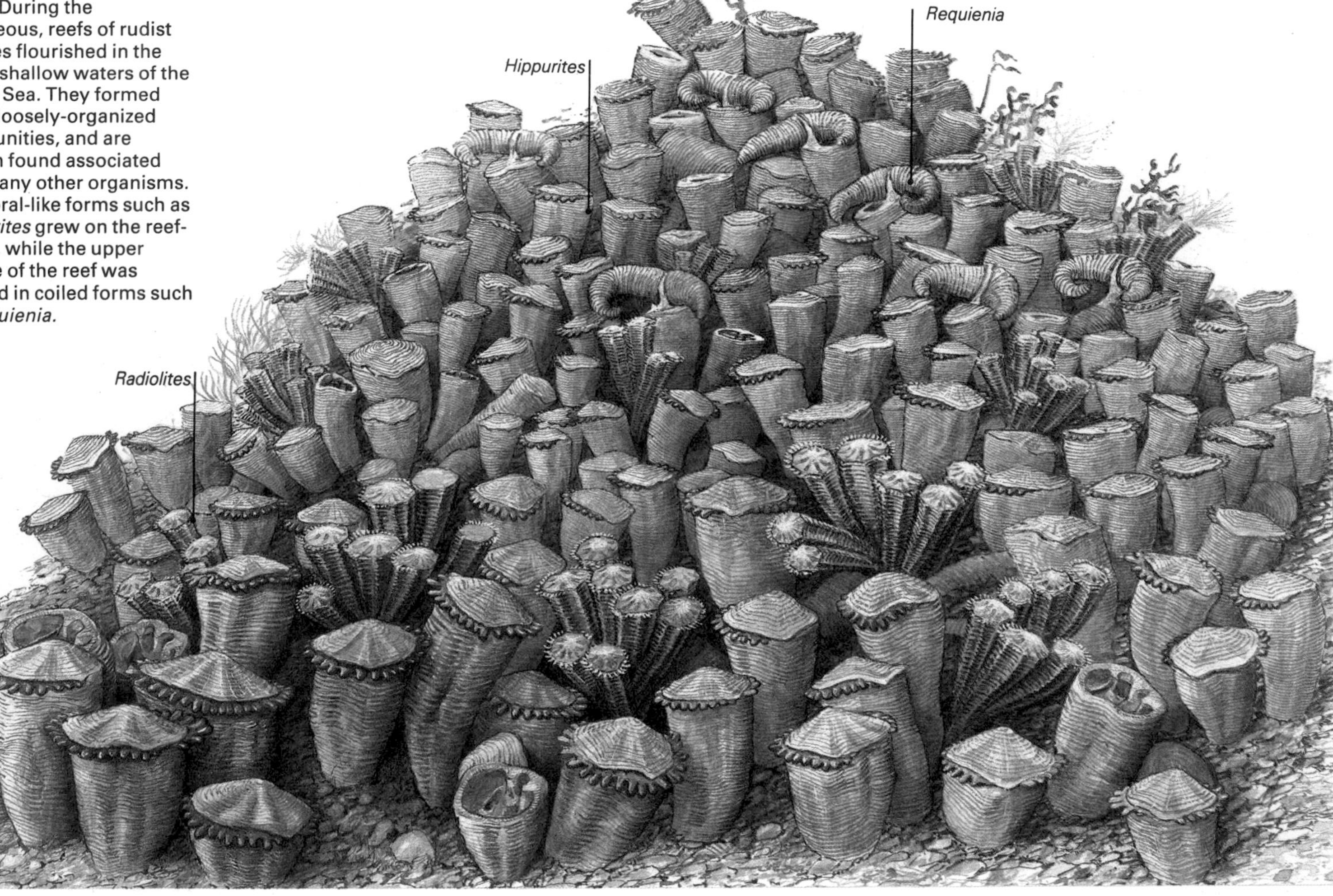

Right: During the Cretaceous, reefs of rudist bivalves flourished in the warm, shallow waters of the Tethys Sea. They formed rather loosely-organized communities, and are seldom found associated with many other organisms. Tall, coral-like forms such as *Hippurites* grew on the reef-slopes, while the upper surface of the reef was covered in coiled forms such as *Requienia.*

H

Hadrosaurs, see DUCK-BILLED.

Heterodontosaurus, or the 'different-toothed lizard', lived in southern Africa during the latter half of the Triassic period. It was an ornithischian or BIRD-HIPPED dinosaur, and noted for its different types of teeth. In many ways its dentition was similar to that of a mammal with large tusk-like canines. *Heterodontosaurus* was a fast-running biped and was probably the ancestor of ORNITHOPOD dinosaurs such as CAMPTOSAURUS and *Iguanodon.* It is likely that 'different-tooth' used its tusks during battles over territory. *Heterodontosaurus* had muscular jaw pouches and it is thought that these were used to move plant material across the mouth to give a chewing effect.

Hippurites is a member of the RUDIST BIVALVE molluscs. It is, like all its relatives, specialized to a reef-dwelling life and is found in sediments of the Upper Cretaceous. The 2 valves of *Hippurites* are unequal in size. The right one is large and coral-like; the left is flat and lid-like. When first described, *Hippurites* was referred to as a 'horn', supposedly by people in southern France who appreciated the cylindrical shape of the lower valve.

Hoplites are a group of the extinct AMMONITES. Thirteen ammonite zones have been recognized in the GAULT CLAY, mainly by their species of *Hoplites.*

I

Ichthyornis, the 'fish-bird', is recorded from the Upper Cretaceous chalk deposits of Kansas, USA. It was a strong flier which looked similar to modern seagulls or terns. *Ichthyornis* was quite small, individuals reaching about 200mm in height. Like ARCHAEOPTERYX, the 'ancient feather', and *Hesperornis,* the 'dawn-bird', *Ichthyornis* had teeth. This is regarded as a primitive character in the evolution of birds. *Ichthyornis* lived at the same time as *Hesperornis* and *Baptornis* and together they provide invaluable information on the evolution of early sea-going birds.

Ichthyosaur was the most highly adapted of all reptiles living in water. The ichthyosaurs lived through the greater part of the Mesozoic, but were especially common

Mussels are invertebrates

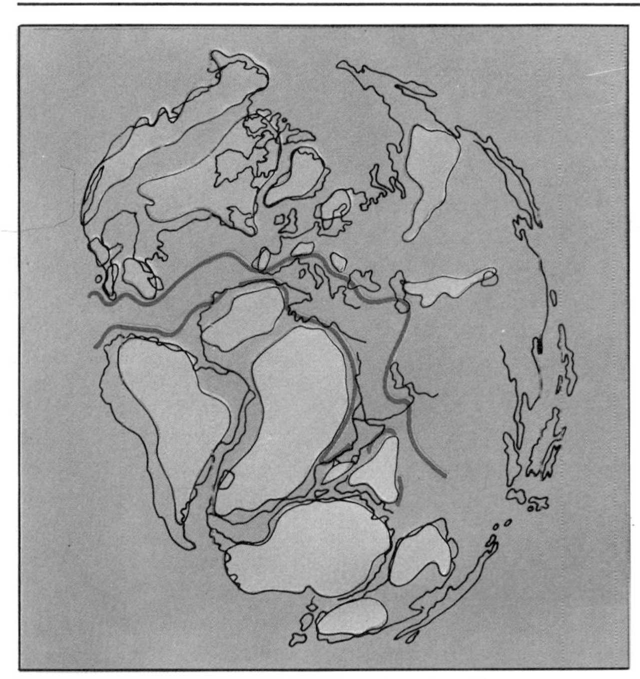

From 'The Ecology of Fossils', McKerrow (Duckworth and Co. Ltd.)

Left: Detailed field studies have enabled the distribution of rudist reefs to be plotted accurately. They follow the ancient shoreline of Tethys, and occur on rather coarse, sandy sea-bottoms. In some areas rudistids are seen to ring ancient sea mounts and even extinct submarine volcanoes. They are therefore helpful in making palaeogeographic reconstructions. From the distribution of the reefs it is clear that the ancient Tethys separated the northern continents from the southern ones which formerly made up Gondwanaland.

known as Tethys extended east–west from the West Indies to the Far East. Its waters encroached on the southern margins of the American and Eurasian landmasses and spread over the northern CONTINENTAL SHELVES (*see page 79*) of South America and Africa. The deeper central waters of Tethys were ruled by free-swimming creatures such as the ammonites, but its coastlines were clearly marked by numerous reef-building organisms. As in other periods, calcareous algae and corals were important members of many reef communities but in Tethys, the RUDIST BIVALVES were by far the most significant reef-formers. Unlike the majority of bivalves, rudistids had two unequal valves, the lower of which was often long and coral-like. The upper valve was flat and acted as a lid. It had two large teeth, and the way in which they fitted into the sockets on the lower valve seems to have restricted their vertical movement. The soft parts of rudist lived inside the thick walls of its lower valve, and organic debris was wafted towards the creature by self-generated currents. Rudistids, unlike many reef-dwelling animals, did not form colonies in the true sense, although they did often exist in closely-packed groups. Most preferred to live in coarse, sandy substrates where the large valve could be partly buried in sediment. As suspension-feeders, rudistids grew mainly in shallow waters, which were warm, with a limited or low rate of sediment deposition. In most reefs the various creatures were cemented together, or intertwined, but in the rudistid reef few organisms encrusted or attached themselves to the bivalve shells. The reasons for this are unknown, although some palaeontologists believe that the rudistids secreted a fluid which repelled other organisms. The rudist reefs are therefore more loosely constructed than the usual coral-algae ones, which also indicates that they existed in relatively calm waters.

Rudistids vary considerably in size and shape, some forms, such as RADIOLITES and HIPPURITES, growing to 300 millimetres in height. These robust coral-like types occurred mostly on the seaward slopes of the reef, whereas more exotic coiled types, such as REQUIENIA and CAPRINA, covered the upper and inner zones.

The success of the rudistids as reef-builders lasted from the middle to the end of the Cretaceous period. From then onwards they are unknown in the fossil record and their demise is probably linked with the host of extinctions that took place at that time. In the case of the rudistids it is likely that the closing of Tethys (following the movement of the African and Indian landmasses northwards) was very important. This resulted in currents changing direction and, with the uplift of land, in increasing amounts of sediment being carried to the sea. The level of turbulence may also have increased, and together these factors would have proved fatal to organisms adapted to living in quiet, clear waters. It is also thought that rudistids were unable to cope with sediment entering their shells, and that if this happened they would die of suffocation.

Right: *Sellathyris sella* is a well-known terebratulid brachiopod from the Cretaceous of Europe. It grew to between 10–30 mm in length, and is often found in 'nests' of several hundred individuals. *Sellathyris* has a smooth shell which has no radial ribbing. It has growth lines, however, and the shell is folded gently at the forward, or anterior, margin.

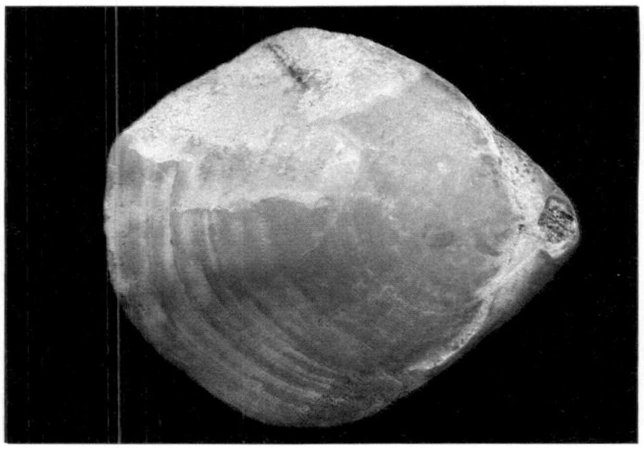

in the Jurassic. They are highly specialized for living in water when they appear in Triassic rocks, yet no earlier forms are known.
Iguanodont is the name given to ORNITHOPOD dinosaurs such as *Iguanodon* and a few related genera. The name means 'iguana-tooth', and refers to the similarity between the teeth of these herbivorous dinosaurs and the living iguana. In *Iguanodon* and CAMPTOSAURUS the teeth are broad and leaf-shaped.
Invertebrates are animals without backbones.

Lagoonal describes a shallow salt-water environment, partly or wholly separated from the sea by a narrow strip of land. It may also describe waters enclosed by an atoll.
Lance and Hell Creek are places in western North America associated with Upper Cretaceous formations rich in dinosaur remains.
Lesothosaurus was a small, primitive, BIRD-HIPPED dinosaur known to have existed in southern Africa during the Upper Triassic, at the same time as HETERODONTOSAURUS. These reptiles were approximately the same size, adults reaching 900 mm long. Unlike *Heterodontosaurus, Lesothosaurus,* the 'Lesotho-lizard', had rather simple teeth and no muscular cheeks. Its head was also smaller but like *Heterodontosaurus* it was an agile animal which ran on its strong hind legs.
Lias rocks are particularly well exposed at Lyme Regis and Charmouth in west Dorset, southern England. They are a fossil collectors' paradise, and it was at Lyme Regis that the famous collector Mary Anning discovered the remains of the large marine reptiles *Ichthyosaurus* and *Plesiosaurus* in the early 1800s. Apart from these spectacular fossils, there are also numerous ammonites and belemnites, as well as some crinoids. Unfortunately, many of the Lias cliffs are constantly crumbling and therefore dangerous.

Lias rocks, Dorset, England

Lizard-hipped dinosaurs, or saurischians, are those in which the pubis bone points downwards and forwards and the ischium bone downwards and backwards. This

Wealden shoreline

Earth movements towards the end of the Jurassic resulted in north-west Europe being uplifted into land. Continental conditions then prevailed in many areas for a considerable period, although in southern England the dawn of the Cretaceous was marked by a transgression of the seas over lowland areas. This flooding was short-lived, however, and swamplands and river deltas became the characteristic environments of the Wealden (Lower Cretaceous). As in the Jurassic, the climate was warm and humid, and we know that the vegetation resembled that found today in the EVERGLADES of Florida, in the USA. MANGROVES spread along the shorelines, while CYCADS, PINES and a few FLOWERING PLANTS grew within the high-level canopy.

Dinosaurs were dominant among larger vertebrates, although sea birds such as ICHTHYORNIS and various pterosaurs ruled the skies. Of the dinosaurs, ornithopods were the most common, and *Iguanodon* and *Hypsilophodon* the best known. *Iguanodon* continued the 'normal' ornithopod line, its likely ancestor being CAMPTOSAURUS from the late Jurassic of North America. 'Iguana-tooth' was almost twice the size of its forebear, and one of the largest of all ornithopods at 10 metres long and 5 tonnes. For most of its life it went on two legs, but with age and increasing bulk it often resorted to four. *Iguanodon* was well equipped to eat plants and its several rows of 'leaf-like' teeth are a considerable advance on the arrangement in *Camptosaurus.* Both ornithopods were rather defenceless creatures, although the famous spike-like thumbs of *Iguanodon* may have been used as a weapon. As far as evolution goes, the discovery at BERNISSART in Belgium, 1877, of a large number of associated IGUANODONTS was the first evidence of herding in higher vertebrates.

In contrast to *Iguanodon, Hypsilophodon* — 'the high-ridged toothed lizard' — was very small. It, too, went on two legs, but its lightly-built frame was perfectly adapted to a more agile life. To this small herbivore speed and agility were invaluable, enabling it to outrun and out-manoeuvre both large and small predators. According to recent research, its hind limb bones were similar in proportion to those of an ostrich or a gazelle. *Hypsilophodon* ran with its head forward, its stiffened tail held high as a counterbalance. It was a small animal, had few teeth, and its horn-covered jaws seem to have been adapted to crushing fruits and soft shoots.

Apart from *Iguanodon* and *Hypsilophodon,* one other ornithischian type was represented in the Wealden community. This was the early ankylosaur *Polacanthus,* which superficially resembled *Scelidosaurus* from the Lower Jurassic. In fact they were about the same length but *Polacanthus,* the 'many-spined lizard', was much more heavily armoured. Large spines ran in two rows along the back, and a thick bony shield covered its hips. The body was low and flattened and its overall design helped *Polacanthus* to withstand all but the most determined predators.

As in the Jurassic, the role of major predator was filled by a carnosaur. Its name was *Altispinax* and it was a direct descendant of creatures such as MEGALOSAURUS and ALLOSAURUS. Most car-

Below: The shorelines of Europe and North America during the Wealden period of the Lower Cretaceous were similar to the Everglades of Florida, USA, today. During the Wealden, however, herds of *Iguanodon* were common. Other dinosaurs, including the agile *Hypsilophodon* and well-armoured *Polacanthus,* were also present, and together these gentle herbivores provided the voracious carnosaurs with a plentiful supply of food.

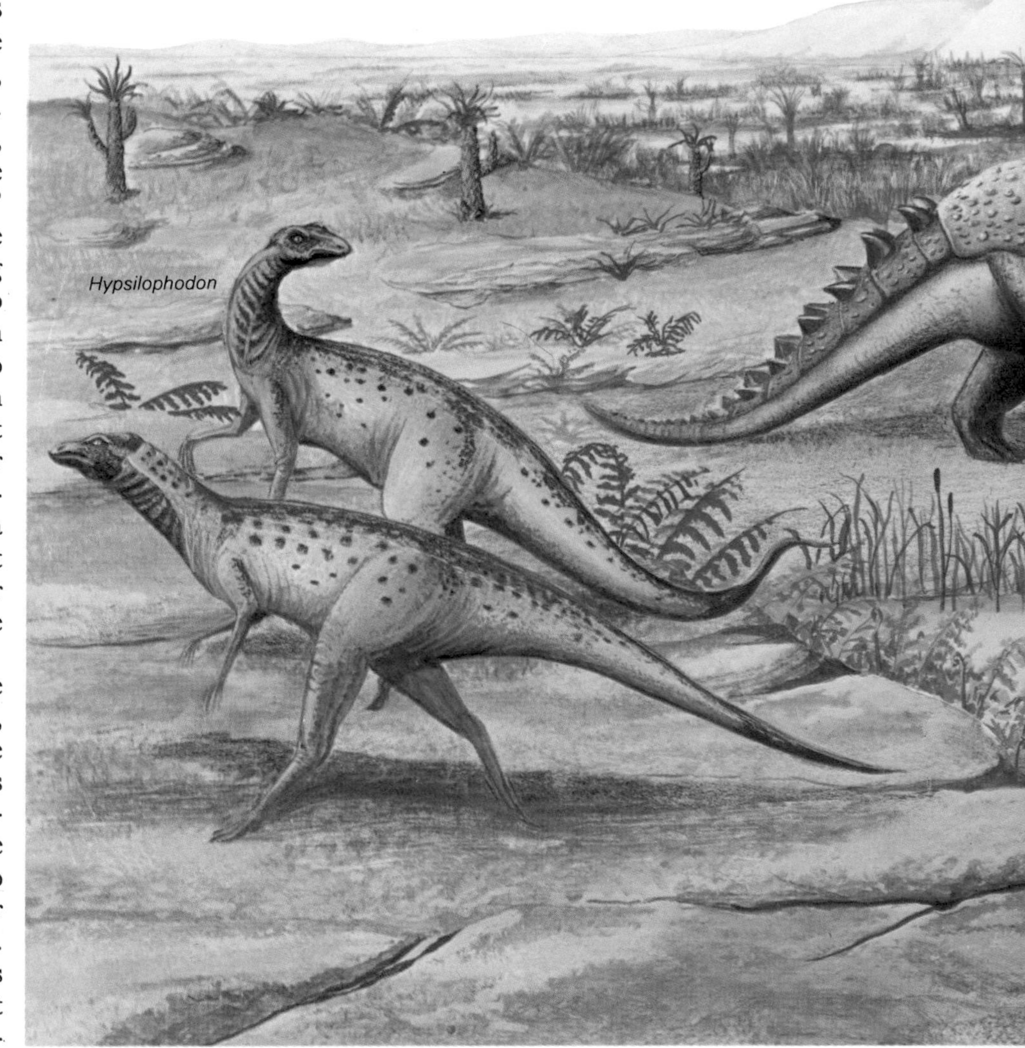

results in a 4-pronged arrangement of the pelvis, similar to the condition found in many other types of reptile. See also BIRD-HIPPED.

Lower Greensand was an unfortunate choice of name for this group of sandstones and its base clay. The term 'Greensand' was first used by the surveyor William Smith (1769–1839) for certain beds in Wiltshire, England. They are indeed green, from glauconite, a mineral of marine origin. The name was then extended to include sandstones exposed along the Kentish coast. But later it was realized that the Greensand of Wiltshire *overlies* the GAULT CLAY, whereas that in Kent *underlies* it. Accordingly, a Lower Greensand and an Upper Greensand were recognized, though only the Upper is really aptly named, for the Lower is more usually red, brown, yellow or white!

William Smith

M

Mangroves are plants specially adapted to a life in water. They have stilt roots that are arched to keep the stem and leaves above tide level. Specialized roots called pneumatophores obtain air from above both mud and water level.

Mastodontosaurus is the largest known of all the LABYRINTHODONT (*see page 85*) amphibians. Its skull alone measured over 1 metre in length and the whole animal was several metres long. Its skull was broad and flat and noted for several large tusk-like teeth at the front. Various species have been recorded from the Triassic rocks of Germany and India. *Mastodontosaurus* is associated with a group of labyrinthodonts called the stereos-

Mangrove swamp exposed at low water

nosaurs have a rather similar form, and the only obvious evolutionary changes are towards a reduction in the length and shape of the forelimbs, and a general overall increase in size. But in Lower Cretaceous Egypt, SPINOSAURUS'S huge '*Dimetrodon*-like' sail was an obvious adaptation to a tropical environment.

Little or no evidence of the coelurosaurs comes from the Wealden of Europe, but in North America, material from sediments of the same age shows that a new and highly specialized group — the DEINONYCHOSAURS — had evolved.

Life in early Cretaceous seas

The deltas and lakes of the Wealden period were

Below: Until recently *Hypsilophodon*, the small 2-legged ornithopod, was portrayed as a tree-dwelling dinosaur. But now *Hypsilophodon* is reconstructed as a fast-running herbivore.

Iguanodon is probably one of the best-known of all dinosaurs. This large herbivore's remains were first discovered in 1822 by Mary Ann Mantell, wife of the pioneer palaeontologist Gideon Mantell.

pondyls, which are characterized by a flattening of the skull and an increased hardening, or ossification, of the vertebrae.

Megalosaurus is one of the largest meat-eaters to have lived on Earth. The name means 'big lizard', for *Megalosaurus* measured 6 to 7 metres long. It stood over 4 metres tall and weighed approximately 2.5 tonnes. *Megalosaurus* lived during the Jurassic and Lower Cretaceous, and is found in association with *Apatosaurus*, the SAUROPOD, and the ORNITHOPOD *Camptosaurus*. It was a typical CARNOSAUR, with huge jaws and large serrated teeth. 'Big-lizard' was bipedal, and numerous tracks of its footprints show that its 3-toed feet turned slightly inwards during movement.

Melanorosaurus was a huge PROSAUROPOD that lived in South Africa during the latter half of the Triassic period. It was 4-legged, and adults grew to almost 12 metres in length. In many respects it looked similar to *Diplodocus* or *Brachiosaurus*, but significant differences in the skeleton separate it from the SAUROPODS proper. Many experts think that *Melanorosaurus* may have been the ancestor of the great 'lizard-footed' creatures of the Jurassic and Cretaceous. *Melanorosaurus* was a close relative of *Plateosaurus*, which lived in Europe at the same time.

Molluscs are an important group of INVERTEBRATE animals. They have an unsegmented body, often enclosed in a calcareous shell. This may be a single structure or a 2-valved unit.

Mosasaurs lived only in Upper Cretaceous times, but were distributed worldwide. They are particularly common in the chalk rocks of Kansas, USA. They swam with snake-like movements, and probably more than any other known animal looked like the popular idea of a monster sea serpent.

Mountain-building movements, or orogenies, are concentrated along long narrow zones called orogenic belts. In these, sediments are folded upwards into mountains. There have been 3 orogenies in Eurasia since Cambrian times. The youngest of them — the Alpine orogeny — threw up the Alps and the Himalayas.

Himalayan mountain range

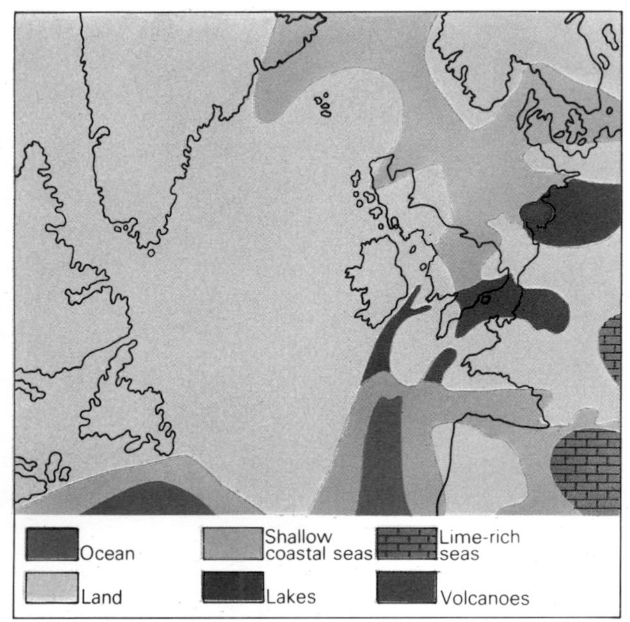

From 'The Ecology of Fossils', McKerrow (Duckworth and Co. Ltd.)

Left: Canada, Greenland and northern Europe during the Lower Cretaceous. We can see that land covered large areas of northern Europe and most of North America. Lakes and swamps also filled large tracts of low-lying land, and shallow seas flowed over much of east and central England, Denmark and northern Spain.

eventually flooded by a transgression of the sea in which the LOWER GREENSAND rock of southern and south-east England was laid down. This was the start of one of the greatest transgressions in the geological record; its climax came in late Cretaceous times, when vast continental areas were submerged. The Lower Greensand is followed by another marine deposit — the GAULT CLAY. To the west, the Upper Gault passes sideways into the Upper Greensand, the reason being that the Upper Gault Clay was laid down in relatively deep water, whereas the Upper Greensand was deposited nearer to the shore.

The completely sandy parts of the Lower Greensand are generally devoid of fossils. This is partly because the sands were continually disturbed as they were being laid down, and partly because fossil shells have been destroyed by acid ground-water percolating through the rock layer after it had been deposited. So only in the Lower Greensand's occasional clays, limestones, silty or clayey sands and CALCAREOUS CONCRETIONS are fossils at all common.

Lower Greensand fossils are mainly of ammonites, bivalves and gastropods, with occasional sponges, echinoids and corals. Careful collecting has shown that on the sandy floor of the Lower Greensand sea lived a wide range of bivalves (such as oysters), numerous terebratulid and rhynchonellid brachiopods and some gastropods. Many bivalves also lived in the sand of the sea floor, nourished by filtering sea-water for the organic matter suspended in it. At some levels in the Lower Greensand crabs and lobsters are preserved. The nekton include coiled and uncoiled ammonites, some of the uncoiled ones being a metre across.

In contrast to the Lower Greensand, the black and grey clays of the overlying Gault are rich in fossils which are often very well preserved. Especially plentiful are ammonites, particularly HOPLITES. Some still have irridescent shells, though many have been preserved by iron sulphide. There are also many belemnites, bivalves (such as *Inoceramus*) and gastropods, together with some brachiopods, crabs and lobsters, and the occasional teeth of sharks and ichthyosaurs.

Certain fossils from the Upper Greensand in Dorset, southern England, match those from the Upper Gault at Kent to the east, and so prove that the two deposits are of the same age. The Upper Greensand, however, accumulated in shallower water than the Gault. Accordingly, the fossils of the Upper Greensand differ somewhat, the benthic animals being less diverse and dominated by bivalves and gastropods. Among the bivalves are the coiled oyster *Exogyra*, several large scallops and various creatures that lived

Below: Cliffs cut in the Gault Clay at Folkestone, Kent, south England. The rock sequence here is reasonably complete and yields many fossils, including ammonites and belemnites.

and also buckled the CHALK of southern England and northern France. The Alpine orogeny reached a peak in Oligo-Miocene times, but it is likely that some areas are still rising.

N

Nodosaurs were a specialized group of ANKYLOSAURS that had a thick, bony armour over both head and body. They were squat, robust plant-eaters and lived in the Upper Cretaceous.

O

Omnivore describes an animal eating a mixed diet of plants and animals.

Ornithischian, see BIRD-HIPPED.

Red squirrel, an omnivore

Ornithopod dinosaurs form the major group of BIRD-HIPPED dinosaurs. Ornithopod describes the 3-toed, bird-like foot of animals such as *Iguanodon* and *Hypsilophodon*.

Over-specialization was once thought to be the outcome of evolutionary adaptation that had eventually overstepped the bounds of usefulness. (For example, it was assumed that the great sabre-toothed cats became extinct because their canines grew so large that they interfered with biting!) The word has also been used to describe organisms that have become highly adapted to a very restricted way of life, where even a small change in the environment could lead to extinction. The first idea cannot be accepted, as competition with other species ensures that inefficient adaptations do not arise. The second is also unacceptable, for though some organisms may not tolerate small changes in the environment, they are perfectly adapted to their way of life so long as the environment remains the same. A better description is 'highly specialized', compared with more adaptable generalized organisms.

P

Pachycephalosaurs, see BONE-HEADED.

Parasaurolophus was one of the most spectacular DUCK-BILLED dinosaurs. It was similar to *Iguanodon* in body form, but its great head was crowned by a huge hollow crest. In one species the crest alone measured 1.5 metres, and scientists have debated over its purpose. As it is hollow, it was once thought to have stored air when the animals swam

Above: *Hoplites interruptus*, a fossil ammonite from the Gault Clay at Folkestone, Kent. Ammonites, particularly *Hoplites*, are important in distinguishing different stratigraphic zones. The fossil shown is preserved in iron sulphide.

partly or entirely in the sand on the sea floor. Sponge communities, including *Siphonia*, were common.

Today the Greensands are widely associated with barren heathlands, often carrying conifer plantations or woods of silver birch. In places they also give rise to marked geographical features, the most imposing being the Lower Greensand hills running within, and parallel to, the chalk downs which rim the southern English WEALD. Damp grasslands, on the other hand, typify the Gault, as do hedges and woods with many oaks. Furthermore, the Gault erodes more easily and so often coincides with areas of low ground.

Late Cretaceous sea life

A variety of large reptiles lived in the Upper Cretaceous seas. They correspond to certain sea

Below: A typical selection of the various animals that lived in the Cretaceous sea in which the Upper Greensand was deposited. As well as these invertebrate creatures, however, there were also marine reptiles and various types of fish, including sharks.

Above right: A fossil skeleton of the sponge *Siphonia*. The tulip-shaped skeleton was attached to the sea floor by a stalk.

underwater, but this is now considered unlikely as the capacity of the chamber was small. Recent theories suggest that the crest was either a display feature, or that it was simply a sound box. *Parasaurolophus* lived during the Upper Cretaceous in western North America.

Pareiasaurs were an important group of COTYLOSAURS (*see page 79*) that lived during the Middle and Upper Permian. They are known from Europe and South Africa and constitute an easily-identifiable group of reptiles. All were plant-eaters and, with a large overall weight, tended to rotate their limbs towards the body for greater support. Their feet were also different from those of their close relatives, and became rather hoof-like. In many forms, including *Scutosaurus*, the large head was covered in warty or horny outgrowths. Most pareiasaurs were slow and cumbersome.

Periodic extinctions of related groups occurred between the MASS EXTINCTIONS (*see page 86*) which brought the Palaeozoic and Mesozoic eras to a close.

Phytosaurs are a group of large, crocodile-like THECODONTIANS recorded from the Triassic period.

Pines are an important group of conifers (cone-bearing trees). They first appeared in the early Mesozoic (possibly late Palaeozoic) and exist today mainly in northern regions.

Plagiosaurs form an unusual group of Permian and Triassic amphibians. Typical among plagiosaurs are *Plagiosaurus* and *Ferrothorax*. Of these, *Ferrothorax* is particularly well known and remains are

Pine trees

quite common in certain late Triassic sediments. It had a broad, short skull and large external gills. The body was also broad and short and armoured on both upper and lower surfaces. The limbs of *Ferrothorax* were much reduced and the tail short and tapered. Adults reached about 1 metre long.

Plesiosaurs are common in many Jurassic and Cretaceous rocks. They first appear in Rhaetic deposits, which mark the changeover from the Triassic to the Jurassic. By Liassic times they were already well diversified.

Above: Some animals of the late Cretaceous seas. Ichthyosaurs (**2**) were scarce by this time, but swan-necked plesiosaurs like *Elasmosaurus* (**3**) were common, as were the mosasaurs (**5**), and such turtles as *Archelon* (**4**). A large flightless diving bird, *Hesperornis*, is also shown (**1**).

mammals of today — the smaller whales, dolphins and sea lions — in their relationship to the environment. Thus the 'fish-lizard' or ichthyosaur strongly resembled a modern dolphin in appearance, the two types of animal providing examples of CONVERGENT EVOLUTION towards fish-like forms at different times in geological history. Remains of ichthyosaurs are often found in black shales, and occasionally their body outlines are preserved as well. They grew to 9 metres or more, and since they had numerous teeth and enormous eyes it is clear that they were predators, mostly of fish. Like all reptiles they had lungs and breathed air, so their nostrils were set far back on the head. However, whereas most reptiles lay eggs in sand or in a nest, this would not have been suitable in the sea, and we know from fossil evidence that they gave birth to live young.

Plesiosaurs were similar in some respects to sea lions, although their necks were generally much longer. They ranged up to 13 metres in length and their limbs were adapted into large, powerful paddles which they used to move forwards or backwards or to rotate their bodies. It seems that they swam through shoals of fish, catching their prey by darting their heads from side to side. (There have been suggestions that the legendary Loch Ness monster may be a plesiosaur, despite the fact that scientists regard these as having died out about 65 million years ago.) The short-necked plesiosaurs, called PLIOSAURS, would have looked rather like whales, as they had elongated skulls and jaws. In *Kronosaurus*, from the Cretaceous of Australia, the skull was almost 4 metres long! They hunted other sea reptiles and large shell-fish.

Other large marine lizards of late Cretaceous times were the MOSASAURS, or sea monitors. Like the reptiles mentioned above, their limbs were formed into paddles, but their tails were more crocodile-like and helped to propel the mosasaurs through water in search of prey such as ammonites. Mosasaurs grew to lengths of 15 metres and had narrow, pointed jaws with ferocious teeth.

During the Upper Cretaceous, most of Europe (apart from a few scattered islands) was covered

Pliosaurs diverged from PLESIOSAURS in the early Jurassic, and soon developed large forms. Both pliosaurs and plesiosaurs almost certainly returned to the shore for breeding.

Procompsognathus was one of the earliest COELUROSAURS. Typically it was a small, 2-legged creature with a fairly large head, long neck and large tail. It was an agile, fast-running carnivore which probably fed on small reptiles or scavenged off large carcasses. *Procompsognathus* is known from Europe and is found in association with the remains of *Plateosaurus*.

Prosauropods are a group of LIZARD-HIPPED dinosaurs from the Middle and Late Triassic. They were heavily-built, ate plants, and seem to be the ancestors of the giant SAUROPODS of the Jurassic and Cretaceous.

Pterosaurs, or flying reptiles, arose in the early Jurassic, near salt water. They glided on air currents, for it is doubtful whether they could have flapped their wing-like membranes. Probably they swooped low over the sea and scooped fish from the water. The arrangement of their leg bones shows that they could not have stood upright on land. It has even been suggested that they never landed on the ground, and that they hung upside-down, like bats, on sea-cliffs. The Cretaceous *Pteranodon* had a wingspan of nearly 8 metres, and an even larger pterosaur has recently been discovered in North America.

Q

Quadrupedal refers to animals with a 4-legged or footed stance, such as the elephant or *Brachiosaurus*, the SAUROPOD dinosaur.

Deer are quadrupedal animals

R

Racial senility, or old age, is a discredited idea

by sea, in which great thicknesses of CHALK were laid down. Chalk is a very pure limestone made up solely of the remains of organisms — mainly of minute PLANKTON (*see page 89*) algae called COCCOLITHS and to a lesser extent of foraminiferids, with some shell debris. The lack of sediments from land suggests that the chalk was deposited far from shore, and that where land did exist it was worn down and so added little sand or mud to the chalk sea.

Many museum displays may give the impression that fossils are plentiful in the chalk, but this is not usually the case. In fact such displays are the result of patient collecting over many years. When deposited, the chalk was in a semi-fluid or thixotropic state, so that the sea-bed animals of the time were often adapted for living on soft bottoms. Bivalves like *Spondylus* developed long spines to distribute the weight of the shell more widely, and the echinoid *Tylocidaris* had club-shaped spines for the same purpose. Dead shells also provided a hard base on which other animals, such as oysters, could live.

Right: Highly magnified fossil coccoliths in chalk, from Oxfordshire, England. Coccoliths are calcareous structures which occur on the cell walls of minute green algae known as coccospheres. Much of the chalk is made up of coccoliths.

Below: Reconstruction of an animal community from the upper chalk seas of Britain. Some of the echinoids and bivalves have clearly adapted in ways which have made it easier for them to live on soft bottoms.

(1) *Parapuzosia* (ammonite)
(2) *Ventriculites* (sponge)
(3) *Tylocidaris* (echinoid)
(4) *Spondylus* (bivalve)
(5) *Parasmilia* (coral)
(6) *Conulus* (echinoid)
(7) *Echinocorys* (echinoid)
(8) *Micraster* (echinoid)

Bivalves, especially *Inoceramus,* are generally the most plentiful fossils in the chalk, along with those of echinoderms, belemnites and brachiopods. Most of the echinoids fed on the organic debris in the original chalk sediment. Certain types, such as *Conulus* and *Echinocorys,* probably ploughed through the sediment. Yet BIOTURBATION of this kind, and the burrows of other animals, are hard to see in the fossil state because the chalk is so pure. Among the nekton, or swimming animals, ammonites become progressively rarer upwards through the chalk, though specimens of the giant ammonite *Parapuzosia* may reach 2 metres across.

The Upper Cretaceous

About 100 million years ago the Earth had entered a period of significant change. The continents, which had been fused together during the Permian and early Triassic, were moving slowly apart and the climate was changing. Of the individual continents, North America had moved from South America and the widening of the south Atlantic was well under way. By the Upper Cretaceous the Gondwana supercontinent had almost completely broken up, and India, Australia, Antarctica and Madagascar

---

that likened the evolution of a particular plant or animal group to the age cycle of an individual organism. Just as the individual can become old and senile, so it was thought that a group such as the dinosaurs would eventually become 'old' and less vigorous. But there is no scientific basis for this.

Radiation, in the evolutionary sense, refers to a rapid increase in the number of types in a given group or groups of organisms. It marks an increase in efficiency followed by greater success.

Radiolites is a large, coral-like RUDIST BIVALVE. The lower valve is erect and cone shaped, and the outer surface is coarsely ridged. The upper valve is flat to conical in shape. *Radiolites* was a reef-forming organism and is known from Upper Cretaceous sediments of Europe, North Africa, north-east Asia and North America. Like many other rudists it is useful in suggesting former environments and in establishing the former coastline of the TETHYS Sea.

Regression, used in the geological sense, refers to a fall in sea-level, which exposes new areas of land. See TRANSGRESSION.

Requienia is a RUDIST BIVALVE. It is rather florid in shape and the 2 valves are of unequal size. Unlike the straight, erect forms such as RADIOLITES and HIPPURITES, *Requienia* is coiled into distinct spirals. The outer wall of both valves is wrinkled. As with CAPRINA, this decorative rudist lived on upper surfaces of reefs during the Lower Cretaceous. Its distribution coincides with the former shorelines of the TETHYS Sea.

Rhynchonellid is a BRACHIOPOD (*see page 77*) which is more or less triangular in outline. It also has a strong fold at the margin of the shell along which the valves open. Rhynchonellids appeared in the Ordovician and survive to the present.

Rhynchonellia

Rhynchosaurs are a group of heavily-built QUADRUPEDAL reptiles from the Triassic. They had jaws modified for slicing and chopping, and it seems that they fed on 'fruits' with a hard outer cover. Classifiers associate rhynchosaurs with the snakes and lizards.

Rudist bivalves had one large, fixed, conical valve, with a small lid-like valve on

had moved away from each other as separate landmasses.

In the northern hemisphere, warm, temperate plants were widespread over much of northern Europe, Siberia and North America. Oak, poplar, walnut, hickory and magnolia were all common to these areas, as were giant redwoods, GINKGOS and ferns. Sub-tropical plants grew slightly to the south, and a vast arid region stretched from Spain across to the Middle East. In the southern hemisphere plants and climate were less varied, with swamplands persisting in many areas.

The more pronounced changes in the northern hemisphere brought about a RADIATION among dinosaurs. This was mainly centred on Mongolia and North America, and the major response came from the ornithischians. Until the Upper Cretaceous this group had included only the 'main line' ornithopods, and the plated and early armoured dinosaurs. But 100 million years ago there was a change, and the specialized DUCK-BILLED, BONE-HEADED dinosaurs and horned ornithischians all appeared.

According to some experts, the 'main-line' ornithopods, such as *Iguanodon* and possibly *Hypsilophodon,* survived to the end of the Cretaceous. This suggests that they were well adapted to their environment and had successfully withstood the great carnosaurs. Of the armoured ankylosaurs, *Polacanthus* had died out, but its place had been filled by animals representing two distinct lines of evolution. Both remained ankylosaurian, but whereas one was noted for squat, heavily-built and armoured creatures, the other included animals with a more upright stance and lighter armour. Members of the first line were termed NODOSAURS and the second, ACANTHOPHOLIDS. At the beginning of the Upper Cretaceous the nodosaurs were represented by *Scolosaurus* and acanthopholids by *Acanthopholis.* Both were low-level browsers but *Scolosaurus* probably lived in more open uplands.

Horned and duck-billed dinosaurs

The first horned dinosaur, or CERATOPIAN, appeared in Mongolia about 100 million years ago. The name of this more specialized ornithischian was *Protoceratops,* and although it was much smaller in both size and weight than its descendant *Triceratops,* it had almost all the family characteristics, with a parrot-like beak

Below: *Protoceratops,* the first of the horned dinosaurs, and *Ornithomimus,* the ostrich-like coelurosaur, were important among the Upper Cretaceous animals of Mongolia. *Protoceratops* laid its eggs in shallow nests and probably protected its young from the nest-robbing coelurosaurs. Another enemy of the horned dinosaur was *Tarbosaurus,* a close relative of *Tyrannosaurus rex.*

top. In the Cretaceous they formed large shallow-water reefs in the TETHYS Sea.

S

Sauropod is the name given to 'lizard-footed' dinosaurs such as *Diplodocus* and *Brachiosaurus.* It refers to the form of the foot, which is rather like that of an elephant. Prosauropods such as *Plateosaurus* and *Melanorosaurus* also have a similar type of foot.

Feet of a sauropod, or 'lizard-footed' dinosaur

Scelidosaurus was a heavily-built, 4-legged ORNITHISCHIAN. This 'limb-lizard' grew to over 4 metres in length and had such a small head and armoured body that it has been suggested as the ancestor for both the plated STEGOSAURS and armoured ANKYLOSAURS.

Sea-floor spreading is a theory or concept inferring that the sea-floors of various oceans spread outwards from an oceanic ridge. The ridge is a continuous swell, several hundred km wide, which is constantly added to by the outpouring of volcanic rocks. Evidence in support of this concept is drawn not only from the age of these rocks, but from ocean-floor magnetism and deep-sea sediments. Sea-floor spreading is a relatively new theory, as the original ideas were presented in the late 1950s and early 1960s.

Seed ferns

Seed ferns are an extinct order of GYMNOSPERMS that lived from Carboniferous to Cretaceous times. As their

and a bony frill covering its neck. *Protoceratops* was four-legged, and many experts think it gained protection as a herd animal. Its major enemies were the coelurosaurs, for we have evidence that it protected its nest against raiders such as VELOCIRAPTOR, 'the swift robber', and *Ornithomimus,* 'the bird imitator'.

Velociraptor was a direct descendant of *Coelurus* and other 'normal' coelurosaurs, while *Ornithomimus* belonged to a specialized side branch. Its long forelimbs, grasping hands and bird-like beak made it the ideal nest-robber or egg-stealer. *Ornithomimus* is also known from North America, and it seems that in common with many other dinosaurs it migrated eastwards over the BERING LAND BRIDGE. Among these others were giant carnosaurs such as *Gorgosaurus* and a host of ornithischians including the horned ceratopians.

The duck-billed dinosaurs probably originated in Asia and then moved east. Though our evidence for this is limited, *Bactrosaurus,* the earliest duck-bill from Mongolia, certainly predates its earliest North American relative, CLAOSAURUS. With time, the duck-billed, horned and bone-headed dinosaurs flourished in western North America, and palaeontologists recognize three distinct communities spanning 20 million years. Our reconstruction is of the BELLY RIVER community, around 90 million years old. It was the first of the three and it seems that the duck-billed dinosaurs such as *Parasaurolophus* made up approximately 70 per cent of its herbivore population.

Lance and Hell Creek community

During the last 5 million years or so of the

Below: During the early part of the Upper Cretaceous, bird-hipped (ornithischian) dinosaurs flourished in the western regions of North America. *Scolosaurus,* an ankylosaur, was a prominent member of the North American communities, as were *Parasaurolophus,* the duck-billed dinosaur, and *Pachyrhinosaurus,* the ceratopian.

name implies, they were seed-bearing plants but otherwise strikingly resembled ferns. They were important among the Carboniferous coal plants of the northern hemisphere.

Selection pressures, such as competition for food, living space or shelter, have a considerable effect on evolution. Successful competitors are obviously better adapted to the prevailing conditions and they will therefore pass on to their offspring the necessary information for success.

Sphenopsid trees were common in Carboniferous times. They resembled giant versions of their only living representatives, the horsetails, which all belong to the single genus, *Equisetum.*

Spinosaurus was a sail-backed CARNOSAUR recorded from the Upper Cretaceous of Egypt. The presence of a sail is unusual in the huge meat-eaters, but *Spinosaurus* obviously supported such a structure. The animal was approximately 11 metres long and its sail extended from the middle of the back to a point behind the hips. Like *Tyrannosaurus, Spinosaurus* had a large head armed with numerous sharp teeth. *Spinosaurus* probably used its sail to control its body temperature.

Horsetails resemble sphenopsid trees

Spiriferid is a BRACHIOPOD (*see page 77*) with a roughly triangular shell in which a straight hinge-line forms the widest part. Its name comes from the fact that the lophophore — the feeding mechanism — is supported by a spiral structure. Spiriferids range from the Ordovician to today.

Stegosaurs were a group of plated dinosaurs. They were QUADRUPEDAL plant-eaters and are known from the Upper Jurassic of North America and Africa. *Stegosaurus* may have been able to control its body

Cretaceous period came the greatest radiation of dinosaurs. Once again the evidence is mainly from North America and Mongolia, and similarities between animals of these two regions argue for the continued existence of the Bering land bridge. Of the two regions the North American is the better known, and its animals represent the third of the three communities mentioned previously. This one takes its name from rocks of the LANCE AND HELL CREEK formations in Alberta and Montana.

In contrast to the Belly River community, that of the Lance and Hell Creek is noted for its numerous horned ceratopians. The most important groups are TOROSAURUS and *Triceratops,* the latter including several species. Duck-bills were still common, but now accounted for only 20 per cent of the plant-eating population. Ceratopians made up 50 per cent and ankylosaurs much of the rest. These animals formed prey for the great predators, the ratio of predators to prey being 1 to 10. Chief predator was *Tyrannosaurus rex* – the 'tyrant-lizard' – which represents the peak of carnosaur evolution.

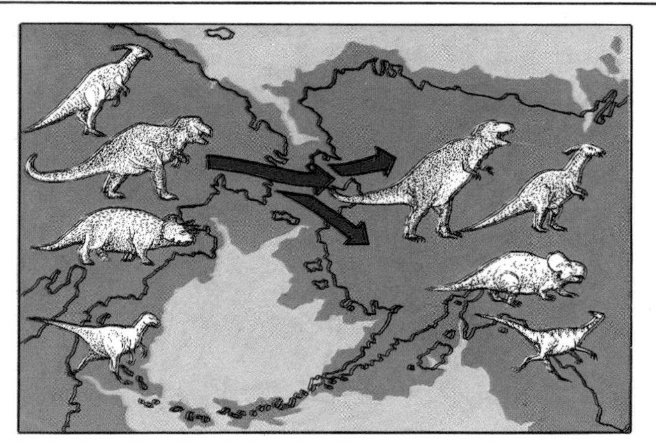

Left: The evolution and distribution of various groups of dinosaurs suggest that the landmasses of North America and Siberia were in contact during the Cretaceous period. The area of contact acted as a land 'bridge' and permitted various stocks to migrate from one continent to the other. In the case of the dinosaurs, this migration was mostly towards the east. The Bering land bridge also aided the distribution of certain mammals.

The great carnosaur

Tyrannosaurus was a giant, 12 metres long and 5 metres high – considerably larger than its Lower Cretaceous ancestor *Gorgosaurus.* It was the largest meat-eater of all time, four to five times bigger overall than Triassic forms. The skull was enormous and its teeth large and serrated. *Tyrannosaurus* was two-legged, and unlike its ancestors had arms reduced to almost ridiculous proportions. There were just two fingers, and much debate has been directed to the use of such restricted limbs. One theory suggests that *Tyrannosaurus* used the arms when rising from a resting position, its tiny forelimbs preventing the animal from sliding forwards. When hunting, *Tyrannosaurus* relied on its powerful legs and huge clawed feet, with which it gripped and tore at its prey. *Tyrannosaurus* ruled North America, while in Mongolia, *Tarbosaurus,* an almost identical animal, was the chief predator.

Herbivores

It is likely that *Tyrannosaurus* attacked mainly weak and old animals, but even so, the plant-eaters had developed various features for defence. Most were herd animals and in the case of

temperature by regulating the flow of blood into the large, bony plates set along its back.

Supernova is an enormous explosion of an old star. These events occur on average at a rate of 2 to 3 per galaxy each century. Some people have argued that a supernova would have generated enough cosmic radiation to cause mass extinctions on Earth.

Lagoon nebula, a supernova

'Supersaurus' was the name used to describe the remains of a huge SAUROPOD dinosaur discovered in Colorado, North America, in 1972. The name was given to the animal by a popular journal, although it is scientifically unfounded. *'Supersaurus'* is known from the remains of the shoulder-blades, hip and 5 vertebrae, and estimates of its size are astounding. *'Supersaurus'* is thought to have stood 15 metres tall, measured 32 metres and weighed 100 tonnes.

Suspension-feeder

Suspension-feeders eat micro-organisms and particles of organic matter suspended in sea water. Most suspension-feeders are also FILTER-FEEDERS.

Suture lines in CEPHALOPODS (*see page 78*) mark the contact between the inner partitions, or septa, and the outer shell.

T **Terebratulid** is a BRACHIOPOD (*see page 77*) which is oval in shape, with 2 convex valves. The lophophore (feeding mechanism) is supported by a calcareous loop. Tereb-

Below: *Triceratops*, probably a herding animal, was the largest ceratopian dinosaur. Also large were the ankylosaurs, or 'reptilian tanks'. *Ankylosaurus* used its heavy armour in defence against *Tyrannosaurus*, which, together with its relative *Tarbosaurus*, was the dominant carnosaur of the Upper Cretaceous. In the background is a group of pachycephalosaurs. Their thick, bony skulls were probably used during territorial battles.

Triceratops, for example, the presence of huge male animals must have deterred *Tyrannosaurus* from attacking too often. *Triceratops* was itself a huge beast, a large male probably exceeding 7 metres in length and weighing from 8 to 9 tonnes. It had a large bony frill over its shoulders and the two brow horns, just above the eyes, were nearly a metre long. *Triceratops* had a parrot-like beak and as a low-level browser it pulled and clipped away at fairly soft vegetation. During the last five million years of the Cretaceous, at least ten species of *Triceratops* flourished on the open lands of North America, a success story probably triggered by CLIMATIC CHANGE. Other ceratopians, such as *Torosaurus*, also flourished in the Lance and Hell Creek community. *Torosaurus* was similar in size to *Triceratops* but its bony frill was exceedingly large. These two represent the peak of ceratopian evolution, which involved not only an increase in overall size, but such details as the development of hoof-like feet and a shortened tail.

Of the remaining plant-eaters, ankylosaurs were represented by the 'reptilian tank' *Euoplocephalus*. This animal was covered from head to toe by thick, bony plates and its heavy, squat body made it a difficult target for a hungry predator. Under attack it would sink to the ground and defy *Tyrannosaurus* to break through its defence or turn it over. Among duck-billed dinosaurs, *Anatosaurus* was the main representative; it lacked the crests of many of its predecessors but overall was similar in shape and size. It ran fast on two legs and its DENTAL 'BATTERIES', made up of hundreds of closely-packed teeth, show that it fed on tough vegetation.

In more upland regions, the PACHYCEPHALOSAURS were prominent members of the Lance and Hell Creek community. They lived rather as do goats and mountain sheep today, and used their thick, bony head-shields as weapons during battles over territory. *Pachycephalosaurus* was a large two-legged creature and, like *Triceratops*, roamed in herds. As a herbivore it naturally attracted *Tyrannosaurus*, but its speed and agility probably helped it to avoid its predator. Together with all the other dinosaurs, *Tyrannosaurus*, the pachycephalosaurs and ceratopians died out at the end of the Cretaceous period, about 65 million years ago.

ratulids enter the fossil record in Devonian times and are the most numerous brachiopod group alive today. *Terebratulina* lives in clear, relatively deep water around the North Atlantic coastline. It occurs in groups, each individual attached to the sea-floor by a short stalk or pedicle.

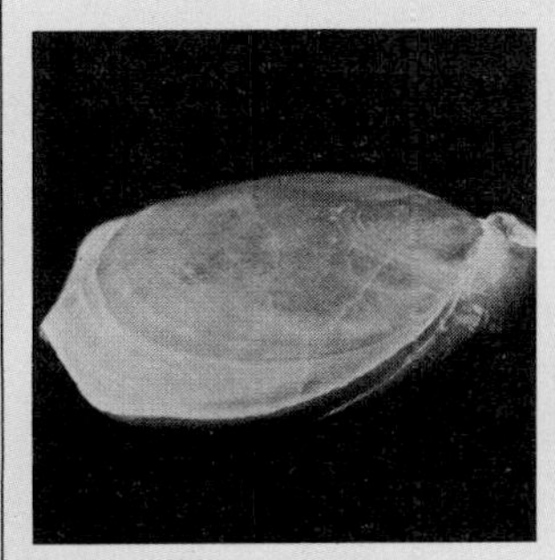
Terebratulid lamp shell

Tethys was an ocean that once existed between the super-continents of GONDWANALAND (*see page 82*) to the south, and LAURASIA (*see page 85*) to the north. The Mediterranean is the central remnant of this once-great seaway.

Thecodontians were early, primitive ARCHOSAUR reptiles which are known to be the ancestors of the dinosaurs, crocodiles and PTEROSAURS. They lived from the Upper Permian to the Upper Triassic.

Theropod describes the meat-eating LIZARD-HIPPED dinosaurs. The word means 'beast-footed' and the group comprises the COELUROSAURS and the CARNOSAURS.

Toothed birds lived during the Cretaceous and reached their peak in *Hesperornis*, a large, flightless diving bird. Although it had many specialized characteristics, the teeth in its lower jaw and the back of its upper jaw are a primitive feature suggesting *Hesperornis's* reptile ancestry. There were also gull- and tern-like toothless birds. Most fossils of toothless birds are found in chalk, and we know very little of the birds that lived on land in the Cretaceous.

Ichthyornis, a toothed bird

Torosaurus is a huge horned dinosaur known from the Upper Cretaceous of western North America. The animal was almost as large as *Triceratops* overall, but its crest was proportionately much bigger. In fact the crest reached enormous proportions, covering the animal's neck and shoulders

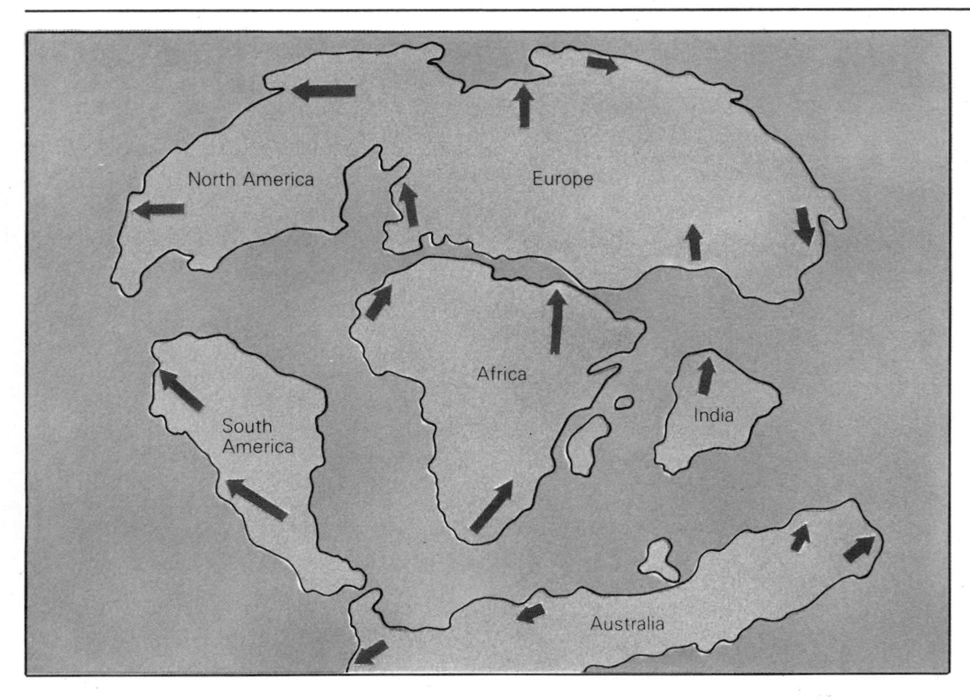

Above: This map shows the approximate positions and also the relative movements (in the directions of the arrows) of the continents at the end of the Cretaceous period.

The Cretaceous extinctions

The mass extinctions which brought to a close the Mesozoic era differed from those which occurred at the end of the Palaeozoic, for they were not confined to the sea (*see page 96*). There had been important extinctions throughout the Mesozoic, but related groups had always appeared to replace those which had been lost. However, at the end of the Cretaceous many forms died out without being replaced. On land all the dinosaurs vanished, as did the flying lizards or pterosaurs and, most probably, the TOOTHED BIRDS. Of the animals which lived exclusively on land, only those with body weights of less than 10 kilograms survived. (The mammals, birds, snakes and lizards fell into this category.) In the sea the ichthyosaurs, mosasaurs and plesiosaurs died out, along with ammonites, rudist bivalves and some types of gastropods. The plant kingdom lost two gymnosperm families in the Cretaceous — the SEED FERNS and the BENNETTITALES. Yet the period as a whole saw the rise to world dominance of the ANGIOSPERMS, and there were no important losses at the Cretaceous–Tertiary boundary (about 65 million years ago).

Left: Representatives of some of the groups of land and sea animals that became extinct at the end of the Cretaceous period, which also marks the close of the Mesozoic era.

with a thick, bony armour. As in *Triceratops*, the brow horns were much larger than the nose horn.

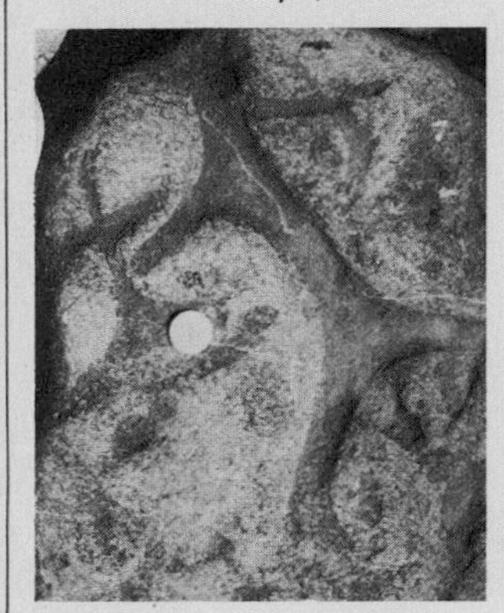

Trace fossils

Trace fossils result from the action of former animals. They include burrows and trails made in once-soft sediments, and borings made in hard areas on an ancient sea floor.

Transgression, in geology, is a rise in sea-level which results in areas of land becoming submerged. For example, as the great ice-sheets of the last glaciation shrank, the water they released led to a world-wide rise in sea-level of over 100 metres, which separated Britain from Europe, and Ireland from Britain. This transgression also caused the deposit of clays in that part of Belgium known as Flanders, and so is called the Flandrian transgression. Indeed, the present inter-glacial period is also known as 'the Flandrian'.

Triassochelys, from the Upper Triassic of Germany, is the earliest recorded turtle. Most of its features are similar to those of living representatives, for example the strongly-developed shell. In contrast to living turtles, however, *Triassochelys* had small teeth and small ribs rising to the side of the neck vertebrae. It is therefore a primitive type, although the shell represents a marked change from its likely COTYLOSAUR (*see page 79*) ancestor.

Terrapins

Tritylodonts were a group of mammal-like reptiles living in South Africa and Europe during the Triassic and Jurassic. They had a unique teeth formation which indicated a close link with mammals. Unlike the mammals, however, the tritylodonts still had several bones in their lower jaw.

Turtles, tortoises and terrapins are a unique group of reptiles in which the bones

The list of late Cretaceous extinctions is impressive, and so too is the variety of explanations for them. Change in climate has often been mentioned as a prime cause. However, climatic changes had occurred before in the Mesozoic without such a wholesale catastrophe; and anyway, why should marine organisms have been so adversely affected? Further, if (as some palaeontologists believe) the dinosaurs were warm-blooded, it becomes even more difficult to accept that a worsening climate extinguished every one of their number — even if we had evidence that a sudden global deterioration of this kind had taken place. Another suggestion involves a SUPERNOVA explosion, or a reversal in the Earth's magnetic field leading to increased cosmic radiation and a rise in fatal MUTATIONS (*see page 87*). The problem is that all higher forms of life would have disappeared.

Why the dinosaurs died

Numerous theories have been concerned solely with the loss of the dinosaurs. They include: OVER-SPECIALIZATION; RACIAL SENILITY; disease; slipped discs; and the development of mammals which specialized in eating dinosaur eggs. Other ideas suggest that carnivorous dinosaurs killed all the herbivorous dinosaurs and then died of hunger; or that there were changes in vegetation which reduced the food supply to the herbivorous dinosaurs. Among these only the last can be regarded as a serious possibility for we know that there was progressive diversification and dominance of the angiosperms during the Cretaceous. However, this growing dominance was accompanied not by a fall, but by a parallel increase in the diversity of large, plant-eating ornithischian dinosaurs!

Explanations based on one cause have not been widely accepted, either for the extinctions in general or for the disappearance of the dinosaurs in particular. More recently a different approach to the problem has been taken — one which attaches importance to MOUNTAIN-BUILDING MOVEMENTS and changes in sea-level. The sequence begins with mountains bordered by lowlands, and surrounded by wide, shallow seas. The mountain barriers allow a rich variety of animal life to evolve in isolation. The seas, too, have a rich variety of life. Over millions of years, the mountains gradually wear down and the seas retreat down the continental shelves. The larger land animals can cross the mountains and migrate to the lowlands. Eventually, with the major barriers gone, no new large animals will evolve to replace those which have dispersed to the lowlands and died out. However, small animals will still be able to diversify, isolated by the lesser barriers of the remaining hilly terrain. Sea life is also less varied after the shrinking of the shallow seas. But animals such as crocodiles and turtles are more numerous as the fall in sea-level increases the area of coastal wetlands and estuaries. Such changes in terrain and sea-level did occur in the late Cretaceous, and so did the same pattern of extinction and survival.

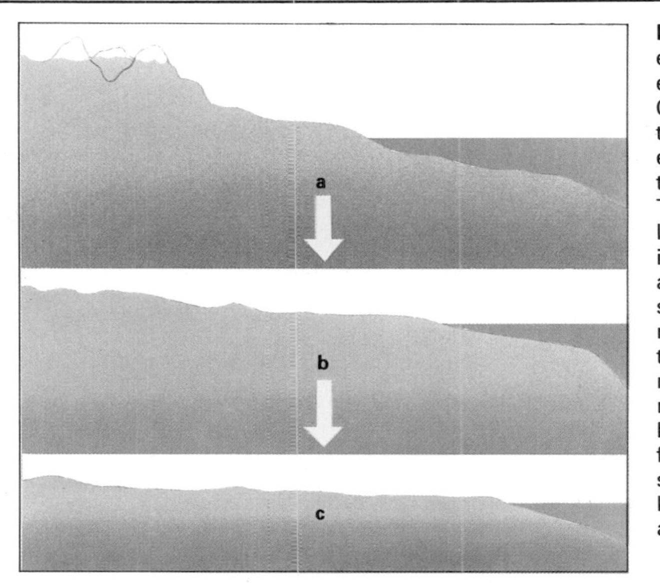

Left: According to one explanation of the mass extinction at the end of the Cretaceous, the character of the land surface and the extent of shallow sea at the time were important factors. Thus in (**a**) new species of large animals could evolve in the mountainous regions and in the extensive shallow seas. However, as the mountains wore down and the seas retreated, in the manner shown in (**b**), such new species of large animals became increasingly less frequent. Eventually, when situation (**c**) was reached, large animals disappeared almost everywhere.

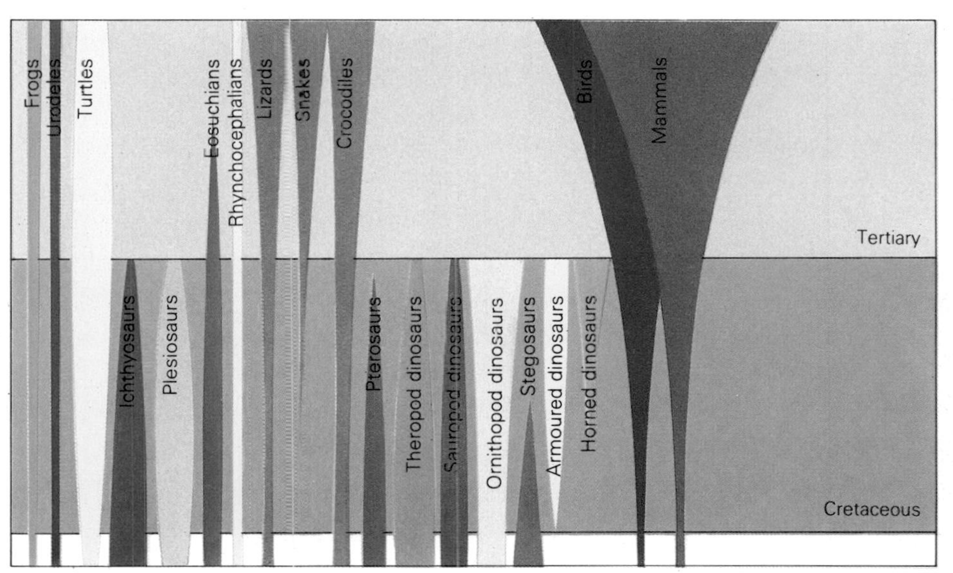

Above: Of the groups of land animals that survived the extinctions at the end of the Mesozoic, the birds and mammals were the most successful in evolutionary terms.

of the shoulder and hip girdles occur between 2 bony units — the upper carapace and the ventral or lower plastron. The first animals from this group appeared in the Upper Triassic.

V **Velociraptor** is also known as the 'swift-' or 'fast-running robber'. It was a COELUROSAUR and lived in Mongolia during the Upper Cretaceous. A carnivore, with strong hind limbs and larger arms than most other coelurosaurs, *Velociraptor* is now associated with another bipedal meat-eater, *Deinonychus*, and is thought to have been among the most intelligent group of dinosaurs. It was a nest-robber and a recent discovery shows that at least once an individual was caught in the act. This discovery is from Mongolia and it shows *Velociraptor* and the horned dinosaur *Proceratops* locked in a death struggle.

Voracious is used to describe the gluttonous feeding habits of flesh-eating dinosaurs.

W **Weald** is an oval-shaped region of south-east England which is made up mainly of Cretaceous sandstones and clays. It is surrounded by chalk downland except at the eastern end where its boundary is the Straits of Dover. The core is known as the High Weald and coincides with sandstone hills; the encircling belt of clay lowlands is called the Low Weald.

Weald, south-east England

Wealden sediments are alternations of sandstone and clay which make up the oldest Lower Cretaceous rocks in the WEALD of south-east England. Each bed of sandstone represents the development of an ancient delta. The clay next to each bed represents in turn the advance of the sea on to land, thus flooding the former delta.

The communities of plants and animals living on different continents today evolved during the Cainozoic era, beginning about 65 million years ago. Mammals, like the dinosaurs before them, adapted to land, sea and air.

Cainozoic Communities

Following the extinctions and reduction in numbers of so many animal groups at the end of the Cretaceous, there was less diversity in the lower Tertiary or PALAEOGENE seas — at least to begin with. The sea also covered a smaller area than in the Cretaceous, and new areas of land were exposed. So in north-west Europe, only south and south-east England were still submerged, together with parts of northern France, Belgium, Holland, Denmark, northern Germany and Poland. The rest was land, with large lakes and lagoons. England and Germany were further south than today and the climate was tropical or sub-tropical. The Atlantic and Indian oceans were still connected by the Tethys Sea.

After the Cretaceous seas had receded, the chalk was gently buckled into vast ANTICLINES and SYNCLINES, and the anticlines were greatly eroded. During the Palaeogene, the Hampshire, London, Paris and Belgian synclines or BASINS experienced repeated influxes and retreats of the sea, so that layers of sea, estuary, delta and marsh sediments were laid down. In the LONDON BASIN the earliest transgression deposited the THANET SAND, which is of early Eocene age. Later, the Hampshire and London basins both had large rivers and brackish-water environments, in which the greater part of the WOOLWICH AND READING BEDS formed. They were submerged in turn by a transgression of the sea which gave rise to the LONDON CLAY, and stretched into northern France, north-west Germany and Denmark. As the London Clay sea grew shallow, the BAGSHOT SANDS and BRACKLESHAM BEDS were formed in rivers, deltas and near-shore waters. The Bracklesham Beds are confined to the Hampshire Basin, where they are overlain by marine sands and clays of the BARTON BEDS. In turn, the Barton Beds pass upwards into lagoon and sea sediments known as the HEADON BEDS, which record the passage from the Eocene to the Oligocene.

Below right: Cliffs in the London Clay, Isle of Sheppey. The London Clay in this area has yielded numerous plant remains of a tropical, or near-tropical, forest that grew around the shores of the Eocene sea in which the London Clay was deposited.

Below left: A reconstruction of a marine community from the Eocene London Clay. There are fewer species than there were in the Cretaceous seas, and gastropods and bivalves were relatively much more important. Turtles, sharks and bony fish were also common. Although the ammonites were by now extinct, the related nautiloids were still in evidence and have in fact survived to the present day.

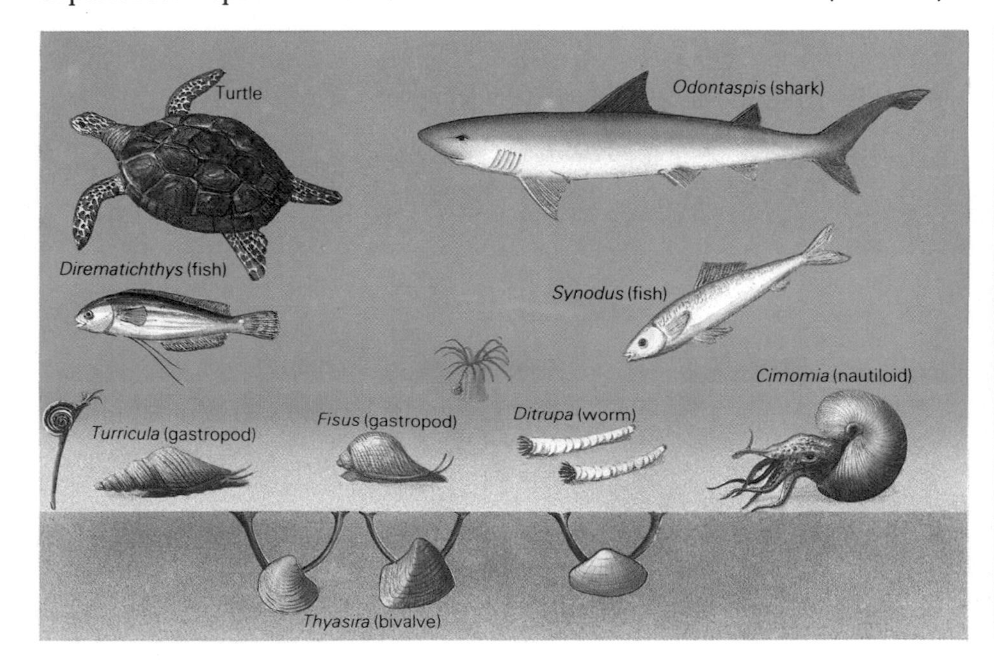

Reference

A **Amblypods** were ancient plant-eating animals that appeared in the Palaeocene. They rapidly developed into large, ponderous creatures, only to die out in early Oligocene times. They were prey for the largest of the oxyaenid CREODONTS.

Anticlines are upfolded or arched rocks, and result from sideways pressures in the Earth's crust. An anticline may be lengthened into a line, or take the form of a dome. The upfolding varies in scale, and the upper parts of anticlines have usually been eroded, revealing older rocks below. Thus erosion of the great chalk anticline of the WEALD (*see page 117*) has exposed underlying Lower Cretaceous sandstones and clays.

Artiodactyls are even-toed UNGULATES. They are very diverse and include pigs, peccaries, hippopotamuses, camels, deer, cattle, sheep, goats, antelopes and their relatives, as well as many extinct forms.

B **Bagshot Sands** form much of the high ground in the LONDON BASIN. They coincide with heathland, much of which has been lost in the last century to birch woodland and fir plantations.

Camels are artiodactyls

Barton Beds were laid down in a sea which inundated Hampshire, England, in late Eocene times. They are extensive in the New Forest, beneath a veneer of flint gravel. Because the Barton Beds and overlying gravels are generally infertile, they tend to be associated with woodland and barren heath.

Basins, in geology, are depressions or SYNCLINES on a regional scale.

Bracklesham Beds are named from the rocks exposed in Bracklesham Bay, southern England. They contain many fossils of creatures associated with tropical and sub-tropical environments, including crocodiles, sea-snakes, cowrie shells and ancestors of the pearly nautilus. There are over 500 kinds of mollusc shells, and they are so common in places that levels of the Bracklesham Beds have been named after them.

Brontornithids, or thunderbirds, were heavily-built, flightless, long-legged birds, and were over 1.5 metres

Sea life

Of the marine animals that survived the late Cretaceous extinctions, BENTHIC types (*see page 67*) underwent important developments in evolution. This was especially true of GASTROPOD predators, and BIVALVES (*see pages 103 and 77*) that lived in sea-floor sediments, feeding off organic matter in the sediments or water. Modern reef-building corals also diversified, although they were not important in north-west Europe.

While rarely plentiful, a large and varied assembly of fossils has been collected from the London Clay. Gastropods and bivalves dominate, but there are also polyzoa, BRACHIOPODS (*see page 77*), worms, FORAMINIFERIDS, remains of bony fish and the teeth of sharks and rays. More spectacular, perhaps, are fossil plants from the tropical or near-tropical forests that grew around the shores of the London Clay sea. Apart from sunken driftwood, the most numerous of these fossils are from the coconut-sized fruit of *Nipa*, a stemless palm that still grows in swamps and deltas in India. To support evidence that conditions in London Clay times were tropical, or nearly so, fossils of crocodiles and turtles are also found.

The more silty and sandy deposits of the Bracklesham Beds and Barton Sands display a richer variety of benthic animals than the London Clay. Very common again, however, were shallow-burrowing bivalves which lived by filtering organic matter suspended in sea water, and gastropods. The latter were mainly predators, but a few were suspension-feeders. The NEKTON (*see page 71*) creatures, too, were more abundant and diverse than in the London Clay, and included sharks, rays, bony fish and cuttlefish.

The Lower Headon Beds, which mark the close of the Eocene in Britain, contain many plant fossils. These indicate a climate cooler than in London Clay times, probably reflecting Britain's continued drift north.

Left: The various Eocene deposits in the Hampshire and London basins today coincide with areas of heathland, often with much birch and oak and plantations of conifers. Here the heathland is growing on the Barton Sands of the New Forest and is dominated by heather and bracken. Birch woodland is in the distance.

The Cainozoic era

By the Palaeocene, at the start of the Cainozoic (about 65 million years ago), the surviving reptiles were already too specialized to adapt to

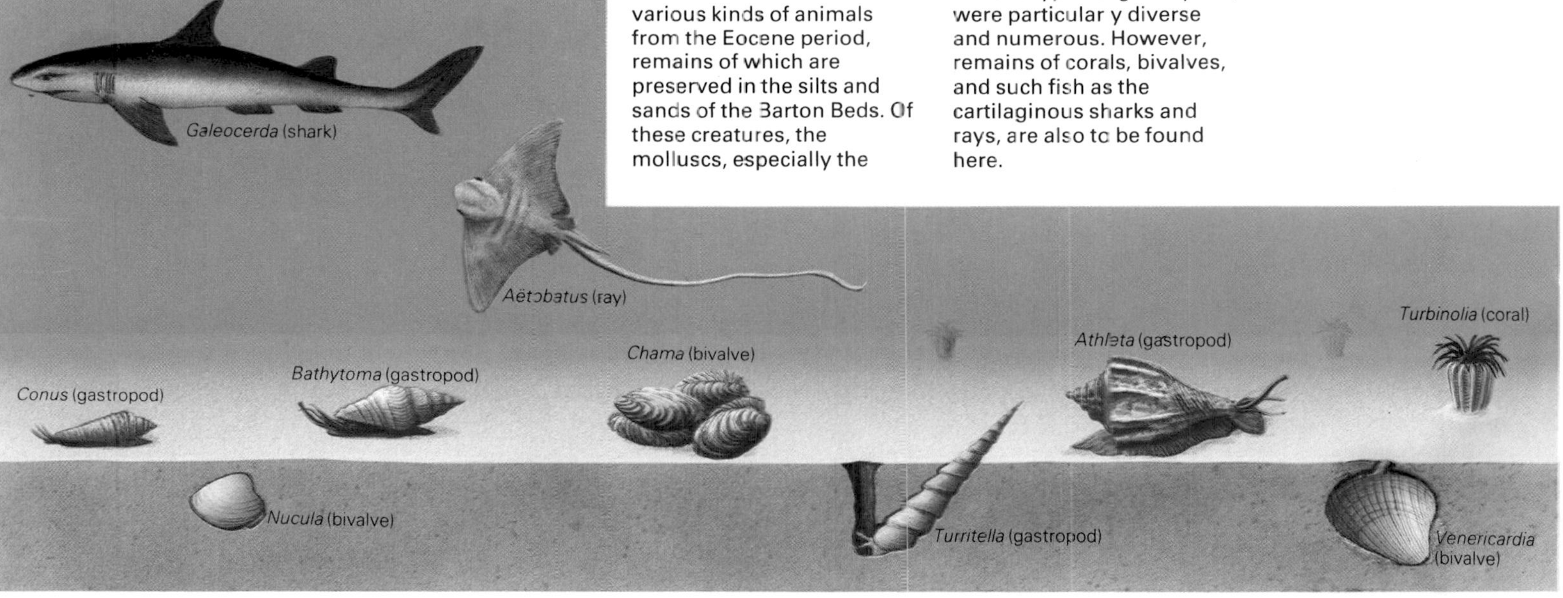

Below: A reconstruction of various kinds of animals from the Eocene period, remains of which are preserved in the silts and sands of the Barton Beds. Of these creatures, the molluscs, especially the various types of gastropods, were particular y diverse and numerous. However, remains of corals, bivalves, and such fish as the cartilaginous sharks and rays, are also to be found here.

tall. They had massive hooked beaks, and preyed on plant-eating mammals.

C Camel-litopterns are extinct South American mammals that had evolved forms similar to the camels that once lived in North America. They may have had a short trunk. But in the advanced forms, which survived into the Pleistocene, the peculiar nostrils had shifted to the top of the head, suggesting a life in water.
Chalicotheres are extinct PERISSODACTYLS. They lived from the Eocene until the failure of large mammals in the late Pleistocene. The later forms looked very like horses, except that they had large claws.

Civet cat

Civet is a small- to medium-sized animal living in forests of the Old World tropics. Civets are rather cat-like and are closely related to the mongooses.
Condylarths were plant-eating mammals of the early Tertiary. They had short legs, a long back, and never became specialized for grazing and running as did the ARTIODACTYLS and PERISSODACTYLS which replaced them.
Coryphodon was an AMBLYPOD that roamed across the northern hemisphere in Lower Eocene times. It was rather like a hippopotamus, about 3 metres long, and probably lived in water for much of the time.
Creodonts were the main flesh-eating mammals of the early Tertiary. They had small brains, and this probably caused the early extinction of most of the group.

D Diatrymas were giant flightless birds of the Eocene that stood about 2 metres tall. They looked like ostriches, but their necks were stouter, to support their fearsome beaks — hence the name 'terror-cranes'. *Diatryma* rivalled the early flesh-eating mammals, as these were generally small.

E Embrithopods are an extinct group known only from the Lower Oligocene of Africa. It includes just one animal — *Arsinoitherium* — which was the size of a rhinoceros and had a huge pair of horns side-by-side on the nasal bones. *Arsinoitherium* possibly lived in marshland.

F Foraminiferids are single-celled aquatic organisms, often less than 1 mm in

Above: A scene pictured in North America at the time of the Lower to Middle Eocene. Among the animals which would have been alive at this time and place were: on the left (**1**) *Uintatherium*, together with 2 individual animals — *Coryphodon* — which are standing in the water in the middle distance (**2**). Also shown is a crocodile (**3**) resting on the shore of the lake, while a pair of condylarths of the genus *Phenacodus* (**4**) are seen making their way towards the lake from the right. Three small horses, belonging to the genus *Orohippus*, are shown front right (**6**). Overlooking them from the rock above is the creodont *Oxyaena* (**5**).

the meat-eating and plant-eating niches left by the dinosaurs and other extinct Mesozoic groups. These were filled by the MAMMALS, although for a while at least there were also great carnivorous birds with awesome claws and beaks. They evolved separately in the northern hemisphere and South America, and in both cases resembled flightless cranes. The northern types were the DIATRYMAS or terror cranes, and their southern counterparts the PHORORHACIDS and the related BRONTORNITHIDS or thunderbirds.

The Palaeocene was a world of luxuriant forests in which the earliest groups of mammal inhabitants had survived from the Mesozoic. There were many small, primitive, often shrew-like INSECTIVORES that lived off the numerous and diverse insects which had evolved parallel with the flowering plants. Similar in appearance (to begin with) were the PRIMATES, but before the end of the Palaeocene they had given rise to the squirrel-like PLESIADAPIDS. Most, if not all of these animals lived in trees, as did many of the RODENT-like MULTITUBERCULATES and the OPPOSSUM-like MARSUPIALS. Some of the larger multituberculates, however, approached the size of a terrier and probably lived on the ground. Also on the ground were the primitive-hoofed UNGULATES or CONDYLARTHS, and early examples of the primitive meat-eating CREODONTS were also present. Apart from these 'old-timers', various new mammal groups made their entrance in the Palaeocene. They included: flying squirrels; the heavily-built, rather dog-like TAENIODONTS; true insectivores; CIVET-like members of the true carnivores; the large, almost bear-like TILLODONTS, with teeth resembling those of rodents; heavy AMBLYPODS (which in the Palaeocene reached the size of a cow) and various South American types of hoofed mammals.

diameter, surrounded by a shell.

G **Giraffe-camels** lived in North America during the Miocene and Pliocene. They had very long necks and stilt-like legs, and seem to have browsed on tall trees, just like the modern giraffe.

H **Headon Beds** are coloured clays with bands of sand and limestone. They contain many fossil shells.
Horse-litopterns are extinct South American animals similar to horses. One type, *Thoatherium*, was more horse-like than the true horses, for the splint bones of its toes were even smaller than those in the modern *Equus*.

Spiny ant-eater is an insectivore

I **Insectivores** are insect-eating MAMMALS. Most modern mammal groups are thought to have evolved from the insectivores. In the Mesozoic they lived off the variety of insects which had evolved parallel with the flowering plants.
Island continents are South America and Australia. Australia is still an island and South America was until nearly 2 million years ago.

L **London Basin** is a broad downfold of chalk, the central parts of which contain Eocene deposits. The Chiltern Hills form the downfold's northern rim, and the North Downs the southern rim.
London Clay extends through much of the LONDON BASIN. Where it occurs at the surface it gives rise to damp grassland, and woodlands and hedgerows with many oak trees.

M **Mammals** are warm-blooded animals which have a protective or insulating cover of hair. They give birth to live young which are then suckled by the mother. Some mammals — the monotremes — lay eggs and have other similarities to reptiles.
Marsupial hippo is the extinct hippopotamus-like *Diprotodon* which lived in Australia during the Pleistocene. The largest known marsupial, it lived off the plants growing on the salt plains of the interior.
Marsupial wolf is another name for the dog-like marsupials that evolved independently in South America and Australia. *Borhyaena* lived in the Miocene of South America, and *Thylacinus* in Au-

Left: In this woodland scene from the late Oligocene of Asia are the giant hornless rhinoceros *Baluchitherium* (**1**) and (in the foreground), the so-called giant pig *Archaeotherium*, one of the entelodonts. Some of the entelodonts grew to the size of a bison. As a group they became extinct in Miocene times, probably displaced by their more intelligent relatives, such as the ancestors of our modern pigs and peccaries. *Baluchitherium* stood over 5 metres high at the shoulder; its head alone was about 1 metre long. Its long front legs and long neck allowed *Baluchitherium* to browse the tree tops in much the same way as a modern giraffe. Despite its great size (*Baluchitherium* was the largest land mammal ever) it was primitive in many important respects and so failed to compete with the more advanced herbivores which had begun appearing in late Oligocene times.

Below: Reconstruction of a scene from the Oligocene of Africa. Tandem-horned *Arsinoitherium* are at the water's edge (**1**). In the middle distance (**2**) are giant dassies (*Megalohyrax*) and (**3**) mastodonts (*Palaeomastodon*).

The Eocene

The Eocene, too, was a time of mainly forest environments. This epoch saw the start of further new mammal types — the rodents, PERISSODACTYLS, ARTIODACTYLS and bats, while ancestors of the whales and sea-cows invaded the oceans. In addition, more advanced primates, little different from the modern lemurs and tarsiers, grew numerous in the tree-tops. During the Eocene giant forms of amblypods arose, such as the bizarre UINTATHERIUM and the hippopotamus-like CORYPHODON. TITANOTHERES and other perissodactyls trended to gigantism as well, but the largest appeared after the Eocene.

The Oligocene

These early giants vanished or dwindled in late Eocene and Oligocene times, along with most of the archaic mammals which had appeared in the Mesozoic and Palaeocene. This was partly as a result of climatic changes which led to the emergence of the first grasslands. But more important was the fact that these groups of animals failed to compete successfully with better-adapted contemporaries. For example, the

---

stralia and New Guinea during the Pleistocene. It survived in Tasmania, but now seems to be extinct.

Marsupials are MAMMALS that give birth to very small young which either crawl into the mother's pouch or cling to her fur.

Mastodonts were rather shorter and heavier relatives of the elephants, and in North America they survived into the present inter-glacial period. Their huge tusks curved up and outwards.

Multituberculates were primitive MAMMALS that resembled RODENTS. Their name comes from their distinctive cheek-teeth.

N

Notoungulates are an extinct and very varied order of mainly hoofed animals. With 2 early exceptions they were restricted to South America. They appeared in the Palaeocene, probably derived from the CONDYLARTHS, and did not die out until the Pleistocene.

O

Okapis are short-necked giraffes, standing about 1.5 metres at the shoulder. They live in the dense equatorial forests of Zaire, and were unknown to scientists until 1901.

Opossum is the name of 2 separate and varied groups of MARSUPIAL animals, one of which lives in the Americas, the other in Australia.

Opossum

P

Palaeogene includes the 3 oldest epochs of the Tertiary period — the Palaeocene, Eocene and Oligocene — while the Neogene normally includes the 2 younger epochs — the Miocene and Pliocene. This division of the Tertiary is a convenient one in many parts of the world.

Perissodactyls are odd-toed UNGULATES, and include horses, asses, zebras, tapirs and rhinoceroses.

Phororhacids were flightless, fast-running birds that lived from Oligocene until Pliocene times in South America. The great *Titanornis* persisted into the Pleistocene in North America. The typical South American type, *Phororhacos*, was as tall as a man, had long legs, and a powerful beaked skull as large as a horse's. These predators could survive on the ground in South America because there were no flesh-eating mammals. In the WORLD CONTINENT, the latter caused the extinction of the terror-cranes or DIATRYMAS as early as the Middle Eocene.

extinction of the multituberculates was matched by the rise of the rodents; condylarths were superseded by their more advanced descendants, the perissodactyls and artiodactyls; and carnivores displaced most of the creodonts. There were far fewer losses in the more isolated southern continents, although the large and peculiar EMBRITHOPODS of Africa did die out.

The Miocene and Pliocene

The Miocene epoch saw great changes in the geography of the world — changes which stimulated the development of modern-looking mammals. Continued cooling and a reduced rainfall in the Pliocene led to extensive steppes and savannas spreading in temperate areas. This prompted further diversification, and refinements to adaptation in the mammals surviving from the Miocene.

In Eurasia, great herds of the three-toed horse *Hipparion* grazed the plains. Other common perissodactyls were the rhinoceroses (horned and hornless) including members of the living African black rhinoceros, *Diceros,* as well as extinct forms such as the elephant-sized SINOTHERIUM. CHALICOTHERES, which resembled large, clawed horses, were also present. But the perissodactyls had been overtaken in numbers and variety by the artiodactyls. There were numerous small, medium and large antelopes, and a range of giraffes. Some of these were long-necked, but most had short necks as in the modern OKAPIS. MASTODONTS also thrived on the Pliocene savannas, those of *Anancus* type being similar to the Pleistocene straight-tusked elephants. In North America at this time the herbivores were rather different. Although mastodonts flourished, rhinoceroses were eventually reduced to the amphibious *Teleoceras.* The remaining ungulates were dominated by the single-toed horse, *Pliohippus;* various camels, such as the 'GIRAFFE-CAMEL' *Alticamelus;* PRONGBUCKS; and the extinct PROTOCERATIDS, including *Synthetoceras.*

A host of predators and scavengers depended on these different herbivores. *Machairodus,* a large, powerful sabre-toothed cat, preyed on

Above: Reconstruction of a scene from the Pliocene of Eurasia. Beneath the trees are short-jawed mastodonts (**4**) of the *Anancus* type, together with the giraffid, *Helladotherium.* The sabre-toothed cats (**1**) are *Machairodus,* which have surprised a herd of antelope, *Palaeoreas* (**2**). However, it is doubtful if these cats could have brought down a healthy antelope. In the foreground (**6**) are 3-toed horses, *Hipparion,* and the large hyaena *Percrocuta* (**5**). The rhinoceroses in the middle distance (**3**) are *Diceros,* to which the modern African black rhinoceros belongs.

Placental mammals give birth to young which have reached an advanced stage of development. Over a lengthy gestation period they are fed inside the mother through a placenta.
Plesiadapids were PRIMATES that existed from Middle Palaeocene to early Eocene times. They were rodent-like, and not part of the evolutionary sequence which led to higher primates.
Primates include the lemurs, monkeys, apes and man, and are therefore the most advanced MAMMALS. The name means 'first mammals'.
Prongbucks are the only living representative of the antilocaprids, a family closely related to the antelopes. They first appeared in the Miocene and have always been restricted to North America.

Prongbucks

Protoceratids were deer-sized ARTIODACTYLS that arose in North America in the Oligocene. The males developed horn-like peaks of bone above the nose, eyes and brain case. *Synthetoceras* was a type that lived from Lower Miocene to Lower Pliocene times. It had a Y-shaped nose bone and horns above the eyes.
Pyrotheres are an extinct group of South American animals which evolved along lines similar to those of the Oligocene elephants of Africa. So close is the likeness that pyrotheres were once thought to be relatives of the elephants. They are known only from Eocene and Oligocene rocks. Some authorities say the pyrotheres are a sub-group of the AMBLYOPODS.

R

Rodents are gnawing animals. They have chisel like incisor teeth which grow throughout the animal's life. They first appeared in the late Palaeocene and diversified into a host of evolutionary lines. They are the most successful of all living MAMMALS, and include the squirrels, beavers, rats, mice, porcupines and guinea pigs.

S

Sinotherium was a gigantic rhinoceros that lived in Asia during Lower Pliocene times. From it was descended *Elasmotherium,* another giant, with a huge horn up to 2 metres long on its forehead. *Elasmotherium* lived on the steppes of Eurasia in the Pleistocene.
Synclines are downfolded

Above: Reconstruction of a Pliocene scene from South America. So-called camel-litopterns, *Macrauchenia,* are standing in the water whilst the hippo-like animals *Toxodon* are at the water's edge. To the right, the sabre-toothed marsupials, *Thylacosmilus,* have killed an old, lame member of the herd of horse-litopterns, *Diadiaphorus.*

heavy, slow-moving animals. Smaller cats were plentiful too and the first examples of the modern group *Felis* appeared. They were joined by several groups of dogs, some of the largest belonging to the extinct *Borophagus.* Hyaenas were widespread in Eurasia, and in the case of *Percrocuta* reached the size of a lion. The ISLAND CONTINENTS of Australia and South America were isolated for much of the Tertiary. Even so, some of the mammals that evolved there were remarkably similar to others on the WORLD CONTINENT. Except through very distant ancestors they were not related; they merely came to look alike in the process of adapting to the same basic ways of life. Living examples of such CONVERGENT EVOLUTION (*see page 101*) from Australia are the marsupial counterparts of the true cats, mice, moles, monkeys, rodents, insectivores and flying squirrels. In the Pleistocene there was a MARSUPIAL 'HIPPO', *Diprotodon,* and what may have been a marsupial 'lion', *Thylacoleo.* The MARSUPIAL 'WOLF' — the thylacine — lived until very recently, but is probably now extinct. In South America, the Miocene marsupial 'wolf' *Borhyaena* and the Pliocene marsupial 'sabre-tooth' *Thylacosmilus* preyed on PLACENTAL MAMMAL herbivores which provided perhaps the most impressive array of evolutionary convergence ever. Thus the litopterns gave rise to the 'HORSE'-LITOPTERNS and the 'CAMEL'-LITOPTERNS. The NOTOUNGULATES diverged into a still wider range: *Toxodon* was hippopotamus-like, the homalodotheres were suggestive of the chalicotheres or clawed 'horses', while a third group, the typotheres, paralleled the rabbits. In an earlier period there were even PYROTHERES that were mastodont-like.

The pyrotheres, litopterns and notoungulates all arose in the Eocene. Whereas the pyrotheres seem not to have survived beyond the early Oligocene, the other two groups lived on in South America throughout the Tertiary. They perished soon after the land connection with North America was re-established, for it exposed them to competition from their more advanced northern counterparts.

rocks. Whereas the upper parts of ANTICLINES are usually destroyed by erosion, sediments in synclines tend to be preserved.

T

Taeniodonts were early Tertiary MAMMALS that were rather large for their times. They were heavily-built, dog-like, and had RODENT-like incisors.

Thanet Sand is the base Eocene deposit in the LONDON BASIN. It is a greenish sand, generally about 12 metres thick, with no fossils.

Tillodonts were, like the TAENIODONTS, large early Tertiary mammals. A further likeness was that tillodonts also had chisel-like incisors.

Titanotheres were mighty PERISSODACTYLS with horn-like outgrowths on their noses.

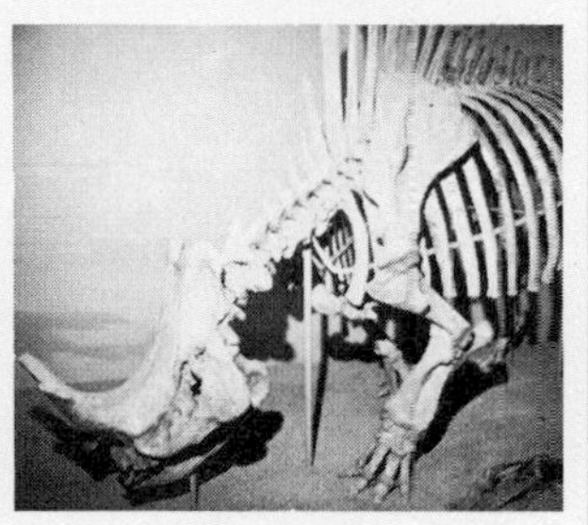

Titanotheres

They lived in the Eocene and early Oligocene and their early extinction probably resulted from their lack of specialized grazing teeth. Their teeth could not take much wear, yet they had to chew vast quantities of soft plant food to support their huge bodies. Some slight change in vegetation could have triggered their end.

U

Uintatherium was a grotesque animal, the size of a rhinoceros, which had 3 pairs of different-sized horns and sabre-like canine teeth. It lived in North America during the Eocene. *Uintatherium* belonged to the *Dinocerata,* a sub-group of the AMBLYPODS.

Ungulates are hoofed, plant-eating mammals.

W

Woolwich and Reading beds display variations known as facies. In the western part of the LONDON BASIN the Reading Beds are vividly mottled, non-marine clays and sands, which pass into the estuarine Woolwich Beds in the London area. Farther east, these in turn pass into marine sands of the Bishopstone facies. Underlying the non-marine and estuarine facies is a marine sand known as the Bottom Bed.

World continent includes North America, Eurasia and Africa. Unlike the situation with the ISLAND CONTINENTS, mammals were able to migrate between the different landmasses of the world continent for large parts of the Cainozoic era. Therefore the animals of the present-day continents have many similarities, whereas those of Australia are unique, as were the Tertiary animals of South America.

The path of evolution which led to man started with changes in the environment. But man's actions have caused even greater changes to the world around him, exerting a powerful influence on evolution itself.

Man and the Ecosystem

A key theme in the evolution of the primate line from RAMAPITHECUS to HOMO SAPIENS is that of further adaptation to a life on open SAVANNAS (*see page 73*). Walking on two legs and keeping an erect posture were significant developments, since they freed the hands for making and using tools. Skill with tools was clearly an advantage, and so evolutionary selection for intelligence, and therefore increased brain-size, was speeded up. This became the main trend in the succession of HOMINIDS from which modern man ultimately emerged.

Early hominids

The line from *Ramapithecus* to *Homo erectus* is something of an evolutionary puzzle. For a long time the AUSTRALOPITHECINES were accepted as immediate descendants of *Ramapithecus.* These pre-humans were no more than 1.5 metres tall. They stood and walked much like humans, but their skulls were more ape-like. Australopithecines lived in Africa from at least 3,000,000 years ago to somewhere between 1,000,000 and 500,000 years ago. There were two types, and they appear to have lived side by side in certain areas, but there is no definite evidence that either of these hominids made tools. Of the two, AUSTRALOPITHECUS ROBUSTUS was taller, heavier and less man-like than the slender, or gracile, AUSTRALOPITHECUS AFRICANUS. The latter was considered the ancestor of HOMO HABILIS, or 'handyman', so called because of the pebble tools and camp found associated with his remains in OLDUVAI GORGE, Tanzania. *Homo habilis* seems to have appeared first about 1,750,000 years ago and was widely regarded as the first true man, mainly because of an increase in the size of the skull. An opposing view was that the oldest *Homo habilis* fossils are actually those of an advanced gracile australopithecine. Either way, discoveries made in East Africa during the last decade show that tool-makers of the group HOMO were definitely living there, alongside the australopithecines, possibly as much as 2,500,000 to 3,000,000 years ago. The great age of these new finds has made uncertain the evolutionary relationships of the early hominids.

Above: Archaeological evidence from Ambrona, 200 kilometres north of Madrid, Spain, suggests that *Homo erectus* used fire to drive elephants on to swampy ground, where they were killed and butchered. Tools apparently employed for butchering the trapped elephants were left scattered over the edge of the swamp, and the odd distribution of elephant leg bones seems to indicate that the legs were positioned to act as stepping stones.

Homo erectus

Most people agree that HOMO ERECTUS represents the next step towards modern man, and that he evolved from *Homo habilis. Homo erectus* lived in Eurasia and Africa between 1,500,000 and 500,000 years ago. This hominid was about 1.5 metres tall, and though his skeleton was very like that of modern man, his skull capacity was roughly 25 per cent less. He also had heavy eyebrow ridges and lacked a forehead. Archaeologists have found that *Homo erectus* was the first big-game hunter, that he made standardized

Reference

A **Acheulean** is the name given to chopper-core stone tools with a pear-shaped outline. The pointed types are known as hand-axes, and those with a cutting edge as cleavers. They have been found all over Africa, and in Europe as far north as southern Britain and a line from the Rhine to the Danube.
Australopithecines means 'southern apes', for when their fossils were first discovered in South Africa they were mistakenly thought to be the remains of apes. We now know that they were primitive members of the family of man. There is no firm evidence that the australopithecines ever lived outside Africa, nor that they made tools. The numerous jaw bones and other bone ends of antelopes found at one South African site were once interpreted as proof that australopithecines used bone, tooth and horn tools. Recent studies have shown that the amount of such bones is that which might be expected in a leopard's lair. Indeed, the australopithecines themselves may well have been preyed upon by leopards.

Acheulean tools

Australopithecus africanus is generally regarded as the older of the 2 australopithecine types. Its teeth and jaws are much smaller than those of AUSTRALOPITHECUS ROBUSTUS, and suggest a mixed diet, including meat. *Australopithecus africanus* was therefore probably a scavenger and small-scale hunter.
Australopithecus robustus had large cheek-teeth, which often show signs of wear. These (together with its powerful jaws and bony skull ridges for the attachment of strong chewing muscles) indicate that it lived largely on a tough diet of seeds, roots and tubers.

B **Biological control** involves fighting pests with natural predators. Modern pest management uses biological control and

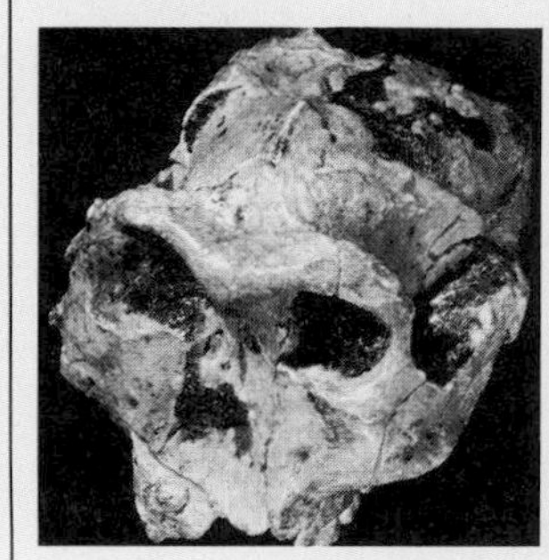

Australopithecus robustus

tools of ACHEULEAN type, and that he used fire. The level of co-operation needed to hunt large game, moreover, shows that he had developed some kind of speech.

Skulls seeming to provide a link with those of modern man are known from Europe, and are between 500,000 and 250,000 years old. But more recent European examples from the last inter-glacial period (200,000 to 100,000 years ago) resemble NEANDERTHAL rather than fully modern skulls. Whereas earlier men had retreated south at the onset of cold conditions, the classic Neanderthals remained in Europe during the last Ice Age, to hunt the game which flourished on the TUNDRAS (*see page 74*). They were sturdy people with physical features well adapted to the frigid climate. Part of the reason for their success was that they had taken tool-making a stage further. The effectiveness of MOUSTERIAN tools is evident from the vast quantities of animal bones found at sites where the Neanderthals lived. The number of flint scrapers also suggests that skins were highly valued, for shelter, clothes and thongs. We know too that they buried their dead, and the presence of grave goods indicates a belief in an afterlife.

Modern man

Although their place of origin is a mystery, examples of HOMO SAPIENS SAPIENS were in Eurasia and Africa 40,000 years ago. The European types, or CRO-MAGNONS, rapidly displaced the Neanderthals. Whether the latter actually belonged to the same species as well is debatable. Nor is it known whether the Cro-Magnons eliminated the Neanderthals deliberately or through competition, or whether they absorbed them into their own population. Like the Neanderthals they were hunters, but their UPPER PALAEOLITHIC culture was far superior. They made fine blade tools and cave paintings, and seem to have had more elaborate rituals and burial customs.

Right: *Homo erectus* must have found the sheer size and weight of elephants a problem when hunting. They may have tried trapping methods still in use today by certain primitive peoples. Perhaps they tried the pitfall to trap elephants (*left*), hardening the points of the sharpened stakes by fire. Another kind of trap consisted of a large and heavy piece of wood, suspended above a track by a grass rope (*right*). As the animal broke through the rope, the spear fell on to the spinal column.

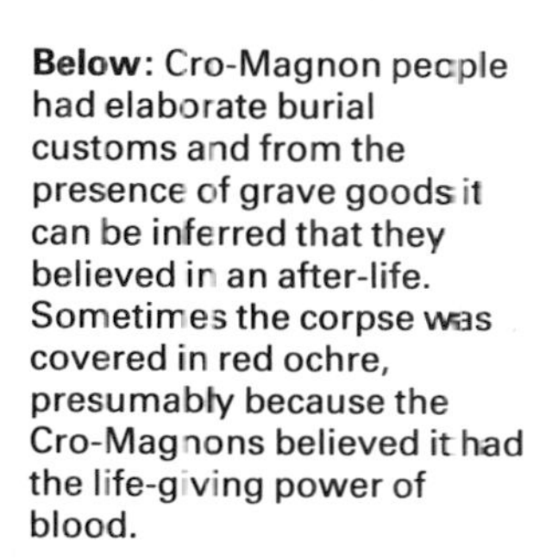

Below: Cro-Magnon people had elaborate burial customs and from the presence of grave goods it can be inferred that they believed in an after-life. Sometimes the corpse was covered in red ochre, presumably because the Cro-Magnons believed it had the life-giving power of blood.

pesticides which break down into less harmful substances in a relatively short time.

Blanket bog is vegetation, mostly moss, which grows in great expanses across the upland plateaus of cool temperate regions, such as north-west Europe. Beneath the moss is a thick layer of peat. Blanket bogs have been much broken down by burning and grazing.

Bronze Age began about 3000 BC in the Near East, when tin bronze was first made (9 parts copper to 1 part tin). Compared with copper ores, tin was scarce, so that bronze was expensive. Bronze was discovered independently in China around 1500 BC, and also in the New World. Bronze melts at a relatively low temperature and so could be easily cast into the shapes required.

Bronze Age figure from Greece

C

Cloning produces living creatures which are exact copies of just 1 parent, either male or female. Cloning was first achieved in 1962, with frogs.

Conservation was first applied to preserving wildlife and the associated habitats. Gradually it also came to include the wise use and re-cycling of NON-RENEWABLE RESOURCES.

Cro-Magnons were the first fully modern people of Europe, and are named after the French site where early discoveries of their remains were made. They lived in caves and in skin huts out on the steppes during the close of the last glaciation.

E

Environmental pollution is the accumulation of substances in forms or amounts which are harmful to life.

F

Fertile crescent extends north along the eastern Mediterranean and swings round into the valleys of the rivers Tigris and Euphrates, which drain into the Persian Gulf.

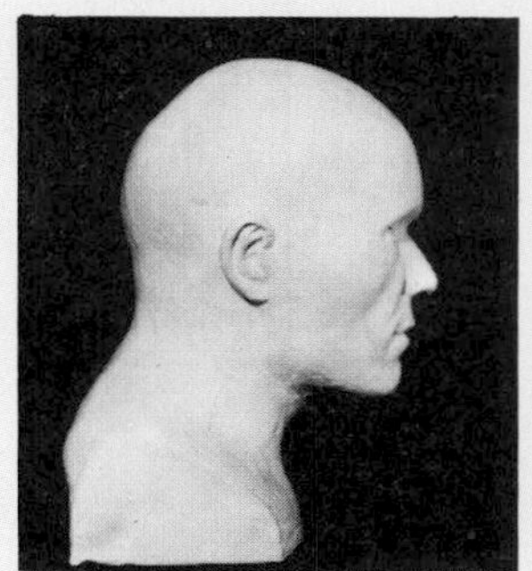

Cro-Magnon man

From hunter to farmer

Before the end of the last Ice Age, about 10,000 years ago, man had colonized every continent. The rapid improvement in climate at the opening of the present inter-glacial period led to great changes in the vegetation of higher latitudes. The tundras of north-west Europe were quickly covered by forests, though in south-west Asia, where conditions were probably drier, more open woodlands and grasslands were established. These changes, together with the late Pleistocene extinction of many large animals, helped to stimulate important developments in human culture. Whereas Upper Palaeolithic peoples hunted animals and gathered wild plants, their NEOLITHIC successors in south-west Asia changed to herding animals and cultivating crops between 9000 and 7000 BC. By this last date, farming peoples were living in permanent settlements in the so-called FERTILE CRESCENT area of the Near East.

In north-west Europe, however, people lived by hunting and gathering for much longer. Their methods were much adapted to fit the forest environment, especially as individual animals rather than herds were pursued. The forest hunters were MESOLITHIC peoples. Although they were nomads and cleared the forest only to make camps, they nevertheless used fire to open out the forest and drive game. Evidence suggests that such activities resulted locally in impoverishing the soil and altering the forest vegetation.

Man changes the landscape

More profound changes occurred as Neolithic farmers spread into north-west Europe. Within roughly 500 years of their arrival around 3500 BC, they were well established in many parts of the British Isles. We know from studies of fossil pollen that they made forest clearances, most of which were small and temporary. The smaller ones were used to grow cereals for a few years until the soil lost its fertility and the clearing was abandoned. Birch and ash — trees which like light and have wind-blown seeds — were usually among the plants which invaded the deserted clearings. Elm and lime, which require more nutrients, rarely recovered their former

Below: Mesolithic people of the post-glacial forests usually lived in marsh and reed-swamp habitats. In addition to stalking such animals as deer and elk, they hunted water fowl and caught fish. At Star Carr, near Scarborough, England, a Maglemosian hunting group established a camp on the edge of one of the early lakes at this site. The remains of their activities have been unearthed in great quantities by archaeological investigations.

G **Gene banks** are the genetic resources contained in plant and animal communities. The genes of wild organisms are potentially valuable for improving plants and animals that provide food and other resources for man. In some cases, wild relatives of domesticated plants are stored in seed form, to ensure that they are available for future plant-breeding programmes.
Genetic engineering involves using bacterial agents to alter the structure of inherited features. At present the technique can be applied only to bacteria themselves. On the one hand genetic engineering could modify bacteria to produce all kinds of useful results. But harmful modifications could also be made, deliberately or accidentally, perhaps with devastating consequences.

H **Hominids** are members of the family Hominidae, which includes AUSTRALOPITHECINES and HOMO. Modern man is a species of *Homo* — *Homo sapiens*. Whether RAMAPITHECUS should also be regarded as a hominid is controversial.
Homo is the group to which all species of true 'men' belong.
Homo erectus was able to range more widely than earlier HOMINIDS because of his increased intelligence and improved tools. In the cooler climates of Pleistocene Eurasia he lived in shelters within caves. Associated with his remains are numerous broken bones of deer, elephant and rhinoceros. Certain broken bones found near a fire made by *Homo erectus* in a cave near Peking were human. This suggests cannibalism.
Homo habilis was, when his bones were discovered in 1964 at OLDUVAI GORGE, Tanzania, generally accepted as the oldest fossil HOMINID belonging to the group HOMO. Some critics, however, argue that the older *habilis* fossils are really those of late AUSTRALOPITHECINES, while the younger ones are from the first representatives of HOMO ERECTUS. *Homo habilis* made the pebble tools at Olduvai Gorge which constitute the 'Oldowan industry'.

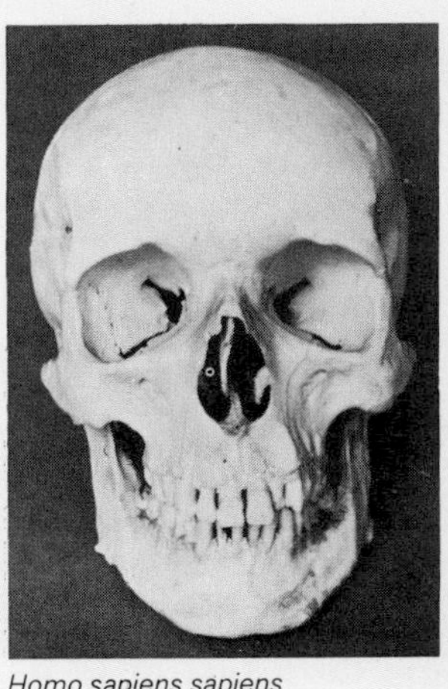

Homo sapiens sapiens

status. So forests in Britain gradually changed, from mainly oak, elm and lime, to oak, birch and ash. The recovery of forest areas was often slower in the wetter uplands, where MOORLAND and BLANKET BOG began to develop instead.

In the following BRONZE AGE, which in Britain began about 1800 BC, the Neolithic way of life was intensified. However, large permanent clearances were also made in areas with light, sandy soils in the lowlands and in some parts of the uplands. Loss of soil fertility led eventually to these large clearings being abandoned. In the uplands they contributed to the expansion of moorland; in the lowlands they developed into heaths.

The destruction of woodland

Neolithic settlers had used polished stone axes to make their clearances, and so too had Bronze Age peoples, for the metal after which their culture is named was in relatively short supply. During the IRON AGE (which in Britain began at roughly 600 BC) iron became widely available. It was used for axes and ploughs, and led to the widespread destruction of forests to gain charcoal for making the iron and to make way for farmland. In Britain only the woodlands in the north-west and on the heavy clay soils of the lowland remained unscathed. They stayed this way throughout the Roman occupation, which lasted from AD 43 to 410, before the final onslaught on these last tracts of woodland began somewhat later in the 400s. The Celts were responsible for further large clearances in the uplands, while Anglo-Saxon invaders tackled the clay soils of the lowlands with their heavy eight-ox plough. The process of destroying woodland was more or less complete by Tudor times, and the countryside of Britain today is wholly the result of man's intervention. Much of it has been maintained for centuries by traditional agricultural practices. Many of these have now been discontinued, so that large parts of the landscape are once again undergoing significant changes.

Urban man

The story of man's evolution is one of increasing dominance over his environment. Scientific, technological and social advances have allowed him to live in ever-larger numbers in industrialized, urban societies. Such societies consume

Right: The Devil's Punchbowl in Surrey, England, was cleared by Bronze Age farmers. It is now bracken heath.
Below: Post-glacial forest (**1**) was cleared by ancient hunters and farmers. Clearance for farming continued (**2**), while industry (**3**) and towns (**4**) brought further changes.

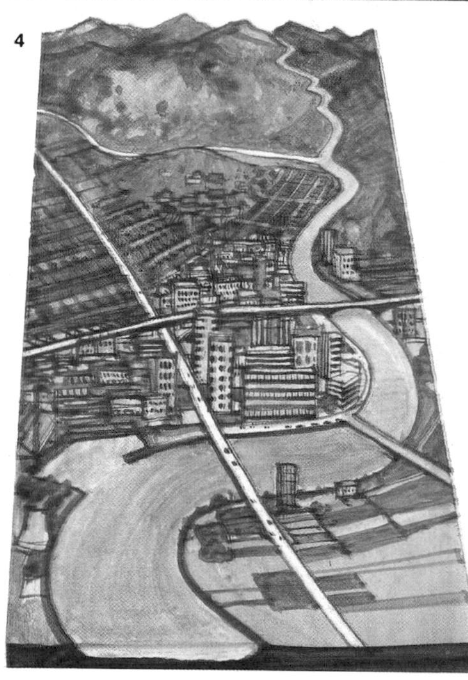

Homo sapiens means 'wise man'. He is the living species of the group HOMO.
Homo sapiens sapiens is the sub-species which includes all living men. We must recognize this sub-species if NEANDERTHAL is also to be considered a variant of modern man, and placed in another sub-species, *Homo sapiens neanderthalensis.*

Iron Age began about 1500 BC in western Asia, when the Hittites of Anatolia succeeded in extracting iron from its ore. Not until the AD 1300s were furnaces developed in the Near East and Europe which could melt iron and so allow it to be cast. Before then, iron articles were forged from red-hot masses of the metal. Unlike tin ores, iron ores were plentiful and so more people owned iron articles than bronze. Cast iron tools are known from the 400s BC in China, where at this early date they must have had extremely high-temperature furnaces.

Mesolithic or 'Middle Stone Age' in Britain begins with the Maglemosian culture, named after the Maglemose ('big bog') site in Denmark. Small flint blades, or microliths, are typical of the Maglemosian. The next Mesolithic culture is called the Sauveterrian. Other Mesolithic groups also used chisel-ended, or tranchet, arrowheads which sliced through the muscle and tendons of small animals.
Moorland is upland vegetation, which includes heathers, grasses, sedges and mosses, growing on soils which are acid and generally peaty.

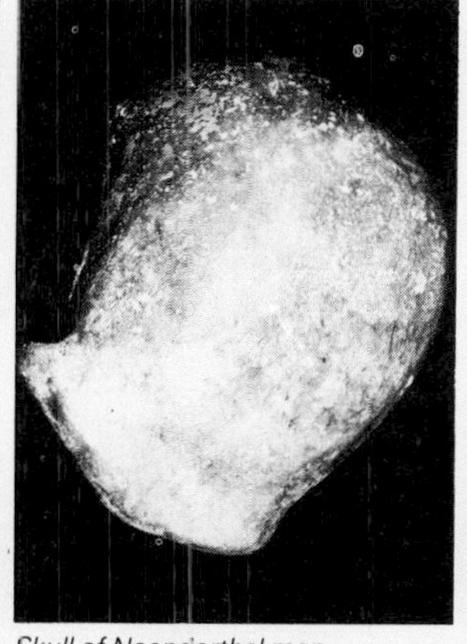

Skull of Neanderthal man

Mousterian culture is attributed to NEANDERTHAL man. It is identified by stone tools made from flakes struck off cores which had been specially prepared in advance. The shape of the flakes could then be better controlled for fashioning into hand-axes, scrapers and triangular points with sharp edges. These last may have been hafted to form spears.

Neanderthal people were short and stocky, had barrel-chested bodies and peculiarly curved thighbones. The brain

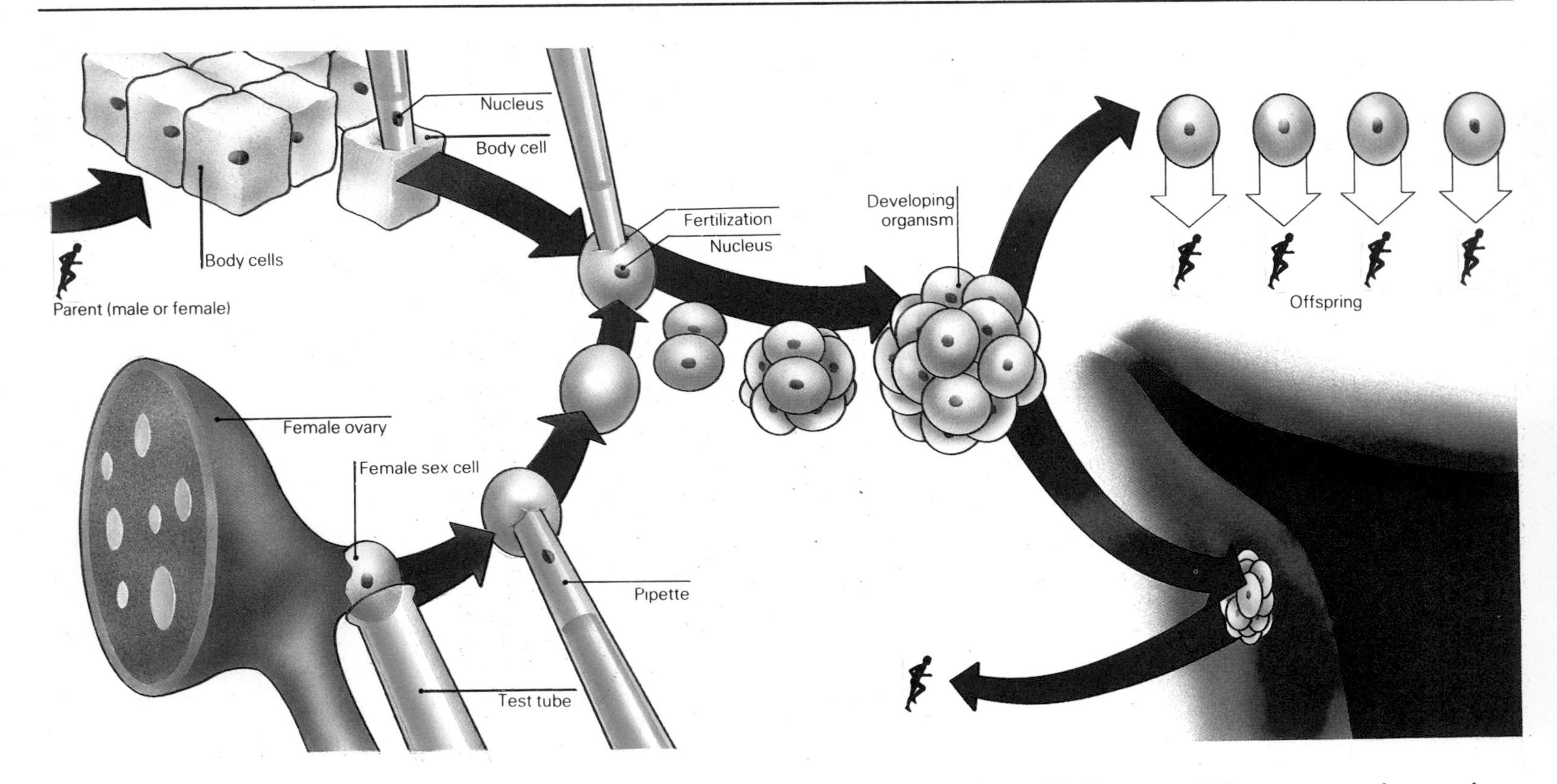

increasing amounts of fossil fuels and other NON-RENEWABLE RESOURCES. Producing and consuming these resources often leads to pollution of the environment, since discarded products and 'waste' are often not re-cycled unless it becomes economically worthwhile. Food consumption also rises as the human population continues to multiply, so the demand for more farmland is relentless. Over-exploitation of land has resulted in SOIL EROSION and the extension of desert, while large-scale use of pesticides and fertilizers has led to further ENVIRONMENTAL POLLUTION. The overall impact of increasing industrialization has thus been massive impoverishment of the environment and depletion of resources, resulting in both ecological and economic instability.

Above: In this cloning technique, a female sex cell is collected as it is released from the ovary and its nucleus is extracted. This is replaced by a nucleus from another type of cell taken from elsewhere in the body of a female (or from a male if it is the same type of organism). In its new surroundings, the nucleus then develops into another organism which is genetically identical to the parent from which the nucleus was taken. This technique can be used to produce one, or (in theory) hundreds of offspring identical to a single parent. Animals such as frogs and newts can be cloned quite easily, because the female eggs are comparatively large and the nucleus readily replaced with one from another part of the frog's body. Mammal egg cells are much smaller and so the problems of exchanging the nuclei are that much greater.

The need for conservation

Many people therefore see CONSERVATION as essential. They feel that every effort should be made to maintain the diversity of living things; to re-cycle non-renewable materials; and to balance the human population with the world's available space and resources. Diverse communities of plants and animals are potentially valuable as GENE 'BANKS', and as we have seen, they also tend to be stable because of the numerous interactions between prey and predators. Various forms of natural BIOLOGICAL CONTROL can also lessen the use of pesticides in farming, and thus the risk of pollution. Cycling of raw materials equally reduces pollution, as well as the rate at which the raw materials themselves are used up. But achieving a sustained balance between population size and the Earth's capacity to carry it is perhaps the greatest challenge facing mankind. Whether the outcome is successful will probably depend as much on political and social factors as on scientific and technological developments. Even so, it is possible that GENETIC ENGINEERING, now in its infancy, might play some part. Since it substitutes choice for chance in selecting which inherited characteristics should be passed from generation to generation, it could alter the whole course of the future evolution of life. Another uncertainty about evolutionary developments concerns CLONING, which can produce exact replicas of parent organisms, male or female. It might be beneficial to have genetic copies of existing organisms, but there is a risk that undesirable organisms, including individual humans, could be duplicated.

---

capacity of a classic Neanderthal was larger on average than that of modern man. His skull had a prominent brow-ridge above high, owlish eye-sockets. The forehead was flattened, there was little or no chin, and the back of the brain-case was swollen into a 'bun'. The cheek bones were swept back and lacked hollows, while the nose was large and broad. Such facial features probably reduced the risk of frostbite and helped cope with the problem of inhaling cold, dry air.

Neolithic means 'New Stone Age', so called because the first prehistoric farmers developed beautiful polished stone-axes and leaf-shaped arrow-heads.

Non-renewable resources are those materials or environments valued by man, which, once they are used or destroyed, cannot be renewed. Coal is one such non-renewable resource; the equatorial rainforest is another.

O

Olduvai Gorge is an offshoot of the East African rift valley, on the edge of the great Serengeti Plain of Tanzania. The Gorge is 40 km long, and cuts through about 90 metres of stratified sediments, which formed in and around a lake. The nearby Lake Eyasi is its shrunken descendant.

R

Ramapithecus is regarded by some authorities as the first HOMINID, by others as an ape which had a few hominid features superimposed.

S

Soil erosion is the process by which water or wind remove soil at an increased rate as a result of the destruction of vegetation cover and soil structure. Soil erosion is frequently associated with poor farming methods, over-intensive farming or excessive grazing.

Olduvai Gorge, Tanzania

U

Upper Palaeolithic is the last part of the 'Old Stone Age'. This saw the development of distinctive cultures recognized by their stone and bone tools. The oldest was the Perigordian-Aurignacian, which was succeeded by the Solutrean and the Magdalenian. The Magdalenian produced a greater variety of advanced tools than the Eskimo culture of today.

Index

Page numbers in **bold** type refer to the reference sections. Page numbers in *italics* refer to illustrations.

Acknowledgements

Contributing artists
Ann Baum, Michael Bilsland, Jim Channell, Drury Lane Studios, John Gosler, Delyth Jones, Chris King, Tom McArthur, Jim Marks, Tony Morris, Peter North, Nigel Osborne, Michael Shoebridge, Ralph Stobart, Dorothy Tucker

The Publishers also wish to thank the following:
Heather Angel 10B, 12B, 18B, 19B, 21BL, 22B, 24B, 25B, 27B, 30B, 32B, 43T, 46B, 55B, 64CL, 68T B, 69T, 73CR, 75B, 77T, 79B, 80B, 82B, 83B, 84B, 90B, 93B, 95B, 99T, 104B, 106BR, 109B, 110B, 114BR, 119T, 127T
Ardea 128B
Ardea/Peter Green 56B
Biophoto Associates 11B, 13B, 15BL BR, 76B
Bruce Coleman Ltd/Hans Reinhard 37T
Mary Evans Picture Library 7B, 8B, 14BL BR, 40B, 51B
Robert Harding Associates/Rainbird 37B
Imitor 3B, 4B, 16B, 21BR, 31B, 39B, 41B, 53T, 69B, 70B, 72B, 75L, 77B, 78B, 84T, 89B, 97B, 98B, 99B, 100B, 106BL, 115BL, 116BL, 118T, 124BL, BR, 126B, 127B
Macdonald Educational 115BR
Macdonald Educational/Kenya High Commission 48B, 94B
/Nancy Durrell McKenna 116BR
/Smithsonian Institution 112BL
Mansell Collection 5B, 17B, 42B, 49B, 112BR
Pat Morris 45B, 52B, 60B, 96B, 121B, 123B
Natural Science Photos 108B
Natural Science Photos/C. Banks 74B
Natural Science Photos/M. Bolton 107B
Natural Science Photos/P.A. Bowman 47B
Natural Science Photos/M. Chinery 87B, 88B
Natural Science Photos/J. Hobday 119B
Natural Science Photos/G. Kinns 53B, 64TL, 73B
Natural Science Photos/G. Newlands 101B
Natural Science Photos/M. Stanley Price 118B
Natural Science Photos/Peter Ward 6B, 36B, 61B, 67B, 92B
Natural Science Photos/Yendall 102B
Novosti 9B
Oxford Scientific Films 111T
Oxford Scientific Films/Kennedy 6TL
Oxford Scientific Films/Ziglesczynski 42T
R.I.D.A./David Bayliss 6TR, 11T, C, 17TL TR, 23T, 73T, 75R, 77C, 83T C, 85T C BC, 92T, 104T, 105T, B, 108T, 109TL TR, 111B
R.I.D.A./D. John 74T
R.I.D.A./R.J. Moody 73T, CL
R.I.D.A./D.J. Taylor 70T
R.I.D.A./Bernard Wood 72T
Bryan L. Sage 71T
Ronald Sheridan 125BL
John Topham Picture Library 28B, 35B, 38B, 43B, 44B, 54B, 57B, 62B, 63B, 81B, 113B, 117B, 120B, 125BR
John Topham Picture Library/Jane Burton 26B
John Topham Picture Library/L. Lee Rue 122B
ZEFA/Photri 114BL